Peanuts

COLLECTIBLES

Identification
&
Value Guide

Andrea Podley
&
Derrick Bang

COLLECTOR BOOKS
A Division of Schroeder Publishing Co., Inc.

Cover Design: Beth Summers
Book Design: Ben Faust

Searching for a Publisher?

We are always looking for knowledgeable people considered to be experts within their fields. If you feel there is a real need for a book on your collectible subject and have a large comprehensive collection, contact Collector Books.

Collector Books
P.O. Box 3009
Paducah, KY 42002-3009

Copyright © 2000 by Andrea Podley & Derrick Bang

Contents

Dedication

For Phillip, my mother, father, and sister: husband and family, who support and honor me with love and laughter.
    –Andrea Podley

For Gayna, my soulmate and best friend, because I cannot imagine bestowing my first dedication on anybody else.
    –Derrick Bang

Acknowledgments

Contrary to the implication of our cover, which might have you believe that absolutely everything inside this book was put together by its two authors, the reality is quite different; as is the case with artistic endeavors, films, plays, etc., we received considerable assistance from other parties who gave generously of their time and talent.

No book is assembled without such behind-the-scenes helpers, and that's particularly true of a book such as this one. In the spirit of integrity and fair play — forever a hallmark of the eternally honorable Charlie Brown — we'd like to thank the following heroes:

•Charles Schulz, of course, without whose talent we'd all be reading vastly inferior newspaper comic strips;

•Liz Conyngham, Meg Troy, Carmen Hartigan, and Michael Posner (United Media), Evelyn Ellison (Creative Associates), and Marcia Aoki (United Media K.K.), who helped with essential permissions, copyright issues, suggestions, and advice;

•George Pipal, who always believed in Andrea's projects and the work she has done for the Peanuts Collector Club; he was its staunchest supporter and mentor, whose absence is keenly felt every day;

•Jeannie Schulz, whose devotion to Canine Companions for Independence has provided our club with its spiritual backbone;

•our photographer, Robert Wess, of Robert Wess Photography, Bellingham, Washington, whose willingness to deal with all these little-bitty things (and LARGE things) made him a saint of the first order;

•our editor, Lisa Stroup, as well as Amy Hopper, who was there with helpful responses every time;

•Chiyo Adachi (Determined Productions), endlessly patient and simply wonderful, who tirelessly researched items for us, identifying numbers, looking up pictures, and every other thankless job thrown at her;

•James Doe of Snoopy's Gallery and Gift Shop, who continually amazes us with the lengths to which he cheerfully goes while "putting on the dog" for members of the Peanuts Collector Club;

•Phyllis Horowitt, who passed away in 1997, and was a dear friend and inspiration;

•Pauline Graeber, seasoned collector and friend, who willingly — and without fear of postal gremlins! — shipped some items to be photographed;

•Kelly Tarigo, who (much to our amazement) let us photograph her large Italian Snoopy bank ... and sent him all the way from Florida;

•Brenda Allen, Jenifer Prystasz, Barbara Palumbo (always there), Victor Lee (whose loyalty and kindness continue to inspire us), Clara Johnson Scroggins, Barbara Erickson, Agnes Lau, Isabelle Bayon, Don Fraser (of Inetics, Inc.), Karen Thompson (of Craft House Corporation), Leslie Kaelin, Richard and Judy White, Dianna McDonnell, Susan Jensen, Nita Obbink, Caryl Hall, and Susie Wildenhus; and Michelle Keller, Alison Novela, and Linda Fewell (of Hallmark Cards), every one a rock of support; and,

•Phil Podley and Gayna Lamb-Bang, who provided patience, moral steadiness, and badly needed shoulder massages; served as first-round editorial sounding-boards; and — most of all — long ago learned the folly of attempting to come between rabid collectors and the objects of our eternal quests. We simply cannot thank them enough. Knowing how to tolerate a super-collector doesn't get addressed in conventional marriage vows, nor can one take classes for such wisdom; it either comes or it doesn't. Phil and Gayna have risen admirably to the challenge; so superbly, in fact, that they no longer lament the absence of empty wall and shelf space in our respective homes (well, not within earshot, anyway). Gayna, in fact, wisely has embraced her own "collector's spirit" to become one of the gang. Now all we need to do is work on Phil ...
    Andrea Podley
    Derrick Bang

Preface

On October 2, 1950, cartoonist Charles M. Schulz first breathed life into a small-town neighborhood whose youthful inhabitants eventually would touch the lives of just about everybody in the so-called "real" world.

We know and love these kids as the Peanuts gang.

What began nearly half a century ago as a comic strip carried in precisely seven newspapers — *The Washington Post, The Minneapolis Star Tribune, The Chicago Tribune, The Morning Call* (Allentown, Pennsylvania), *The Bethlehem Globe-Times, The Denver Post,* and *The Seattle Times* — has grown to be included now in over 2,600 newspapers, every day, in 75 countries. Fans throughout the world wouldn't dream of life without their daily dose of wisdom or whimsical humor from Charlie Brown and his friends.

Comic strips — cartoons, if you prefer that designation — are an art form: a means of expressing an idea or a great truth in an abbreviated space. Schulz uses words sparingly, and his line drawings are uncomplicated and pleasing to the eye. In this modern era of media and artistic overkill where no concept is expressed unless accompanied by a shrill commentator and bombastic, rapid-fire eye-candy, Schulz's brevity is a breath of fresh air, his art a delightful echo of gentler times.

First came The Word: the comic strip itself. It soon was accompanied by books, television specials, feature films, and two musical plays, one of the latter, "You're a Good Man, Charlie Brown," which recently enjoyed an exciting Broadway revival. All have inspired an array of merchandise that has marched off store shelves and into our homes and hearts. Those who cherish such treasures — statues, figurals, plates, bells, ornaments, toys, and so much more — are historians as well as collectors. Just as we now read excitedly about the "reappearance" of a long-lost Gershwin manuscript or a hitherto unknown painting by Picasso, one day future researchers will be grateful for those collectors who so meticulously catalogued and cared for the items on the subsequent pages.

The items themselves have become easier to find since *The Official Price Guide to Peanuts Collectibles* was published back in 1990. Peanuts-themed gift shops may not be as ubiquitous as the mall-entrenched Disney and Warner Brothers stores — not yet, at least! — but quality can be just as important as quantity. And, thanks to the Internet, some of our favorite shopping spots are within reach of collectors the world over. Some make pilgrimages to various parts of the United States to spend time with Charlie Brown and his friends. Santa Rosa, California, where Charles Schulz lives and works, is home to Snoopy's Gallery and Gift Shop, not to mention the Redwood Empire Ice Arena and its annual "Snoopy on Ice" show. Knott's Berry Farm Camp Snoopy theme parks are located in Buena Park, California, Bloomington, Minnesota, and Sandusky, Ohio. In Japan, where Snoopy runs a close second to Mickey Mouse, enthusiastic fans spend time and money in the seven malls devoted wholly to Peanuts. When tourists visit the Peanuts shops located at such venues, they often need a book to help channel their spending desires.

We hope that this book will address such needs. It is intended as a colorful and informative guide for a special journey into the world of Peanuts collectibles. It is our hope that you will find it fun to read and easy to use. Our book is international in scope, reflecting Peanuts' increased popularity with our Asian and European neighbors. But be advised: this is by no means an exhaustive analysis of the subject. No single book could possibly meet that challenge, with new collectibles and household items being produced literally every day. Think of this, instead, as a jumping-off point: a comprehensive overview of Peanuts merchandising we intend to supplement with future editions that will focus more specifically on foreign items and everything else that we lacked space to include between these two covers.

Perhaps some of what follows will rekindle fond memories. Better still, you may become hopelessly transfixed, just like the thousands of people already familiar with the joys of collecting Peanuts memorabilia.

Foreword

I've never been asked to write a foreword to a book before and must beg forgiveness of the reader for my inexperience in this area.

I have been working at United Media, the company that syndicates and licenses the Peanuts comic strip by Charles M. Schulz, since 1983. Over the years I have always worked exclusively on the Peanuts property in a variety of roles as a Licensing Assistant, Coordinator, Sales Executive, Manager, Director, and Worldwide Property Director for these wonderful characters.

Many things have changed in our business over the last decade, but one constant that we have grown to depend on and appreciate is the many Peanuts collectors around the world. At United Media, we feel that the devotion given to the property by its fans and collectors is part of why Peanuts has such a permanent place in our culture, and in the hearts of consumers worldwide.

I have been fortunate to work with the Peanuts Collector Club since its early days under the tutelage of my mentor in this business — George Pipal — who worked for United Media for over 50 years. One of the first projects I assisted George on for the club was a book on Peanuts Collectibles that was published by Random House. It was my job to gather information on the property and licensees, and fact check contract and product dates. In a sense, this project for the club was a great help to me in learning about the history of the merchandising of the property and developing a knowledge of the property that still serves me well today.

We rely on the collectors as a great resource of Peanuts trivia knowledge as well as giving us historical perspective on our extensive merchandise programs that have grown over the last 40 years to a business of over $1 billion in retail sales. Today, we have over 700 active licensing contracts all over the world, with over 20,000 new products produced each year.

Unlike other licensed properties, we are extremely fortunate to be able to rely on the creator, Mr. Schulz, for all the quality and art control for our licensed products. Mr. Schulz's studio sees for approval every single product submitted from every country in which we do business. There are plenty of products that never make it to store shelves because they don't meet the high standards that Mr. Schulz expects of the merchandise that bears his creation. We believe these standards are the reason that Peanuts licensed products have had such a successful history and continue to grow today.

The Peanuts Collector Club provides a great network for Peanuts fans to share their love of the property, their knowledge of the strip, and the joy of collecting the wonderful products that bear the Peanuts image. Through their newsletter, swap meets, and Beaglefest conventions, the Peanuts Collector Club has become a very important aspect of what the Peanuts property is all about.

We at United Media salute Andrea Podley, all the members of her Peanuts Collector Club, and devoted fans of Peanuts everywhere, for their tireless devotion and endless energy on behalf of the property through the years and on to the future.

Liz Conyngham, VP & Worldwide Property Director, Peanuts

Cast of Characters

It has been said that you cannot fully appreciate the play without a program, so let's begin with the lead players:

Charlie Brown

Snoopy

Woodstock

Linus

Lucy

Peppermint Patty

Marcie

Sally

Schroeder

Rerun

These ten characters are the most frequent stars to appear on merchandise. At times, it might even seem that everything to be found revolves around Snoopy and Woodstock, but that just means you're not looking hard enough!

You can expect to encounter these ten characters quite frequently during your Peanuts collecting journey. Because Snoopy has more alter-egos than even Walter Mitty, he can be or do just about anything, which partly explains his enduring popularity with merchandisers. Snoopy isn't your average hound, and manufacturers have been quick to release goodies in the likeness of the World War I Flying Ace, or Joe Cool, or the "legal beagle," or any of several dozen other personalities. And, since Woodstock is Snoopy's "friend of friends," he'll frequently be found in the company of the world-famous beagle.

We next come to the supporting cast, which has varied a bit over the years as new characters have replaced others who slowly faded into comic-strip limbo:

The Daisy Hill Puppies (Snoopy's four brothers and one sister)
   Spike (the skinny one, who lives in Needles, California)
   Belle (the sister, who lives in Kansas City, Missouri)
   Olaf (the chunky one)
   Andy (the "fuzzy" one, frequently seen in Olaf's company)
   Marbles (the brown-spotted one)

Pig Pen

Franklin

The Beaglescouts (birds who resemble Woodstock)
   Conrad
   Oliver
   Bill
   Harriet
   Raymond
   Fred

Shermy

Patty (no, not Peppermint Patty; this is a different girl)

Violet

Frieda

And, finally, as a play or movie might have its cameo guests who wander on stage just long enough to be noticed, the Peanuts world boasts similar significant — albeit only briefly seen — visitors:

Eudora

Molly Volley

Crybaby Boobie

Roy

5

Cormac

Collections are as varied as the collectors who put them together. Some concentrate on Snoopy exclusively, while others are just as fiercely determined to gather items that feature Lucy, or Linus, or even Peppermint Patty and Marcie. There are no right or wrong approaches to collecting; all that matters is that the process itself should bring joy to those who embrace it ... and there's little doubt of that, when dealing with the Peanuts gang.

How to Use This Book

Although we've tried to make this tome as user-friendly as possible, it would be impossible to anticipate all the ways that a single item could be described. Would a ceramic Christmas ornament be listed under Figurines, or would Seasonal be a better choice?

For the sake of simplicity, we have restricted ourselves to eleven primary collectible categories, which are so noted in the Contents. The index is alphabetized by specific items, and therefore is much handier for collectors just getting started.

Within each of the primary categories, we have organized items as logically as possible. Thus, the section on books will be located near similar sections on magazines and comic books, while a section on cookie jars will be close to that on drinking glasses and dish sets. Since our concept of logic might differ from yours, we strongly suggest that you quickly skim through the entire book just to get a sense of where everything can be found. That way, you'll know precisely where to look when you unearth a particularly delightful surprise during your next visit to an antiques mall.

The memorabilia associated with Charlie Brown and his friends is assorted and diverse. Throughout the years, though, specific trends have been set. As with most comic character collectibles, it appears that collectors are most fond of ceramic items, music boxes, Christmas-themed items, and banks. We therefore have endeavored to provide an extensive sampling of these categories, along with various other topics we have judged critical.

We cannot include everything. You may wonder why a certain topic has been left out. Rest assured, it was not overlooked; we plan to write several books on the subject of Peanuts collecting, and we urge you to look for our future titles.

Research and expertise have resulted from many factors, including but not exclusive to the following:

The authors' own records;
Contact with licensees and manufacturers;
Contact with United Media in the United States and
    Japan;
Observing auctions;
Attending antique and collectibles shows;
Attending flea markets;
Attending events designed as "Peanuts-only;"
The Peanuts Collector newsletter and its classified ads;
Discussion and correspondence with fellow collectors;
Researching related material, such as magazine articles;
    and
Tracking catalogs and brochures issued by
    licensees.

Because many items resemble each other — consider the overwhelming number of plush Snoopy dolls that have been produced during the past 30 years — we've taken care to include full descriptions along with manufacturer, item number, and date of release, and any other tidbits of information that might be useful (such as a title or caption, if appropriate).

This is perhaps a good moment to cite the all-important distinction between a copyright date and an item's date of production. Copyright date refers to the year of the character's first publication: 1958 and 1965 for Snoopy and Woodstock, for example. Properly licensed — that is to say, legitimate — items made through 1994 always will include such dates. It's proof that the manufacturer, known as the "licensee," has properly purchased the right to produce goods with the character's likeness.

Things have changed.

Newspapers, books, films, recordings, and other forms of publication will carry complete copyright lines, including the year-dates, as before.

During the latter half of 1994, licensees for non-published products were advised that they now have the option of using a new form without year-dates, which is:

PEANUTS © United Feature Syndicate, Inc.

If you see this form on a product, you will know it was produced no earlier than the latter half of 1994.

Copyright dates have absolutely no bearing on when an item has been manufactured, which in most cases will be years or even decades later. We could not count the number of times folks have asked us about, say, "a plush Snoopy made in 1958." Very little was made or released before the 1960s, so that's the first clue to the error of that question; the second clue lies in the fact that 1958 is, as mentioned above, one of Snoopy's copyright dates.

The dates you will find associated with items throughout this book reflect each item's date of production. Market saturation isn't necessarily consistent or uniform; many times items will be much more readily accessible, say, in the eastern United States than on the West Coast. Thank goodness for the Internet, which has shortened such frustrating distances with respect to the newest collectibles!

We are not all-knowing or all-seeing, particularly with older items. Sometimes our release dates are approximations. Then, too, not every manufacturer bothers with item numbers. If you come across a listing that does not include a date of release or a product number, don't automatically assume that we forgot such information ... it could well be that it never existed in the first place!

On the other hand, it could mean that we simply didn't know, in which case we'd love to hear from fellow collectors with incontrovertible proof regarding a missing date, or anything else.

With few exceptions, all the values contained between these covers assume that the item is in mint condition, and, where applicable, is packaged in its original box or wrap. Not all packaging is of consequence, and we tell you when this is so.

A few words about condition: when we say mint-in-the-package, we mean it. The item must be packaged just as it was when it left the factory. The packaging (box, shrink-wrap, etc.) must be just as flawless as the item it contains.

Mint-in-the-package therefore is distinguished from mint, which refers only to the item itself, which must be absolutely and utterly perfect. No scratches. No chipped paint. No fading or yellowing. No rips or tears. A book should look as though it just arrived from the publisher. A ceramic ornament should be bright and colorful, without any Christmas tree sap gumming up the glaze finish. Board games should include all pieces which should be present in their original wrappers. Stickers should be shrink-wrapped. Plush clothing should not look as though it has been through the wash half a dozen times.

True, you're unlikely to find older items in such condition, but this gives everybody a starting point. It's difficult to distinguish between "used" and "slightly used," and some collectors are more tolerant than others of items that have that "well-loved" look. We've been known to pick up a less-than-perfect ceramic Christmas ornament with hidden chips or scratches in the rear, while waiting to find the identical item in better condition. (We use the terms "ceramic" and "porcelain" interchangeably.) But if we all agree what mint means, then we'll all know when an item is in less than mint condition.

You can usually assume that a clearly used but still well-treated item — one that shows its age but is not broken in any way — is worth roughly 70% of its mint value; we'd probably identify such an item as being in fine condition. Similarly, an item with noticeable damage or staining would be worth roughly 50% of the mint value; we'd probably call that good condition. In either case, however, both seller and buyer should be fully aware of a non-mint item's shortcomings: *Caveat emptor* is still the rule of the day.

Our price range, therefore, runs from good (low end) to mint (high end). These prices are based on experienced judgment and market analysis: an item's actual long-term value as a relation of its availability and appeal to a broad spectrum of collectors. As a result, you will not find us justifying the often crazy prices that items have fetched via Internet auctions (for example), when deep-pocketed collectors allow excitement to overwhelm common sense. Nor do we take fads-of-the-moment into account, such as the buying frenzy that greeted 1998's "World Tour" PVCs when first released in Singapore. The initial prices paid by some collectors for those items bore no relation to their actual value, which will assert itself over time.

Our values are based on the big picture and, as a result, we've tried to be fair both to potential sellers and potential buyers. Bear in mind that our book is only a guideline, and one whose contents had to be set in stone when our publication date arrived. (Next to late-winter snowmen, price guides are among the world's most ephemeral endeavors.) If you find an item for sale at a slightly higher price, that could just be market forces at work; it doesn't necessarily mean that the seller is looking to gouge potential customers. But if you find an item marked at double (or more) what we show ... well, forewarned is forearmed.

Copyright Information

Contrary to what some folks might think, particularly those on the Internet who inappropriately trade images of Charlie Brown, Snoopy, and the rest of the gang, all of Charles Schulz's characters are licensed and fully protected by copyright laws. United Media controls that copyright and guards it with great care, as is only proper.

More than anything else, we at the Peanuts Collector Club get e-mail requests from folks wanting us to send them images of Charlie Brown, or Snoopy, or Lucy at her psychiatrist's booth, or Schroeder at his piano. Some people ask nicely. Others do not.

Our answer, regardless of the manner in which the question is phrased, is always the same: We can't.

We're not allowed to, for the simple reason that we do not own the right to do so! United Media strictly forbids us or anybody else from sharing or sending licensed art of Charles Schulz's characters in any way, shape, or form.

The sole exceptions are the graphics that United Media provides at their web site for individual home-page use as an illustrated link to United Media's pages. Under specific circumstances that you are obliged to follow, you may use those pictures on your page(s). But they are the only ones.

By the same token, we've seen countless unauthorized and "pirate" collectibles over the years, produced and/or sold by folks who either don't know that they're doing something wrong, or know full well and couldn't care less (until and unless they get caught). We feel very strongly about this issue and can sound positively self-righteous under certain circumstances. Our way of toeing that line is to list only legitimate, licensed items in this book. In a few cases we do include prototypes or one-of-a-kind items, as we know that collectors love to see anything rare or difference. But we carefully note these exceptions.

Please do not shoot us as the messenger here. We do not make the rules, but we are obliged to follow them.

It does no good to whine or snarl about "that expletive-deleted United Media and its big-shot lawyers," or phrases even less pleasant than that. If you do, you're merely demonstrating your own ignorance.

Rule #1 in life: We don't always get what we want. Sad, but true.

Look at it this way. Copyright laws are in place to protect Charles Schulz and the work that is rightfully his.

Take his artwork, even for something as harmless as a home-made silver pin in the shape of Snoopy, or an Internet homepage, and you are, in effect, stealing from the man who created Charlie Brown, Snoopy, and the rest of the Peanuts gang. It's that simple.

If you still do not understand this or simply are curious about the intricacies of copyright law, please visit Brad Templeton's web site at this address, where you'll find his words of wisdom on "Ten Big Myths About Copyright Explained:" http://www.clari.net/brad/copymyths.html.

Brad goes through it all simply, with specific references to Internet use that are no less applicable to real-world collectibles.

And please, be mature. Your humble editors like to think we're nice, pleasant, sensitive folks, and part of that sensitivity concerns our understanding and appreciation of Charles Schulz's wishes and the best way to protect his property.

United Media explains the issue quite clearly in the following statement:

The U.S. Copyright Act in effect prior to January 1, 1978, provided that when a copyrighted work was published it was required to bear a copyright notice containing three elements — the copyright symbol (or the word copyright or a specified abbreviation for the word); the year date of first publication; and the name of the copyright owner. The U.S. Copyright Act which went into effect January 1, 1978, retained these requirements, but made the failure to comply with them less onerous. The copyright notices on Peanuts merchandise produced up through the 1990s reflected these requirements. The year dates on such merchandise represented the year date of first publication in the Peanuts strip of the characters represented (for example, Charlie Brown in 1950 and Snoopy in 1958).

So there's a quick copyright primer: in a nutshell, licensed products will include a copyright notice. Sometimes this information is hard to find, either because it's very tiny, or because it's located in an unexpected place. But look closely, because it'll almost always be there some place.

On rare occasions, some legitimate products have been released without the copyright information; perhaps the stamping machine was broken that day. Whenever possible, we try to point that out to you.

If you can't find any such indication on an item other than those specific few we mention, and if you're dealing with somebody you don't know — say, a total stranger at a weekend flea market instead of a known dealer — then you should be very cautious, because the item(s) may not be legitimate. It would be bad enough to allow such "black market" product into your collection, but it would become positively embarrassing if you later attempted to sell said item(s) to another collector who knew better.

And that's enough time spent on the soapbox. We promise: no more preaching during the rest of this book. The object here is to have fun!

Adding to Your Collection

Just as there are two types of people in this world (those who insist that there are only two types and those who know better), collectors can be broken down into two basic types: those content to build up a collection comprised solely of new merchandise readily available at stores, and those more fascinated by older items no longer available in such primary markets.

It's easy to help the first type, and our first suggestion is to join the Peanuts Collector Club. Aside from helpful information about new products — very important, considering how many items are released only regionally or perhaps only in specific countries — we also include advertisements from some of our more ambitious members who run their own businesses selling Peanuts merchandise. Not a bad way to combine business with pleasure, hmm?

We endorse the efforts of the following such businesses, starting with the one that doubles as a fan pilgrimage site:

Snoopy's Gallery and Gift Shop
1665 W. Steele Lane
Santa Rosa, California 95401
(800) 959-3385; FAX (707) 546-3764
http://www.snoopygift.com

Located next to the Redwood Empire Ice Arena, where the annual Snoopy ice show is a must-see event, this two-story complex is both store and museum in one. The first floor is devoted entirely to Peanuts merchandise, except for a small corner filled with skating and hockey supplies. You name it, and you'll find it: books, clothes, jigsaw puzzles, posters, stickers, Christmas ornaments, greeting cards, computer software, a very nice selection of infant clothes and toys, and anything else that friendly manager Jim Doe can dig up. The second floor is filled with Charles Schulz's many awards and magazine covers, along with several displays of original sketches and newspaper strips, all displayed attractively in glass showcases. The building is surrounded on two sides by a huge wraparound carpet (on the walls!), and two large moving displays of the characters keep patrons amused. Snoopy (a large, human-sized version) has even been known to make the occasional appearance.

Additionally, don't miss

The Snoopy Shop: On-line shopping from United Media
http://www.snoopy.com

Cartoon Collections (Robert Casterline)
37 Public Square
Wilkes-Barre, Pennsylvania 18701
(717) 821-2291

The Crazy Collector (Leslie Kaelin)
5703 Spring Bluff Dr.
Crestwood, Kentucky 40014
(502) 241-2035; FAX (502) 241-2396

Fun Art Galleries (Robert Casterline)
1307 Celebrity Circle, B-115
Myrtle Beach, South Carolina 29577
(803) 444-3233
http://www.funart.com

Joe Collector (Carla and Steve Olson)
673 Sheridan Court
Lake Zurich, Illinois 60047-2774
(888) 563-2655; FAX (847) 726-8618
e-mail: joecollect@aol.com

Mark J. Cohen Originals Artwork
P.O. Box 1892
Santa Rosa, California 95402-1892
(707) 528-3440; FAX (707) 528-2451
http://www.markomics.com/
(Mark sends a portion of his sales to CCI, a favorite charity of Mr. and Mrs. Schulz)

Nuts Design (Hedwig Keek)
Zeil Straat 50, 1076 SJ
Amsterdam, Holland
(020) 670-2131; FAX (020) 670-2132

Philosiuupie (Fanny Ko)
Flat C @ Onion Court
176 Ede Road
Kowloon, Hong Kong
okynnaf@iohk.com

Play House
Harajuku Omotesando
1-13-18, Jingumae
Tokyo, Japan
3470-6107

Snodgrass Sales, Inc. (Marsha Snodgrass)
8085 Wabash Avenue
Terre Haute, Indiana 47803-3971
(812) 877-1897; (800) 373-9871; FAX (812) 877-6971
e-mail: snodgras@indy.net
http://www.al.com/snodgrass/

Snoop to Nuts, Ltd. (Sandra Cramer)
P.O. Box 1066
Bellmore, New York 11710
(516) 868-6036; FAX (516) 868-6148
e-mail: s2n@pipeline.com
http://www.snoop2nuts.com

Snooping Around
297 Brookfield Rd.
Brimfield, Massachusetts
Phone & FAX: (413) 245-7187
e-mail: snoopy@hey.net (Karen Olson)

The Mall of America in Minneapolis/St. Paul, Minnesota, has two different stores in and around Camp Snoopy. Joe Cool's Hot Shop can be reached at (612) 883-8789, and Snoopy's Boutique is at (612) 883-8630. The full address is:

Mall of America
5000 Center Court
Bloomington, Minnesota 55425

Knott's Berry Farm in southern California sells Peanuts merchandise at two shops: the Snoopy Boutique and Snoopy's Camp Store. The latter can be reached at (714) 220-5302, and the park's general access number is (714) 827-1776. Snoopy's Boutique can be reached at extension 4131 or 4132. The full address is:

Knott's Berry Farm
8039 Beach Blvd.
Buena Park, California 90620

Cedar Point
One Cedar Point Dr.
Sandusky, Ohio 44870
(419) 626-0830
http://www.cedarpoint.com

The Camp Snoopy Park houses a Snoopy Boutique shop.

Overseas travelers should take note of the new Snoopy Town in Osaka, Japan. The place is pretty overwhelming. Their address is 2-7-70 Matta Omiya, Tsurumi-ku, Osaka City 538, Osaka Prefecture, Japan. Their phone number is 81-6-913-8800. Their stores include the Gallery House, the Theme House, the Garden House, the Woodstock Shop, the Lucy Shop, the Peppermint Patty Shop, Restaurant Snoopy, and Olaf's Snacks.

As for the second type of collector, our first suggestion is to join the Peanuts Collector Club! (Is there an echo in here?) Every quarterly issue of our newsletter is jammed with pages and pages of buy/sell/trade classified ads from our members; sooner or later, you'll find references to just about everything.

But there also are plenty of other places to look, starting with local flea markets, antique malls, and garage sales. Don't scoff: just about every serious collector has one or two stories of great finds along with one or two equally frustrating tales of the ones that got away. Although the entire concept of collecting has become much more popular during the past decade, with prices often reflecting more in the way of greed than reality, not everybody is out to make a killing. Antiques shops that specialize in early Americana won't necessarily be

as fussy when it comes to stray lots of Peanuts products. Remember: many antiques shops pick up new merchandise in "house lots" that are gathered in bulk, and not all dealers will pay as much attention to a ceramic Sally bank from Italy while pricing paintings, furniture, and sterling silver.

Bottom line: it never hurts to try. Whenever you visit a new area, while spending the holidays with friends or family, take a few hours to investigate antiques shops, Goodwill stores, and the like. You just never know what you might find.

Publications such as *Toy Shop* and *Antique Trader* also are a great place to look, although you're less likely to find bargains; those who advertise in such publications are pretty savvy about their target audience.

The Internet also is invaluable, starting with a voluminous and quite popular auction site that goes by the name of eBay. It has a sub-category devoted specifically to Peanuts collectibles, and it can be found at http://pages.ebay.com/aw/listings/list/category773/index.html. At any given moment, you'll find literally hundreds of Peanuts goodies for sale ... but be warned: although it is possible to find great deals on eBay, it's just as easy to be caught in the grip of "auction fever." Before you know it, you'll be bidding far in excess of an item's actual value. This site is not for the faint of heart or the light of wallet!

If you're seeking one or two specific items, try posting a notice in the UseNet "newsgroup;" think in terms of a gigantic bulletin board, organized around a single theme, devoted to Peanuts: alt.comics.peanuts. You also can send messages through the Peanuts-themed list server, snoopy@onelist.com.

As you can see, there's no excuse for complacency!

Inventorying Your Collection

How may I collect thee? Let me count the ways ...

Collectors do a lot of counting. They also make a lot of lists. They make lists of things they have, and lists of things they don't have. They do this to keep track of things — particularly once the collection has outgrown your ability to display it, and things start finding their way into boxes stored in closets or under the bed — and also because it's fun. (And some of us keep lists because our memories aren't what they used to be!)

Some folks organize their collections by type: rooms devoted exclusively to plush toys, shelves designed for commemorative plates and bells, bulletin boards holding buttons, badges, and pins. Some folks prefer the "organized clutter" approach, with everything tossed into a glorious jumble that can take visitors weeks to fully appreciate.

We're big on display;

we've never really seen the point of accumulating so much that you're literally unable to show it all at once. One's family, spouse, or significant others also play a part in this equation; such folks generally will draw the line eventually ... unless you're all collectors, in which case, good luck, and don't overtax the bank account!

Obviously, the better you are at keeping the entire collection on display, the easier it is to keep track of what you actually own. We've seen all sorts of great display techniques, from cabinets designed for specific ceramic items, to rows upon rows of plush Snoopy dolls, each carefully protected beneath a transparent dust cover. Take note when stores go out of business; you sometimes can find great display racks and cabinets. An old stationery store greeting card rack is a great way to display a collection of Peanuts greeting cards. Electrical rotating display units that once housed watches or jewelry are superb for small ornaments, ceramic eggs, or the like. Posters look great on the ceiling. PVC figures fit perfectly in racks designed to hold CDs, cassettes, or videotapes. Old lawyer's bookshelves — the type with glass panels that drop down in front of each shelf — both showcase a collection and prevent dust from accumulating.

And if you're lucky enough — and wealthy enough — to have an understanding roommate who won't mind turning an entire room over to a collection, you can have fun for months while designing and building (or buying) custom-made shelves, racks, and so forth.

Checklists are an excellent way to proceed with all this; so are index cards. Computers are very handy for tracking one's collection, and the World Wide Web is a great place to download shareware indexing programs that will help sort your collection in every imagineable manner.

Keeping track of everything is much easier if you religiously take notes as you go along; woe to those who wait a couple of years, and then are faced with a task that would rival the labors of Hercules!

Maintaining such a list also comes in handy, when ...

Selling Your Collection

We don't like to think about it, but it happens.

Sometimes we just gradually lose interest, the way one eventually tires of a certain musician or clothing style. Sometimes the tail begins to wag the dog, and we recognize the need to go "cold turkey" to escape a collecting mania that has consumed us. Sometimes money becomes tight, and it becomes necessary to part with treasures in order to survive in comfort. Sometimes — and this can be the worst — a favorite relative will die, and we're left with the need to itemize and sell a collection that wasn't even ours to begin with.

Whatever the reason, the first step is to make sure the entire collection is inventoried (a much easier task for those who've kept careful records all along). Take note of each and every item, making notes as to condition, quantity, and any other applicable information. Check the relevant sections in this book for examples; you should think in terms of including as much information as we do. We could not count the times that folks have written, e-mailed, or called us with some variant of this question: "I have a Charlie Brown coffee mug ... what's it worth?"

We know that folks don't deliberately intend to make life difficult, but it's simply impossible to answer such a question as presented. What condition is the mug in? Does it have coffee or tea stains? Is it chipped or scratched? What makes it a Charlie Brown mug ... is he pictured on the outside of the mug, or is the mug actually shaped like his head? What color is it? Can any copyright information be distinguished?

You see the point: be as precise as possible. Only then, perhaps with the help of this book, can you accurately determine your collection's value.

Having gotten that far, your next step is to find the best possible buyer: one or many who desire what you're selling. Parting with a collection is like playing the stock market: it's all a matter of timing. If you're not in a hurry and can wait for the best possible offer, then do so. Be willing to put some effort into the process; you're bound to do better by selling items individually than by insisting on parting with everything as one huge lot. Both options have advantages and disadvantages; selling items individually, while potentially more lucrative, is time-consuming, requires trusting perhaps scores (hundreds?) of individuals, and generally leaves you still holding the final 20% that nobody wanted. Selling a collection as a unit will limit you to a relatively small number of "deep pockets" purchasers who invariably will negotiate you down to a lower per-item price.

As for where to start and how to publicize such a sale, the avenues are identical to those described in our section on Adding to Your Collection. Place an ad in the quarterly Peanuts Collector Club magazine, where eager buyers breathlessly await such entries and read the For Sale ads before anything else, in the hopes of being the first to pounce on a particular item or an entire collection. Place ads in collector publications. Rent a table at a flea market or antiques store. Visit Internet newsgroups and Peanuts-themed web sites. Try eBay. In this era of Internet-driven commerce, it's now pretty easy to be in reach of collectors from all over the world ... quite a change from the days when we all had to rely on yard sales and garage sales!

The Peanuts Collector Club

Yes, it's time for a shameless plug.

Chances are, though, that if you've purchased this book, you're either already a member, or definitely the sort of person who'd seriously think about becoming a member. Our organization picked up quite a few new members after the appearance of 1990's *Official Price Guide to Peanuts Collectibles*, which now is long out of print and has become a highly-prized collectible in its own right. (Go figure.) We're all here for the same reason: to honor Charles Schulz and his cartooning genius, which created an empire just as powerful 50 years later as it was shortly after Charlie Brown and Snoopy took their first newsprint steps.

So indulge us, for a moment, as we briefly explain the history of our little band of merry individuals.

In 1983, Phil Podley trumpeted wife Andrea's Peanuts fixation by placing an ad in a national collector's magazine. Phil intended to prove, once and for all, that Andrea was the only person in the entire universe whose devotion to Snoopy had become so all-consuming.

Imagine his surprise when Andrea received 42 replies to that ad.

Word spread quickly, and soon Andrea could not keep up with the mail and phone calls. The next step was inevitable: she founded the Peanuts Collector Club, with the blessings of United Media and Charles "Sparky" Schulz.

The first newsletter, quite modest by later standards, appeared in August of 1983.

Now, more than 16 years later, the club has blossomed with the vigor of a healthy pumpkin patch. Over 3,000 new and ongoing world-wide members eagerly await each quarterly newsletter, jam-packed with at least 40 pages of information about the Peanuts gang, new products, informative articles by and concerning individual members and their collecting preferences, comments from Sparky himself, and current updated definitive lists of books, videos, posters, ink-stampers, Christmas ornaments, and all the other hundreds of licensed items which have displayed Snoopy and the gang.

The club has become Andrea's full-time occupation, and she cherishes both her involvement and the contact with so many like-minded people. The club is an outlet for all those who love Charlie Brown and his friends and wish to share their interest, either by trading information or collectible merchandise, or expressing delight over the latest Peanuts newspaper strip.

In Andrea's own words:

I believe collecting is an extraordinary learning experience, as well as a hobby. Remember, collectors are historians in their own right. We learn a lot about one another and about ourselves. Without this hobby, I would never have met so many of you, whom I'm privileged to call my friends.

Annual membership dues are as follows:

United States: $25.00
Mexico & Canada: $35.00
All other countries: $50.00

These dues entitle an individual to one year's membership in the Peanuts Collector Club, which includes four consecutive issues of the club newsletter. Note: $1.00 of each subscription is donated to Canine Companions for Independence, the organization near and dear to the hearts of Charles and Jeannie Schulz. Members also receive a card entitling them to discounts at select Snoopy shops.

Checks — U.S. funds only, please (foreign subscribers should use international money orders, which can be obtained at a local bank) — should be made payable to the Peanuts Collector Club, Inc., and mailed to this address:

Peanuts Collector Club, Inc.
539 Sudden Valley
Bellingham, Washington 98226
USA

Washington residents need to add sales tax. All newsletters are mailed at bulk rate, so it is essential for you to let us know of any change of address. The post office will not forward bulk rate parcels!

If you write us with a question, please include a self-addressed and stamped return envelope; we're not made of money! E-mail is cheaper and easier, and you may direct queries to either of these addresses:

acpodley@nas.com
bang@dcn.davis.ca.us

Be sure to include your name, address, and phone number, and don't forget to mention how you heard about us! (Was it from this book?)

Banks

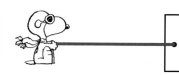

Applause

These banks are plastic and were issued in 1989 in a plain gift box. Prices are based on mint condition, with no scuffs or paint missing. The box has no impact on the value.

Woodstock Nest Egg Bank, Woodstock sits on a large egg, #15982, $14.00 – 17.00; Snoopy's Beagle Bank, Snoopy wears a blue business suit and sits on the roof of his doghouse, on one side he's holding briefcase, on the other side he's holding a yellow coin with Woodstock's likeness, Joe Banker is printed over doorway, #15984, $16.00 – 22.00.

Determined Productions, Inc.

Banks are one of the most interesting and collectible categories in the Peanuts arena. As with most Peanuts collectibles available in the United States after the mid 1970s, Snoopy became "top dog" and appeared on most items; Woodstock sometimes accompanied him.

The earlier releases from Determined Productions sit on the top shelf of the Peanuts bank pyramid. As with all Determined items, they had style and class, and always touched our heartstrings.

Due to the age of the comic strip, banks with Charlie Brown, Linus, Schroeder, and Lucy are almost a gleam in the eye of the distant past. They are still produced in countries like Japan, but recent U.S. licensees usually focus on Snoopy and Woodstock.

In this category, the Snoopy Santa bank is the most desirable. Produced by Determined in 1982, it is an absolutely gorgeous item and one we wouldn't dream of using for its original purpose.

The price range is based on very good to mint condition. There should be no paint missing and no cracks and — very important — the original stopper should be included. *Inspect banks closely for hairline cracks.* Make certain the paint on Snoopy's collar is intact. Papier-mâché and composition banks should be examined carefully, as many times pieces are missing. All writing should be legible.

All sizes are approximate heights.

• Ceramic Egg Shape •

Snoopy reclines, petite red, yellow, and blue design against white background, 2½", #1561, 1976, $20.00 – 30.00; ceramic egg shape with flat base, each is the approximate size of a large egg, series #1560, 1976; "Surprise a friend with a hug!!", Snoopy hugs Woodstock; "This has been a good day!", Snoopy lies on his house, Woodstock, in a nest, rests on his tummy; "I feel free!", Snoopy holds a basket of flowers and dances; "How nice!", Woodstock hands flowers to Snoopy. $24.00 – 38.00 each.

• Ceramic Figures, Hand Painted in Italy •

Each bank (in particular Lucy, Charlie Brown, and Linus) may have variances in color, because each was hand painted. Snoopy came with different colored collars, including gold, yellow, green, pink, and blue, 1969. Snoopy, 16¾", #938, $375.00 – 575.00; Snoopy, 8½", #933, $65.00 – 90.00; Snoopy, 6½", #923, $50.00 – 70.00.

Snoopy, varied polka dots against white background (Italy only), 8½"; Snoopy reclines on his tummy, 10½" long. $160.00 – 240.00 each.

Charlie Brown, 7" (left and right), #920, $65.00 – 85.00; 9⅛", #930, $90.00 – 150.00.

Lucy, 7" (left and right), #922, $65.00 – 85.00; 8¾", #932, $90.00 – 150.00.

Sally, 9", $175.00 – 300.00.

Linus, 7" (left and right), #921, $65.00 – 85.00; 9", #931, $90.00 – 150.00.

Not Pictured
Linus sitting, 9". . . . . .$175.00 – 300.00

• Ceramic "Happy" Banks •

Snoopy in a sitting position. Mid 1970s. 5", $15.00 – 20.00; 16", #1558, $200.00 – 280.00; 11", #1557, $150.00 – 225.00; 6", #1556, $18.00 – 25.00.

• Ceramic Snoopy Santa Claus Bank •

15", #1709-8, 1982, $475.00 – 650.00.

• Ceramic Two-Dimensional •

These banks were produced for Japan, although some managed to find their way to stores in Europe. Approx. 5½". Early to mid 1980s. The Flying Ace in a sitting position, $45.00 – 65.00. Snoopy walks and holds Woodstock, who is asleep in his arms, $40.00 – 60.00; Snoopy sits and holds Woodstock, $40.00 – 60.00.

• Ceramic Prototype •

Woodstock sits in a woven basket full of bubbles, 4", mid 1970s, $90.00 – 125.00.

• Snoopy Sports Ball Series (papier-mâché or composition) 1976 •

Snoopy reclines on a basketball, 4½", #8538, $18.00 – 28.00; Snoopy reclines on a blue bowling ball, 4½", #8539, $40.00 – 60.00; Snoopy reclines on a soccer ball, 4¼", #8535, $20.00 – 35.00; Snoopy reclines on a football, 4¼", #8534, $20.00 – 35.00; Snoopy reclines on a baseball. 4¾", #8531, $25.00 – 40.00.

• Snoopy Vehicle Series (papier-mâché or composition, 3½") 1977 •

Snoopy pilots an orange airplane with a green "Flying Ace" caption on one side, #8475, $20.00 – 40.00; Snoopy drives a blue convertible car, #8472, $25.00 – 35.00; Snoopy steers a yellow, white, and green motor boat with a "Sailor" caption in red on one side, #8474, $22.00 – 32.00.

Snoopy drives a red sports convertible with "Racer" captioned in black on one side, #8473, $25.00 – 35.00. Snoopy drives a green truck with "the Express" captioned in orange on one side, #8476, $22.00 – 32.00; Snoopy drives a yellow truck with "Express" captioned in orange on one side, $22.00 – 32.00.

• Baseball Series (papier-mâché or composition, 7½") 1973 •

Charlie Brown #0925, $45.00 – 64.00; Snoopy #0928, $50.00 – 70.00; Schroeder #0924, $45.00 – 64.00.

Peppermint Patty #0929, $45.00 – 64.00; Linus #0926, $45.00 – 64.00; Lucy #0927, $45.00 – 64.00.

• Snoopy Doghouse Bank (papier-mâché or composition) 1969 •

6", #918, $8.00 – 12.00; 7", #915, $14.00 – 20.00.

• Snoopy with Animal (papier-mâché or composition, 4¾") mid to late 1970s •

Snoopy sits on a blue chicken, #8441; Snoopy lies on top of a gray elephant, #8442; Snoopy sits on a white swan, #8443, $58.00 – 75.00 each.

• Snoopy with Fruit (papier-mâché or ceramic, each was issued in both mediums) 1976 •

Snoopy reclines on an orange with a single green leaf, 3½", $65.00 – 80.00; Snoopy sits on a strawberry with a green hull, 4", #8461, $30.00 – 40.00; Snoopy reclines on a banana with "Snoopy" captioned in black, 3¼", #8462, $30.00 – 40.00.

Snoopy lies face down on a lemon, Woodstock reclines on Snoopy's head, 3¾", #8464, $40.00 – 52.00; Snoopy reclines on a red apple with a single green leaf, 3½", $65.00 – 80.00; Snoopy sleeps atop a slice of watermelon, 4", #8466, $30.00 – 40.00.

• Snoopy Wears Hat (ceramic, approx. 5") 1979 •

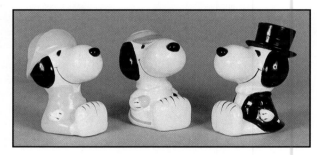

Snoopy wears a red baseball cap, #8546, $30.00 – 40.00; Snoopy wears a gold football helmet with a gold stripe, #8544, $20.00 – 30.00; Snoopy wears a silver hard hat, #8547, $25.00 – 35.00.

Snoopy wears a yellow rain slicker hat, #8548, $20.00 – 30.00; Snoopy wears a blue tennis visor, #8545, $25.00 - 35.00; Snoopy wears a black top hat, #8549, $25.00 – 35.00.

• Snoopy with Junk Food (ceramic) 1979 •

Snoopy lies on top of a mustard-lined hot dog nestled in a bun, 4", #1536, $52.00 – 70.00; Snoopy's upper body in a box of fries, 4¾", #1534, $52.00 – 70.00; Snoopy lies atop a hamburger sandwich with lettuce, onion, and tomato, 3½", #1535, $35.00 – 45.00. Snoopy sits in front of an ice cream cone that holds a scoop of chocolate, 4", #1533; $52.00 – 70.00. (The hot dog and hamburger banks were also issued in composition for overseas markets, but the ceramic composition versions are the most prized.)

Snoopy sits in front of an ice cream cone that holds a scoop of strawberry, 4", Europe, $52.00 – 70.00.

• Daisy Hill Puppies (ceramic, Japan, series #740740, each approx. 4½", must include box) early 1990s •

Snoopy plays a guitar, $30.00 – 42.00; Andy plays a drum, $25.00 – 35.00; Spike plays the bass, $27.00 – 37.00; Olaf plays a jug, $30.00 – 42.00; Marbles plays a banjo, $25.00 – 35.00; Belle plays a fiddle, $25.00 – 35.00.

• Baseball (ceramic, Japan, Determined Productions with Phoenix Corporation, Ltd., green or brown hat, each stands 6" unless noted, series #134, must include box) 1989 •

Schroeder wears catcher's equipment, $43.00 – 55.00; Peppermint Patty leans on a baseball bat, Snoopy wears a catcher's mitt, $43.00 – 55.00; Charlie Brown stands and wears a baseball mitt, 8½", $55.00 – 80.00; Charlie Brown stands and wears a baseball mitt on his left hand, $43.00 – 55.00; Lucy holds a baseball bat over her shoulder, Linus wears a baseball mitt, $43.00 – 55.00.

• Musician (ceramic, Japan, 5¾" – 6½", must include box) early 1990s •

Lucy holds a trumpet; Linus plays a bass, $36.00 – 46.00; Schroeder with a piano, $36.00 – 46.00; Charlie Brown plays a guitar, $36.00 – 46.00; Snoopy holds a saxophone, $40.00 – 50.00.

• Snoopy in Happi Coat (ceramic, Japan, DP-215 series, must include box, each of the different colors is pictured, but not in both sizes) 1989 •

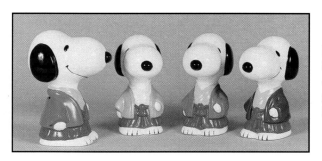

Dark green robe, 5", $35.00 – 42.00; dark green robe, 5¾", $44.00 – 58.00; light green robe, 5", $35.00 – 42.00; light green robe, 5¾", $44.00 – 58.00; blue robe, 5", $35.00 – 42.00; blue robe, 5¾", $44.00 – 58.00.

• Miscellaneous (ceramic) •

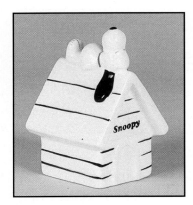

Snoopy Ceramic Doghouse Bank. The bank is white with black trim. Snoopy wears his traditional red collar. San-Rio, for Determined, 3¾", #72-10, 1972, $45.00 – 65.00.

Baby Block with A B C D and E and Snoopy and Woodstock designs, 3", #1505, mid 1970s, $22.00 – 30.00; Baby Block with yellow and white gingham background, Snoopy and Woodstock, 3", mid 1970s, $22.00 – 30.00.

Woodstock figural, standing, 5¾", #1502, mid to late 1970s, $20.00 – 28.00; Snoopy's upper half, he wears a red bowtie and his arms are up, Determined Productions, Inc. with Phoenix Corporation, Ltd., Japan, #DP-259, 1990, $25.00 – 32.00.

Dog Bone, small picture of Snoopy, caption: "Spike's Parcel Service. Handle with care." 2" tall x 10¼" long, Japan, #EL-87, 1982, $110.00 – 175.00.

• Miscellaneous (composition or papier-mâché) •

Snoopy Joe Cool Bank, Snoopy as Joe Cool, 6", #8554, 1970s; 6", distributed by Ideal for Determined, #5272-0, 1970s, $25.00 – 35.00 each; with box, $30.00 – 45.00 each.

Not Pictured:
Snoopy Tuxedo Bank, 6", distributed by Ideal
    for Determined, #5273-8, 1970. . . . .$30.00 – 40.00
                    with box, $45.00 – 75.00

Snoopy & Woodstock Doghouse Bank, Snoopy rests on his doghouse with Woodstock at his feet, 5½", #8555, 1970s, $20.00 – 25.00, with box $30.00 – 50.00. Snoopy Fireman Bank, Snoopy as a fireman in a red uniform, 5¾", distributed by Ideal for Determined, #5255-2, $28.00 – 38.00, with box $40.00 – 55.00.

Belle sits, wears a pink dress with darker pink polka dots, #1500-7, 1981, $18.00 – 25.00. Snoopy wears a blue jogging suit, Woodstock is behind him, 5¼", $22.00 – 38.00; Snoopy wears a blue turtleneck and sunglasses, stands on a green base with his arms folded, 5½", #1516-4, $20.00 – 35.00.

Snoopy lies on a gold and red savings book, "Savings" captioned on front, 5¾", #8532(A); Snoopy lies on a penny dated 1982, 6", #1503, 1982; Snoopy lies on a blue savings book with red trim and "Savings" captioned on front, 5¾", #8532(B), $30.00 – 40.00 each.

Snoopy lies on a rainbow, 4¾", #8533, $12.00 – 18.00; "Baby's first bank." Snoopy sits with pink or blue ribbon around his neck, 4", early 1980s, $20.00 – 25.00.

Snoopy wears a green cap and holds a golf club in one hand, 7", prototype from early 1970s, $90.00 – 140.00; Snoopy wears a red cap and carries his bag of golf clubs, United Kingdom, 6¼", late 1970s, $35.00 – 55.00.

Snoopy as a football player, wears a red helmet with a black stripe and holds a football under one arm, prototype pictured, 7", early 1970s, $90.00 – 140.00; Snoopy as a baseball player, 4½", 1971, $65.00 – 95.00.

• Miscellaneous (plastic, Japan) •

Snoopy stands with his face pointing upward, 4½", 1984, $18.00 – 25.00; Snoopy sits with his face pointing upward, 4", 1984, $18.00 – 25.00; Snoopy is a businessman, dressed in a blue bowler hat and red bow tie. He carries a yellow briefcase, 6", 1984, $30.00 – 40.00; Snoopy holds his blue hat in one hand and stands next to Woodstock, they wear red bowties, 4½", 1984, $22.00 – 35.00; Snoopy sits as he talks on a red telephone, 4", 1984, $22.00 – 35.00.

Cylindrical shape, clear plastic, Snoopy and Woodstock play basketball and a net hangs inside the bank, Japan, 4½" tall x 2⅛" dia., #08203-1, mid 1980s, $4.00 – 6.00; Snoopy hugs Woodstock, Japan, 6", #30438-7, mid 1980s, $18.00 – 25.00; Japanese lantern shape with wire handle, Snoopy and Woodstock are dressed in Japanese attire, Japan, 6½", 74101-9, 1984, $15.00 – 22.00.

Snoopy sits and holds a spoon to his mouth. Place a coin on the spoon and Snoopy's mouth automatically opens to digest the coin, 5¼", Determined/Tomy, #M-31, early to mid 1980s, $45.00 – 60.00; with box, $65.00 – 90.00.

• Miscellaneous (metal) •

"Fresh Up," three metal soda cans function as banks. They are affixed to a plastic backing. Made to be hung from the wall, Japan, 15" long x 2" wide x 9" tall, #EM-34, 1984, $75.00 – 100.00.

Snoopy holds a branch with three nests, a bird in each, made to be hung from the wall, Japan, 8¾" dia., #HG-69, mid 1980s; Linus, Lucy, Charlie Brown, and Sally sit in a convertible driven by Snoopy, each wears sunglasses, 8¾" dia., Determined Productions, made for Familiar, a children's department store in Japan, #740932, 1988, $25.00 – 40.00 each.

"Powerful," battery-shaped with twist-off coin receptacle on top, Snoopy's upper half, he flexes his arms, black background with red lettering, Japan, 6¾" x 4¼" dia., #BS-33, 1932; Snoopy has one arm in the air, red background with blue lettering, Japan, 6¾" x 4¼" dia., #DS-33, 1982, $20.00 – 28.00 each.

"40 Years of Happiness," Snoopy and Woodstock wear top hats and bowties. Behind them are Eudora, Schroeder, Pig Pen, Olaf, Lucy, Franklin, Sally, Marcie, Peppermint Patty, Charlie Brown, Linus, and Spike, all dressed up to celebrate. Japan, 7⅜" tall x 5⅜" dia., #DP-282, 1990, $30.00 – 40.00.

Godinger Art Company

When Godinger became a licensee of Peanuts items, they offered an extensive line of silverplated products designed for gift giving — especially to new parents — each packaged in a delightful box.

Prices are based on mint-in-the-box condition; the bank itself should be shiny or returnable to its original sheen.

Snoopy, as the Literary Ace, sits on top of his doghouse, #500, 1990; Snoopy, as the Flying Ace, sits on top of his doghouse, #501, 1990, $25.00 – 35.00 each.

Leonard Silver

These banks are silverplated. Prices are based on the bank being mint-in-the-box, although not all the stores used the original boxes. If the bank is tarnished, it must respond to proper cleaning. 1979.

Snoopy standing figural wears a baseball cap and mitt, and holds a ball, #9683, $40.00 – 65.00; Woodstock savings bank, gold tone, #9673, $25.00 – 35.00; Snoopy doghouse bank, #96670, $18.00 – 25.00; Snoopy Alphabet, block-style bank, #9669, $25.00 – 35.00; Snoopy sits, #9672, $18.00 – 25.00. All from 1979 production year.

Ohio Art

Metal globe shape on stand. Flags of the world on bottom portion. Snoopy performs various sports on upper portion. Captioned "Snoopy Bank." The globe in on a stand, but the bank is one piece. 1984. $18.00 – 29.00.

Vilac

The box which houses this bank is somewhat plain and does not affect the value of this charming and unusual bank.

Snoopy sits, wood, 6½", 1990, $60.00 – 80.00.

Willitts Designs

Banks produced by Willitts are ceramic with prices based on mint-in-the-box condition. (Some of the banks did not have boxes, and those will be noted.) There should be no chips or paint off the bank. The bank should have its stopper.

Lucy's Advice Bank, Lucy leans on her elbows at her stand, 4" x 4", #8118, 1988, $26.00 – 32.00; Peanuts Nest Egg Banks, Joe Cool stands in front of his house, no box, 3" tall, #88071, 1989, $10.00 – 14.00.

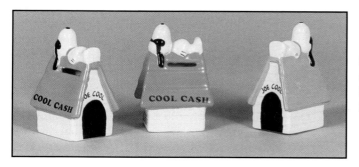

Snoopy rests on top of his doghouse, wearing sunglasses, "Cool Cash" is painted on the roof, "Joe Cool" over the doorway. Roof colors: lavender, red, blue. No box. 3½" tall, #400190, 1990, $8.00 – 12.00.

Uncle Sam Snoopy. Snoopy wears formal Uncle Sam outfit which includes red and white striped jacket and striped hat with a blue band bearing white stars. He holds a baton, 10¼" tall, #45007, 1990, $95.00 – 140.00.

Snoopy sits, Woodstock is perched on his head, 40th Anniversary edition, 8" tall, #19017, 1990, $40.00 – 55.00; Snoopy as railroad engineer, 8" tall, #45033, 1991; $40.00 – 55.00.

The Disney Studios, echoing the words of Walt himself, liked to say, "It all started with a mouse."

With Charles Schulz and Peanuts, it all started with three kids, a dog, and seven American newspapers.

Although that's easy to forget, particularly in view of the subsidiary merchandising goodies discussed elsewhere in this guide, the facts are inescapable: without the daily newspaper strip, there'd be no plush Snoopy dolls, no Christmas ornaments, no greeting cards.

It's therefore essential to devote some space to the books that have allowed collectors to accumulate the comic strips we all love. While there are undoubtedly a few people who've faithfully clipped and archived every strip as it appears, most of us — either not alive in 1950 or not perceptive enough to do the same — have relied on the many reprint books.

It has not been an easy task.

Multiple publishers and varied formats have turned what should have been an easy task into a chore of often Herculean proportions. There's really no such thing as a "Peanuts book;" the term covers considerable territory. Some books collect newspaper strip reprints, while others present popular storylines, such as *Snoopy and the Red Baron*, in a form somewhat akin to modern comic graphic novels. Some are kid-oriented adaptations of the movies and television specials, and others — *Love is Walking Hand in Hand*, for example — are gift-book collections of one-panel illustrations and philosophical observations on the mysteries of life.

Just assembling a more-or-less chronological collection of Peanuts strips can be daunting, since there's really no uniform series of titles. Worse yet, the strips reprinted in American books rarely display their date of original publication, and often are not in sequence.

The very first collection of Peanuts comic strips appeared in a book appropriately titled *Peanuts* and first published by Rinehart & Company (later Holt, Rinehart & Winston) in July of 1952. It reprinted strips from late 1950 through early 1952. By 1960 it had already gone through 20 printings.

Among book collectors, the "true First Edition" is always the prize. A First Edition in excellent condition will always fetch a premium price. (This information usually can be determined by examining the left-handed page either facing or behind the title page.) All prices shown in this guide are for First Editions; later editions should be correspondingly less expensive. Never tolerate a dealer who charges First Edition prices for third (or fifth, or seventh) edition merchandise.

Paperback books enjoying even the most attentive care are unlikely to remain in mint condition over the course of 20 years; color will fade, and covers will become dog-eared. (This is particularly true of early Holt, Rinehart & Winston titles, which were cursed with very soft covers.) A well-treated book should look as pristine as possible; all pages should be intact and firmly attached (although yellowing is permitted); covers should be flat (not bent), with no rips or tears; the spine should be intact and show no sign of having been curled back on itself; there should be no stains or writing on the inside cover, title page, or any interior pages (unless, of course it happens to be Charles Schulz's signature).

Hardcover books should bear witness to similar care. If there is a dust-jacket, it should be intact, with crisp edges. Hardcover books with missing dust-jackets are, of course, worth significantly less.

Prices shown throughout this chapter are for First Edition books in mint condition (or as near to that as possible); lesser condition will of course reduce the value. We've listed those books which are both quite popular with fans and collectors and should be a mainstay of any serious Peanuts fan's book collection. With respect to books still in print or fairly easy to obtain, we have listed "NR," which stands for "Near Retail." In this case the value would be within $5.00 of the cover price.

 ## Chronological Reprints

Early Holt, Rinehart & Winston (HRW) titles appeared in two formats: the familiar 5" x 8" books, or a horizontal 8" x 5" version. Daily strips were reprinted in the vertical manner, while Sunday strips were printed in the horizontal form. Later editions of the Sunday collections were changed to the vertical format for the sake of uniformity. During the middle 1960s, books began mixing daily and Sunday strips instead of segregating them under different titles.

The following titles are listed in their order of publication. Numbered titles reflect the first appearance of the cartoons contained therein, and also are used later for reference purposes. Date and month (when known) of first publication are shown. While this list is ordered more or less chronologically, such progression cannot be assumed; *It's a Dog's Life, Charlie Brown* and *You Can't Win, Charlie Brown* both include numerous strips from 1960 through 1962. Furthermore, the contents of all these books were completely random until *Thompson is in Trouble, Charlie Brown*, which initiated an ongoing tradition of assembling the strips in their (mostly) proper order.

Title	Value
1. *Peanuts* (7/52)*	$25.00
2. *More Peanuts* (9/54)	15.00
3. *Good Grief, More Peanuts* (10/56; Sunday strips only)	15.00
4. *Good ol' Charlie Brown* (8/57)	15.00
5. *Snoopy* (6/58)**	15.00
6. *You're Out of Your Mind Charlie Brown* (12/58; Sunday strips only)	15.00
7. *But We Love You, Charlie Brown* (8/59)	15.00
8. *Peanuts Revisited* (10/59)***	15.00
9. *Go Fly a Kite, Charlie Brown* (1960)	10.00
10. *Peanuts Every Sunday* (4/61; Sunday strips only)	10.00
11. *It's a Dog's Life, Charlie Brown* (2/62)	10.00
12. *You Can't Win, Charlie Brown* (8/62)	10.00
13. *Snoopy, Come Home* (2/63)**	10.00
14. *You Can Do It, Charlie Brown* (8/63)	10.00
15. *We're Right Behind You, Charlie Brown* (1/64; Sunday strips only)	10.00
16. *As You Like It, Charlie Brown* (10/64)	10.00
17. *Sunday's Fun Day, Charlie Brown* (9/65; Sunday strips only)	10.00
18. *You Need Help, Charlie Brown* (3/66)	10.00
19. *The Unsinkable Charlie Brown* (3/67)	10.00
20. *You'll Flip, Charlie Brown* (9/67)	10.00
21. *You're Something Else, Charlie Brown* (1968)	10.00
22. *You're You, Charlie Brown* (1968)	10.00
23. *You've Had It, Charlie Brown* (1969)	10.00
24. *You're Out of Sight, Charlie Brown* (1970)	8.00
26. *Ha Ha Herman, Charlie Brown* (1972)	8.00
28. *You're the Guest of Honor, Charlie Brown* (1973)	8.00
29. *Win a Few, Lose a Few, Charlie Brown* (1974)	8.00

1. *Peanuts*; 3. *Good Grief, More Peanuts*.

8. *Peanuts Revisited*.

* The cartoons in this debut book have never been gathered in any other title, unlike those found in almost all other books, which have been reprinted many more times. That makes this book something of a prize, although not a phenomenal prize, because its several dozen printings guarantee the existence of an awful lot of copies.
** This title is devoted exclusively to cartoons starring Snoopy, some unique, others collected in earlier books.
*** This book is a prize. It is different in three respects: it is a hardcover, complete with dust-jacket; it has roughly twice as many pages (224, to be exact); and it reprints selected cartoons from the previous four titles, in addition to containing cartoons from 1957 – 59 not found anyplace else. Although published in three different printings through April 1968, it is very hard to find. Beware of the Weekly Reader version, which contains only 80 pages.

Beginning in 1975, HRW switched to a new format, known as the Peanuts Parade Paperbacks. They are larger books, 7" x 10", with more pages, and equal to exactly 1½ of the first books. In addition to showcasing new strips, the Parade format also was used to reprint the contents of the aforementioned titles. This was done almost at random and made organizing them confusing because the Parade books were themselves assigned numbers which bore no relation to chronological order or the strips' original appearance.

The subsequent list begins with titles reprinting older material, as indicated, and then continues with collections of new strips. The numbers shown in parentheses refer to the "Peanuts Parade Paperback number," and reflect the order in which these books were published.

Title	Value
There Goes the Shutout (PPP#13; 1977), reprints *More Peanuts* and the first half of *Good Grief, More Peanuts*	$12.00
Always Stick Up for the Underbird (PPP#14; 1977), reprints the second half of *Good Grief, More Peanuts* and *Good Ol' Charlie Brown*	12.00
What Makes You Think You're Happy? (PPP#5; 1976), reprints *Snoopy* and the first half of *You're Out of Your Mind, Charlie Brown*	12.00
Fly, You Stupid Kite, Fly! (PPP#6; 1976), reprints the second half of *You're Out of Your Mind, Charlie Brown* and *But We Love You, Charlie Brown*	12.00
Thank Goodness for People (PPP#9; 1976), reprints *Go Fly a Kite, Charlie Brown* and the first half of *Peanuts Every Sunday*	12.00
What Makes Musicians So Sarcastic? (PPP#10; 1976), reprints the second half of *Peanuts Every Sunday* and *It's a Dog's Life, Charlie Brown*	12.00
The Mad Punter Strikes Again (PPP#7; 1976), reprints *Snoopy, Come Home* and the first half of *You Can't Win, Charlie Brown*	12.00
A Kiss on the Nose Turns Anger Aside (PPP#6; 1976), reprints the second half of *You Can't Win, Charlie Brown* and *You Can Do It, Charlie Brown*	12.00
There's a Vulture Outside (PPP#3; 1976), reprints *We're Right Behind You, Charlie Brown* and the first half of *Sunday's Fun Day, Charlie Brown*	12.00
What's Wrong with Being Crabby? (PPP#4; 1976), reprints the second half of *Sunday's Fun Day, Charlie Brown* and *As You Like It, Charlie Brown*	12.00
Who's the Funny-Looking Kid with the Big Nose? (PPP#1; 1976), reprints *You Need Help, Charlie Brown* and the first half of *The Unsinkable Charlie Brown*	12.00
It's a Long Way to Tipperary (PPP#2; 1976), reprints the second half of *The Unsinkable Charlie Brown* and *You'll Flip, Charlie Brown*	12.00
A Smile Makes a Lousy Umbrella (PPP#17; 1977), reprints *You're Something Else, Charlie Brown* and the first half of *You're You, Charlie Brown*	12.00
My Anxieties Have Anxieties (PPP#18; 1977), reprints the second half of *You're You, Charlie Brown* and *You've Had It, Charlie Brown*	12.00
It's Great to Be a Super Star (PPP#19; 1977), reprints *You're Out of Sight, Charlie Brown* and the first half of *You've Come a Long Way, Charlie Brown*	12.00
Stop Snowing on My Secretary (PPP#20; 1977), reprints the second half of *You've Come a Long Way, Charlie Brown* and *Ha Ha Herman, Charlie Brown*	12.00
It's Hard Work Not Being Bitter (PPP#15; 1977), reprints *Thompson is in Trouble, Charlie Brown* and the first half of *You're the Guest of Honor, Charlie Brown*	12.00
How Long, Great Pumpkin, How Long? (PPP#16; 1977), reprints the second half of *You're the Guest of Honor, Charlie Brown* and *Win a Few, Lose a Few, Charlie Brown*	12.00

Title	Value
30. *Speak Softly, and Carry a Beagle* (PPP#11; 1975; first with new material)	12.00
31. *Don't Hassle Me with Your Sighs, Chuck* (PPP#12; 1976)	12.00
32. *Summers Fly, Winters Walk* (PPP#21; 1977)	12.00
33. *The Beagle Has Landed* (PPP#22; 1978)	12.00
34. *And a Woodstock in a Birch Tree* (PPP#23; 1979)	12.00
35. *Here Comes the April Fool* (PPP#24; 1980)	12.00
36. *Dr. Beagle and Mr. Hyde* (PPP#25; 1981)	12.00
37. *You're Weird, Sir!* (PPP#26; 1982)	12.00
38. *Kiss Her, You Blockhead!* (PPP#27; 1983)	12.00
39. *I'm Not Your Sweet Babboo!* (PPP#28; 1984)	12.00
40. *The Way of the Fussbudget is Not Easy* (PPP#29; 1986)	12.00

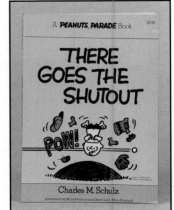

There Goes the Shutout.

Things changed again in 1985, when Topper, a division of Pharos Books, took over the publication of new chronological reprint titles. Topper did not reissue older material under different titles but concentrated solely on new collections. These are numbered in order of release. During its short run, this company produced horizontal books in three sizes: the first four are 8½" x 5", the next three are 10" x 7", and the last is 11" x 8½".

Title	Value
41. *Dogs Don't Eat Dessert* (#1; 1987)	NR
42. *You're on the Wrong Foot Again, Charlie Brown* (#2; 1987)	NR
43. *By Supper Possessed* (#3; 1988)	NR
44. *Talk is Cheep, Charlie Brown* (#4; 1988)	NR
45. *It Doesn't Take Much to Attract a Crowd* (#5; 1989)	NR
46. *If Beagles Could Fly* (#6; 1990)	NR
47. *Don't Be Sad, Flying Ace* (#7; 1990)	NR
48. *Could You Be More Pacific?* (#8; 1991)	NR

Dogs Don't Eat Dessert.

Andrews and McMeel took the reins in 1990 and released two titles in the ongoing chronological series, both 8½" x 9". They are not numbered.

Title	Value
49. *Being a Dog is a Full-Time Job* (1994)	NR
50. *Make Way for the King of the Jungle* (1995)	NR

Concurrent with most of the previous editions, Fawcett Crest issued standard, wallrack-size paperback collections of the same cartoons. Each of the early HRW titles generated two Fawcett Crest books, while the Parade-sized books produced three each. Up to this point, it was almost possible to gather the same material with Fawcett Crest books; with the sole exception of *Snoopy, Come Home* (which inexplicably generated only one Fawcett Crest title), each of the larger books' contents was faithfully reproduced in these smaller books, in easily identified pairs or runs of three.

This was not the case once Topper took over the primary reprints. Due to their unusual size, each Topper book corresponds to roughly 1½ Fawcett Crest books; thus, it takes three of the latter to equal two of the former. The contents of these later Fawcett Crest titles are not as organized and do not necessarily collect strips in the same order.

Fawcett Crest has not released any collections of material from the Andrews and McMeel books.

The Fawcett Crest titles below are arranged in sequence corresponding to the books from which their contents are drawn. The numbers in parentheses refer back to the latter, with the letters reflecting which portion of each original title is gathered.

Title	Value
2A. *The Wonderful World of Peanuts*	$6.00
2B. *Hey, Peanuts*	6.00
3A. *Good Grief, Charlie Brown*	6.00
3B. *For the Love of Peanuts*	6.00
4A. *Fun with Peanuts*	6.00
4B. *Here Comes Charlie Brown*	6.00
5A. *Here Comes Snoopy*	6.00
5B. *Good Ol' Snoopy*	6.00
6A. *Very Funny, Charlie Brown*	6.00
6B. *What Next, Charlie Brown?*	6.00
7A. *We're On Your Side, Charlie Brown*	6.00
7B. *You Are Too Much, Charlie Brown*	6.00
9A. *You're a Winner, Charlie Brown*	5.00
9B. *Let's Face It, Charlie Brown*	5.00
10A. *Who Do You Think You Are, Charlie Brown?*	5.00
10B. *You're My Hero, Charlie Brown*	5.00
11A. *This Is Your Life, Charlie Brown*	5.00
11B. *Slide, Charlie Brown, Slide*	5.00
12A. *All This and Snoopy Too*	5.00

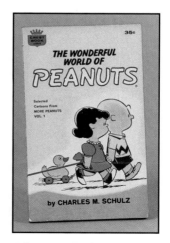

The Wonderful World of Peanuts.

Title	Value	Title	Value
12B. *Here's to You, Charlie Brown*	$5.00	32A. *Think About It Tomorrow, Snoopy*	$4.00
13. *We Love You, Snoopy*	5.00	32B. *Love and Kisses, Snoopy*	4.00
14A. *Nobody's Perfect, Charlie Brown*	5.00	32C. *Stay With It, Snoopy*	4.00
14B. *You're a Brave Man, Charlie Brown*	5.00	33A. *Jogging Is In, Snoopy*	4.00
15A. *Peanuts for Everybody*	5.00	33B. *Snoopy, Top Dog*	4.00
15B. *You've Done It Again, Charlie Brown*	5.00	33C. *Sing for Your Supper, Snoopy*	4.00
16A. *Charlie Brown and Snoopy*	5.00	34A. *You're Our Kind of Dog, Snoopy*	3.00
16B. *You're the Greatest, Charlie Brown*	5.00	34B. *Blaze the Trail, Snoopy*	3.00
17A. *It's for You, Snoopy*	5.00	34C. *This is the Best Time of Day, Charlie Brown*	3.00
17B. *Have It Your Way, Charlie Brown*	5.00	35A. *Look Out Behind You, Snoopy*	3.00
18A. *You're Not for Real, Snoopy*	5.00	35B. *Don't Bet on It, Snoopy*	3.00
18B. *You're a Pal, Snoopy*	5.00	35C. *Up and At 'Em, Snoopy*	3.00
19A. *What Now, Charlie Brown?*	5.00	36A. *It's Chow Time, Snoopy*	3.00
19B. *You're Something Special, Snoopy*	5.00	36B. *We're All in This Together, Snoopy*	3.00
20A. *You've Got a Friend, Charlie Brown*	5.00	36C. *Go For It, Charlie Brown*	3.00
20B. *Take it Easy, Charlie Brown*	5.00	37A. *Sweet Dreams, Charlie Brown*	3.00
21A. *Your Choice, Snoopy*	5.00	37B. *How Does She Do That, Charlie Brown?*	3.00
21B. *Try It Again, Charlie Brown*	5.00	37C. *You're Hopeless, Charlie Brown*	3.00
22A. *Who Was That Dog I Saw You With, Charlie Brown?*	5.00	38A. *Take Charge, Snoopy!*	3.00
22B. *There's No One Like You, Snoopy*	5.00	38B. *Let's Party, Charlie Brown*	3.00
23A. *You've Got It Made, Snoopy*	5.00	38C. *Good Morning, Snoopy*	3.00
23B. *Don't Give Up, Charlie Brown*	5.00	39A. *Go Fish Snoopy*	3.00
24A. *You're So Smart, Snoopy*	5.00	39B. *She Likes You, Charlie Brown*	3.00
24B. *Watch Out, Charlie Brown*	5.00	39C. *Get Physical Snoopy*	3.00
25A. *It's All Yours, Snoopy*	5.00	40A. *You're an Ace, Snoopy*	3.00
25B. *You've Got To Be You, Snoopy*	5.00	40B. *How Romantic, Charlie Brown*	3.00
26A. *You're On Your Own, Snoopy*	5.00	40C. *Nice Shot, Snoopy*	3.00
26B. *You Can't Win Them All, Charlie Brown*	5.00	41A. *You're Supposed to Lead, Charlie Brown*	3.00
27A. *You've Come a Long Way, Snoopy*	5.00	41B. & 42A *Hold the Fort, Snoopy*	3.00
27B. *That's Life, Snoopy*	5.00	42B. *Have No Fear, Snoopy*	3.00
28A. *It's Your Turn, Snoopy*	5.00	43A. *You're a Knockout, Charlie Brown*	3.00
28B. *You Asked For It, Charlie Brown*	5.00	43B. & 44A *It's Party Time, Charlie Brown*	3.00
29A. *Play Ball, Snoopy*	5.00	44B. *School's Out, Charlie Brown*	3.00
29B. *They're Playing Your Song, Charlie Brown*	5.00	45A. *Get Back to Nature, Snoopy*	3.00
30A. *You've Got to Be Kidding, Snoopy*	4.00	45B. & 46A *Hats Off to You, Charlie Brown*	3.00
30B. *It's Show Time, Snoopy*	4.00	46B. *Have a Ball, Snoopy*	3.00
30C. *Keep Up the Good Work, Charlie Brown*	4.00	47A. *Guess Who, Charlie Brown?*	3.00
31A. *It's Raining on Your Parade, Charlie Brown*	4.00	47B. & 48A *You're Not Alone, Charlie Brown*	3.00
31B. *Think Thinner, Snoopy*	4.00	48B. *Lead On, Snoopy*	3.00
31C. *Let's Hear It for Dinner, Snoopy*	4.00	*Strike Three, Charlie Brown**	3.00
		*Good Catch, Snoopy**	3.00

*This Fawcett Crest title gathers the contents of *Big League Peanuts* (see subsequent section on Anthology books).

Confused yet? We hope not, because it gets worse.

Since 1990, Henry Holt's Owl Books has been reprinting the HRW titles (both original and Parade-sized). These new books are the same size, 5" x 8", as the earliest HRW titles, but have solid-color covers with the banner PEANUTS CLASSICS across the top. The perplexity arises from the titles of these newest books; sometimes the titles duplicate those of the first HRW printing, and sometimes the Peanuts Parade reprinting. In the latter cases, since the Parade books were larger, the additional contents are inserted into Peanuts Classics books with entirely new titles. Owl has reprinted almost all the original HRW titles in this format with entirely new titles.

Early editions of these Classics books betray many errors: repeated pages, missing pages, and occasionally incorrect, and incomplete, contents. While in print and easier to locate, they should not be regarded as the collections of record.

As before, the Classics titles which follow are arranged in sequence corresponding to the books from which their contents are drawn. The numbers in parentheses refer back to the latter, with the letters reflecting which portion of each original title is gathered.

Title	Value
2. *There Goes the Shutout*	NR
3. *Good Grief, More Peanuts!*	NR
4. *Always Stick Up for the Underbird*	NR
5. *What Makes You Think You're Happy!*	NR
6. *You're Out of Your Mind, Charlie Brown*	NR
7. *Fly, You Stupid Kite, Fly!*	NR
9. *Thank Goodness for People*	NR
10. *Peanuts Every Sunday*	NR
11. *What Makes Musicians So Sarcastic?*	NR
12. *The Mad Punter Strikes Again*	NR
13. *You Can't Win, Charlie Brown*	NR
14. *A Kiss on the Nose Turns Anger Aside*	NR
15. *There's a Vulture Outside*	NR
16. *What's Wrong with Being Crabby?*	NR
17. *Sunday's Fun Day, Charlie Brown*	NR
18. *Who's the Funny-Looking Kid with the Big Nose?*	NR
19. *The Unsinkable Charlie Brown*	NR
20. *It's a Long Way to Tipperary*	NR
21. *A Smile Makes a Lousy Umbrella*	NR
22 & 25. *You've Come a Long Way, Charlie Brown*	NR
23. *My Anxieties Have Anxieties*	NR
24. *It's Great to Be a Superstar*	NR
26. *Stop Snowing on My Secretary!*	NR
27. *It's Hard Work Being Bitter*	NR
28. *You're the Guest of Honor, Charlie Brown*	NR
29. *How Long, Great Pumpkin, How Long?*	NR
30A. *Speak Softly, and Carry a Beagle*	NR
31A. *Don't Hassle Me with Your Sighs, Chuck*	NR
30B & 31B. *Duck, Here Comes Another Day*	NR
32A. *Summers Fly, Winters Walk*	NR

Title	Value
33A. *The Beagle Has Landed*	NR
32B & 33B. *The Cheshire Beagle*	NR
34A. *And a Woodstock in a Birch Tree*	NR
35A. *Here Comes the April Fool*	NR
34B & 35B. *Nothing Echoes Like an Empty Mailbox*	NR
36A. *Dr. Beagle and Mr. Hyde*	NR
37A. *You're Weird, Sir!*	NR
36B & 37B. *I Heard a D-Minus Call Me*	NR
38A. *Kiss Her, You Blockhead!*	NR
39A. *I'm Not Your Sweet Babboo!*	NR
38B & 39B. *Sarcasm Does Not Become You, Ma'am*	NR
40. *The Way of the Fussbudget is Not Easy*	NR

Sarcasm Does Not Become You, Ma'am.

 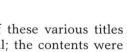

Anthologies

Equivalent to Greatest Hits music collections, the HRW anthologies began to appear in the late 1960s. The first five were large (8½" x 11") hardbound books with dust-jackets; one was also issued in trade paperback. Some feature full-color Sunday strips. Although these books are filled primarily with strips also published in the preceding chronological series, they cannot be ignored by completists, because most have at least some strips which do not appear elsewhere (except, in a few cases, in another anthology).

After these first five, both size and state (hardcover, paperback) varied widely, although the books were always much smaller. Other companies also released similar themed collections, and none of these various titles contained previously unseen material; the contents were always excerpted from other books.

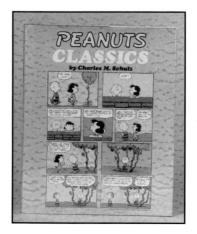

Peanuts Classics.

Title	Value
The Peanuts Treasury (10/68)	$40.00
Peanuts Classics (1970)	45.00
The Snoopy Festival (10/74 hardcover)	20.00
(1980 paperback)	10.00
Sandlot Peanuts (1977)	40.00
Classroom Peanuts (1982)	25.00
Snoopy's Tennis Book (with 8 pgs. new color art)	
(1979 hardcover)	12.00
(1979 paperback)	7.00
And the Beagles and the Bunnies Shall Lie Down	
Together (1984 paperback)	6.00
Big League Peanuts (1985 paperback)	6.00

The Snoopy Festival.

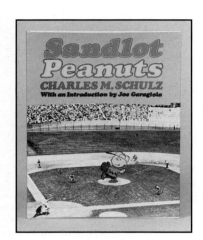

Sandlot Peanuts.

Classroom Peanuts.

• Pharos/Topper •

Title	Value
Charlie Brown: This is Your Life (1988 hardcover album)*	NR
Snoopy: My Greatest Adventures (1988 hardcover album)*	NR
Sally: School is My World (1988 hardcover album)*	NR
Schroeder: Music Is My Life (1988 hardcover album)*	NR
Brothers and Sisters: It's All Relative (1989 paperback)	NR
An Educated Slice (1990 paperback, with 16 pgs. new color art)	NR

*Translated from title originally published in Italy

• Henry Holt & Co. •

Title	Value
Snoopy's Love Book (1994 hardcover, with dust-jacket)	NR

Retrospectives

Starting in 1975 we began to see larger books which blended a mix of reprinted strips and autobiographical text by Charles Schulz. Each is a little different, with some concentrating on the comic strips themselves and others acknowledging the by-now massive ancillary merchandising explosion. As with the anthology titles, each includes some strips not previously reprinted. Publisher and date are noted for each.

Title	Value
Charlie Brown and Charles Schulz	
(1970 World hardcover)	.$25.00
(11/71 Signet paperback)	.5.00
Peanuts Jubilee	
(1975 HRW hardcover, 15" x 11¼")	.45.00
(10/76 HRW paperback)	.15.00
Happy Birthday, Charlie Brown	
(1979 Random House hardcover)	.25.00
(10/80 Ballantine paperback)	.12.00
Charlie Brown, Snoopy and Me	
(1981 Fawcett Columbine Books paperback) . .	.10.00
You Don't Look 35, Charlie Brown	
(1985 HRW hardcover)	.20.00
(1985 HRW paperback)	.10.00
Charles M. Schulz 40 Years Life and Art	
(Deluxe 9¾" x 12¾" slipcovered Pharos Books hardback, edited by Giovanni Trimboli, translated from the Italian original; 1990)	.NR
Around the World in 45 Years	
(1994 Andrews & McMeel hardcover)	.NR
(1994 Andrews & McMeel paperback)	.NR

Around the World in 45 Years.

Storybooks

Some of the more popular and extended storylines were modified from their original four-panel format and turned into themed "graphic novelettes." These were all published by HRW in hardcover.

Title	Value
Snoopy and the Red Baron (1966)	.$10.00
Snoopy and His Sopwith Camel (1969)	.10.00
It Was a Dark and Stormy Night (1971)	.10.00
Snoopy's Grand Slam (1972)	.10.00
I Never Promised You an Apple Orchard (1976)	.10.00

***Snoopy** and the Red Baron; Snoopy and His Sopwith Camel.*

Gift Books

Although Charlie Brown and his friends had become household names by the mid 1950s and an international phenemenon by the mid 1960s, no single book achieved near the impact of a modest little collection first published by Determined Productions in 1962, *Happiness is a Warm Puppy*. It became the gift to be passed between husband and wife, boyfriend and girlfriend, parent and child. Its success spawned numerous sequels and generated an equally popular series of Scholastic paperback reprints. Many of the original titles resurfaced in the 1970s, with greatly modified contents that reflected the absence of some characters (Violet, Shermy, Patty, Frieda) and the introduction of newer characters (Marcie, Peppermint Patty, Woodstock). The original hardcovers have dust-jackets, as do the later hardcover reprints.

Hallmark, long known for its extensive line of Peanuts greeting cards, got into the act with its "Peanuts Philoso-phers" series of small hardcover books (no dust-jackets), as well as highly-prized children's pop-up books (all hardback). HRW and Andrews & McMeel also released a few titles clearly designed to capture part of this market.

Starting in 1996, HarperCollins began an ambitious release program of Peanuts gift books in a variety of different sizes and styles. Most are square-shaped hardcovers that collect newspaper strips according to a certain theme, such as Christmas, Valentine's Day or Snoopy in his "Joe Legal" mode. Others are storybooks aimed at younger readers, while still others are prestige blends of commentary and comic strips revolving around a specific character. And still others are hard to categorize, so we haven't even tried! All HarperCollins titles are in print, so you should not expect to pay more than cover price for any of them. We've grouped them alphabetically according to size, rather than by subject.

• Determined/Scholastic •

Title	Value
Happiness is a Warm Puppy	
(1962 hardcover) $14.00	
(1971 paperback) 2.00	
(1979 hardcover) .6.00	
(1983 paperback) .2.00	
Security is a Thumb and a Blanket	
(1963 hardcover) .14.00	
(1971 paperback) .2.00	
(1982 hardcover) .6.00	
(1983 paperback) .2.00	
I Need All the Friends I Can Get	
(1964 hardcover) .12.00	
(1977 paperback) .2.00	
(1981 hardcover) .6.00	
(1983 paperback) .2.00	
Christmas is Together Time	
(1964 hardcover) .12.00	
(1981 hardcover) .10.00	
(1983 paperback) .4.00	
Love is Walking Hand in Hand	
(1965 hardcover) .12.00	
(1971 paperback) .2.00	
(1979 hardcover) .8.00	
(1982 paperback) .2.00	
Home is On Top of a Doghouse	
(1966 hardcover) .12.00	
(1982 hardcover) .8.00	
(1983 paperback) .4.00	

Title	Value
Happiness is a Sad Song	
(1967 hardcover) $6.00	
Suppertime (1968 hardcover) 6.00	
Peanuts Cook Book	
(1968 hardcover) .6.00	
(1970 paperback) .3.00	
Peanuts Lunch Bag Cook Book	
(1970 hardcover) .6.00	
(1974 paperback) .3.00	
It's Fun to Lie Here and Listen to the Sounds of the Night	
(1970 hardcover) .7.00	
Winning May Not Be Everything, but	
Losing Isn't Anything (1970 hardcover) 7.00	
For a Nickel I Can Cure Anything (1970 hardcover) .7.00	
It Really Doesn't Take Much to Make a Dad Happy	
(1970 hardcover) .7.00	
Snoopy's Doghouse Cook Book (1979 paperback) . . .8.00	
Great Pumpkin Cook Book (1981 paperback) 10.00	
Snoopy and the Gang Out West (1982 hardcover) . .20.00	
Snoopy Omnibus	
(1982 hardcover) .15.00	
(1983 paperback) .7.00	
Snoopy and the Twelve Days of Christmas	
(1984 hardcover; pop-up book) 25.00	
Mischief on Daisy Hill (1993 hardcover) . . . . .NR	

Home is On Top of a Doghouse.

Peanuts Cook Book.

Great Pumpkin Cook Book.

Snoopy & the Gang Out West.

Snoopy Omnibus.

Snoopy and the Twelve Days of Christmas.

• Hallmark •

Title	Value
Charlie Brown's Reflections (1967)	$5.00
The Wit and Wisdom of Snoopy (1967)	5.00
Lucy Looks at Life (1967)	5.00
The Meditations of Linus (1967)	5.00
The World According to Lucy (1968)	5.00
Snoopy's Philosophy (1968)	5.00
Linus on Life (1968)	5.00
The Wisdom of Charlie Brown (1968)	5.00
Thoughts on Getting Well (1968)	7.00
All About Friendship (1968)	7.00
The Peanuts Platform (1968 paperback)	12.00
We All Have Our Hangups (1969)	8.00
Help Stamp Out Things that Need Stamping Out (1969)	8.00
It Always Rains on Our Generation (1969)	8.00
Everything I Do Makes Me Feel Guilty (1969)	8.00
A Peanuts Valentine (1971)	9.00
Love, Sweet Love (1971)	8.00
The Flying Ace (1971)	10.00
All About Birthdays (1971)	$7.00

Title	Value
Yes, Santa, There is a Charlie Brown (1971)	8.00
Live and Learn (1971)	7.00
Charlie Brown's World (1971)	8.00
A Woman's World (Ambassador Division of Hallmark 1971)	9.00
Cheery Sayings of Snoopy (Ambassador Division of Hallmark 1971)	7.00
Everybody and His Dog Wishes You a Happy Birthday! (Ambassador Division of Hallmark 1971)	8.00
It's the Thought That Counts (Ambassador Division of Hallmark 1972)	8.00
A Letter from Me (Ambassador Division of Hallmark 1972)	8.00
All I Want for Christmas Is... (1972)	10.00
Snoopy's Home Medical Advisor (1972)	8.00
Reflections of You (1972)	7.00
The Very Best Dad of Them All (1972)	7.00
This is Your Day (1972)	8.00
I Would Have Written Sooner But... (1972)	8.00

Title	Value	Title	Value
What Makes This Country So Great? (1972)	$10.00	*It's Good to Have a Friend* (1972 pop-up)	$40.00
The Peanuts Philosophers (1972 pop-up)	40.00	*Wishing You a Very Merry Christmas* (1973)	10.00
Snoopy's Secret Life (1972 pop-up)	40.00	*Christmas Time With Snoopy And His Friends*	
Love A La Peanuts (1972 pop-up)	40.00	(1978 pop-up)	45.00

The Peanuts Platform.

The Peanuts Philosophers.

Snoopy's Secret Life.

It's Good to Have a Friend.

• Hallmark boxed sets of four books •

Title	Value
The Peanuts Philosophers (contains *The World According to Lucy, Snoopy's Philosophy, The Wisdom of Charlie Brown,* and *Linus on Life*)	$25.00
More Peanuts Philosophers (contains *The Wit and Wisdom of Snoopy, Lucy Looks at Life, Charlie Brown's Reflections,* and *The Meditations of Linus*)	25.00

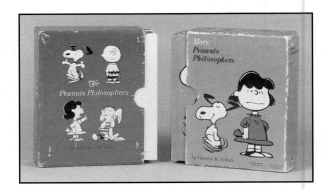
The Peanuts Philosophers; More Peanuts Philosophers.

• Holt, Rinehart & Winston/Owl •

Title	Value
Things I Learned After It Was Too Late (1981 hardcover)	$10.00
Things I've Had to Learn Over and Over (1984 hardcover)	10.00
(1989 paperback)	6.00

• Andrews & McMeel •

Title	Value
Dr. Snoopy's Advice to Pet Owners (1993 hardcover)	NR

• HarperCollins •

Title	Value
4¼" square hardcovers:	
Bah, Humbug!	NR
Birthdays Are No Piece of Cake	NR
Bon Voyage!	NR
Born Crabby	NR
Eating Is My Business	NR
Friends for Life	NR
Happy Halloween!	NR
Happy New Year	NR
I Love You	NR
Laughter Is the Best Exercise	NR
Lighten Up, It's Christmas	NR
Love Is in the Air	NR
Season's Greetings	NR
You Can Count on Me	NR
You're Divine, Valentine!	NR
6¼" square hardcovers:	
The Doctor Is In(sane)	NR
Dogs Are from Jupiter (Cats Are from the Moon)	NR
A Good Caddie Is Hard to Find	NR
Happy Birthday! (And One to Glow On)	NR
Have Another Cookie (It'll Make You Feel Better)	NR
Here's to You, Mom!	NR
Insights from the Outfield	NR
It's Christmas!	NR
Life's Answers (And Much, Much More)	NR
Life Is Like a 10-Speed Bicycle	NR
The Literary Ace Strikes Again	NR
Love Isn't Easy	NR
Me, Stressed Out?	NR
Once You're Over the Hill, You Begin to Pick Up Speed	NR
Our Lines Must Be Crossed!	NR
Peanuts Christmas Ornament Book	NR
Punt, Pass and Peanuts	NR
See You Later, Litigator!	NR
Siblings Should Never Be in the Same Family	NR
Somebody Loves You	NR
Tis the Season to Be Crabby	NR
Way Beyond Therapy	NR
You're the Tops, Pops!	NR

Title	Value
8" square children's storybook softcovers:	
Aaugh! A Dog Ate My Book Report!	NR
Beware of the Snoring Ghost!	NR
Everyone Gets Gold Stars But Me	NR
A Flying Ace Needs Lots of Root Beer	NR
Have Fun at Beanbag Camp!	NR
I'll Be Home Soon, Snoopy	NR
It's the First Day of School!	NR
I've Been Traded for a Pizza!	NR
Kick the Ball, Marcie!	NR
Leaf it to Sally Brown	NR
My Best Friend, My Blanket	NR
Travels with My Cactus	NR
You Have a Brother Named Spike?	NR
Your Dog Plays Hockey?	NR
You're Our New Mascot, Chuck	NR
9¼" square children's storybook hardcovers:	
Happy Halloween, Great Pumpkin	NR
Happy Valentine's Day, Sweet Babboo!	NR
The Round-Headed Kid and Me	NR
Sally's Christmas Miracle	NR
Sally's Christmas Play	NR
9¼" square hardcover character books:	
Charlie Brown: Not Your Average Blockhead	NR
Lucy: Not Just Another Pretty Face	NR
Snoopy: Not Your Average Dog	NR
Miscellaneous size and format:	
Funny Pictures: Cartooning with Charles M. Schulz	NR
Good Grief! Some Dates Are Hard to Remember Datebook	NR
Memories and Mistletoe: A Christmas Keepsake Album	NR
Pop! Goes the Beagle (musical)	NR
Snoopy's Christmas Tree (musical)	NR
Trick or Treat, Great Pumpkin (musical)	NR

Film & Television Adaptations

Just as popular mainstream films inevitably generate written novelizations, the Peanuts films and television specials and the first play were adapted to the written form. Designed primarily as children's storybooks, they blend cels (individual hand-drawn and painted images) with dialog lifted directly from the source. Some titles were produced by more than one publisher; World handled the first TV adaptions, but this duty soon fell to Random House, which issued its own version of some first published by World.

Many titles appeared in both hardcover and paperback editions, but from different publishers. Signet released the paperback versions of World titles, Scholastic handled most published by Random House, and Fawcett Crest released those from Holt, Rinehart & Winston.

• World/Signet •

Title	Value
A Charlie Brown Christmas	
(1965 hardcover)	$20.00
(9/67 paperback)	3.00
Charlie Brown's All-Stars	
(1966 hardcover)	20.00
(7/67 paperback)	3.00
It's the Great Pumpkin, Charlie Brown	
(1967 hardcover)	25.00
(8/68 paperback)	3.00
You're in Love, Charlie Brown	
(1968 hardcover)	30.00
(1/69 paperback)	3.00
He's Your Dog, Charlie Brown	
(1968 hardcover)	15.00
(9/69 paperback)	3.00
It Was a Short Summer, Charlie Brown	
(1970 hardcover)	20.00
(2/71 paperback)	3.00
Play It Again, Charlie Brown (1971 hardcover)	15.00
You're Not Elected, Charlie Brown	
(1973 hardcover)	15.00

Title	Value
Charlie Brown's Yearbook (1970 hardcover, includes *Charlie Brown's All-Stars*; *He's Your Dog, Charlie Brown*; *It's the Great Pumpkin, Charlie Brown*; and *You're in Love, Charlie Brown*)	$35.00

Charlie Brown's Yearbook.

• Random House/Scholastic •

Title	Value
A Charlie Brown Christmas (1965 hardcover)	$22.00
You're a Good Man, Charlie Brown	
(1967 hardcover)	15.00
A Charlie Brown Thanksgiving (1974 hardcover)	10.00
There's No Time for Love, Charlie Brown	
(1974 hardcover)	10.00
It's a Mystery, Charlie Brown (1975 hardcover)	10.00
Be My Valentine, Charlie Brown (1976 hardcover)	10.00

Title	Value
It's the Easter Beagle, Charlie Brown	
(1976 hardcover)	$11.00
You're a Good Sport, Charlie Brown	
(1976 hardcover)	9.00
It's Arbor Day, Charlie Brown (1977 hardcover)	10.00
It's Your First Kiss, Charlie Brown (1978 hardcover)	7.00
What a Nightmare, Charlie Brown (1978 hardcover)	8.00
You're the Greatest, Charlie Brown (1979 hardcover)	9.00
Bon Voyage, Charlie Brown (And Don't Come Back)	
(1980 paperback)	15.00

Title	Value
It's the Great Pumpkin, Charlie Brown	
(1980 hardcover)	.$12.00
She's a Good Skate, Charlie Brown	
(1981 hardcover)	.10.00
Life is a Circus, Charlie Brown (1981 hardcover) . . .	.9.00

Title	Value
Someday You'll Find Her, Charlie Brown	
(1982 hardcover)	.$9.00
Is This Goodbye, Charlie Brown? (1984 hardcover)	. .7.00
Snoopy's Getting Married (1986 hardcover)	.7.00
Happy New Year, Charlie Brown (1986 paperback)	. .5.00

• Holt, Rinehart & Winston/Fawcett Crest •

Title	Value
A Boy Named Charlie Brown (1969 hardcover) . . .	.$25.00
(10/71 paperback)	.8.00
The Snoopy Come Home Movie Book	
(1972 hardcover)	.22.00
(1973 paperback)	.6.00
Race for Your Life, Charlie Brown (1978 hardcover)	. .18.00

• Topper •

Title	Value
Why, Charlie Brown, Why?	
(1990 hardcover)	.NR
(1990 paperback)	.NR

Books About Peanuts

Although Robert Short's two superb studies of Peanuts' theological content are the best known examinations of Schulz's deeper subtexts, they are by no means alone. Peanuts is actually unique in this respect. Very few newspaper strips have been deemed worthy of academic or even popular analysis; fewer still have seen books published on such research. All these titles include reprints of numerous Peanuts comic strips and excerpts.

Title	Value
The Gospel According to Peanuts by Robert Short	
(12/64 John Knox paperback)	.$6.00
(2/68 Bantam paperback)	.3.00
The Parables of Peanuts by Robert Short	
(1968 Harper & Row hardcover)	.8.00
What's It All About, Charlie Brown? by Jeffrey H. Loria	
(1968 HRW hardcover)	.8.00
Why Salt the Peanuts: Sayings of the 5-Cent Psychiatrist	
by Benjamin Weininger and Henry Rabin	
(1979 Guild of Tutors Press paperback)	.6.00
The Doctor is In, by Maurice Berquist	
(1981 Warner Press hardcover)	.NR
(1986 Henry Holt & Co. paperback)	.NR
The Peanuts Trivia and Reference Book, by Monte Schulz	
and Jody Millward	
(1986 Henry Holy & Co. paperback)	.NR
When Do the Good Things Start? by Abraham J. Twerski	
(1988 Topper paperback)	.NR

The Peanuts Trivia & Reference Book.

Miscellaneous Peanuts Titles

Some books simply defy easy description, while others have been packaged in particularly unique formats. With respect to the latter, value always depends on the condition of the packaging, in addition to the appearance of the books themselves.

Title	Value
The Snoopy Collection, by J.C. Suares, from World Almanac Publishing (1982)	$18.00
The Charlie Brown Dictionary, complete in one book, from World, later from Random House (1973) each book in the original eight-volume set, from World (1973)	8.00
Charlie Brown's 'Cyclopedia, complete fifteen volume set, from Funk & Wagnalls (1980 – 81)	24.00
Mattel's Boxed Set, contains nine hardcover double books reprinting 18 of the original Holt, Rinehart & Winston, chronological titles (1979)	100.00
Charlie Brown Boxed Set, contains five Fawcett Crest paperbacks (1970s)	20.00

Title	Value
Snoopy Boxed Set, contains five Fawcett Crest paperbacks (1970s)	$20.00
Snoopy Boxed Set #2, contains six Fawcett Crest paperbacks (1970s)	24.00
Peanuts Box Set #2, contains six Fawcett Crest paperbacks (1970s)	24.00
Snoopy in Fashion, from Chronicle Books (1984)	20.00
Snoopy Around the World: Dressed by Top Fashion Designers, text by Charles M. Schulz; photos by Alberto Rizzo, Henry N. Abrams, Inc. hardcover (1990)	35.00
Official Price Guide to Peanuts Collectibles, written by Andrea C. Podley and Freddi Margolin, from House of Collectibles Division of Random House (1990)	40.00

Charles Schulz Biography

Title	Value
Good Grief: The Story of Charles M. Schulz, by Rheta Grimsley Johnson (1989 Pharos hardcover)	NR

Books by Charles Schulz with *No* Peanuts Content

Before Peanuts became such a recognized phenomenon, Schulz divided his time between this strip and other cartooning assignments. He produced quite a number of one-panel gags for various Christian youth periodicals, which were later gathered and published in book form. He also contributed illustrations for a few other titles, notably the two bestsellers drawn from Art Linkletter's popular adventures with children and live television.

Title	Value
Kids Say the Darndest Things, by Art Linkletter (1957 Prentice hall hardcover)	. . . .$16.00
Kids Still Say the Darndest Things, by Art Linkletter (1961 Prentice Hall hardcover)	. . . . .14.00
Teenager is Not a Disease (1961 Warner Press hardcover)	. . . . .18.00
Teenagers Unite (1961 Warner Press hardcover)	. . . . .18.00
(6/67 Bantam Books paperback)	. . . . .5.00
Young Pillars (1961 Warner Press hardcover)	. . . . .8.00
(1958 Warner Press paperback	. . . .
Dear President Johnson (1964 William Morrow hardcover)	. . . . . . .15.00
(6/65 Avon paperback)	. . . . .5.00
Two-By-Fours (1965 Warner Press hardcover)	. . . .20.00
What Was Bugging Ol' Pharaoh? (1964 Warner Press hardcover)	. . . . .15.00
(1970 Warner Press paperback)	. . . . .3.00
Tennis Love: A Parents Guide to the Sport, by Billie Jean King (1978 MacMillan Press)	. .12.00

Dear President Johnson.

 # Foreign Titles

While a complete listing of all foreign Peanuts books would undoubtedly fill a guide twice this size, we feel compelled to cite two countries, England and France, because of their superior presentations.

England's Ravette Books Limited was very ambitious with its Peanuts collections during the 1980s and released paperback books in several different formats. All are numbered within each format. Some reprint strips in chronological order and are similar in content and appearance to the American books from Topper. Others, notably the "Snoopy Stars As" series (identical in size to the American Fawcett Crest paperbacks), assemble cartoons from the numerous decades according to a particular theme. Still others reprint Sunday strips in full color. Unlike most American collections, all the Ravette books reprint strips with their original dates, an invaluable bonus for researchers. These books have all gone out-of-print, although they sometimes turn up on the bargain tables in American and Canadian bookstores. (They should be grabbed quickly when so located!) The listing is simply for your reference.

The Sportsman.

"Snoopy Stars As..."

1. *The Flying Ace*
2. *The Matchmaker*
3. *The Terror of the Ice*
4. *The Legal Beagle*
5. *The Fearless Leader*
6. *Man's Best Friend*
7. *The Sportsman*
8. *The Scourge of the Fairways*
9. *The Branch Manager*
10. *The World-Famous Literary Ace*
11. *The Great Pretender*
12. *The Dog-Dish Gourmet*
13. *The Fitness Freak*
14. *The Pursuit of Pleasure*
15. *The Weatherman*
16. *The Thinker*
17. *The Mixed Doubles*
18. *Brotherly Love*
19. *Ludwig Van Beagle*
20. *The Holiday Maker*
21. *The Entertainer*

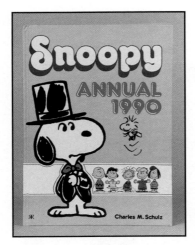

Snoopy Annual 1990.

Black & White Chronological Series
1. *It's a Dog's Life*
2. *Roundup*
3. *Freewheelin'*
4. *Joe Cool*
5. *Chariots for Hire*
6. *Come Fly with Me*
7. *Are Magic*
8. *Hit the Headlines*

Color Sunday Landscapes
1. *First Serve*
2. *Be Prepared*
3. *Stay Cool*
4. *Shall We Dance?*
5. *Let's Go*

Weekender
Weekender #1

Annuals
1990
1991
1992
1993

Dargaud, which publishes books in France and Canada, also has done very well by Peanuts over the years. The major attraction here is that these collections reprint all the strips in full color, Sunday and daily. The drawback is that the colors are not necessarily "accurate." For example, Linus' shirt sometimes turns up with red and yellow stripes, when we usually see him with a green and black striped shirt. As with Ravette, Dargaud includes original dates on all strips. All titles are numbered. Again, the following lists are for reference only.

Paperback 16/22 Collections
60. *Snoopy Super Champion*
69. *Bonne Annee Snoopy*
76. *Snoopy, Toujours Pret!*
81. *Snoopy et Le Baron Rouge*
96. *Snoopy et Les Femmes*
115. *Snoopy Ecrivain*
122. *La Maison de Snoopy*
129. *Snoopy et Les Chats*
136. *Snoopy, La Vie Est Belle!*
143. *Snoopy et Le Sport*
152. *Snoopy et Le Grand Braque*
159. *Snoopy et Ses Amis*

Hardcover albums
1. *Reviens Snoopy*
2. *Incroyable Snoopy*
3. *Intrepide Snoopy*
4. *Imbattable Snoopy*
5. *Inegalable Snoopy*
6. *L'infaillible Snoopy*
7. *Irresistible Snoopy*
8. *Ineffable Snoopy*
9. *Invincible Snoopy*
10. *Inattaquable Snoopy*
11. *Inepuisable Snoopy*
12. *Inenarrable Snoopy*
13. *Elementaire Mon Cher Snoopy*
14. *Fantastique Snoopy*
15. *Snoopy, Vive Les Vacances*
16. *Snoopy, Feu d'Artifice!*
17. *Snoopy, Noel Blanc*
18. *Snoopy, Poisson d'Avril*
19. *Snoopy, Chienne de Vie*
20. *Snoopy, Chaud Devant*
21. *Bons Baisers de Snoopy*
22. *Snoopy Garde Le Cap*
23. *Snoopy Reste Dans La Note*
24. *Snoopy Est un Drole D'oiseau*
25. *Snoopy Vise Toujours Plus Haut*
26. *Snoopy Se Fait Mousser*

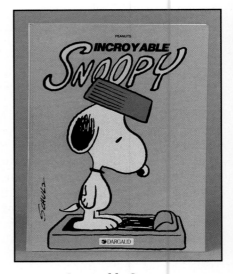

Incroyable Snoopy.

 # Coloring Books

Coloring books remain under-appreciated treasures, if only because they give us an opportunity to admire Charles Schulz's artwork in a much larger format. (Besides, few of us can resist the chance to rekindle our love affair with a fresh box of unmashed crayons!)

Thanks to misguided parents who discarded them as the kids grew up, or — horrors! — children who actually colored them, mint coloring books have become much more scarce that many other collectibles. The older Saalfield books, with their now-classic character poses, are particularly desirable.

Completists take note: some coloring books include four-panel newspaper strips which have not been reprinted elsewhere.

Prices reflect books in excellent to mint condition. There should be no writing or drawing inside. The cover should have no wear or tear on it, and the binding should be intact (not split).

Books are listed by each publisher chronologically. All measurements are approximate.

• Allan Publishers, Inc. (Baltimore, MD) •

These books measure 11" x 14".

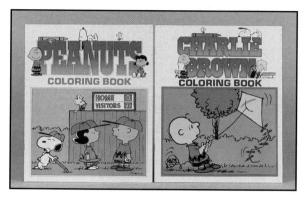

*"**Peanuts** Coloring Book,"* Lucy and Charlie Brown talk baseball, Snoopy stands nearby and Woodstock reads a book as he sits on a fence, ISBN #0-8241-7050-4, 1982; *"Charlie Brown Coloring Book,"* Charlie Brown tries to manage his kite, ISBN #0-8241-7051-2; $8.00 – 10.00 each.

*"**Snoopy** Coloring Book,"* Snoopy looks up at Woodstock, who has fashioned a nest from crayons, ISBN #0-8241-7052-0, 1982; *"Snoopy & Woodstock Coloring Book,"* Snoopy paints a portrait of Charlie Brown, Woodstock approves, ISBN #0-8241-7053-9, 1982; $8.00 – 10.00 each.

• Artcraft (Saafield Publishing Co., Akron, OH) •

These books measure 8⅛" x 10¾".

*"**Peanuts** Coloring Book featuring Peppermint Patty,"* Snoopy and Peppermint Patty dance, "He's a funny looking kid, but he sure can dance..." #3965, 1969, $10.00 – 18.00.

*"**Peanuts** Coloring Book,"* seven members of the Peanuts gang stand together, with Snoopy off to one side, "I would have made a good sheep dog...", #5328, early 1970s, $14.00 – 22.00; *"Peanuts Coloring Book featuring Charlie Brown,"* Charlie Brown leans against his mailbox and thinks, "Happiness is getting a letter," #3991, 1970, $12.00 – 20.00; *"Peanuts Coloring Book featuring Charlie Brown,"* Charlie Brown stands on the baseball mound, "Rats," #4647, 1970; $12.00 – 20.00.

*"**Peanuts** Coloring Book,"* Snoopy has a puzzled look as Woodstock sleeps on top of his head, "Suddenly I can think of about ten things I'd rather be doing right now...", #5330, 1971; *"Linus Coloring Book,"* Linus points in one direction, #A1834, 1972; *"Peppermint Patty Coloring Book,"* side view of Peppermint Patty as she runs excitedly, #A1836, 1972; $10.00 – 14.00 each.

• Child Art Productions, Inc. (Akron, OH) •

These books measure 8⅛" x 10¾".

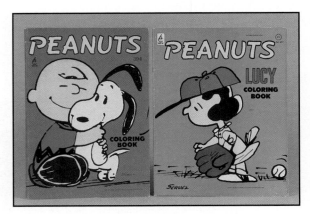

*"**Peanuts** Coloring Book,"* Charlie Brown hugs Snoopy, 1972; *"Peanuts featuring Lucy,"* Side view of Lucy wearing a baseball cap and glove, #6014, 1972; $10.00 – 14.00 each.

• Determined Productions (San Francisco, CA) •

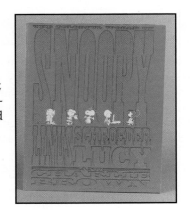

"The Colorful World of Snoopy, Linus, Schroeder, Lucy, and Charlie Brown," each character pictured, early 1960s, two sizes: 9⅞" x 12½" and 14⅛" x 19⅝", $25.00 – 40.00.

• Golden Books (Racine, WI) •

These books measure 7⅞" x 10⅞".

*"**Charlie Brown** Colouring Book,"* Charlie Brown stands on the baseball mound, #4010-16, 1984 (Canadian version); *"Snoopy and Friends. A Big Coloring Book,"* football star Snoopy kisses cheerleader Lucy, #1110, 1987; $2.00 – 4.00 each.

*"**Snoopy** and Friends: A Giant Coloring Book,"* Snoopy windsurfs, Woodstock rides an inner tube, #3143-87, 1987, $2.00 – 4.00; *"Snoopy and Friends: A Giant Coloring/Activity Book,"* Charlie Brown hugs Snoopy very tightly, #3143-88, 1988, $3.00 – 7.00; *"Snoopy and Friends Colouring Book,"* artist Snoopy paints a picture for Woodstock, #91610-98, 1987 (Canadian version), $2.00 – 4.00.

• Hallmark (Kansas City, MO) •

These books measure 8" x 10¾".

*"**Peanuts** Coloring Book for Preschoolers,"* Snoopy holds balloons for Woodstock (includes four pages of stickers), #125PF121-5, 1976, $18.00 – 25.00; *"Peanuts Great Pumpkin Coloring Book,"* Linus and Snoopy in the pumpkin patch, #100HPF901-6, 1978, $20.00 – 32.00.

• Happy House (a division of Random House, New York, NY) •

These books measure 8" x 10⅞".

*"**Charlie Brown** and the Gang: Travels with Snoopy,"* Snoopy stands on a trunk and Woodstock stands next to directional signs, 1984, $2.00 – 4.00; *"Snoopy's Christmastime Coloring Fun,"* Santa Snoopy and Woodstock sit on a chimney, reading Snoopy's Christmas list, 1984, $4.00 – 6.00; *"Woodstock's Woodland Adventures,"* Beagle Scouts Snoopy and Woodstock stand near a Forest Trail sign, 1984, $2.00 – 4.00.

"You're A Good Sport, Charlie Brown," Charlie Brown holds a load of sporting equipment, Woodstock stands in a football helmet, 1984; *"School Days: Learn-to-Read Coloring Book,"* Sally holds Woodstock and his nest for Lucy and Charlie Brown at Show and Tell, 1984; *"Early Words,"* four panels, each with a different character, 1984; $2.00 – 4.00 each.

• Ottenheimer Publishers, Inc. (New York, NY) •

These books measure 8½" x 10¾".

"The Snoopy Busy Day Coloring Book," Snoopy, with umbrella, watches Woodstock sail in his supper dish, 1979, $2.00 – 4.00; *"The Peanuts Gang Coloring Book,"* Schroeder, Charlie Brown, and Lucy on the baseball mound, 1979, $4.00 – 6.00; *"The Snoopy Playtime Coloring Book,"* Snoopy and Woodstock fishing, 1979, $2.00 – 4.00.

"*The Peanuts Christmas Coloring Book,*" Charlie Brown looks confused, as Snoopy sits in the midst of his unwrapped Christmas gifts, 1979; "*The Charlie Brown Christmas Coloring Book,*" Charlie Brown receives shopping tips from a snowman stationed at Lucy's psychiatrist booth, 1979; "*The Snoopy Christmas Coloring Book,*" Snoopy looks at Woodstock sleeping in his nest, a Christmas stocking hangs over the side, 1979; $4.00 – 6.00 each.

"*Good Ol' Charlie Brown! Coloring Book,*" Charlie Brown shows Lucy his self-portrait, 1980, $2.00 – 4.00; "*The Gang's All Here Coloring Book,*" Snoopy juggles balls while riding a unicycle, Woodstock sits on his hand, Linus, Sally, and Charlie Brown watch, 1980, $4.00 – 6.00; "*Good Grief, Charlie Brown Coloring Book,*" Charlie Brown receives psychiatric help from Lucy, 1980, $2.00 – 4.00.

"*Peanuts Funtime Coloring Book,*" Lucy pulls the football from a running Charlie Brown, Linus stands in left corner holding a football, 1980; "*Snoopy Playtime Coloring Book,*" Snoopy uses a phone from Woodstock's nest, Charlie Brown stands in the right corner talking on phone, 1980; "*Peanuts Rainy Day Coloring Book,*" Charlie Brown delivers dinner to Snoopy who dances on the roof of his doghouse in the rain, Woodstock sits in lower right corner, 1980; $2.00 – 4.00 each.

"*Snoopy Funtime Coloring Book,*" Peppermint Patty and Snoopy watch Charlie Brown fly a kite, 1980; "*Charlie Brown All Day Coloring Book,*" Foreign Legionnaires Snoopy and Woodstock join Lucy in her inflatable pool, Charlie Brown in lower right-hand corner, 1980; "*Snoopy Busy Day Coloring Book,*" Snoopy as a scarecrow guards a field while Woodstock rides a tractor, Lucy stands in right-hand corner, 1980; $2.00 – 4.00 each.

"*Curtains Up, Snoopy Fun Coloring Book,*" theater usher Snoopy holds an intermission sign for Charlie Brown and Lucy, 1980, $8.00 – 10.00; "*Not Again, Charlie Brown Fun Coloring Book,*" Charlie Brown looks at Snoopy and Woodstock, tangled in his kite string, 1980; "*Snoopy, the One and Only Fun Coloring Book,*" Snoopy stands on a rock and kisses Peppermint Patty, 1980; $2.00 – 4.00 each.

Not Pictured:
"*The Peanuts Fun Time Coloring Book.*" Snoopy gives a "Pawpet Theater" performance for Charlie Brown and Lucy, 1979. . . . .$4.00 – 6.00

• Price/Stern/Sloan Publishers, Inc. (Los Angeles, CA) •

These books measure 10⅞" x 8⅜".

"Snoopy Antique Planes Coloring Book," Snoopy and Woodstock view a 1930 Bellanca aircraft, #0-8431-0836-3, 1980; *"Snoopy Railroad Trains Coloring Book,"* Snoopy and Woodstock as engineers stand near a red caboose, #0-8431-0837-1, 1980; $14.00 – 22.00 each.

"Snoopy Boats & Ships Coloring Book," Snoopy fishes as a freighter floats by, #0-8431-0839-8, 1981; *"Snoopy Antique Autos,"* Snoopy stands on the running board of an E.M.F. Model 30 Touring Car, #0-8431-0838-X, 1981; $14.00 – 22.00 each.

"Snoopy Cars" (Spanish version shown *"Snoopy Carachas"*), Snoopy drives a 1919 Baillot, distributed by Fernandez Editors in Mexico, #101, 1987; $14.00 – 22.00.

• Rand McNally & Co. (Chicago, IL) •

These books measure 8⅜" x 10¾".

"We Lost Again, Gang!" Charlie Brown and Lucy stand on the baseball mound, #3085, 1980; *"Have a Good Time, Snoopy,"* Snoopy and Woodstock each wear party hats, #3086, 1980; $4.00 – 6.00 each.

"It's Your Serve, Snoopy," Woodstock watches Snoopy serve a tennis ball, #3088, 1980; *"It's Suppertime, Snoopy,"* Charlie Brown hands Snoopy his supper dish, 1980; $2.00 – 4.00 each.

• Saalfield (Akron, Ohio) •

These books measure 8¼" x 10⅝".

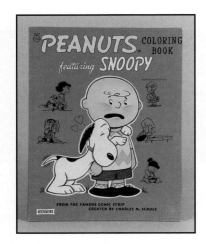

"Peanuts Coloring Book featuring Snoopy," Snoopy hugs Charlie Brown, smaller black outline drawings of Lucy, Linus, Patty, Schroeder and his piano, and Violet are in the background, #1517, 1959, $25.00 – 35.00; *"Peanuts Pictures to Color,"* Lucy and Charlie Brown watch Snoopy ride a toy train, #5626, 1959, $25.00 – 40.00; *"Peanuts Pictures to Color,"* four panels of Snoopy, Charlie Brown, and a beach ball, #5652, 1960, $22.00 – 35.00.

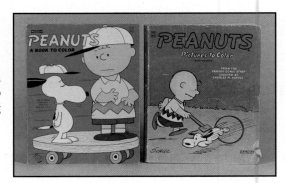

"Peanuts A Book to Color," Snoopy and Charlie Brown share a skateboard, #4549, 1965, $25.00 – 40.00; *"Peanuts Pictures to Color,"* Charlie Brown plays hoop stick with Snoopy jumping through the hoop, #5631, 1960, $22.00 – 35.00.

"Peanuts Coloring Book featuring Charlie Brown," four-panel strip with Charlie Brown on the pitcher's mound, #9510, 1967; *"Peanuts Coloring Book featuring Linus,"* four-panel strip with Linus and Lucy, #9511, 1967; $22.00 – 37.00 each.

"Peanuts Coloring Book featuring Lucy," four-panel strip with Lucy and Linus, #9512, 1967, $22.00 – 37.00; *"Peanuts Coloring Book featuring Violet,"* four-panel strip with Lucy, Violet, and Snoopy, #9513, 1967, $28.00 – 42.00.

"Peanuts Linus Coloring Book," Linus asks, "Do thumbs ever spoil?", #4563, 1968, $22.00 – 37.00.

"*Peanuts Coloring Book,*" Linus hugs blanket as Lucy, Charlie Brown, and Snoopy look on, "Not everyone needs a blanket for happiness, Charlie Brown!", #5675, 1969, $22.00 – 35.00. "*Peanuts Coloring Book,*" Lucy and Charlie Brown stand by a gutter where Charlie Brown has lost his kite, "Don't you know we're not supposed to fly kites underground?" #5694, 1969; $22.00 – 35.00. "*Peanuts Coloring Book,*" Charlie Brown wheels Snoopy in a baby stroller, #5695, 1969, $25.00 – 40.00.

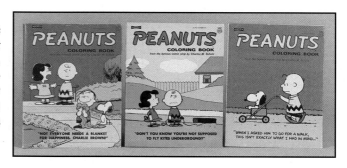

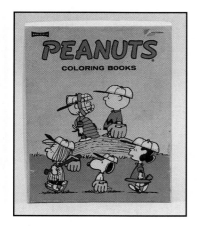
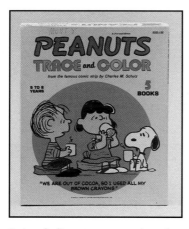

Set of five coloring books in a cardboard box: #4562, 4596, 4564, 4574, 4560. Box cover is a picture of the gang on baseball mound, late 1960s, $23.00 – 38.00.

Set of five trace and color books in a box. Cover: Linus tells Lucy and Snoopy, "We are out of cocoa, so I used all my brown crayons," #5022, 1968, $23.00 – 38.00.

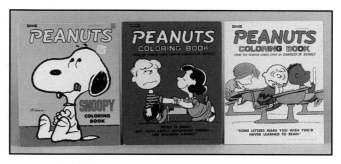

"*Peanuts: Snoopy Coloring Book,*" Snoopy sits and licks his lips, #A1852, 1972, $14.00 – 22.00; "*Peanuts Coloring Book,*" Lucy and Schroeder, "Music is great. But, how about important things — like holding hands?", #3512A, 1972; $14.00 – 22.00; "*Peanuts Coloring Book,*" Peppermint Patty, Charlie Brown, and Franklin sit at their desks, "Some letters make you wish you'd never learned to read!", #3513A, 1972, $25.00 – 35.00.

"*Peanuts Coloring Book,*" Peppermint Patty and Charlie Brown sit against a tree trunk, "Growing up would be simple, Chuck, if our parents hadn't made so many mistakes they don't want us to make!", #3514A, 1972, $18.00 – 30.00; "*Peanuts Coloring Book featuring Snoopy,*" Snoopy ice skates in front of a frowning Lucy, "Looking for a partner, sweetie?", #3703A, 1972, $8.00 – 12.00; "*Peanuts Coloring Book featuring Sally,*" Sally sits attempting to put on shoes, "You'd think someone could have invented a shoe that fits both feet!", #3602A, 1972, $12.00 – 18.00.

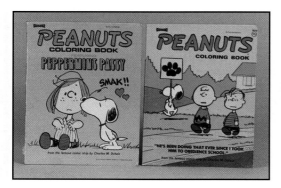

"*Peanuts Coloring Book featuring Peppermint Patty,*" Snoopy kisses Peppermint Patty, #3603A, 1972, $18.00 – 22.00; "*Peanuts Coloring Book,*" Charlie Brown and Linus walk along a street with Snoopy holding a paw-print sign, "He's been doing that ever since I took him to obedience school," #5674, 1972, $20.00 – 32.00.

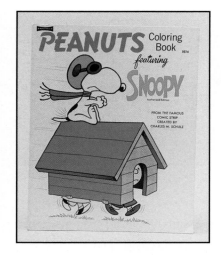

"*Peanuts Coloring Book featuring Snoopy,*" The WWI Flying Ace pilots his house hoisted by Charlie Brown and Lucy, #9574, 1972, printed in Canada, $25.00 – 40.00.

Peanuts Trace and Color, cover: Charlie Brown advises Snoopy, "Never pick a fight with a hundred-pound cat!" Five books in a cardboard box: "*Good Ol' Charlie Brown,*" "*Peppermint Patty's Busy Day,*" "*Linus Looks at the World,*" "*Snoopy, the Head Beagle,*" and "*Lucy Does it Again,*" #6122, late 1960s or early 1970s, $23.00 – 38.00.

• Sanrio (Japan) •

Snoopy leans against Charlie Brown as both sit on a baseball bench, #044253, 7³⁄₁₆ x 10⅛", 1990; Charlie Brown and the gang all dance among flowers, #044326, 7³⁄₁₆" x 10⅛", 1990; $4.00 – 6.00 each.

Snoopy hugs Woodstock and his buddies, and other birds circle while holding letters of the alphabet, #131997, 10³⁄₁₆" x 12¾", 1991; Lucy and the gang watch Charlie Brown put on his shoe, #132004, 10³⁄₁₆" x 12¾", 1991; Snoopy wears red baseball cap and holds blue baseball bat, #132039, 10³⁄₁₆" x 12¾", 1991; $10.00 – 15.00 each.

 # Peanuts Comic Books

Peanuts first appeared as a secondary feature in the United Feature Syndicate comic known as Tip Top Comics, beginning with issue #173 (March – April 1952). This book routinely starred UFS newspaper comic strip favorites such as Tarzan, Li'l Abner, Nancy and Sluggo, and the Captain and the Kids (the Katzenjammer Kids). The Peanuts gang shared some covers and soloed on others until the book concluded its run with #225 (May – June 1961), but it should be noted that they did not appear in every issue; the next issue to follow #173 was #184 (Jan. – Feb. 1954), after which the run was sequential until #225.

During this time, United Feature Syndicate rotated the Peanuts gang through several different titles, but usually for no more than a few pages. They appeared in several issues of Tip Topper Comics and numerous non-consecutive issues of United Comics and Fritzi Ritz (actually the same book; Fritzi Ritz became United Comics, and later went back to being Fritzi Ritz). UFS also released one issue called Peanuts, dated 1953/54; but although it displayed a #1, there were no more issues in this particular run. Despite the "star billing," the Peanuts kids shared this book with other back-up features.

Charlie Brown and his friends later debuted as a back-up feature in Dell Comics' *Nancy*, beginning with issue #148 (Sept. 1957). Their consecutive run in this book lasted through issue #192 (Oct. 1963). The title became *Nancy and Sluggo* with issue #174 (Jan. – Feb. 1960) and the publisher became Gold Key with issue #188 (Oct. 1962).

Peanuts finally received solo billing with issue #878 (Feb. 1958) of Dell's *Four Color* comic, which always took its title from each issue's feature. The second issue of their solo title came a year later with #969 (Feb. 1959), and the third followed with #1015 (Aug. – Oct. 1959). Dell then gave Peanuts its own title and began with #4 (Feb. – April 1960). It was revived by Gold Key a year later, with a new #1 (May 1963); this second run concluded with #4 (Feb. 1964).

Charles Schulz drew the covers of these later books but delegated the interior artwork to good friends Dale Hale and Jim Sasserman, associates from the Art Instruction School in Minneapolis.

Condition is of critical importance when dealing with comic books, and it's also important to verify that the contents are intact; sometimes center pages separate from the staples and disappear. While professional comic book collectors recognize nearly a dozen different grades, you can get by with these three:

MINT: Like new, as you'd expect to see on a magazine at a newsstand. Minor fading of color is allowed, as is a slightly off-center or mis-cut cover. It must not, however, appear dog-eared or heavily browsed.

FINE: Covers should be crisp, colorful, and flat; no folds allowed. Detectable wear around the staples and spine, along with possible color loss (flaking) around the spine and edges.

GOOD: A reading copy, but wholly intact: both covers present, and no missing pages. The spine might be rolled, and minor tears are allowable. Noticeable color flaking. No tape marks or tape.

Title	Value		
Tip Top Comics	Good	Fine	Mint
173	5.00	15.00	30.00
184 – 210	4.00	12.00	20.00
211 – 225	3.00	10.00	15.00
Tip Topper Comics			
17 – 22, 24 – 28	3.60	9.00	18.00
United Comics/Fritzi Ritz			
21 – 28, 30 – 33	4.00	10.00	20.00
37, 38, 41, 43 – 47, 57 – 59	3.00	8.00	15.00
Nancy/Nancy and Sluggo			
146	5.00	15.00	30.00
147 – 173	4.00	8.00	20.00
174 – 192	3.00	6.00	15.00
Peanuts Special			
1	15.00	35.00	75.00
Four-Color/Peanuts			
878	10.00	30.00	75.00
969, 1015	8.00	20.00	60.00
4	6.00	12.00	25.00
5 – 13	5.00	10.00	20.00
1 (Gold Key)	6.00	12.00	25.00
2 – 4 (Gold Key)	5.00	10.00	20.00

Peanuts. No. 1. United Feature Syndicate. Copyright 1948 – 51, 1953.

Tip Top Comics. No. 185. Mar. – April 1954.

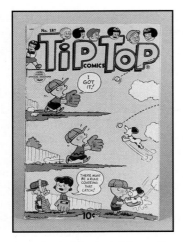

Tip Top Comics. No. 187.
United Features Syndicate,
Inc. July – Aug. 1954.

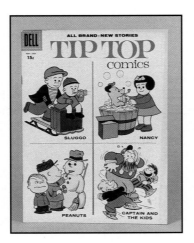

Tip Top Comics. No. 211.
Dell. Nov. – Jan. 1958.

Tip Top Comics. No. 214.
Dell. Aug. – Oct. 1958.

Tip Top Comics, No. 219.
Dell. Nov. – Jan. 1960.

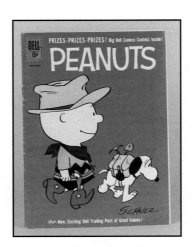

Peanuts. No. 10. Dell. Aug.
– Oct. 1961.

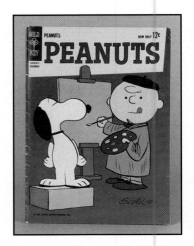

Peanuts. No. 3. Gold Key.
Nov. 1963.

 # Hallmark Flip Book on Keyrings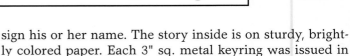

These little items are real charmers. The covers are plastic-coated paper. The first page contains a greeting, such as "With warmest thoughts," where the sender may sign his or her name. The story inside is on sturdy, brightly colored paper. Each 3" sq. metal keyring was issued in the early 1970s.

"*Love, Sweet Love,*" Snoopy gives Charlie Brown a big hug, red cover, #100RB2-1; "*Sayings of Snoopy,*" Snoopy does his happy dance, yellow cover, #100RB2-2, "*Lucy's Philosophy,*" Lucy reads a letter, hot pink cover, #100RB2-4, "*It's Only a Game,*" Lucy's kicked football lands on Snoopy's head, orange cover, #100RB2-5; "*The Flying Ace,*" Snoopy as the World War I Flying Ace, blue cover, #100RB2-7.

Magazines

Ever since the famed and highly prized 1965 cover for *Time* magazine, Charlie Brown and his friends have popped up unexpectedly in many different publications. Not all articles have been devoted to Charles Schulz and his artwork; the characters' universal appeal has made them excellent critics and instructors for a wide array of subjects.

Finding such a magazine at a newsstand, at cover price, is exciting enough; getting a subscription copy in the mail is even more thrilling.

Fortunately, it's not hard to track down such issues with a library periodicals index, but finding the actual magazine often requires patience and repeat visits to used magazine stores. What follows is just a small sampling.

Value is based on excellent to mint condition, with no dog-eared corners and absolutely no writing other than original print. Address labels are acceptable, and the cover may show a bit of wear due to its age.

Title	Value

Time, April 9, 1995. Cover: Snoopy, Linus, Charlie Brown, Schroeder, and Lucy. A cartoon and introdution appear in the index. Article: "Good Grief." . . . .$20.00 – 30.00

Life, March 17, 1967. Cover: Snoopy and Charlie Brown. Article: "Inept Heroes, Winners at Last." . . . .20.00 – 30.00

Family Circle, April 1969. Cover: Snoopy doll with decorated Easter eggs. Article: instructions on how to make the eggs. . . . . .14.00 – 22.00

Junior Scholastic, January 12, 1970. Cover: logo of the movie, "A Boy Named Charlie Brown." Article: "A small-town boy named Charlie Brown CAN find fame and happiness in a full-length movie called 'A Boy Named Charlie Brown!!!'" . . . . .12.00 – 14.00

Liberty, Winter 1973. Cover: Snoopy, Sally, Charlie Brown, Linus, Lucy, and Woodstock read the comics. Article: "Peanuts — How it All Began." . . . . .16.00 – 22.00

Dynamite, No. 35, 1977. Cover: Charlie Brown and Snoopy — Snoopy dances. Article: "You're a Superstar, Charlie Brown." . . . . .12.00 – 14.00

The Plate Collector, Feb. 15, 1980. Cover: Snoopy paints a portrait of Charles M. Schulz. Article: "After 30 years 'Peanuts' and Schulz Are As As (sic) As Ever." .15.00 – 25.00

World Tennis, May 1985. Cover: Lucy yells at tennis player Snoopy. A drawing of Snoopy with the article, "Cheating — It's Your Call." . . . . .8.00 – 12.00

Science Digest, February 1986. Cover: Linus sucks his thumb and holds his security blanket. Article: "Coping with Anxiety." . . . . .8.00 – 12.00

Jazziz, January 1990. Cover: Joe Cool holds his saxophone. He is one of many artists featured. Article: "Desire — Why Charlie Brown Never Kicks the Ball." . . .10.00 – 12.00

Snoopy Magazine. A quarterly magazine that premiered with its Winter 1988 issue (on sale November 1987) and ended with Spring 1990. . . . . .6.00 – 8.00 each.

Life.

Time, Family Circle, Junior Scholastic, Liberty, Dynamite.

The Plate Collector, World Tennis, Science Digest, Jazziz, Snoopy Magazine.

Avon

Avon became a licensee just in time to enjoy the popularity of the first full-length movie release, "A Boy Named Charlie Brown," and their products are classic. All items were very popular with the children who used them, but we suspect adults also bought them for their own use. Each came boxed.

Even back then, fans carefully collected or saved Avon products, and despite the passing years, it's still possible to possess the Avon products listed here in their original boxes. It doesn't really matter whether the original contents are in the container, because it's the container itself that counts.

The products listed below, with one exception, were issued in the very late 1960s or early 1970s. Avon then gave up the license until 1989, when they released children's sunscreen products as well as a Snoopy and Woodstock soap set.

Prices are based on mint-in-the-box but, again, original fluid contents are not important to the value.

Snoopy Comb & Brush, brush is black, white, and red, white comb, $17.00 – 22.00; Charlie Brown Comb & Brush, Charlie Brown wears a white hat with red band, white comb, $15.00 – 20.00; Woodstock Brush & Comb, yellow brush, green comb, $15.00 – 20.00.

Snoopy's Pal Soap Dish & Soap, Snoopy's red dog dish holds plastic figural of Woodstock and two 2 oz. bone-shaped soaps, $18.00 – 24.00; Snoopy Soap Dish & Soap, rubber two-dimensional figure of Snoopy lying down, indention in stomach serves as dish for 3 oz. soap bar, $15.00 – 25.00; Snoopy Soap Refill, 3 oz. bar of soap with no Peanuts graphics on red box, $3.00 – 4.00.

Peanuts Gang Charlie Brown, Snoopy & Lucy Soap, three-dimensional molded soap figures, 1¾ oz. each, Lucy is pink, Snoopy is white, and Charlie Brown is yellow, $25.00 – 37.00.

Snoopy Come Home Soap Dish & Soap, plastic raft is soap dish; sail depicts Snoopy and Woodstock, comes with 3 oz. bar of soap, $20.00 – 24.00; Great Catch, Charlie Brown Soap Holder & Soap, plastic two-dimensional Charlie Brown holds large baseball mitt that serves as soap dish for 3 oz. bar of soap (included), $20.00 – 25.00.

Linus Gel Bubble Bath & Helpful Holder, rubber upper half of Linus' body has suction cup to affix to surface, holds 4 oz. tube of bubble bath, $17.00 – 22.00; Snoopy Ski Team Bubble Bath, plastic figurals of Snoopy and Woodstock on red skis, 7 fl. oz., $18.00 – 24.00.

Snoopy the Flying Ace Bubble Bath, plastic Snoopy figural sits, wearing blue helmet and plastic goggles, 4 fl. oz., $16.00 – 20.00; Snoopy's Bubble Tub Bubble Bath, plastic container of Snoopy in tub filled with blue bubbles, 12 fl. oz., $18.00 – 22.00; Schroeder Bubble Bath, plastic figural of Schroeder sitting, box serves as piano, picture of Beethoven's bust included on box (can be removed), sheet music inside box, 6 fl. oz., $20.00 – 25.00.

Snoopy & Doghouse Non-Tear Shampoo, plastic Snoopy cap, red doghouse container, 8 fl. oz., $8.00 – 12.00; Snoopy's Snow Flyer Bubble Bath, plastic figural of container, 10 fl. oz., $15.00 – 18.00; Surprise Package Wild Country After Shave, milk glass figural Snoopy sits and wears blue plastic baseball hat, 5 fl. oz., $8.00 – 12.00.

Snoopy Shampoo Liquid Soap Mug, milk glass mug with decal of Snoopy, blue metal cap with white plastic knob, 5 fl. oz., $12.00 – 16.00; Snoopy Shampoo Liquid Soap Mug, milk glass mug with decal of Snoopy, red metal cap with white plastic knob, 5 fl. oz., $10.00 – 14.00; Lucy Shampoo Mug, milk glass mug with decal of Lucy, yellow metal lid with white plastic knob, 4 fl. oz.; $8.00 – 12.00.

Not Pictured
Charlie Brown Shampoo Mug, milk glass mug with decal of Charlie Brown. Blue metal lid with white plastic knob, 4 fl. oz. . . . .$8.00 – 10.00

Lucy Bubble Bath, Lucy plastic figural containing bubble bath, she wears red dress and cap, 4 fl. oz., $18.00 – 24.00; Charlie Brown Non-Tear Shampoo, plastic, figural of Charlie Brown wearing red and black baseball cap, 4 fl. oz., $18.00 – 24.00; Linus Non-Tear Shampoo, plastic Linus figural sucks thumb and wears sailor cap, 4 fl. oz., $18.00 – 24.00. Peanuts Pals Charlie Brown & Snoopy Non-Tear Shampoo, plastic figural of Snoopy hugging Charlie Brown, Charlie Brown wears yellow plastic baseball cap, 6 fl. oz., $15.00 – 18.00.

Snoopy & Woodstock Soaps, white figural of Snoopy holding half of Easter egg, small yellow Woodstock sits on top of egg, 1989, $4.00 – 6.00.

Creative Specialties, LTD.

All issued in 1987 and boxed, unless noted. Values are based on items being mint in the box.

Belle Cologne, white glass figure of Belle with pink hat which serves as lid, 2 fl. oz., #01902, $14.00 – 20.00; Snoopy Cologne, white glass figure Snoopy with black top hat that serves as lid, #01906, 2 fl. oz., $18.00 – 24.00.

Snoopy Pin (with Belle solid cologne inside), the pin is two-dimensional plastic, #01914, $8.00 – 14.00; Snoopy & Belle Puff & Talc, #01903, $6.00 – 10.00; Belle Powder & Lip Glow, #01909, $6.00 – 10.00. Belle Lip Glow, Blush, and Roll-On Cologne, #01917, $8.00 – 12.00.

Belle & Snoopy Gift Set, includes Snoopy and Belle talc, bath bubbles, and Snoopy and Belle hand cream, #01915; Snoopy Bath Time Gift Set, includes Snoopy bath bubbles, Woodstock soap, and Snoopy shampoo, #01919; Snoopy Bath Time Gift Set, includes Snoopy bath bubbles, Woodstock soap, and Snoopy and Belle Shaker talc, #01918, $15.00 – 20.00 each.

Snoopy Dresser Set, comb, brush, and mirror, #01910, $12.00 – 18.00.

Not Pictured

Snoopy & Belle Hand Cream, not boxed, 4 oz., #01904 . . . . $2.00 – 4.00
Belle Roll-On Cologne, ⅓ oz., #01905. . . . . .3.00 – 4.00
Belle Blush & Lip Glow, #01907 . . . . .6.00 – 8.00
Snoopy Shampoo, not boxed, 8 oz., #01908 .4.00 – 6.00
Snoopy Bath Bubbles, not boxed, 16 oz., #01916 . . . . .4.00 - 6.00

Determined Productions, Inc.

This appealing line of cosmetics and toiletries was created by Lisa Dutton, the niece of Connie Boucher, one of the founders of Determined Products, Inc.

Products should be in their original boxes. There should be no leakage or stains from any of the containers holding liquid.

The items listed below were produced in 1979.

• Snoopy Beauty Boutique •

Dresser Set with Comb, Brush & Mirror, white plastic accessories in a box, mirror has a red insert design of Snoopy and Woodstock among flowers, caption on mirror: "I feel free!", style #7900; Dresser Set with comb, brush, and mirror, white plastic accessories in box, mirror has a yellow and green insert, Woodstock holds flowers for Snoopy, caption on mirror: "How nice," style #7900, $15.00 – 22.00 each.

Quartet Collection, 1 fl. oz. each of shampoo, cologne, and hand lotion in glass bottles, .9 oz. talc in cardboard container, #7940, $14.00 – 17.00; Flavored Lip Pomades, three tubes: strawberry, orange, and grape in box, #7945, $4.00 – 8.00; Powder Puff Mitten, cloth mitten filled with talcum powder, boxed, Snoopy and Woodstock design, #7949, $8.00 – 10.00; Shampoo & Lotion, 1 fl. oz. each in glass bottles, #7960; Cologne & Talc, .9 oz. talc in cardboard container, 1 fl. oz. cologne in glass bottle, #7970, $6.00 – 8.00.

• Snoopy Bath Boutique •

Toothbrush Holder, Snoopy hugs Woodstock, both sit on Snoopy's house, self-adhesive tab on back, plastic, #7853, $2.00 – 4.00; Toothbrush Holder, Snoopy on bended knee, star background, "Super Smile," self-adhesive tab on back, plastic, #7854, $2.00 – 4.00; Wall Mirror, 6½" x 8¼" mirror with plastic border, white background features Joe Cool and Woodstock, caption: "Mirror, Mirror, on the Wall — Who's the Coolest of Them All?", #7851, $12.00 – 18.00.

Scrubbin' Mitten, Snoopy lathers up under the shower as Woodstock watches, #8088, $8.00 – 12.00; Snoopy Bubble Bath, orange plastic bottle, 12 oz. #16-7961-2, $6.00 – 8.00; Snoopy Soap Pump, green plastic dispenser, 12 oz., #16-7963-4, $6.00 – 8.00.

Snoopy Bath Boutique, continued...

Soap Friends, 3.5 oz., three-dimensional molded soap figures. Snoopy, white, #8061, $6.00 – 8.00; Charlie Brown, light brown, #8060, $5.00 – 7.00; Woodstock, yellow, #8062, $5.00 – 7.00.

Mini Soap, paper wrapped, with various designs, ¾ oz. ea., #8090, 50¢ – 75¢ each.

Display Accessories

Bells – Mother's Day

Only Schmid produced Mother's Day bells. Each was ceramic, came in a box, and was a limited edition. The bells were designed to complement Schmid's limited edition Mother's Day plates. The box is nice but does not contribute greatly to the value. 5¾" tall.

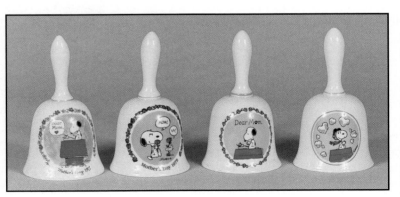

1977, Snoopy sits on his doghouse and types a letter, "Dear Mom" (heart symbol included), #279-027, in box, $23.00 – 33.00; no box, $20.00 – 30.00. 1978, Snoopy and Woodstock hold red roses, "Mother's Day 1978," #279-029; 1979, Signature Series Annual Bell, First Edition (The Signature Series alternated with a Mother's Day bell and a Christmas bell), Snoopy sits at his typewriter and types "Dear Mom," #279-017; 1981, Signature Series, Third Edition, Snoopy as the Flying Ace sits on his doghouse, heart-shaped clouds surround him, #279-326. (There is no 1980 Mother's Day bell.) Last three bells, in box, $20.00 – 30.00 each; no box, $17.00 – 27.00 each.

Bells – Various Categories

Prices are based on mint condition with no cracks, chips, or missing paint. A Certificate of Authenticity, if issued, should be included with the number of the bell purchased. With most of these bells, the box has no bearing on the value.

• Schmid – Face Series •

Each bell is ceramic and stands 5⅞"

Linus, avocado green trim, #278-418, $35.00 – 60.00; Lucy, red trim, #278-417, $45.00 – 75.00; Schroeder, avocado green trim, #178-419, $35.00 – 60.00.

Charlie Brown wears a baseball cap, orange trim, #278-416; Snoopy, yellow trim, #278-415, $45.00 – 75.00 each.

•Schmid – Bicentennial •

Limited Edition, "1776 – 1976," ceramic, 5¾" tall, Snoopy lies on top of the Liberty Bell; in box, $15.00 – 25.00; no box, $12.00 – 23.00.

• Schmid – Annual Series •

Each ceramic bell was issued in conjunction with a music box and plate. The series began in 1983, and production was limited to 10,000 of each design. Certificate of Authenticity included.

Schmid – Annual Series, continued...

1983, "Peanuts in Concert," band leader Snoopy uses his baton to lead Lucy, Linus, Sally, Charlie Brown, Woodstock, and Schroeder in song, red ribbon top, 6⅜" tall, #279-750; in box, $55.00 – 70.00; no box, $50.00 – 65.00. 1984, "Snoopy and the Beaglescouts," Beaglescout leader Snoopy heads up his flock of bird scouts, green ribbon top, 3⅞" tall, #279-751; in box, $45.00 – 55.00; no box, $38.00 – 50.00.

1985, "Clown Capers," handle is figure of Snoopy with Woodstock standing on his head, bell design is the gang dressed in clown clothing in an old-time jalopy, 5⅞" tall, #279-752; 1986, "Flyin' Tamer Snoopy," handle is figure of Snoopy as ringmaster of a circus, bell design is Snoopy taming a lion portrayed by Woodstock, 3⅞" tall, in box, $50.00 – 65.00 each; no box, $45.00 – 60.00 each.

• Willitts •

Handle is figure of Snoopy, who sits on the bell which has a 40th Anniversary logo of Charlie Brown, Woodstock, and Snoopy, ceramic, 5½" tall, #19003, 1990; in box, $25.00 – 35.00; no box, $20.00 – 30.00.

• Prototype •

This bell with a figure of a frowning Lucy was never released to the public, probably by Schmid, 5" tall, 1976, $150.00 – 200.00.

Candleholders & Candles

Although considered a temporary type of art, many early Peanuts candles managed to avoid being touched by a match. Hallmark, the most prolific in this category, also produced candleholders.

It can be difficult to find an absolutely mint candle. Age takes its toll on the brightness of the design, and sometimes the candle takes on a "crumbly" effect. The cellophane wrap often is torn. The prices reflected here are based on good condition, with bright colors and no major scratches.

Value of the candleholders, however, is based on excellent to mint condition: no chips, missing paint, or cracks. Check carefully for hairline cracks, especially on Hallmark composition holders; they tend to crack around the neckline.

• Candleholders – Composition •

Figures in red, black, and white, Hallmark, early 1970s

Lucy stands next to part of her psychiatrist booth, caption: "The Doctor is in," 7", $20.00 – 35.00; Linus sucks his thumb and holds his blanket, 7¼", $15.00 – 30.00; Snoopy wears a night cap, 7¼", $25.00 – 40.00; Charlie Brown wears a baseball cap, 8", $20.00 – 35.00.

• Candleholders – Ceramic •

Each of the following holders came with a candle inside

Charlie Brown sits, wearing a baseball hat and glove, 5½", Hallmark, #CDM73125, early 1970s, $35.00 – 45.00; Charlie Brown and Lucy flank Snoopy and Woodstock, who stick out their tongues at Lucy, caption, "Bleah!" 3" tall, 2" dia., Hallmark, early 1970s, $10.00 – 15.00; Woodstock looks in a mirror, Peppermint Patty touches her hair, Lucy faces Schroeder as he sits by his piano, and Snoopy wears a blue jacket, each scene is by candlelight, caption, "Everyone looks better by candlelight," 2⅜" tall, 1⅞" dia., Hallmark, #CDM8701, early 1980s, $10.00 – 15.00; Romeo and Juliet scene played by Snoopy, birds, and Lucy, caption, "Hark! What light through yonder window breaks? Tis just sweet, precious me up in the balcony," 2⅜" tall, 1⅞" dia., Hallmark, #CDM8700, early 1980s, $10.00 – 15.00; Snoopy sits next to a candle, which looks like a cup filled with different flavors of ice cream, both sit on a white ceramic base, 2¾", Japan, Hallmark/Tokyo Candle Products Co., Ltd., #SN-2, mid 1980s (pictured top row), $25.00 – 35.00.

Snoopy sits in a sleigh, wearing a red and green knit cap, the sleigh is pulled by bird "reindeer," 4¼", Willitts, #8621, 1989, $20.00 – 30.00; Snoopy sits and holds a candy cane and wears a black top hat and green muffler, a candle accompanies the holder which is in Snoopy's hat, 7", Willitts, #7864, 1987, with box $15.00 – 29.00, no box $13.00 – 25.00; Snoopy wears a blue muffler and sits next to a red Christmas boot with a candle inside, 2½", Japan, Hallmark/Phoenix Corp. Ltd., #34044-8, 1988, $20.00 – 30.00; Santa Snoopy rides in his sleigh, his gift pack holds a red candle, 3", Japan, Hallmark/Phoenix Corp. Ltd., #34044-8, 1988, $25.00 – 35.00; Santa Snoopy sits next to a decorated Christmas tree which holds a candle, 2¾", Japan, Hallmark through Sanrio, #03434-7, 1988 (pictured top row), $25.00 – 35.00.

Candleholders – Ceramic, continued...

Charlie Brown, Lucy, and Snoopy wear ice skates and stand around the edge of snow, a plain glass candle-holder is in the middle, 3½", Willitts, #8447, 1989; with box, $35.00 – 45.00; no box, $30.00 – 40.00.

Snoopy wears a witch's cape and eye mask, he eats candy from his trick-or-treat bag as he sits next to a pumpkin, which holds a candle, 2", Willitts, #7907, 1987; with box, $35.00 – 45.00; no box, $30.00 – 40.00.

• Candleholders – Plastic •

Chef Snoopy works on a three-layer chocolate cake, Woodstock sits on the cake with frosting on his nose, cake caption, "Happy Birthday," 2½", Hallmark, #CDB8611, early 1980s; with box, $45.00 – 70.00; no box, $35.00 – 55.00.

• Candleholders – Glass •

Baseball field with players Thibault, Woodstock, Snoopy, Lucy, Linus, Schroeder, Charlie Brown, 5, and Peppermint Patty, 2⅝" tall x 1⅞" dia., Hallmark, early 1970s, $20.00 – 32.00; Linus in the pumpkin patch, 2⅝" tall x 1⅞" dia., Hallmark, early to late 1970s, $18.00 – 30.00.

Snoopy and birds decorate a Christmas tree, the birds also pull a sled and make a snowman, caption, "Friends help make the season brighter," 2⅝" tall x 1⅞" dia., Ambassador division of Hallmark, early to mid 1970s, $15.00 – 20.00; Glass disk of Snoopy riding a sleigh, with Woodstock acting as his reindeer, all sitting on a plastic base, a plain glass votive candle holder sits behind the disk, 4¾", Willitts, #8513, 1986; with box, $22.00 – 30.00; no box, $18.00 – 25.00.

Series of three holders, Japan, Marimo Craft, Inc., 1987. 4", #SN073, $15.00 – 25.00; 2", #SN071, $8.00 – 12.00; 2½", #SN072, $10.00 – 18.00.

• Candles – Figures •

Snoopy sits, Woodstock is in front of him, 6", Hallmark, early 1970s, $15.00 – 20.00; Snoopy sits, wearing a red dog collar, 5½", Hallmark, early to mid 1970s, $15.00 – 20.00; Snoopy stands on a blue base and wears a red turtleneck sweater and sunglasses, caption on sweater, "Joe Cool," 6", Hallmark, mid 1970s, $20.00 – 28.00; Charlie Brown stands wearing a red shirt with black zig-zag and black pants, 7¾", Hallmark, 1970s, $22.00 – 32.00; Charlie Brown looks forlorn as he sits with his elbows on his knees, 6", Diplomat Candles division of Ambassador/Hallmark, 1970s, $20.00 – 25.00.

Snoopy wears a Santa hat and holds a large red gift sack filled with toys, 3½", Hallmark, mid 1970s, $10.00 – 15.00; Snoopy wears a red muffler and holds a green gift box tied with red ribbon, 2⅜", Hallmark, #CDD9009, mid 1980s, $10.00 – 12.00; Woodstock wears a Santa cap and green scarf, sits on a white gift box tied with red ribbon, 2⅜", Hallmark, #CDD9010, mid 1908s, $8.00 – 10.00; Santa Snoopy holds a little metal bell and stands next to a chimney, 2⅞", Japan, Hallmark/Phoenix Corp. Ltd., #3494201, 1988, $15.00 – 22.00; Snoopy wears a Santa cap and rests on his doghouse which is decorated with a Christmas wreath and snow, 3¾", Willitts, #7863, 1987, $14.00 – 18.00.

Lucy wears a blue dress, sits, and holds a football, 4", Hallmark, #CDD7417, mid to late 1970s, $15.00 – 20.00; Snoopy wears a yellow tennis visor and holds a yellow and white tennis racket, 4", Hallmark, #CDD7416, mid to late 1970s, $17.00 – 22.00; Charlie Brown wears a red baseball cap with black rim and a red shirt with the caption "Manager," 4¼", Hallmark, #CDD7413, mid to late 1970s, $15.00 – 20.00.

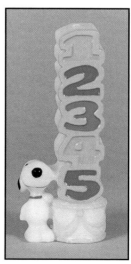

Snoopy stands next to a cake with a large candle on it, the candle bears the numbers "1, 2, 3, 4, and 5," 7", Hallmark, #CDD8100, early 1980s, $14.00 – 20.00.

Not Pictured
Snoopy hugs Woodstock as he sits on a heart base, 2¾",
Hallmark, #CDD8718, mid 1980s. . . .$4.00 – 6.00.

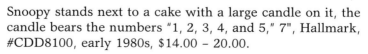

• Candles – Pillar •

Approx. 5⅞" – 6" tall x 3" dia. Each is by Hallmark and from the 1970s.

Three poses of Joe Cool; Snoopy kisses Peppermint Patty, as Charlie Brown and Lucy stand nearby; Woodstock flies upside down near Charlie Brown, Linus, and Snoopy, $8.00 – 12.00 each.

 # Aviva Ceramic Eggs

Some of the designs were printed against a plain white background. Others appeared within an oval, surrounded by a small band of color. It is possible to find designs with both backgrounds. The eggs did not come packaged and were issued in the early to mid 1970s. Prices are based on mint condition with none of the design scratched off and gold seal at the bottom intact. There may be manufacturing flaws in most eggs, such as a wavy pattern in the ceramic.

"A Little Love Goes a Long Way." Snoopy sits, surrounded by lots of hearts; "Aaugh!" Snoopy bites his tennis racket (two versions); "Gee!" Snoopy sits and holds a flower; "Give Me a Smile...I Deserve It!", Snoopy stands and rolls his eyes, Woodstock leans against him, $15.00 – 20.00 each.

"Giving is More Fun Than Receiving," Snoopy stands holding a bunch of flowers; "Hi, Sweetie!", Snoopy winks; "Hummm..." Snoopy enjoys an ice cream cone; "I Love You", Woodstock looks up at Snoopy, who reclines on top of a large red heart; $15.00 – 20.00 each.

"I'm So Cute", Snoopy stands holding his supper dish (two versions); "Joe Gourmet" Snoopy wears a chef's hat and holds cooking utensils; "Love is for Sharing", Snoopy and Woodstock in a nest; $15.00 – 20.00 each.

"MMMMM", Snoopy hugs Charlie Brown; "Security is a happy home" Snoopy listens to music as he rests on top of his doghouse (two versions); "SMAK!", Snoopy kisses Lucy; $15.00 – 20.00 each.

"Snif!", Snoopy has tears rolling down his cheek as he holds a heart in one hand; "Work is for the birds", Snoopy sits at typewriter as Woodstock stands nearby; "World's Greatest Mom", Snoopy leaps over the letter "O" in the word "MOM"; "World's Greatest Dad", rim of Snoopy's Beaglescout cap holds several birds; $15.00 – 20.00 each.

"You Crack Me Up", Snoopy and Woodstock sit and giggle; "You're the Best", Snoopy and Woodstock share a nest; "You're the Cutest", Snoopy sits in front of a rainbow; "Zzzz", Snoopy and Woodstock sleep on ground, their heads resting against a rock; $15.00 – 20.00 each.

Not Pictured
"Let's Be Friends", Woodstock perches on
    Snoopy's nose and sings. . . . .$15.00 – 20.00
"You Make Me Smile", Snoopy leans on a
    tree stump, "Sigh!" . . . . .15.00 – 20.00

Eggs with flat bottom; a pattern of flowers surrounds the design and caption. The eggs sit flat, with the design and caption facing up. "Surprise a friend with a hug," Snoopy hugs Woodstock; "How nice," Woodstock holds a bouquet of flowers for Snoopy; "This has been a good day," Snoopy and Woodstock rest on top of Snoopy's doghouse; "I feel free," Snoopy dances and holds a basket full of flowers; $25.00 – 35.00 each.

 # Ceramic Tiles

Although not nearly as popular as ceramic or porcelain plates, tiles are another way collectors can display a fondness for a particular subject.

Prices are based on tiles being absolutely mint, with no chips or flaws. In the case of the Christmas tile, it is based on mint-in-the-box condition.

• Christmas •

"Merry Christmas 1978." Snoopy holds a check list for "Good Boys and Good Girls." Several birds help getting toys ready to put on Snoopy's sleigh. 6" square. Determined Productions, Inc., 1978. $35.00 – 50.00 MIB.

• Non-Holiday •

Non-holiday, "World Famous Beagle Snoopy and His Friend Woodstock" series. Each came in two different sizes, Japan, mid 1980s.

Snoopy carries a branch containing Woodstock asleep in his nest; Snoopy sprinkles seeds on three birds; Snoopy sits on the top of his doghouse and types a letter as Woodstock watches. 5¾" square, $25.00 – 35.00 each; 4¼" square, $15.00 – 18.00 each.

 # Jewelry – Character Pins

Some collectors try to amass every Peanuts character pin released over the years, no easy task since some designs are available in more than one size. It's an endless search, and one must be up for the challenge. This chapter touches just the tip of the iceberg.

Value is based on very good to excellent condition: no missing paint, chips, or scratches. Be sure to look for the copyright information because many unauthorized pins were manufactured. Some legitimate pins came with a paper tag bearing the copyright information instead of being imprinted on the pin.

Dimension refers to height.

• Aviva •

Two-dimensional figures with hollow back. Hand-painted metal. These pins are quite heavy for their size.

Difficult to find without some paint missing, so prices take this into consideration. Approx. 1½". Late 1960s.

Linus in a green and blue striped shirt; Schroeder in a shirt with Beethoven's bust; Pig Pen in green overalls; Lucy in a red dress; $65.00 – 90.00 each.

Painted metal, 1970s

Schroeder plays his piano, his shirt is green, and his pants are red, 1¾"; Charlie Brown in a green shirt with silver zigzag, and a baseball cap and mitt, 1¼"; The Flying Ace's face, 1"; Lucy in a blue dress, holding an apple, 1¼"; $12.00 – 18.00 each.

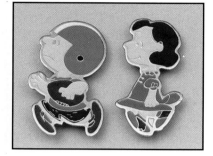

Charlie Brown holds a football and runs, his helmet is red, 1⅝", $12.00 – 18.00; Lucy in a red dress, side view, 1⅝", $10.00 – 15.00.

Charlie Brown wears a yellow shirt with gold zigzag, 1¼", late 1960s (shown on original card), $18.00 – 22.00.

Cloisonne, 1970s – 1980s

Snoopy in an orange and blue baseball uniform and cap with a brown baseball mitt, 1"; Snoopy in a light green and yellow baseball uniform and cap with a light brown baseball mitt, 1", $10.00 – 14.00 each. Linus sucks his thumb and holds his blue blanket, 1¹⁄₁₆"; Schroeder plays his piano, 1¹⁄₁₆; $8.00 – 12.00 each.

Snoopy holds an Uncle Sam hat, ⅞", $16.00 – 24.00. Snoopy holds a Union Jack flag, ¹⁵⁄₁₆"; Snoopy holds an American flag from 1776, 1", $18.00 – 30.00 each.

"I Love N.Y.", Snoopy as the Statue of Liberty, 1"; Snoopy reclines on top of a cable car, 1"; $10.00 – 14.00 each. Spike wears a brown hat and sits, 1"; "Belle," Belle wears a red and blue outfit and holds a heart, $6.00 – 8.00 each.

• Snoopy's Pin Pals •

Plastic, approx. 2½", 1972. The packaging affects the value slightly.

The Flying Ace sits, in pkg., $20.00 – 30.00; no pkg., $18.00 – 24.00; Lucy wears a red dress with no shoes, in pkg., $12.00 – 19.00; no pkg., $10.00 – 16.00; Snoopy wears a blue sweater while he roller skates, in pkg., $12.00 – 19.00; no pkg., $10.00 – 16.00; Snoopy plays a guitar, in pkg., $15.00 – 24.00; no pkg., $15.00 – 18.00; The Flying Ace stands, in pkg., $20.00 – 30.00; no pkg., $18.00 – 24.00.

Not Pictured
Snoopy wears a baseball cap and mitt and holds apple.
in pkg., $20.00 – 30.00
no pkg., 18.00 – 24.00
Snoopy wears a red and blue sweater and dances for joy.
in pkg., 12.00 – 19.00
no pkg., 10.00 – 16.00
Snoopy wears a blue nightshirt and cap and holds a candlestick.
in pkg., 12.00 – 19.00
no pkg., 10.00 – 16.00

Snoopy wears a fireman's hat and holds a bucket.
in pkg., $18.00 – 28.00
no pkg., 15.00 – 22.00
Snoopy holds a basket of flowers. in pkg., 12.00 – 19.00
no pkg., 10.00 – 16.00
Linus holds his yellow blanket and sucks his thumb.
in pkg., 12.00 – 19.00
no pkg., 10.00 – 16.00
Charlie Brown wears a baseball cap and mitt.
in pkg., 20.00 – 30.00
no pkg., 18.00 – 24.00

• Snoopy Ceramic Collection •

Approx. 1¼". The card on which the pin was sold does not affect the value.

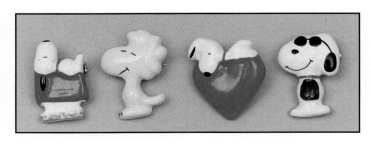

Snoopy sleeps on his doghouse; Woodstock; $6.00 – 9.00 each. Snoopy on top of a heart; Joe Cool wears a blue shirt and sunglasses; $5.00 – 8.00 each.

• Mini Trophy Pin •

Plastic, approx. 2½". Each comes with a slogan. The prices here reflect the absence of a package; increase the price by $2.00 – 3.00 if the package is included.

"Have a great one," Snoopy wears a party hat and holds balloons; "You don't know what you're missing," Woodstock sits inside Snoopy's dog dish as Snoopy sits nearby; $6.00 – 9.00 each. "I care not for fame and glory," the Flying Ace with his arms folded, $7.00 – 10.00 each.

• Pin Sets •

Snoopy 35th Anniversary Celebration. Cloisonne. Large inset plaque of Snoopy and Woodstock surrounded by smaller pins of Charlie Brown, Snoopy playing tennis, Snoopy playing hockey, Lucy, Flying Ace, Beaglescout, Linus, Literary Ace, football player, Sally, Joe Cool, and Flashbeagle. Six-sided wood frame with glass. Sequentially numbered, limited edition. Total issued is not known. 12¼" long x 9¾" wide. Quantasia, 1984. $110.00 – 165.00.

"40 Years of Happiness. World's Best Read Comic Strips Since 1950." A picture of Snoopy with one of the 40th anniversary logos is in the middle of the frame. Surrounding him are character pins with their names underneath: Snoopy, Charlie Brown, Sally Brown, Linus, Peppermint Patty, Lucy Van Pelt, and Woodstock. 12" square wood frame with glass. A small pamphlet is included with pictures and a write-up about Charles M. Schulz and the Peanuts characters. Japan, Glory Co., Ltd., 1990. $125.00 – 195.00.

"Peanuts 45th Anniversary." Cloisonne. Five pins: Snoopy with Woodstock; Snoopy kissing Lucy; Snoopy bringing Charlie Brown his dog dish; Snoopy and Linus sharing a blanket and sucking their thumbs; and in the middle, Snoopy lying on top of a plate with "Peanuts Comics, 45th Anniv." Light wood frame with glass. 8" x 8". Japan, manufacturer unknown, 1995. $55.00 – 70.00.

"Peanuts Collector's Edition." Set of six pins: Lucy, Linus, Sally, Snoopy, Charlie Brown, and Woodstock in a velvet-lined box with a mirror on the inside lid. Limited edition of 500, sequentially numbered. QVC (shopping channel), 1994. $40.00 – 55.00.

"Peanuts Collector's Edition." Set of five Christmas-themed pins: Charlie Brown, Woodstock, and three Snoopy designs in a velvet-lined box with a mirror on the inside lid. Limited edition of 1,000, sequentially numbered. QVC (shopping channel), 1994. $38.00 – 48.00.

Pinbacks

The Peanuts pinbacks — items of adornment related to campaign buttons — are especially attractive to collectors because they team a favorite character with a memorable slogan, phrase, or pose.

Simon Simple produced the bulk of their pinbacks in the late 1960s and continued until the early 1970s. Their designs, using the characters in the older depictions, remain the most desirable. Some warehouse finds of older Simon Simple pinbacks have affected prices.

Aviva produced the MOVEE butons, a series of twelve pinbacks that, when moved back and forth, change scenes. These, as well as the three Hallmark "flasher" buttons, are a plus for collectors.

Butterfly took over the pinback license in the 1970s and made a colorful contribution to the world of Peanuts collectibles. Whereas Simon Simple employed many of the Peanuts kids on their buttons, Butterfly mostly relied on the popularity of the world's most lovable beagle. They also complemented the usual plastic-covered metal buttons with some of cloth-covered metal, or very heavy plastic.

Japan produced a lovely supply of pinbacks in the early 1980s, many of which made their way into the collections of both Peanuts and non-Peanuts fans. These pinbacks are a highlight of any collection.

Advertisers often used pinbacks to promote a particular product, knowing that fans would cheerfully turn themselves into walking billboards.

Price ranges reflect pinbacks in very good to mint condition. There should be no scratches; colors should be bright, and the original pin should be intact.

Unless the description indicates otherwise, all pinbacks are metal with plastic covering. Sizes are approximate diameters, unless noted.

• Applause •

Plastic, 2½", 1990. Each is colored with a yellow background.

"I'm Irish," Joe Beagle wears a green cap and turtleneck sweater, and puckers up for a kiss; "Blarney Beagle," Snoopy looks like a Leprechaun and wears a green hat and bowtie, three-leaf clovers are in the background; $4.00 – 6.00 each.

• Aviva "Movees" •

Early 1970s, 2⁷⁄₁₆". Reverse side has Snoopy standing in director's chair; the scene changes as you move the button.

Woodstock flies over Snoopy's head, $10.00 – 12.00. "Strike One," "Strike Three," Snoopy holds a baseball bat and misses the ball; "Pow!", Charlie Brown on the baseball mound; $12.00 – 15.00 each.

Not Pictured

"Aaugh!", Lucy pulls a football away from
    Charlie Brown. . . . .$10.00 – 12.00
Snoopy dances as leaves fall nearby. . . . . .10.00 – 12.00
"I Hate It When They Serve Hard," Snoopy falls
    when he misses a tennis shot. . . . . .10.00 – 12.00
"Aaugh," The Flying Ace falls off his
    bullet-riddled house. . . . . .12.00 – 15.00

"Smak." Snoopy kisses Lucy. . . . . .10.00 – 12.00
"Ahchoo!", Snoopy sneezes as Woodstock
    flies over his house. . . . . .10.00 – 12.00
"Bonk!", Snoopy throws a football over Woodstock's
    head. .10.00 – 12.00
Snoopy walks behind a flock of birds. . . .10.00 – 12.00
Snoopy wears a ten-gallon hat and plays a
    guitar. .10.00 – 12.00

• Butterfly Originals •

Hard plastic, 2½", Assortment #2510, late 1970s

"Ace," Snoopy as a tennis player, $3.00 – 5.00.
"Boss," Snoopy as a film director wears a beret
and holds a megaphone, $4.00 – 6.00; "Cool,"
Snoopy as Joe Cool; "Friends," Snoopy and
Woodstock shake "hands"; "High Roller,"
Snoopy performs a handstand on a skateboard;
$3.00 – 5.00 each.

"Hustle," Snoopy wears a blue jacket and
dances, $4.00 – 5.00. "Jog," Snoopy jogs, Wood-
stock flies behind him; "Smile," Snoopy sits and
smiles; $3.00 – 5.00 each. "Snoopy Fan,"
Snoopy sleeps on the roof of his home; "Suave,"
Snoopy looks smug and wears a top hat and
bowtie; $4.00 – 6.00 each.

Not Pictured

"Love," Snoopy hugs Woodstock. . . . .$4.00 – 6.00
"T.G.I.F.", Snoopy leans over the roof of
    his home. . . . . .4.00 – 6.00

2¼", Assortment #2501, late 1970s

Not Pictured

No caption. Snoopy sits with a smaller identical
    image in a circle. . . . .$2.00 – 4.00
"All American," Snoopy holds a large trophy. 3.00 – 5.00
"Beaglescout," Snoopy wears a Beaglescout
    hat and necktie. . . . . .3.00 – 5.00
"Bike It," Woodstock performs wheelies on a
    bicycle. .2.00 – 4.00
"Born to Sleep," Snoopy snoozes on top of his
    doghouse. . . . . .2.00 – 4.00
"Boss," Snoopy wears a beret and sunglasses
    and holds a megaphone. . . . . .3.00 – 5.00
"Cool," Snoopy wears sunglasses and shorts
    and holds a drink to his mouth. . . . . .2.00 – 4.00
"Enjoy, Enjoy," Happy Snoopy with ears partially
    sticking up. . . . . .2.00 – 4.00
"Gal Friday," Lucy writes on a stenographic
    pad. . . . . .2.00 – 4.00

"Go Fly a Kite," Charlie Brown flies a kite. .3.00 – 5.00
"Go Ride a Bike," Snoopy rides a bike. . . . .2.00 – 4.00
"Good Luck," Peppermint Patty and Snoopy
    shake hands. . . . . .3.00 – 5.00
"Hike It," Snoopy dressed as a hiker. . . . . .2.00 – 4.00
"Hot Gear — Hot Gear," Snoopy dressed
    in rollerskating gear and sunglasses. . . .2.00 – 4.00
"I'd Rather Be Sailing," Snoopy's face appears
    in the middle of a life preserver. . . . . .2.00 – 4.00
"I'll Do It Tomorrow," Snoopy and Woodstock
    (lying on Snoopy's tummy) rest on Snoopy's
    roof. . . . . .2.00 – 4.00
"I'm Afraid My Brain Has Left for the Day!",
    Snoopy leans against a rock. Woodstock
    is on Snoopy's foot. . . . . .2.00 – 4.00
"I'm Still Hoping That Yesterday Will Get Better,"
    Snoopy looks at an unhappy Charlie
    Brown. . . . . .3.00 – 5.00

"Just Call Me 'Sugar Lips'," Snoopy kisses
Peppermint Patty. . . . . .3.00 – 5.00
"Left Fielder," Baseball player Snoopy's side
view. . . . . .3.00 – 5.00
"Let's Be Friends," Snoopy's extended arm
wears a huge mitt. . . . . .3.00 – 5.00
"Let's See Eye To Eye," Woodstock is on
Snoopy's foot. . . . . .2.00 – 4.00
"Life is Full of Surprises," Detective Snoopy holds a
magnifying glass to Woodstock's face. .2.00 – 4.00
"Love," Classic pose of Snoopy hugging
Woodstock. . . . . .3.00 – 5.00
"Love Me," Snoopy wears a lovable
expression. . . . . .2.00 – 4.00
"Music Power," Snoopy plays the piano. . . . .2.00 – 4.00
"Nests are Best," Woodstock at home in his
nest. . . . . .2.00 – 4.00

"Out to Lunch," Side view of Snoopy
walking. .2.00 – 4.00
"Score!", Snoopy and Woodstock as hockey
players. . . . . .2.00 – 4.00
"Somewhere I Can Hear Someone Eating a
Chocolate Chip Cookie!", Snoopy's ear
sticks out. . . . . .2.00 – 4.00
"Sundays Beat School Days," Snoopy blows
bubbles from a bubble wand. . . . . . . .2.00 – 4.00
"Ten-four, Good Buddy!", Snoopy wears a hat
and holds a microphone. . . . . .2.00 – 4.00
"The Cutest of the Cute," Peppermint Patty puts
her arm around Snoopy. . . . . .3.00 – 5.00
"Try to Understand Me," Upside-down Woodstock
chirps to Snoopy. . . . . .2.00 – 4.00
"When My Stomach Talks I Listen," "Hi There,"
Snoopy pats his tummy. . . . . .2.00 – 4.00

Cloth covered, Valentine theme, 2¼", Assortment #2502 (six in the series), 1980

Not Pictured
Beaglescout Snoopy holds a staff with heart
on top. . . . .$5.00 – 7.00
"You're Sweet," Snoopy hugs Woodstock. . . .5.00 – 7.00
"Hearts & Flowers," Snoopy looks at Woodstock,
who holds three flowers. . . . . .5.00 – 7.00

"Happy Valentine's Day," Snoopy lies on the
roof of his home. Valentines in the shape
of a heart decorate part of the roof. . . .5.00 – 7.00
"One of the best things in the whole world is
a friend," "Snoopy & Woodstock." Snoopy
shakes hands with Woodstock. . . . . . .5.00 – 7.00
"Love Me," Snoopy sits and wears a big grin. 5.00 – 7.00

Cloth covered, Halloween theme, 2¼", Assortment #2503 (six in the series), 1980

From back: Lucy as a witch holds a broom; Woodstock and Snoopy howl at the moon; "Trick or Treat," Snoopy holds his goodie bag; "Happy Halloween," Snoopy reads ghost stories to Woodstock; Snoopy as Joe Cool stands next to a large pumpkin; Snoopy lies on a large carved pumpkin; $6.00 – 8.00 each.

Cloth covered, Christmas theme, 2¼", Assortment #2504 (six in the series), 1980

From back: "Happy Holidays," Charlie Brown tangled up in Christmas lights; "Ho-Ho-Ho," Santa Snoopy standing; "Happy Holidays," Snoopy and Woodstock wear green Santa caps; Snoopy as Joe Cool Santa stands next to a house decorated with Christmas lights; Woodstock stands in the center of a Christmas wreath; "Merry Christmas," Snoopy and Woodstock on a sled; $6.00 – 8.00 each.

Cloth covered, Easter theme, 2¼", Assortment #2505 (six in the series), 1980

"Happy Easter," Snoopy holds an Easter basket; Snoopy wears bunny ears; "Happy Easter," Snoopy hugs a bunny; Sally and Lucy wear elaborate Easter bonnets; Snoopy rides a unicycle; Snoopy holds a large Easter egg, Woodstock paints it; $6.00 – 8.00 each.

• Butterfly •

Miscellaneous

"Only 25 Years Old and They're Doing My Life Story!", Charlie Brown stands on top of the baseball mound. He wears a baseball cap, traditional red shirt with black zigzag stripe, and a baseball mitt, 4", 1975. $27.00 – 32.00.

• Hallmark •

Moving Scene Buttons, 2⅞", early 1970s

Schroeder holds a sign which says, "Halloween's Here!", picture changes to "Only 40 Shopping Days 'till Beethoven's Birthday," $20.00 – 30.00.

Not Pictured

"The Great Pumpkin is Watching You," Linus in
    the pumpkin patch. . . . .$25.00 – 35.00
Snoopy does his classic dance, "Snoopy for
    President" .15.00 – 20.00

1½". These buttons came packaged on cardboard, issued 1990.

Not Pictured
"Party Animal!", Woodstock. #JF6112. . . . .$1.50 – 2.50
"Cowabunga!", Snoopy rides a skateboard.
    #JF6114. . . . . .1.50 – 2.50
"Happy Birthday!", Snoopy's upper half.
    #JF6115. . . . . .1.50 – 2.50
"Laugh It Up!", Snoopy's paw covers a portion
    of his mouth. #JF6116. . . . . .1.50 – 2.50

These 3" buttons came packaged on cardboard, 1992.

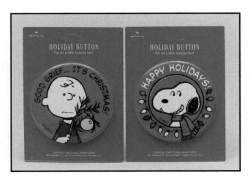

"Good Grief...It's Christmas!", Charlie Brown's upper half. He holds a tree branch with one Christmas ball. #XLP3681; "Happy Holidays!", Snoopy's upper half, a portion of the circle is decorated with Christmas lights, #XLP3691; $2.00 – 4.00 each.

These 3" buttons came packaged on cardboard, issued 1990.

Not Pictured
"Let's Party!", Snoopy and Woodstock.
    #JF6117. . . . .$2.00 – 4.00
"Whoopee!", Snoopy dances. #JF6118. . . . .$2.00 – 4.00

• Simon Simple •

Each ¾" pin has the face of a character along with his/her name.
At least two different background colors are known: cream or white, 1960s.

Charlie Brown; Linus; Lucy; Patty; Pig Pen; Schroeder; Shermy; Snoopy; Violet; $3.00 – 6.00 each.

1¹¹⁄₁₆"

"All I Need is One Hit, and I Can Raise My Lifetime Batting Average to .001!", Lucy and Charlie Brown wear baseball hats, late 1960s, $18.00 – 23.00; "Big Man on the Campus!", Snoopy stands and looks smug, late 1960s, $15.00 – 20.00; "Curse You, Red Baron!", The Flying Ace on a house, late 1960s, $18.00 – 23.00; "Good Grief," Charlie Brown watches Snoopy play golf, late 1960s, $18.00 – 23.00.

"Here's 'Beau' Snoopy of the Foreign Legion Marching Across the Desert," Snoopy as a Foreign Legionnaire wears a topi, late 1960s, $18.00 – 23.00; "Here's the World-Famous Tennis Player Walking Out Onto the Court," tennis player Snoopy and Woodstock, early 1970s, $8.00 – 13.00; "I Don't Care if Anybody Likes Me...Just So I'm Popular!", Lucy tells this to Charlie Brown, late 1960s, $18.00 – 23.00; "I Kissed a Crabby Face!", Snoopy kisses Lucy, late 1960s, $18.00 – 23.00.

"I Think My Feet Need Sharpening!", Snoopy has fallen on the ice, late 1960s, $12.00 – 17.00; "I'm on the Moon!", Astronaut Snoopy on the lunar surface, late 1960s, $20.00 – 25.00; "It's Good to Have a Friend," Snoopy and bunny lean against one another, late 1960s, $18.00 – 23.00; "It Always Rains on our Generation!", Linus and Lucy in the rain, late 1960s, $18.00 – 23.00.

"Surf's Up!", Snoopy runs with his surfboard on his head, late 1960s; "To those of us with real understanding, dancing is the only pure art form," late 1960s; "Vote for Lucy," "Diplomatic Service," Lucy flexes her arm muscles, late 1960s, $15.00 – 20.00 each. "You're A Good Man, Charlie Brown," Charlie Brown stands, late 1960s, $12.00 – 15.00.

Not Pictured
"Happy Birthday, America, 1776 – 1976,"
  Bicentennial. Snoopy and Woodstock
  flank a birthday cake, 1976. . . . . . .$25.00 – 30.00
"Snoopy, Come Home," pose from the movie
  of the same name. Snoopy with supper
  dish on head, hobo pack over shoulder,
  Woodstock walks behind Snoopy,
  early 1970s. . . . . .4.00 – 8.00
"Snoopy for President," Snoopy stands with his
  paw over his heart, late 1960s. . . . . .12.00 – 15.00

2½"

2¹⁵⁄₁₆"

Not Pictured
"Snoopy For President," Snoopy stands with his
   paw over his heart, late 1960s. . . . .$15.00 – 20.00

Not Pictured
"The In Crowd," Frieda, Schroeder, Violet, Snoopy,
   Patty, Pig Pen, Sally, Linus, Lucy, and Charlie
   Brown, late 1960s. . . . .$30.00 – 40.00.

6"

"All Secretaries Need a Little Compliment Now and Then,"
Woodstock sits at his typewriter and is patted on the head by
Snoopy, late 1960s, $20.00 – 30.00; "Curse You, Red Baron!" Fly-
ing Ace Snoopy on his house, late 1960s, $25.00 – 30.00.

"Help Stamp Out Things That Need Stamping Out!", Linus shows his sign to
Snoopy and Lucy, late 1960s; "I've Developed a New Philosophy...I Only
Dread One Day at a Time!", Charlie Brown and Linus with elbows on wall,
late 1960s; "My Home is Always Open to Those Who Enjoy Discussion
Groups!", Snoopy with a flock of birds on top of his house, late 1960s; "No
Problem is So Big or So Complicated That it Can't Be Run Away From,"
Linus voices his opinion to Lucy and Snoopy (who is sleeping), late 1960s;
$20.00 – 30.00 each.

Not Pictured
"Snoopy, Come Home," (Pose from the movie of the
   same name.) Snoopy with supper dish on head,
   hobo pack over shoulder, Woodstock walks
   behind Snoopy, early 1970s. . . . . . .$5.00 – 10.00.

• Butterfly •

Japan, early-mid 1980s, 1½"

Woodstock wears a Japanese headband and holds a hand fan, yellow
background, Series 67245-9; Snoopy's upper half, he wears Japanese
attire and holds a lantern, red background, Series 93316-3; Snoopy
wears Japanese attire and uses sticks to bang on a Japanese drum,
blue and red background, Series 67245-9, $5.00 – 7.00 each.

Snoopy sits at an easel and paints Woodstock's portrait. Trees
in the background, blue sky, Series JXJZ, $5.00 – 7.00; "Dear
Mom," Snoopy types a letter to his mom, yellow background,
Series JXJZ; "Friends," Charlie Brown and Schroeder shake
hands, Schroeder holds his piano under one arm, green and
tan background, Series JXJZ; $4.00 – 6.00 each.

1¾"

"Charlie Brown," Charlie Brown's face, blue background; "Linus Van Pelt," Linus' face, yellow background; "Sally Brown," Sally's face, white background; Lucy Van Pelt," Lucy's face, red background; $4.00 – 6.00 each. "Superbeagle Snoopy," Snoopy's face, blue background, $6.00 – 8.00.

2⅜", Series ES-38

"Snoopy & Sally," they are sharing a tropical drink, palm tree in the black background; "Linus & Snoopy," Linus stands and sucks his thumb while he holds his blanket, Snoopy sits and leans against Linus as they both nap, blue background; "Peanuts," top portion of both Woodstock and Snoopy wearing traditional English bowler hats, yellow and purple background; $6.00 – 8.00 each.

6", 1991

"It's the Great Pumpkin, Charlie Brown," Lucy, Snoopy, Charlie Brown, Linus, Peppermint Patty, Woodstock, and Sally are dressed in Halloween costumes, blue background, $15.00 – 25.00.

• Promotional (Advertising, Premiums & Mail-Aways) •

All Nippon Airlines

"84 ANA Ski Tour," Snoopy skis as birds follow him, plastic, 2⅝" square, 1984, $4.00 – 6.00.

Beaglefest

"Beaglefest IV," "Celebrating 45 Years" "July 1995," Franklin, Lucy, Linus, Peppermint Patty, and Sally hoist Snoopy and Charlie Brown up, Woodstock flies nearby (limited circulation), 2⅜", 1995, $3.00 – 5.00; "Beaglefest V," "Christmas in July," Snoopy reclines on top of his decorated doghouse (limited circulation), 2⅜", 1997, $2.00 – 4.00.

Not Pictured
"Beaglefest III." "Happiness is being a Peanuts Collector," Logo of the Peanuts Collector Club (limited circulation), 2⅜", 1992. . . . .$5.00 – 7.00

Dog Museum (St. Louis, MO)

Not Pictured
"Snoopy's in St. Louis at the Dog Museum," Flying Ace Snoopy's upper half, 1¼", 1990. . . . .$2.00 – 4.00

Ford Falcon

"I Love Falcon," Snoopy sits inside white heart set against red background, 1¼", early 1960s, $25.00 – 35.00.

GRP Records

"Happy Anniversary, Charlie Brown!" Released in conjunction with their album of the same name, Snoopy's face, he wears shades with two patterns, 2½", 1990, $5.00 – 7.00.

Hallmark Keepsake Ornament, 2½", 1990

Charlie Brown stands next to a Charlie Brown snowman, $12.00 – 18.00.

Knott's Berry Farm, Camp Snoopy, California
Each has "Knott's Berry Farm" as well as the depicted character's name, 1⅜". The first five are all 1990.

"Snoopy," Snoopy dances; "Peanuts," Snoopy and Woodstock recline on Snoopy's roof; "Charlie Brown," Charlie Brown with one hand to chin; "Peppermint Patty," Peppermint Patty wears green blouse, black pants, and brown sandals; "Lucy," Lucy in yellow dress; $2.00 – 4.00 each.

"Knott's Berry Farm," "Camp Snoopy," Snoopy lies on red tent, Woodstock peeks from side or underneath tent, 2¼", 1984; $2.00 – 4.00.

Not Pictured

"Knott's Berry Farm," "Camp Snoopy," Snoopy as Beaglescout. Birthday cake holds one candle for Camp Snoopy's first birthday, 2¼", 1985. . . . .$4.00 – 7.00

Camp Snoopy — Minnesota

Not Pictured

"Happiness is...Our First Birthday," "Minnesota 1993," 2¹⁵⁄₁₆". . . . .$3.00 – 5.00

Interstate Brands (Butternut Bread, Dolly Madison, Weber's Bread)

"Curse You Red Baron," Snoopy sits and shakes his fist at his unseen nemesis, red background, white drawing, tab button, 2", early 1970s, $10.00 – 14.00.

"Snoopy for President," inset design is upper portion of Snoopy wearing an Uncle Sam hat and a huge grin, red, white, and blue, 2⅞", mid 1970s, $10.00 – 12.00.

Not Pictured

"The Prince of Sandwiches," crown on Snoopy's head, tab button, 1½", early 1970s. . . . . .$10.00 – 14.00

"Butternut Bread," "Snoopy's Spotters Club," Flying Ace Snoopy looks through binoculars, 2⅜", early 1970s. . . . .$10.00 – 12.00

"Snoopy for President," "Weber's for Bread," Snoopy has a big grin, he wears a red, white, and blue top hat, 3", early 1970s. . . . .$10.00 – 14.00

"Snoopy for President," "Weber's for Lunch," Snoopy with his arms outstretched, tab button, 2", early 1970s. . . . .$14.00 – 17.00

McDonald's

"McDonald's," Snoopy in McDonald's uniform, 2¾" x 1⅝", late 1980s, $12.00 – 14.00.

Met Life

"Healthy Me," "Award Winner," "Metropolitan Life Foundation," Pig Pen, Sally, Franklin, Linus, Lucy, Charlie Brown, Peppermint Patty, Schroeder, and Woodstock flank Snoopy, who is the Met Life representative, 2¾", early 1990s, $5.00 – 8.00.

"Get Met, It Pays." Side view of Snoopy carrying his Met briefcase, white, black, and blue (U.S. and French Canadian versions pictured), 2¼", late 1980s, $2.00 – 4.00.

Redwood Empire Arena, Santa Rosa, CA. 1¾", available through the 1980s

Snoopy holds a hockey stick; Snoopy wears a knit cap and ice skates; $2.00 – 4.00 each.

Saint Paul Winter Carnival

"Celebrate 1990 Saint Paul Winter Carnival," Snoopy and snowman on sled, 6", 1990, $15.00 – 20.00.

Snoopy Fan Club

"Snoopy Fan Club," Snoopy in front of a colorful striped background, 1½" square, early 1980s, $4.00 – 6.00; "Snoopy Fan Club," Snoopy walks along, his ears are partially up, 2⅜", early 1980s, $3.00 – 5.00; "Snoopy Fan Club," Snoopy sits and smiles, 1½", early 1980s, $3.00 – 5.00.

Snoopy The Musical

Not Pictured
"Snoopy The Musical," Snoopy in his pose used
    as the musical's logo. He wears a top hat,
    formal shirt, and jacket and carries a
    baton, 2¼", England, early 1980s. . . . .$5.00 – 8.00

Snoopy's Ice Cream & Cookie Store. (The first one opened in San Francisco, CA.)

Not Pictured
"Snoopy for President," "Snoopy's Ice Cream & Cookie Store," 3", 1984. . . . .$18.00 – 24.00

UNICEF, 2", early 1990s

The gang holds hands around the globe, $5.00 – 10.00.

Coins

Determined Productions issued one coin. While not made of a precious metal, collectors really love and seek it because of the subject: Snoopy as an astronaut, in conjunction with the Apollo moon mission.

Coins in fine silver or gold were produced by Rarities Mint in 1987 and 1988. Each sported a different picture on the front and back. The coins were limited and numbered sequentially through an accompanying certificate or on the cardboard packaging.

We're also including the unique bronze medal offered as a premium by Interstate Brands (Mrs. Karl's, Dolly Madison, Butternut, and Weber's Bread).

Value is based on absolutely pristine condition: the coin must be in the original package.

• Determined Productions, Inc. •

"All Systems Are Go," Snoopy Astronaut Commemorative Coin. Snoopy is dressed as an astronaut. Reverse: "First Landing on the Moon, Commemorative 1969." Snoopy as an astronaut on his doghouse. In either gold or silver tone metal. Packaged on a red, white, and blue cardboard display card, 1½" dia., 1969, $35.00 – 60.00.

• Interstate Brands •

"E Pluribus Snoopy," bronze medal, Snoopy wears a garland of leaves on his head. He also wears a "Hero" medal. Comes in a velvet pouch, 2", early 1980s, $30.00 – 45.00.

• Rarities Mint, Inc. •

"Merry Christmas 1987," Snoopy adds an ornament to the Christmas tree; Woodstock stands on top of it. Reverse: "Happy New Year 1988." Schroeder, Lucy, Charlie Brown, and Snoopy wear party hats; Woodstock looks on. Housed in a clear plastic, fitted case, inside a red velvet box, 2½" dia., five troy ounces, .999 fine silver, 3,000 issued, $75.00 – 120.00.

"Merry Christmas 1987," Snoopy adds an ornament to the Christmas tree; Woodstock stands on top of it. Reverse: "Happy New Year 1988." Schroeder, Lucy, Charlie Brown, and Snoopy wear party hats; and Woodstock looks on. Housed in a clear plastic case, on a cardboard paper display case which opens to reveal Snoopy and Linus in the snow, ¾" dia., one-fourth troy ounce, .999 fine gold, 2,500 issued, $175.00 – 220.00.

"My Heart is Yours 1988," Sally shows a heart to Linus. Reverse: Snoopy hugs Charlie Brown. Coin is housed in a clear plastic case in a cardboard paper display case which opens to reveal birds surrounding Snoopy's doghouse. 1" dia., one troy ounce, .999 fine silver, 30,000 issued., $15.00 – 25.00.

Patches

While patches are not particularly high on the collecting ladder, they remain an inexpensive way to advertise one's interest in a favorite character: Snoopy, Schroeder, or even crabby ol' Lucy.

Determined was creative and original with patches from the beginning, and in the 1980s produced patches for the Familiar Department stores in Japan. There are many, many patches, and what follows is only a sampling.

Value is based on mint condition. There should be no fading. The design should remain very crisp. The value indicated here is based on the patch being in the original packaging. If not, deduct a dollar or two.

• Determined: USA •

Each patch is approximately 3" in diameter and made from cloth, late 1960s and early 1970s.

"I Love Beethoven," Schroeder holds his piano, blue background, red stitched edge, gold letting, $7.00 – 10.00; "I Need All the Friends I Can Get," Charlie Brown walks with a baseball bat over his shoulder, green background, red stitched edge, yellow lettering, $5.00 – 8.00; "The Mad Punter," Snoopy kicks a football, orange background, blue stitched edge, green lettering, $5.00 – 8.00; "Curse You Red Baron," the Flying Ace sits on top of his home, red background, blue stitched edge, green lettering, $7.00 – 10.00; "Tennis Anyone?", Snoopy holds a tennis racket, blue background, red stitched edge, gold lettering, $5.00 – 8.00.

"Jamming," Snoopy rollerskates, wearing protective helmet and a scarf, red background, blue stitching, green lettering, $7.00 – 10.00; "Joe Cool," Snoopy as Joe Cool, orange background, blue stitched edge, green lettering, $5.00 – 8.00; "Ice is Nice," Snoopy ice skates, wearing a red knit cap and scarf, blue background, red stitching, gold lettering; "America You're Beautiful," Snoopy holds an Uncle Sam hat, white background, red stitched edge, blue lettering; "World's Crabbiest Female," Lucy stands, green background, red stitched edge, gold lettering; $7.00 – 10.00 each.

"Jogging is My Thing," Snoopy jogs, orange background, blue stitched edge, green lettering; "World Famous Ski Champion," Snoopy skis, wearing a red knit cap and scarf, green background, red stitched edge, gold lettering; "Strike," Snoopy holds a bowling ball, green background, red stiched edge, gold lettering; "It's Hero Time," Snoopy wears HERO badge, blue background, red stitched edge, gold lettering; "Raw Strength & Courage," Snoopy flexes his muscles, orange background, blue stitched edge, green lettering; $5.00 – 8.00 each.

Not Pictured
"Come Dance with Me," Snoopy dances, orange background, blue stitching, green lettering. . . . .$7.00 – 10.00

• Determined Productions for Familiar: Japan •

Japan, 1½" diameter, cloth, early to mid 1980s

From top: "Snoopy," Snoopy's face, blue background, red stitching, red lettering, Series #740261; Charlie Brown's face, yellow background, turquoise blue stitching, Series #740262; Sally's face, pink background, pink stitching, Series #740262, Japan; Woodstock's profile, blue background, blue stitching, Series #740261; Snoopy holds his paws up to his face and smiles, Series #740261; Snoopy's upper body, blue background, red stitching, Series #740262, Japan; Snoopy wears a hockey uniform and carries a hockey stick over his shoulder, yellow background, yellow stitching, Series #740261; $3.00 – 4.00 each.

2" diameter, cloth, Determined Productions through Familiar Department Stores, Japan, Series #740265, late 1980s

"Merry Christmas," Charlie Brown's face, he wears a Santa cap, blue background, gold stitching, gold lettering, $4.00 – 6.00; "Snoopy," Snoopy as Santa Claus holds gift, gold background, red stitching, red lettering, $6.00 – 8.00.

Determined: USA. Each of the 12 patches in this is approximately 3⅛" in diameter and made from cloth. Issued 1984 in conjunction with the Summer Olympics held in Los Angeles, CA.

Snoopy as a runner, blue background, red border, gray stitching, lettering; Belle playing basketball, gold background, red border, gray stitching, lettering; Snoopy as a pole vaulter, gold background, green border, gray stitching, lettering; Snoopy on the handrings, red background, black border, gray stitching, lettering; Snoopy holds discus, gold background, blue border, orange stitching, lettering; Belle as a gymnast wears leotard and ballet slippers, red background, gold border, blue stitching, lettering; $4.00 – 8.00 each.

Snoopy rides a bicycle, green background, gold border, blue stitching, lettering; Snoopy dives into the swimming pool, blue background, gold border, red stitching, lettering; Snoopy rows a kayak, blue background, green border, gold stitching, lettering; Snoopy as a fencer, green background, blue border, gold stitching, lettering; Snoopy lifts weights, red background, gold border, blue stitching, lettering; Snoopy on pommel horse, red background, blue border, gold stitching, lettering; $4.00 – 8.00 each.

Mother's Day Plates

Plate collecting is a favorite national hobby favored by thousands of people. What better way to tell Mom you love her than through words and an appealing Peanuts drawing on a plate?

Prices are based on mint-in-the-box. There should be no nicks or chips; the lettering and drawing should be bright and clear. The box should not show signs of wear.

• Schmid •

Schmid is regarded as a company that produced quality items any Peanuts collector would be proud to own. Each Mother's Day plate is 7½" in diameter and made of porcelain. In addition, many are sequentially numbered, so the total number of issued plates is part of the plate's record. A Certificate of Authenticity accompanies each plate. Not all plates have item numbers.

1972, "Linus," Linus stands and holds a single red rose. First edition. $15.00 – 25.00.

1973, Snoopy reads a sign held by Woodstock, which says "Mom?" Second edition; 1974, "Snoopy and Woodstock on Parade." Snoopy and Woodstock holds banners with tassels. Snoopy's banner has a heart; Woodstock's has the word "MOM." Third edition. $18.00 – 30.00.

1975, "A Kiss for Lucy," Snoopy holds a red rose and leans over to kiss Lucy, who is not amused. Fourth edition; 1976. "Linus and Snoopy," Linus, Snoopy, and Woodstock each hold a yellow and orange flower. Fifth edition. #279-009. $18.00 – 30.00 each.

1977, "Dear Mom," Snoopy sits on top of his doghouse and types a letter beginning, "Dear Mom." A heart appears in his thoughts. Sixth edition. #279-011; 1978, "Thoughts that Count," Snoopy and Woodstock each hold a red rose and think of their mothers. Seventh edition. #279-013. $18.00 – 30.00 each.

1979, "A Special Letter," Snoopy sits on his doghouse and types, "Dear Mom." The "O" in "MOM" is a pawprint. Eighth edition. 10,000 issued. #279-015; 1980, "A Tribute to Mom," Snoopy leans through the "O" spelling "MOM," Woodstock holds several flowers. Ninth edition. 10,000 issued. #279-315. $18.00 – 30.00 each.

1981, "Mission for Mom," The Flying Ace pilots his doghouse; clouds spell out "MOM." Tenth edition. 10,000 issued. #279-316; 1982, "Which Way to Mother?", Snoopy and Woodstock look at direction sign indicating "Mom" in several different languages. Eleventh edition. 10,000 issued. #279-317. $18.00 – 30.00 each.

• Willitts •

Mother's Day Signature Series

A Certificate of Authenticity accompanied each limited edition Mother's Day plate. The descriptions below are quoted from the back of each plate. Each plate is 7½" in diameter and made of porcelain. A Mother's Day plate was not issued by Willitts for the year 1991.

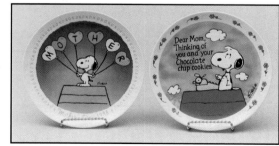

1988, "Snoopy's Mother's Day balloons spell a name that means so much — from loving hearts to loving hugs, Mothers have that special touch!", first edition, #8116, $25.00 – 35.00; 1989, "Snoopy's Thoughts of Mom are of the happiness she makes with her smile, her warmth, her patience — and the cookies that she bakes!", second edition, #9361, $20.00 – 30.00.

1990, "Mom's that special person who brightens every day, and this happy dance from Snoopy is for her on Mother's Day!", third edition, #40009; 1992, "Chef Snoopy's brought his special cake and Woodstock his bouquet, to honor Mom and wish her joy today — and every day!", fourth edition, #40012; $20.00 – 30.00 each.

Valentine's Day Plates

Schmid was the sole producer of collector Valentine's Day plates. Snoopy appeared on each plate, which was a limited edition and accompanied by a Certificate of Authenticity.

Prices are based on mint-in-the-box condition. All lettering and pictures should appear bright, with no chips or nicks on the plate.

1977, "Home is Where the Heart Is," Snoopy lies on top of a gingham heart trimmed in lace, first edition, #279-306; 1978, "Heavenly Bliss," hearts rain all around Snoopy who holds an umbrella, second edition, #279-310; $18.00 – 26.00 each.

1979, "Love match," Snoopy holds a tennis racket and gets ready to receive the heart that is coming his way, third edition, #279-308, $18.00 – 26.00; 1980, "From Snoopy with Love," Snoopy blows a heart-shaped bubble with his bubble pipe, fourth edition, #279-309, $20.00 – 28.00.

1981, "Hearts-A-Flutter," Charlie Brown flies his heart-shaped kite; Snoopy watches in the background, fifth edition, #279-310; 1982, "Love Patch," Snoopy, as a scarecrow, stands in an open field of hearts, sixth edition, #279-311; $20.00 – 28.00 each.

Decorative Plates (Non-Holiday)

Manufacturers always are challenged to find novel ways to present their designs to the public. In this chapter, we've listed some of the plates that do not have a holiday connection but are, nonetheless, collectible.

All prices are based on mint-in-the-box condition. Lettering and design should appear bright, and the plate should not have any chips or nicks.

• Carrigaline Pottery Co. Ltd. •

Plates from this Irish pottery company were produced in the 1970s and have a plain off-white, or cream-colored background. 6⅞" dia.

"I Love My Home," Snoopy reclines on top of his doghouse, $40.00 – 50.00; "Security is Having Someone to Lean On," Charlie Brown and Snoopy sit, leaning against one another, $45.00 – 55.00.

• Danbury Mint •

Peanuts collectors became quite excited when they learned that Danbury Mint was planning a series of Peanuts plates. But, alas, it was not to be. Danbury was unable to fill all the orders and, consequently, the two plates issued were released in such limited numbers that they are desired by plate collectors and especially Peanuts collectors. Each plate has a gold edge and carries the title, "Snoopy and Friends," 8" dia., 1990.

Charlie Brown tells Snoopy, "No, I didn't hear any chocolate chip cookies calling you...", #A391, $225.00 – 300.00.

Charlie Brown hangs upside-down from a tree, all tangled up in kite string, Snoopy holds his supper dish in his mouth, Charlie Brown sighs, #A396, $225.00 – 300.00 each.

• Determined Productions •

Two very special plates were issued in Japan in the late 1980s. Each is 10¾" in diameter and was limited to a production of 1,000 units.

Snoopy wears traditional Japanese attire, Woodstock flies nearby, captioned "40th," $280.00 – 450.00.

Snoopy and Woodstock are dressed in formal attire as they stand by the American flag, $280.00 – 450.00.

• Peanuts 45th Anniversary Series •

These four plates were issued in Japan in 1995 in conjunction with the comic strip's 45th anniversary. An imprinted gold stamp, "Peanuts Comics 45th Anniv.", appears with a gold border on each plate. 8¼" diameter.

"Friends Share with Each Other," Linus and Snoopy sit next to one another, each holding Linus' blue blanket and sucking a thumb; "Would You Like to Share My Supper?", Snoopy hands Charlie Brown his supper dish; $45.00 – 80.00 each.

"Crabby Faces Need Lots of Kisses," Snoopy kisses a disgusted Lucy; "It's Good to Have a Best Friend," Snoopy wears his supper dish on his head and carries a hobo pack over one shoulder, Woodstock walks behind him; $45.00 – 80.00 each.

• Determined Productions (The Dupont Collection Limited Editions) •

"Happy Birthday," Snoopy and Woodstock are in the center of the plate, each holding several ballons, a train encircles them, carrying many of their friends: Linus, Schroeder, Charlie Brown, Lucy, Sally, and Peppermint Patty, #1509, 9¼" dia., mid 1970s, $27.00 – 35.00.

• Sasaki •

This Japanese manufacturer produced glass Peanuts plates that may not have originally been intended for decoration. Collectors, though, had other ideas. Not all the plates are round; some have wavy edges while others have lips as part of their edge. They came in red, black, and white boxes decorated with Snoopy and Woodstock. Captions indicated are those appearing on the plate.

"Snoopy," Snoopy sits on his doghouse rooftop and watches Woodstock fly away, #DT84-4620, 8⅞" x 7¾", mid 1980s, $18.00 – 25.00.

"Snoopy," circus master Snoopy holds a ring for Woodstock to fly through, #DT84-4619, 8⅞" x 7¾", mid 1980s, $18.00 – 25.00.

"40 Years of Happiness," Charlie Brown and Snoopy shake hands, Woodstock flies above holding a banner which reads, "Since 1950," this was a promotional plate and not widely distributed, 1990, $150.00 – 225.00.

• Schmid •

Bicentennial, 1776 – 1976, Snoopy sleeps on top of the Liberty Bell, 7½" dia., $12.00 – 20.00.

30th Anniversary Collector Plate, 1950 – 1980, "Happy Anniversary," the plate features many of the major characters, Snoopy, Linus, Peppermint Patty, Spike, Sally, Charlie Brown, Woodstock, Schroeder, Lucy, and Franklin, 10½", limited edition of 15,000, #279330, $40.00 – 75.00.

World's Greatest Athlete Collection. A series of four plates, each accompanied by a Certificate of Authenticity. Production was limited to 10,000 units of each design, 6½" diameter, 1983.

"Go Deep," Snoopy throws a football to Woodstock who watches, first limited edition, #279-701; "The Puck Stops Here," Snoopy and Woodstock play ice hockey, second limited edition, #279-702; $40.00 – 60.00 each.

"The Way You Play the Game," Snoopy poises his racket to hit a tennis ball, third limited edition, #279-703, $35.00 – 50.00; "The Crowd Went Wild," Snoopy swings his baseball bat, fourth and final limited edition, #279-704, $45.00 – 70.00.

Annual Collector Plate, 7½" dia.

First issued in 1983, these 7½" plates were quite popular with collectors. The designs are extremely colorful and imaginative, taking either Snoopy and/or other characters out of their everyday surroundings, A Certificate of Authenticity accompanies each plate. 20,000 of each design were issued.

1983, "Peanuts in Concert," bandleader Snoopy conducts Lucy, Linus, Sally, Charlie Brown, Schroeder, and Woodstock in a concert, first edition, #279-740, $50.00 – 65.00; 1984, "Snoopy and the Beaglescouts," Beaglescout leader Snoopy leads his troup of birds on a walk, second edition, #279-741, $45.00 – 60.00.

1985, "Clown Caper," Linus, Peppermint Patty, Schroeder, Franklin, Marcie, Sally, Charlie Brown, Lucy, Snoopy, and Woodstock wear clown outfits, their antics center around an old jalopy, third limited edition; 1986, "Flyin' Tamer Snoopy," Snoopy is the tamer of Woodstock, who is dressed as a lion, #279-743, fourth limited edition; $45.00 – 60.00 each.

1987, "Big Top Blast Off," Snoopy is dressed in top hat and formal jacket as he acts as the circus ringmaster. Woodstock gets ready to light the fuse of the cannon which contains a very concerned Charlie Brown. Although intended to be part of the Annual Collector Plate series, Schmid gave up the license; subsequently, this plate did not go into production and is extremely difficult to locate. It did not come in a box; the price here is for the plate only, $175.00 – 250.00.

• Willitts Designs •

"40 Years of Happiness," Charlie Brown, Woodstock, and Snoopy wear red bowties, accompanied by a Certificate of Authenticity, limited edition, 7½" dia., 1990. $28.00 – 40.00.

• Manufacturer Unknown •

"Around the World and Home Again: A Tribute to the Art of Charles M. Schulz, September 18 to October 2, 1994." This was issued in conjunction with an art exhibit held at The Mall of America, Bloomington, Minnesota. The plate did not come with a box, 8⅛" dia., $22.00 – 35.00

Trinket Boxes

Little boxes hold precious treasures; with Snoopy, they're safe.

The boxes are made from many different materials, including porcelain, silverplate, enamel, and glass.

Prices are based on very good to mint condition, no scratches or hairline cracks, and no paint missing. If there is a lid, it should seat securely.

"Love," silverplated, heart-shaped box with three-dimensional figure of Snoopy sitting on top. Red, velvet-lined container, 2½" x 2⅝" x 1½", Leonard Silver, 1979; "Love," ceramic, heart-shaped box with three-dimensional figure of Snoopy sitting on top, 2½" x 2⅝" x 1½", Determined Productions, Inc., #8835, 1978; $15.00 – 25.00 each.

Not Pictured

"Love," silverplated. A three-dimensional Snoopy leans on his elbows. The dish is heart-shaped and lined with red velvet. 6" x 6" x 4", Leonard Silver, 1979. . . . .$90.00 – 145.00

Ceramic, peanut-shaped box with three-dimensional figure of Snoopy reclining on top, 4" x 2" x 3", Determined Productions, Inc., #8920, 1979; ceramic, walnut-shaped box with three-dimensional figure of Snoopy reclining on top, 3" x 2¼" x 3½", Determined Productions, Inc., #8921, 1979; $75.00 – 110.00 each.

"Snoopy," Snoopy's face, design of little yellow stars spells out his name, clear glass, star-shaped, Japan, 3" x 1½", Sasaki Glass Co., Ltd. for Determined Productions, Inc., #DT63-4728, mid 1980s, $10.00 – 16.00; "Snoopy," Snoopy sits, Woodstock is in Snoopy's dog dish, mirrored box, 3¾" x 3½" x 1", Italy, manufacturer unknown, mid 1980s, $12.00 – 20.00; Snoopy and Woodstock deliver several valentines to a U.S. mailbox, clear glass, heart-shaped, Japan, Sasaki Glass Co., Ltd. for Determined Productions, Inc., 3¾" x 5" x 2", #DT49-4519, mid 1980s, $14.00 – 25.00.

"Let's Be Friends," Snoopy holds a red flower, interior caption, "Always," enamel box, 1⅝" dia. x 1", Bilston & Battersea Enamels for Cartier, 1978, $275.00 – 325.00; Woodstock holds an envelope in his mouth, this enamel box does not open, but rather is for decoration. (Because the similar Bilston & Battersea Enamels for Cartier box is in this section, we placed this design here.) ⅞" dia. x ½", Halcyon Days Enamels for Cartier, 1978, $95.00 – 140.00.

Ceramic with lid, raised design of Santa Snoopy with arms outstretched, 2¾" x 4½" x 1¹⁵⁄₁₆", Determined Productions, Inc., #1718-0, 1982; "Merry Christmas," Woodstock and Snoopy are both dressed in their Santa Claus outfits, a green gift box tied with red ribbon is between them, 4½" x 2¾" x 1¹⁵⁄₁₆", Determined Productions, Inc., #1719-1, 1982; $45.00 – 65.00 each.

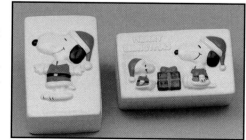

A wooden figure of Snoopy is the cover on the box, limited edition. (Note: this box was also given to United Media licensees at a California meeting in 1985 and had a plaque attached to the front.) Japan, Another Determined Production for Toybox Corporation, 6¼", 1984; in box, $150.00 – 200.00; no box, $135.00 – 185.00.

Plastic Trophies (Aviva)

Don Fraser of Aviva designed the first plastic trophy: Snoopy as the Flying Ace with the caption, "Curse You, Red Baron!" These colorful trophies have remained very popular throughout the years, with their appeal and reasonable price encouraging collectors to seek out as many different designs as possible.

Don't be surprised if you encounter the same design with a different caption; many of the captions appeared on more than one style of trophy. Be careful, however, because the slips of metal on which the captions are printed slide out quite easily, and many folks customized their own trophies by mixing and matching different captions.

Encountering a combination not shown below does not necessarily suggest that it left the factory that way.

The trophies were sold with or without mailer-type boxes. The price is not affected if the box is not included.

The following list attempts to be definitive, but it's entirely possible that a few have been missed along the way. Prices are based on mint condition. The trophy should be firmly attached to the base with no cracks or chips at the point of contact. The caption plate should be firmly intact, with no scuffs, missing paint, or missing letters. The base can be any color, although most are black. All were issued during the 1970s.

Title	Value
"1776 – 1976: Happy Anniversary," Snoopy holds red, white, and blue electioneering hat.	$8.00 – 12.00
"Affection needed immediately," Snoopy, surrounded by hearts, puckers up for a kiss.	5.00 – 7.00
"A friend is a present you give yourself," Snoopy and Woodstock sit close together and smile.	3.00 – 5.00
"Ahhhh! Retirement!", Snoopy sits in a comfy chair.	8.00 – 12.00
"A kiss a day deeps the blahs away," Snoopy kisses Peppermint Patty.	5.00 – 7.00
"America, you're beautiful," Snoopy stands, holding an Uncle Sam hat.	8.00 – 12.00
"Aquarius," Snoopy holds a book.	8.00 – 10.00
"Atlanta launching pad," Atlanta Braves Snoopy wears baseball cap, looks grim.	5.00 – 9.00
"Be kind to nature," Snoopy in safari hat and jacket holds binoculars.	5.00 – 7.00
"Best of luck," Linus wears a wizard's hat and ponders a crystal ball.	8.00 – 12.00
"Bon Voyage," Snoopy as an aviator, wears red scarf, jacket, and goggles.	3.00 – 5.00
"Bon Voyage," Snoopy tips his cap, carries a travel bag over one arm.	3.00 – 5.00
"Boogie Down," Snoopy wears a John Travolta-style disco outfit.	6.00 – 8.00
"Cancer," Snoopy sits among Woodstocks while one talks.	8.00 – 10.00
"Capricorn," Snoopy holds a heart.	8.00 – 10.00
"Cheers," Belle in pink dress with two blue megaphones.	8.00 – 12.00
"Cheers," Flying Ace shares a root beer with Woodstock.	3.00 – 5.00
"Cold nose ... warm heart!" Snoopy reclines on a bunch of pink and red hearts.	3.00 – 5.00
"Congratulations," Snoopy sleeps on pink blanket on word "Baby."	5.00 – 7.00
"Congratulations," Snoopy wears top hat and tails.	5.00 – 7.00
"Cowabunga," Surfer Snoopy tackles a big wave.	5.00 – 7.00
"Curse this stupid war," Snoopy in his Flying Ace garb.	8.00 – 10.00
"Curse you, Red Baron," Snoopy, in his determined Flying Ace pose.	5.00 – 7.00
"Doctor Beagle," Snoopy sits next to Woodstock's nest, with stethoscope.	5.00 – 7.00
"Don't throw in the towel yet," Snoopy wears swimming trunks.	3.00 – 5.00
"Downhill racer," Snoopy skis down a hilll.	3.00 – 5.00
"Do you mind if I admire you?" Snoopy and Woodstock wear top hats, bow ties.	6.00 – 9.00
"Every good day begins with a little love," Flying Ace holds a bunch of flowers.	3.00 – 5.00
"Feeling groovy," Snoopy dances, wearing red turtleneck with blue stripes.	3.00 – 5.00
"Femme fatale," Belle strikes a model's pose.	5.00 – 7.00
"Friendship is for sharing," Hobo Snoopy has dish on head, Woodstock follows.	3.00 – 5.00
"Friendship is for sharing," Lucy and Charlie Brown at Lucy's psychiatric booth.	5.00 – 7.00
"Front runner," Snoopy in blue jogging suit, Woodstock alongside.	3.00 – 5.00
"Get well soon," Snoopy, dressed as a doctor, holds bag and needle.	5.00 – 7.00
"Get well soon," Snoopy wears a blue robe, Woodstock holds a thermometer.	3.00 – 5.00
"Girls are smarter than boys," Lucy, in orange dress, holds up arm and opens her mouth.	8.00 – 10.00
"Good luck," Woodstock stands with a four-lear clover.	5.00 – 7.00
"Grandmother!" The Flying Ace holds a bunch of flowers.	5.00 – 7.00

Title	Value
"Happiness is a good friend," Snoopy lies on his doghouse, Woodstock on his tummy.	$3.00 – 5.00
"Happiness is a happy birthday," Charlie Brown, wearing party hat, holds out his arms.	8.00 – 10.00
"Happiness is love," Peppermint Patty stands and smiles.	8.00 – 10.00
"Happiness is love," Snoopy dances, wearing orange and red turtleneck.	3.00 – 5.00
"Happiness is love," Snoopy wears blue sports coat, holds out his arms.	3.00 – 5.00
"Happiness is love," Woodstock wears a top hat, carries a rose.	5.00 – 7.00
"Happiness is me and you," Snoopy and Woodstock in blanket, hold pennants.	3.00 – 5.00
"Happiness is togetherness," Snoopy leans to see what Charlie Brown is reading.	3.00 – 5.00
"Happy birthday," Chef Snoopy holds cake in dog dish, with one red candle.	5.00 – 7.00
"Happy birthday," Snoopy and Woodstock wear top hats and red bow ties.	5.00 – 7.00
"Happy birthday," Snoopy wears a party hat.	5.00 – 7.00
"Happy birthday to you," Snoopy holds a green and yellow package.	3.00 – 5.00
"Happy Easter," Woodstock sits in a cracked egg.	5.00 – 7.00
"Happy Monday," Snoopy, bleary-eyed, lies on his doghouse.	3.00 – 5.00
"Happy Valentine's Day," Snoopy reclines on a bed of hearts.	5.00 – 7.00
"Have a beautiful day," Snoopy holds a heart over his chest	3.00 – 5.00
"Have a beautiful day," Woodstock sits in front of a rainbow.	5.00 – 7.00
"Have a good one," Snoopy wears supper dish on head and carries a hobo pack.	3.00 – 5.00
"Have a happy one," Lucy wears a red dress and party hat.	8.00 – 10.00
"Have a happy one," Snoopy holds a green gift tied with yellow ribbon.	3.00 – 5.00
"Have a heart," Snoopy holds a basket of flowers and a heart.	3.00 – 5.00
"Have fun," Snoopy wears tennis gear and holds bag.	3.00 – 5.00
"Hello," Snoopy extends his paw in friendship.	3.00 – 5.00
"Hope you're feeling better," Snoopy as the world-famous surgeon.	5.00 – 7.00
"I (heart symbol) New York," Snoopy as the Statue of Libery, in front of New York.	8.00 – 12.00
"I can't get you off my mind," Charlie Brown leans back; Snoopy sleeps on his head.	3.00 – 5.00
"I can't stop loving you," Snoopy wears 10-gallon hat and strums guitar.	5.00 – 7.00
"If you need a friend, I'm available," Woodstock wears red bowtie and holds top hat, flower.	3.00 – 5.00
"I hope you're feeling better," Snoopy as a doctor, in blue scrubs.	5.00 – 7.00
"I like you," Snoopy dances in a red and orange turtleneck.	3.00 – 5.00
"I like you," Snoopy hugs Charlie Brown tightly	3.00 – 5.00
"I'll make you an offer you can't refuse," Snoopy wears trench coat, brown hat, carries bank.	3.00 – 5.00
"I love you THIS much," Snoopy, wearing blue coat, stands with arms outstretched.	3.00 – 5.00
"I'm in the mood for love," Snoopy sits, holding flowers, with a goofy grin on his face.	5.00 – 7.00
"I'm in the mood for love," Snoopy smiles while holding three flowers.	3.00 – 5.00
"I miss you," Snoopy stands with 3-D tear in one eye.	5.00 – 7.00
"I'm lost without you," Snoopy wears a backpack and carries a map.	5.00 – 7.00
"I'm sorry," Snoopy stands with 3D tear rolling down his cheek.	5.00 – 7.00
"I need all the friends I can get," Snoopy leans against Charlie Brown, who wears a green shirt.	3.00 – 5.00
"Isn't it nice we're both living in the same world?", Snoopy and Woodstock recline on blue cloud.	5.00 – 7.00
"I think the world of you," Snoopy, with dog dish on head, holds a globe.	5.00 – 7.00
"I think you're wonderful," Snoopy hugs Woodstock.	3.00 – 5.00
"I think you're wonderful," Snoopy leans on his paws on a tree stump.	3.00 – 5.00
"I think you're wonderful," Woodstock wears a top hat, carries a rose.	5.00 – 7.00
"It's the little things that count," Snoopy stands, surrounded by admiring Woodstocks.	5.00 – 7.00
"Joe Family," Snoopy stands, surrounded by admiring Woodstocks.	5.00 – 7.00
"Joe Gourmet," Chef Snoopy holds frying pan and utensils.	8.00 – 10.00
"Joe Rembrandt," Snoopy, in mustache and beret, holds palette.	5.00 – 7.00
"Keep smiling," Snoopy dances while Woodstock sits on the doghouse.	3.00 – 5.00
"Keep the corners of your mouth turned up," Lucy and Charlie Brown smile at her psychiatric booth.	5.00 – 7.00
"Leo," Snoopy sits on red cushion, wearing a crown, paw raised.	8.00 – 10.00
"Libra," Snoopy	8.00 – 10.00
"Life is like a brown bag ... full of wonderful surprises," Snoopy sits on a school bench.	5.00 – 7.00

Title	Value
"Life is one big thrill after another," The Flying Ace holds a baton.	5.00 – 7.00
"Love from San Francisco," Snoopy reclines on top of a cable car.	8.00 – 10.00
"Love me now and beat the crowd," Snoopy dances among pink and red heart background.	3.00 – 5.00
"Love me tender," Snoopy hugs Woodstock tightly.	3.00 – 5.00
"Love one another," Snoopy hugs Woodstock tightly.	3.00 – 5.00
"Merry Christmas," Santa Snoopy holds a sack filled with gifts.	8.00 – 10.00
"Merry Christmas," Snoopy holds a large green gift box.	5.00 – 7.00
"My pal," Snoopy hugs Woodstock tightly.	3.00 – 5.00
"Never underestimate the effect of a pretty face," Snoopy admires himself in a small mirror.	3.00 – 5.00
"Ordinary beagle," Snoopy carries his lunch pail.	3.00 – 5.00
"Poor sweet baby," Snoopy researches medical journal to help Woodstock.	3.00 – 5.00
"Raindrops keep falling on my head," Snoopy wears 10-gallon hat and strums guitar.	3.00 – 5.00
"Saturday Night Beagle," Disco Snoopy.	5.00 – 7.00
"Scorpio," Snoopy sits by Scorpio sign.	8.00 – 10.00
"Security is having someone to lean on," Snoopy leans against Charlie Brown.	3.00 – 5.00
"Simply super sister," Snoopy and Belle flank a large pink heart.	5.00 – 7.00
"Ski bum," Snoopy walks with skis, wears striped cap.	3.00 – 5.00
"Smile," Woodstock stands and smiles.	5.00 – 7.00
"A smile goes up not down," Snoopy sits, with Woodstock on his head.	3.00 – 5.00
"Sorry I Haven't written, my secretary's been ill," Snoopy watches Woodstock type.	5.00 – 7.00
"Spirit of '76: 1776 – 1976," Snoopy wears George Washington-style hat, holds axe.	10.00 - 15.00
"Superstar," Snoopy and Woodstock playing tennis against a net.	5.00 – 7.00
"Superstar," Snoopy with red hat, grins with teeth showing.	5.00 – 7.00
"Taurus," Snoopy and Woodstock both sing.	8.00 – 10.00
"Tennis ace," Snoopy wears tennis visor and holds racquet.	3.00 – 5.00
"Tennis is my racquet," Snoopy walks, holding a racquet.	3.00 – 5.00
"Thank you," Beau Snoopy wears a yellow sports coat.	3.00 – 5.00
"Thank you," Snoopy, in red and blue turtleneck, dances.	3.00 – 5.00
"Thank you this much," Charlie Brown wears a dinner jacket and party hat.	8.00 – 10.00
"Thank you," Woodstock stands and smiles.	3.00 – 5.00
"There is no heavier burden than a great potential," Snoopy wears green coat, top hat, and cane.	5.00 – 7.00
"They're playing our song," Snoopy plays piano while Woodstock dances on it.	3.00 – 5.00
"Thinking about you makes my whole day!" Snoopy dances and holds basket of flowers.	3.00 – 5.00
"Think snow," Snoopy stands, wearing red and orange sweater, holding red skis.	3.00 – 5.00
"This is a difficult time. I'm going through life," Snoopy, grinning, walks in front of blue background.	3.00 – 5.00
"Top grandpa," Snoopy stands with blue hat on, brown pipe in mouth.	8.00 – 10.00
"We all have our hang-ups," Linus holds blue blanket while sucking his thumb.	3.00 – 5.00
"Welcome back," Snoopy in astronaut's gear, holds life-support pack.	8.00 – 10.00
"We're in tune," Snoopy plays a bugle while Woodstock sings.	5.00 – 7.00
"What did I do to deserve this?", Beaglescout Snoopy surrounded by four bird scouts.	3.00 – 5.00
"What did I do to deserve this?", Snoopy seems to have been attacked by the cat next door.	3.00 – 5.00
"What did I do to deserve this?", Snoopy wears a big grin.	3.00 – 5.00
"What's cooking," Chef Snoopy bangs his bowl with a bone.	8.00 – 10.00
"What's your handle, good buddy?", Snoopy sits on doghouse with CB radio.	5.00 – 7.00
"Winning isn't everything. It's the only thing," Snoopy holds large trophy and plaque.	5.00 – 7.00
"Wish you were here," Woodstock sits on large travel case; pennant reads "SOUTH"	5.00 – 7.00
"Work is for the birds," Joe Cool relaxes under tree while Woodstock gardens.	5.00 – 7.00
"World's best bicycle racer," Snoopy in red, white, and blue biking gear, on bicycle.	3.00 – 5.00
"World's best cook," Chef Snoopy holds red dish, with his tongue out.	5.00 – 7.00
"World's best driver," Snoopy in a blue helmet and red suit, leans against a tire.	5.00 – 7.00
"World's best friend," Snoopy in dancing pose wearing red shirt with black trim	3.00 – 5.00
"World's best friend," Snoopy wears a yellow jacket with tie.	3.00 – 5.00
"World"s best salesman," Snoopy wears red jacket and a bowtie.	3.00 – 5.00
"World's best secretary," Snoopy and Woodstock, who types, sit on doghouse.	3.00 – 5.00

Title	Value
"World's best skipper," Snoopy wears a naval jacket and cap.	3.00 – 5.00
"World's best student," Snoopy sits at a school desk.	5.00 – 7.00
"World's best teacher," Snoopy sits at a school desk.	5.00 – 7.00
"World's biggest clown," Snoopy dressed in multi-colored clown suit.	8.00 – 12.00
"World's greatest assistant," Woodstock carries a pencil.	5.00 – 7.00
"World's greatest backpacker," Woodstock struggles beneath huge green backpack.	3.00 – 5.00
"World's greatest baseball player," Snoopy, in baseball cap, tries to hit baseball with bat.	5.00 – 7.00
"World's greatest baseball player," Snoopy in red and blue uniform, holds baseball glove.	5.00 – 7.00
"World's greatest basketball player," Snoopy holds a basketball, wears blue shorts and yellow top.	5.00 – 7.00
"World's greatest boss," Snoopy wears jacket, top hat, and holds cane.	3.00 – 5.00
"World's greatest boss," Snoopy wears orange coat and holds lots of greenbacks.	3.00 – 5.00
"World's greatest bowler," Snoopy wears orange shirt and throws bowling ball.	3.00 – 5.00
"World's greatest bowler," Snoopy wears red bowling outfit and throws bowling ball.	3.00 – 5.00
"World's greatest coach," Snoopy wears red sweater, carries baseball and bat.	3.00 – 5.00
"World's greatest coach," Snoopy wears turtleneck and whistle, holds equipment.	3.00 – 5.00
"World's greatest cyclist," Snoopy on yellow motorcycle, wears green helmet.	5.00 – 7.00
"World's greatest dad," Snoopy as scoutmaster, with birds on his green hat.	5.00 – 7.00
"World's greatest dancer," Snoopy dances in his best Arthur Murray style.	5.00 – 7.00
"World's greatest dieter," Snoopy stands and looks down on a scale.	5.00 – 7.00
"World's greatest doctor," Snoopy wears white shirt and stethoscope, bag in hand.	5.00 – 7.00
"World's greatest fan," Snoopy in fake fur coat and porkpie hat, holds pennant.	3.00 – 5.00
"World's greatest fireman," Snoopy wears fireman's outfit and holds a fire hose	5.00 – 7.00
"World's greatest fisherman," Snoopy wears fishing gear and holds fish.	5.00 – 7.00
"World's greatest football player," Snoopy, in orange jersey and helmet, throws football.	3.00 – 5.00
"World's greatest golfer," Snoopy wears blue shirt, golf club over shoulder.	3.00 – 5.00
"World's greatest graduate," cap-and-gowned Snoopy and Woodstock, with diploma.	5.00 – 7.00
"World's greatest hairstylist," Snoopy wears red bouffant wig and styles Woodstock's comb.	5.00 – 7.00
"World's greatest handyman," Snoopy holds hammer and nails, with two nails in his mouth.	5.00 – 7.00
"World's greatest hockey player," Snoopy skates in outfit, with hockey stick in hands.	5.00 – 7.00
"World's greatest hockey player," Snoopy wears yellow cap and carries yellow hockey stick.	5.00 – 7.00
"World's greatest hunter," Snoopy wears a safari suit, with binoculars.	5.00 – 7.00
"World's greatest math student," Snoopy sits at a school desk	5.00 – 7.00
"World's greatest mom," Snoopy leans over the "O" in the word "MOM."	8.00 – 12.00
"World's greatest neighbor," Snoopy delivers a potted houseplant	5.00 – 7.00
"World's greatest nurse," Lucy tends to an ill and bedridden Snoopy.	8.00 – 10.00
"World's greatest partygoer," Snoopy and Woodstock wear party hats, hold balloons.	8.00 – 10.00
"World's greatest policeman," Snoopy as policeman holds a whistle in one paw.	3.00 – 5.00
"World's greatest roller skater," Snoopy wears red helmet and roller skates.	3.00 – 5.00
"World's greatest secretary," Snoopy and Woodstock at the typewriter.	5.00 – 7.00
"World's greatest secretary," Snoopy walks with pencils in his paw, mouth, and on ear.	5.00 – 7.00
"World's greatest skateboarder," Snoopy glides along on a yellow skateboard.	3.00 – 5.00
"World's greatest skateboarder," Snoopy jumps on red skateboard with yellow wheels.	3.00 – 5.00
"World's greatest skater," Snoopy in red sweater with yellow trim, red and yellow cap.	3.00 – 5.00
"World's greatest skater," Snoopy wears green boots and ice skates, with muffler.	3.00 – 5.00
"World's greatest skater," Snoopy wears striped scarf and green skates	3.00 – 5.00
"World's greatest skier," Snoopy, in goggles, stands on blue skis with yellow trim.	3.00 – 5.00
"World's greatest skin diver," Snoopy wears scuba gear.	5.00 – 7.00
"World's greatest slam dunker," Snoopy runs, mouth open wide, basketball over his head.	5.00 – 7.00
"World's greatest," Snoopy as the Flying Ace.	3.00 – 5.00
"World's greatest soccer player," Snoopy kicks a soccer ball.	3.00 – 5.00
"World's greatest soccer player," Snoopy runs, in green and yellow uniform; he's angry.	3.00 – 5.00
"World's greatest swimmer," Snoopy wears trunks, sunglasses, and gold medals.	3.00 – 5.00
"World's greatest teacher," Joe Cool carries school books.	3.00 – 5.00
"World's greatest tennis player," Snoopy holds racquet, wears yellow shirt trimmed in red.	3.00 – 5.00
"World's greatest tennis player," Snoopy wears green visor and carries tennis racquet.	3.00 – 5.00

Title	Value
"World's greatest water skier," Snoopy skis on blue water, wearing yellow water skis.	3.00 – 5.00
"World's greatest weight watcher," Snoopy stands on yellow scale.	5.00 – 7.00
"You are a rare gem," Peppermint Patty stands and smiles.	5.00 – 7.00
"You are a real winner," Snoopy carries a trophy.	3.00 – 5.00
"You captured my heart," Snoopy with a valentine.	5.00 – 7.00
"You crack me up," Woodstock sits in a cracked egg.	5.00 – 7.00
"You make me smile," Snoopy dances	3.00 – 5.00
"You make my sun shine," Woodstock stands in front of orange sun.	3.00 – 5.00
"You're a real winner," Snoopy holds a huge trophy cup and plaque.	3.00 – 5.00
"You're close to my heart," Snoopy hugs Woodstock.	3.00 – 5.00
"You're close to my heart," Snoopy stands with a red heart over his own heart.	3.00 – 5.00
"You're close to my heart," Woodstock stands in a rainbow.	5.00 – 7.00
"You're grrreat!" Snoopy wears a magician's cape and hat, holds baton.	5.00 – 7.00
"You're number one," Snoopy wears a "hero" ribbon.	5.00 – 7.00
"You're one of the few good guys left," Snoopy, as sheriff, holds a star.	5.00 – 7.00
"You're sweet," Snoopy holds basket of flowers and heart.	3.00 – 5.00
"You're the coolest," Snoopy wears shades and green turtleneck, throws a Frisbee.	3.00 – 5.00
"You're the fairest," Snoopy holds a mirror.	3.00 – 5.00
"You're the greatest," Snoopy wears a magician's cape and hat, holds baton.	5.00 – 7.00
"You're the Joe Coolest," Snoopy wears blue shirt and sunglasses.	3.00 – 5.00
"You're the world's greatest mom," Snoopy leans over the "O" in the word "MOM."	8.00 – 10.00
"You're the world's greatest," Snoopy wears red shirt, dances.	3.00 – 5.00
"You're the world's greatest," Woodstocks sit on top of Snoopy's head.	3.00 – 5.00
"Your fault or mine?", Snoopy holds a tennis racquet, with a big smile.	3.00 – 5.00
"Your wish is my command," Snoopy appears as a knight, wearing a mantle.	4.00 – 6.00
"You've got me on Cloud 9," Snoopy sleeps, Woodstock on stomach; rainbow.	3.00 – 5.00
"You've got rhythm," Snoopy plays the drums.	5.00 – 7.00

"Ahhhh! Retirement!"

"Cheers."

"Curse you, Red Baron."

"Do you mind if I admire you?"

"Femme Fatale."

"Girls are smarter than boys."

"Grandmother!"

"Happy Birthday."

"Happy Monday."

"Have a happy one."

"I like you"

"Life is one big thrill after another!"

"Merry Christmas"

"Spirit of '76: 1776 – 1976"

"Thinking about you makes my whole day!"

"We all have our hang-ups"

"World's Greatest Hair Stylist"

"World's Greatest Nurse"

"World's Greatest Skin Diver"

"You are a rare gem"

• Double Trophies •

These have more than one plastic design on them. We've listed just a few.

"World's Greatest Bowler," Snoopy gets ready to roll his bowling ball at Woodstock, who sits on the pins in the background, $14.00 – 18.00.

"World's Greatest Skier," Snoopy stand on his skis, mountains are in the background, $14.00 – 18.00.

"You're the Fairest One of All," Snoopy admires himself in a mirror, $14.00 – 18.00.

"You've Captured My Heart," Snoopy dances, Woodstock sits on Snoopy's house in the background, $14.00 – 18.00.

Not Pictured
"You've Captured My Heart," Snoopy aims a
Cupid's arrow at Woodstock, who sits
on a heart in the background. . . . . .$16.00 – 22.00

Sparkies

We could call these products "Happiness on a Spring," because they're so charming. A little plastic scene stands on a teakwood base and features Snoopy. Woodstock can be found in a corner of each scene, assuming the poor little guy hasn't disappeared. Alas, many of these scenes turn up without Snoopy's little "friend of friends." He's supposed to be glued on, but the design leaves him exposed, so be prepared: you may not find Sparkies in a condition that is as mint as you'd like. As you can see, Woodstock is absent in one of the scenes pictured here. The pricing is based on mint condition with Woodstock.

These are charmers and well worth having. Finding them packaged is a plus because the orange box features Snoopy on the cover and a sticker of the product housed inside, 1972.

Joe Cool tosses a frisbee to Woodstock; Snoopy holds onto a kite string; in box, $20.00 – 30.00; no box, $15.00 – 25.00 each.

Snoopy walks along with a flock of birds; in box, $25.00 – 35.00; no box, $20.00 – 30.00. Snoopy holds his arms outstretched; in box, $20.00 – 30.00; no box, $15.00 – 25.00.

The Flying Ace (note hole where Woodstock is missing); Snoopy kisses Lucy; in box, $25.00 – 35.00; no box, $20.00 – 30.00 each.

Banners & Pennants

Those who love the Peanuts gang often wish to declare this love to the world. A banner, pennant, or flag is the way to go. They first were issued by Determined in the 1960s. Many feature characters in their older incarnations, before their features softened up.

The Determined banners and pennants are made from felt and stamped with black drawings and writing. The felt came in various colors, but only one color to each banner or pennant. Some have the character's name printed on them as well.

While most of the banners and pennants listed below were available for purchase in the United States, some of the same designs were available in other countries.

Pricing is based on excellent to mint condition, with no tears or holes. The background color must be bright, with no fading. The drawing and lettering are black.

• Banners •

15" at widest point x 33" long, 1960s to mid 1970s

Title	Value
"Actually, we Joe Cools are scared to death of chicks," Snoopy as Joe Cool, #5703.	$7.00 – 12.00
"A Friend is Someone Who Accepts You for What You Are!", Pig Pen and Snoopy walk together.	7.00 – 12.00
"All Systems Are Go!" Snoopy as an astronaut.	35.00 – 45.00
"America, You're Beautiful!", Snoopy holds his Uncle Sam hat. This is the only felt banner issued with a multicolor background, white with a red and blue design, #5704.	16.00 – 22.00
"Bleah!" Lucy sticks her tongue out.	7.00 – 12.00
"Curse You, Red Baron!", The Flying Ace Snoopy steers his imaginary Sopwith Camel, #5708.	10.00 – 14.00
"For a nickel, I can cure anything!", Lucy waits for customers to arrive at her psychiatrist's booth.	7.00 – 12.00
"Happiness is Loving Your Enemies," Snoopy hugs two bunnies.	8.00 – 14.00
"I am suddenly overcome by a burst of wishy-washiness!", Charlie Brown wears baseball mitt and cap.	7.00 – 12.00
"I feel the need to have the feeling that it's good to be alive," Charlie Brown, #5727.	7.00 – 12.00
"I Hate People Who Sing in the Morning," Snoopy tries to sleep on his rooftop as Woodstock sings, #5715.	7.00 – 12.00
"I Love Mankind...It's People I Can't Stand!", Linus holds his trusty blanket and sucks his thumb.	7.00 – 12.00
"I'm frustrated, inhibited, and no one understands me!", Lucy stands with outstretched arms.	7.00 – 12.00
"I'm My Own Person!" Lucy opens her big mouth, #5713.	7.00 – 12.00
"I Need All The Friends I Can Get!" Charlie Brown stands, #5709.	7.00 – 12.00
"It Doesn't Matter What You Believe As Long As You're Sincere!", Linus stands and holds up one arm.	7.00 – 12.00
"I Think I'm Allergic to Morning!", Snoopy very tired and bleary-eyed on his doghouse roof, #5711	5.00 – 10.00
"It's amazing how stupid you can be when you're in love...", Lucy sits.	7.00 – 12.00
"I've Become Allergic to People!" Snoopy sits inside his mailbox.	7.00 – 12.00
"I've Got to Start Acting More Sensible ... Tomorrow!", Snoopy does his happy dance, #5707	7.00 – 12.00
"Love is Walking Hand-in-Hand," Linus and Sally hold hands as they walk, #5710.	8.00 – 14.00
"Merry Christmas From All of Us, The Peanuts Gang," Sally, Charlie Brown, Violet, Frieda, Snoopy, Lucy, and Linus near Schroeder as he plays his piano, 20¼" x 28".	35.00 – 50.00
"Mi Pesa Pensare Alle Prossime Scadenze," Snoopy looks puzzled as Woodstock sleeps on his nose (Italy).	7.00 – 12.00
"No One Understands My Generation Either," Snoopy sits on the rooftop of his home, #5714.	7.00 – 12.00
"PEACE," Linus holds his fingers to symbolize peace.	7.00 – 12.00
"Polluted snowflakes!", Linus stands as snowflakes fall, #5718.	6.00 – 10.00
"Smile," Snoopy wears a big smile.	7.00 – 12.00
"Snoopy For President," Snoopy puckers up for a kiss and holds a sign.	8.00 – 14.00
"Somehow I have the feeling that a crisis has arisen...", Snoopy hugs Charlie Brown for dear life.	7.00 – 12.00
"Suddenly I Can Think of About 10 Things I'd Rather Be Doing Right Now," Snoopy looks puzzled as Woodstock sleeps on his nose, #5717.	7.00 – 12.00
"The Moon is Made of American Cheese!", Snoopy as an astronaut.	35.00 – 45.00
"The Planting of a Tree Shows Faith in the Future," Linus and Lucy get ready to plant a tree, #5720.	7.00 – 12.00
"There are times when life is pure joy.", Snoopy and Woodstock dance, #5723.	7.00 – 12.00
"The secret of life is to reduce your worries to a minimum!", Snoopy on doghouse.	7.00 – 12.00
"To Know Me is to Love Me!", Linus stands with arms outstretched, #5712.	7.00 – 12.00

"America, You're Beautiful."

"Curse You, Red Baron!"

"I Need All the Friends I Can Get!"

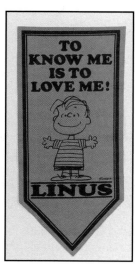

"To Know Me is to Love Me!"

"I'm My Own Person!"

"Polluted Snowflakes."

"There are times when life is pure joy."

"PEACE."

"Bleah!"

"It's amazing how stupid you can be when you're in love..."

"The secret of life is to reduce your worries to a minimum!"

"Somehow I have the feeling a crisis has arisen..."

"Mi Pesa Pensare Alle Prossime Scadenze."

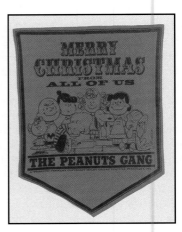

"Merry Christmas From All of Us. The Peanuts Gang."

• Pennants •

14½" at widest point x 31" long, 1970s.

Title	Value
"BASEBALL," Snoopy swings his baseball bat, Woodstock is nearby.	$5.00 – 7.00
"FOOTBALL," Woodstock runs as Snoopy catches football.	5.00 – 7.00
"Gee...somebody cares!", Snoopy hugs Woodstock.	3.00 – 5.00
"HIKE," Woodstock follows Snoopy, who wears backpack and cap.	3.00 – 5.00
"I Hate It When It Snows on My French Toast!", Snoopy sits near his dog dish as snowflakes fall.	3.00 – 5.00
"Snoopy for President," Snoopy smiles and closes his eyes, Woodstock sits nearby.	3.00 – 5.00
"SOCCER," Snoopy runs toward the soccer ball, Woodstock watches.	3.00 – 5.00
"TENNIS," Snoopy is poised to hit a tennis ball with his racquet.	3.00 – 5.00
"To Dance is to Live, to Live is to Dance!", Snoopy and Woodstock dance.	3.00 – 5.00

"Gee...somebody cares!"

"Snoopy for President."

"BASEBALL."

"FOOTBALL."

Determined Products, Japan

Two heavy cloth Christmas banners on wooden dowels were produced for Familiar Department Stores in the mid 1980s.

"Merry X'Mas Snoopy & Friends," Santa Snoopy enjoys the company of three "party" birds, 13" x 14¾", $20.00 – 30.00.

"Merry Christmas," "Snoopy, Charlie Brown, Lucy, Sally, and Linus," Each character is pictured wearing a party hat, #84-072, $40.00 – 50.00.

Advertising

• Knott's Berry Farm — Camp Snoopy •

Pennants were among the first souvenirs available from Knott's Berry Farm when they opened their "Camp Snoopy" amusement park in 1983. 12" at widest point, 19¾" long, unless otherwise noted.

Title	Value
"40 Years of Happiness," "Knott's Berry Farm," Snoopy, Charlie Brown, and Woodstock 40th Anniversary logo, also pictured is Snoopy in several poses, 1990.	$4.00 – 7.00
"Camp Snoopy," "Knott's Berry Farm," Snoopy lifts his Beaglescout hat in a greeting, 1983.	10.00 - 12.00
"Knott's Berry Farm," "Camp Snoopy," the gang participates in all sorts of outdoor camping activities, 1990, 8" at widest point, 25" long.	4.00 – 7.00
"Knott's Berry Farm," Snoopy stands on a podium; he wears a gymnast's outfit and holds a gold medal.	8.00 – 10.00

"Camp Snoopy."

Movie: "A Boy Named Charlie Brown."

This felt pennant came in a variety of colors with black writing and drawing, issued 1969, $20.00 – 25.00.

Football Team Pennants

Issued in 1990 by Wincraft, each of these pennants is an NFL Officially Licensed Product bearing the team logo. Each pennant is of thin felt, 8⅞" at widest point, 24" long.

Title	Value
"49ERS," Snoopy practically runs over Woodstock to score a touchdown.	$6.00 – 10.00
"Buccaneers," Snoopy throws the football down the field.	6.00 – 8.00
"Cardinals," Snoopy kicks the football.	6.00 – 8.00
"Chiefs," Snoopy wears a Native American headdress, and several birds wearing helmets flock toward him.	6.00 – 8.00
"Colts," Snoopy practically runs over Woodstock to score a touchdown.	6.00 – 8.00
"Dolphins," Snoopy wears underwater gear including fins and mask as football heads toward him.	6.00 – 8.00
"Falcons," Snoopy as the Flying Ace sits and holds the football.	6.00 – 8.00
"Oilers," Snoopy runs to catch a pass.	6.00 – 8.00
"Seahawks," Snoopy runs with the football, a flock of Woodstocks precedes him.	6.00 – 8.00
"Steelers," Snoopy and Woodstock are wrapped in a blanket, each holds a pennant.	6.00 – 8.00

Cardinals.

Snoopy Fan Club

Not Pictured
Felt pennant was included with the membership
kit sent to Snoopy Fan Club members in
the early 1980s, 8¾" wide at widest point,
21½" long. . . . .$3.00 – 5.00

Soft Sculpture Wall Hangings

Silgo International introduced several large nursery wall hangings which captivated collectors. We've provided a small sampling of the company's original line.

Price is based on unused condition, with no tears or marks. Colors should be bright, and the material should be crisp.

Silgo International. 1990. Each is approximately 22" high x 14" wide, unless noted.

Snoopy sits and hugs several birds, #186-201 (24" x 22"), $45.00 – 70.00.

Charlie Brown stands with outstretched arms, #186-208; Lucy stands with outstretched arms, #186-209; $35.00 – 60.00 each.

Schroeder carries his piano, #186-210, $25.00 – 50.00.

Two Dimensional Wall Plaques

• Ceramic •

Among the loveliest of all Peanuts collectibles are the 1989 offerings from the short-lived licensee, Bai Dotta. They were a licensee for less than a year, and any plaques

listed below are highly desirable.

Value is based on excellent to mint condition, with no chips or paint missing or cracks in the glaze.

Charlie Brown, in his traditional red shirt with black zigzag, $80.00 – 120.00; Peppermint Patty, in purple shirt, black pants, and brown sandals, $65.00 – 95.00; Lucy wears a blue dress and nurse's cap, as well as her traditional saddle shoes, a stethoscope is around her neck, $90.00 - 110.00.

Snoopy, in his classic Joe Cool pose, $55.00 – 80.00; Woodstock stands with his feathers outstretched, $35.00 – 50.00.

Pig Pen stands in a dust cloud. His shirt is light blue, his pants are black. Yellow background, $55.00 – 80.00.

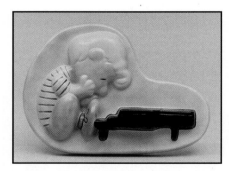

Snoopy wears a purple baseball shirt and cap and black shades, he leans on baseball bat, Woodstock also wears shades and sits on a baseball, they're on green grass against blue sky, $85.00 – 110.00.

Schroeder sits and plays his piano, his shirt is blue with dark blue stripes; his trousers are brown, rosy pink background, $80.00 – 105.00.

Lucy kicks back and waits for business in her yellow stand, "Psychiatric help – 5¢. The doctor is in." $85.00 – 110.00; Snoopy sleeps on his yellow doghouse, grass surrounds base of house, $75.00 – 95.00.

Baseball manager **Charlie Brown** looks forlorn as he sits by his stand, "Manager's Office. The buck starts here..." $105.00 – 125.00.

Snoopy as the Flying Ace, sits and guides an imaginary plane, his scarf is yellow, background is a large blue cloud, $85.00 – 110.00; Linus sits and sucks his thumb, while holding blue blanket, his shirt is orange with black stripes, $65.00 – 95.00.

Frontal view of Snoopy, $90.00 – 135.00.

• Plastic – Manufacturer Unknown •

These pictures are framed vacuform (similar to celluloid) with either a green or tan colored background. Issued 1960s. The name of the character should be intact, and there should be no chipping or missing paint. They are very delicate.

Charlie Brown, $25.00 – 60.00; Snoopy, $35.00 – 70.00.

Lucy; Linus; $25.00 – 60.00 each.

Dolls

Rubber

• Hungerford Plastics Company •

Large Hungerford dolls, 1958.

This company produced the very first Peanuts dolls: seven figures, plus Schroeder's piano. A set has become a prized goal for serious collectors who hold vintage items as a priority.

The dolls originally were packaged in clear plastic wrap with a cardboard header. A cartoon panel of the character was on the header. Having at least one of the dolls in the original packaging is a great find, and a real piece of Peanuts history. Dolls in these original bags are, unfortunately, few and far between.

Value is based on excellent condition. There should be no missing paint, and very few (if any) scuffs or scratches. We do allow for the ravages of time, so some minor wear is acceptable.

Charlie Brown and Snoopy are shown in their original packages.

Schroeder as a baby, 7", Schroeder's piano, 3¾"; in bag $300.00 – 400.00 (both items), $125.00 – 175.00 (Schroeder or piano), $250.00 – 325.00 (Schroeder with piano); Sally as a baby, 6½", in bag, $200.00 – 240.00, no bag, $90.00 – 120.00; Lucy, 9", her hat came painted two ways, either completely yellow or yellow with a red top, in bag, $160.00 – 205.00; no bag, $75.00 – 95.00; Charlie Brown, 8¾", in bag, $160.00 – 205.00; no bag, $75.00 – 95.00; Snoopy, 7¼", in bag, $200.00 – 240.00; no bag, $90.00 – 120.00; Linus, 8½", in bag, $160.00 – 205.00; no bag, $75.00 – 95.00; Pig Pen, 8¾", in bag, $200.00 – 240.00; no bag, 90.00 – 120.00.

Small Hungerford dolls, 1958

Aside from height, these differ from the larger dolls in a few other details. For example, Linus' shirt is red instead of red with black stripes; Lucy's cap is red instead of yellow, and there is no red trim on the front of her dress.

Lucy, 7"; Linus, 6¾"; in bag, $175.00 – 220.00 each; no bag, $90.00 – 110.00 each; Snoopy, 6", in bag, $215.00 – 255.00; no bag, $105.00 – 135.00; Charlie Brown, 7½", in bag, $175.00 – 220.00; no bag, $90.00 – 110.00.

Bendy Toys by Newfeld Ltd., England

These foam rubber dolls have a unique charm. The Charlie Brown doll is especially beautiful, due to its coloring. The original boxes are quite colorful and have graphics of characters — but not any from the Peanuts gang, and thus are not taken into consideration in the value.

Value is based on good to very good condition. Because of the nature of the material, it is quite difficult to find one in perfect condition. The foam tends to dry out and crumble.

Charlie Brown with painted clothing, 8", $45.00 – 75.00; Snoopy, dressed in blue jeans and red top, 10", $48.00 – 80.00.

Determined Productions

Snoopy Astronaut, he wears a NASA flight suit with a United States flag on the side, his equipment includes a plastic bubble and Flight Safety kit. He wears blue shoes, 9½", 1969; in box, $125.00 – 200.00; no box, $120.00 – 195.00.

PVC Collector Dolls

These PVC dolls are jointed. Their ears and tails are plush, and the clothing is removable.

Many were available in Europe and Asia. While many, but not all, of the dolls in the United States came in very colorful boxes with pictures of the dolls on them, some were sold loose, with no packaging. In other parts of the world, the packaging differed.

A series of these dolls was made only for the Japanese market; they appear to wear finer-made clothing. We offer a sampling here.

Value is based on excellent to mint condition, with all clothing and accessories, 8½", 1984.

Snoopy as a roller skater, #3401, in box, $50.00 – 80.00; no box, $40.00 – 70.00; Snoopy as a tennis player, #3403, in box, $45.00 – 75.00; no box, $30.00 – 50.00; Snoopy as a jogger, #3402, in box, $40.00 – 70.00; no box, $25.00 – 45.00.

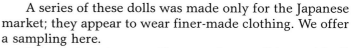

Snoopy as a soccer player, with a soccer ball in the net, #3404, in box, $45.00 – 75.00; no box, $30.00 – 50.00; Snoopy as a baseball player, #3405, in box, $50.00 – 80.00; no box $35.00 – 65.00; Snoopy as a sailor, #3406, in box, $45.00 – 75.00; no box, $25.00 – 40.00.

Snoopy as a Boy Scout, Japan, $50.00 – 80.00; Snoopy in wool school uniform carrying books wrapped with a string, Japan, $45.00 – 75.00.

Belle as a bride, #06-3411-1, in box, $55.00 – 85.00; no box, $45.00 – 75.00; Belle in nightgown and cap, holding a small pillow, #06-3412-2; Belle in a jogging outfit, with a cassette player, #6-3413-3; in box, $30.00 – 50.00; no box, $20.00 – 40.00 each; Belle in a red and white cotton blouse and velvet overall pants, carrying a pink purse made of felt, Japan, $35.00 – 60.00.

Snoopy with cassette player, #06-3407-6, in box, $40.00 – 70.00; no box, $25.00 – 45.00; Snoopy as a golfer, he carries a gold bag with three clubs in it, #06-3408-7, in box, $45.00 – 75.00; no box, $25.00 – 40.00; Snoopy as a bridegroom, #06-3409-8, in box, $55.00 – 85.00; no box, 45.00 – 75.00.

• Pocket Dolls by Boucher Associates (Another Determined Production) •

These remain popular with collectors, especially when they're found mint in the plastic bag, 7", 1967.

Linus in a red and white striped shirt and black pants, holding a red flannel blanket, #801; Lucy in a pink dress with lavender trim and panties, she looks like she might be yelling, #802; Lucy in a pink dress with lavender trim and panties, she is smiling, #802A; Schroeder in black pants and an orange shirt with a picture of Beethoven on it, #804; Snoopy in a felt aviator helmet, black goggles, and blue scarf (scarf does not appear in photo), #803, Charlie Brown wears a red shirt with black zigzag, black pants and a baseball cap, #800; in bag, $28.00 – 42.00; no bag, 20.00 – 32.00 each.

• Knickerbocker Toy Co., Inc. •

These were not particularly popular when first introduced in 1983, but have caught on recently with collectors. Separate outfits are available, as well as "The Snoopy & Belle Show 'n Go House," which stores either a Snoopy or Belle doll and clothing (item #1582).

Snoopy in red and yellow top with blue jeans, a plastic Woodstock is included, 8", #1580, in box, $33.00 – 43.00; no box, $11.00 - 21.00; Belle in a pink dress with blue and white flowers, trimmed in blue ribbon and white lace, a plastic Woodstock is included, 7½", #1581, in box, $25.00 - 35.00; no box, $8.00 – 15.00.

Cloth & Rag Dolls

Determined Productions, Pillow dolls. Each is approx. 18" high and screen printed, 1967.

Charlie Brown wears a blue shirt with black zigzag, #810, in pkg., $25.00 – 35.00, no pkg., $15.00 – 25.00; Linus wears a hot pink shirt with black stripes and holds a red blanket, #811, in pkg., $20.00 – 30.00, no pkg., $10.00 – 15.00.

Lucy wears a hot pink dress with black trim, her mouth is wide open and her arms are up, #812, in pkg., $20.00 – 30.00, no pkg., $10.00 – 15.00; Snoopy sits and shows his side view, #813, in pkg., $30.00 – 40.00, no pkg., $25.00 – 35.00.

Peanuts Playmate, Snoopy is of brushed velour material, he sits; his black collar holds a plastic red heart captioned, "Official Dog from the Peanuts Comic Strip," 7" tall, 1970, in pkg., $35.00 – 50.00, no pkg., $18.00 – 25.00.

Not Pictured
Schroeder wears a blue shirt with a large drawing
of Beethoven, #814. . . . . . .in pkg., $20.00 – 30.00
no pkg., 10.00 – 15.00

• Thumb and Blanket Rag Dolls •

Snoopy often imitates Linus by sucking his thumb. Determined used this idea to produce these two dolls. The faces and hands are made of soft plastic. Each wears a one-piece sleeper and holds a blanket and came packaged either in a box or clear plastic bag, 1983.

Snoopy, 7" tall, #8813, in pkg., $25.00 – 38.00, no pkg., $15.00 – 25.00; Linus, 8" tall, #8814, in pkg., $20.00 – 30.00, no pkg., $10.00 – 18.00.

"Happy Holiday" dolls, mid 1980s.

Snoopy is dressed in red corduroy pants and green shirt dotted with candy canes, 12", $30.00 – 45.00; Belle is dressed in a green dress dotted with candy canes, 11", $15.00 – 25.00.

• Ideal Toy Corp./Another Determined Production •

With or without the original package, these dolls are charming, but the packaging makes them more so, mid 1970s.

Snoopy wears blue jeans and a red shirt with the gang on front, 13½", #1410-0, in box, $45.00 – 62.00; no box, $18.00 – 38.00; Lucy wears a red dress with blue trim, 13½", #1411-8, in box, $38.00 – 52.00; no box, $15.00 – 28.00; Charlie Brown wears an orange shirt with black zigzag and black short pants, 13½" tall, #1412-6, in box, $38.00 – 52.00; no box, $15.00 – 28.00.

Peppermint Patty wears a green shirt with white stripes and black short pants, 13½", #1413-4; Linus wears a green and blue striped shirt and black short pants, 13½", #1414-2; in box, $38.00 – 52.00 each; no box, $15.00 – 28.00 each.

Snoopy as an astronaut, wearing a NASA space suit, 14", #1441-5, in box, $180.00 – 295.00; no box, $85.00 – 140.00.

Not Pictured
Snoopy as the World War I Flying Ace. His jacket and helmet are brown, and his neck scarf is blue, 22" tall, #1420-9 . . .in box, $180.00 – 295.00
. . . . .no box, $85.00 – 140.00

Plush Dolls

• Applause •

When this company became a licensee in 1989, it produced many plush dolls, mostly with Snoopy. A few of the more interesting, theme-type dolls are listed here.

Snoopy Beach Beagle, he's dressed in a yellow tank top, blue, green, and yellow pants, and blue beach sandals with yellow thong strap as well as a sun visor, 11", #15820, 1989, $30.00 – 45.00; **Belle Beach Beagle**, she's dressed in a one-piece blue, green, yellow, and black outfit, her floppy hat is blue and yellow, and her blue beach sandals have a yellow thong strap, 10", #15821, 1989, $20.00 – 35.00.

Snoopy as a groom, dressed in a black coat, gray slacks, white shirt with pink bowtie and cummerbund, 11" tall, #36019, 1989; **Belle** as a bride, dressed in a white dress and veil with pink flower trim, 10" tall, #36018, 1989; $35.00 – 48.00 each.

• Dakin •

Dress-Up collection, Western, limited 1993 edition

Each doll wears a brown hat with red band and a brown vest with a star on it. Snoopy and Belle wear boots and bola ties.

Snoopy wears a red and white gingham shirt with blue trim and blue jeans with brown velvet trim, 14" tall, #05409, $60.00 – 85.00; **Belle** wears a blue shirt with red and white gingham trim, her panties are red and white gingham, and her skirt is brown velvet, 12" tall, #05417, $40.00 – 65.00; **Woodstock** wears a red kerchief and brown vest, he holds a rope, $38.00 – 55.00.

• Determined Productions •

Determined had the license to produce the first plush dolls, which were introduced in 1968. We therefore thought it would be informative to look at the first plush dolls Determined issued for different characters.

Belle wears a pink dress with red pictures of herself, she also wears a red ribbon by one ear, #8734, 10" tall, $8.00 – 14.00; #0822, 15" tall, $14.00 – 25.00; #8737, 25" tall, $75.00 – 90.00; #0787, 32" tall, $95.00 – 125.00; #8738, 45" tall, $175.00 – 250.00.

Not Pictured
Snoopy. He wears a black dog collar.
#0821, 11" tall. . . . .$10.00 – 16.00
#0823, 18" tall. . . . . .20.00 – 30.00
#0826, 24" tall. . . . . .50.00 – 75.00
#0838, 30" tall. . . . . .90.00 – 125.00
#0786, 40" tall. . . . . .135.00 – 190.00
#0830, 60" tall. . . . . .200.00 – 250.00

Woodstock. His feathers are yarn and his feet are felt.
#4509, 9" tall. . . . .$10.00 – 15.00

Spike, his whiskers are felt and he wears a light-brown felt slouch hat with a black band, #8743, 12", $15.00 – 20.00; #875, 18", 25.00 – 35.00; #8747, 30", $75.00 – 120.00; #8748, 60", $225.00 – 300.00.

Peanuts Family Dolls. First introduced in 1983, each has remained popular.

Charlie Brown. 11", #05-7442-6, $20.00 – 30.00; 14", #05-7452-5, $35.00 – 45.00; 30", $175.00 – 225.00.

Linus. 11", #05-7443-7, $20.00 – 30.00; 14", #05-7453-6, $35.00 – 45.00; 30", $175.00 – 225.00.

Lucy. 11", #05-7450-3, $20.00 – 30.00; 14", #05-7452-5, $35.00 – 45.00; 30", $175.00 - 225.00.

Peppermint Patty. 11", #05-7441-5, $20.00 – 30.00; 14", #05-7451-4, $35.00 – 45.00; 30", $175.00 – 225.00.

Limited Edition Snoopy

Each stands 18" and is accompanied by a certificate of authenticity and arrives inside a special plastic-coated shopping bag, 1985 – 1986.

35th Anniversary Snoopy, he wears a gold and silver lamé tuxedo, limited to 2,500 sequentially numbered; the Flying Ace wears a brown bomber jacket, helmet, and boots, tan pants, and red fringed scarf, limited to 2,500 sequentially numbered; $145.00 – 225.00 each; Joe Cool wears a red shirt with "Joe Cool" on it, blue jeans, red sneakers, and sunglasses, limited to 2,500 sequentially numbered, $125.00 – 205.00.

• Determined Productions, Inc. for Hallmark Cards, Inc. •

Hallmark Card stores ran a contest: Enter your name and address to win a 36" plush Snoopy hugging Woodstock. Snoopy's hands have velcro inside to enable him to securely hug Woodstock, 1985, $120.00 – 170.00.

• Determined Productions, Inc./FAO Schwarz •

Belle wears a blouse and ribbon, along with a red felt 1950s-type skirt with a picture of Snoopy, 15", #352054, $55.00 – 80.00; Snoopy, the back of his shirt has "Team Snoopy — FAO Schwarz" printed on it along with his picture, he also wears a cap, 18", #352112, $75.00 – 95.00.

• Worlds of Wonder •

Collectors loved the "talking" plush Snoopy, and he still remains a popular guy on the secondary market. By placing a cassette inside his battery-operated body — he requires four C-sized alkaline batteries — Snoopy's mouth moves and tells a story. There's a book to follow along. Although everybody loved Snoopy, we were promised a talking Charlie Brown doll, and he never appeared. Poor ol' Charlie Brown!

Prices are based on mint-in-the box condition. We find that it's quite difficult to locate a box that's pristine, and so we allow for wear and tear due to shelf life.

Storybook and cassettes sold separately.

Title	Value
Snoopy's Talent Show.	$10.00 – 15.00
Rock-A-Bye Snoopy.	10.00 – 15.00
Snoopy Goes Camping.	10.00 – 15.00
Snoopy's Land of Make-Believe.	10.00 – 15.00
Snoopy's Baseball Game.	10.00 – 15.00
Snoopy's Show and Tell.	10.00 – 15.00
Snoopy and The Great Pumpkin.	10.00 – 15.00
Snoopy's America.	10.00 – 15.00
Snoopy at the Dog Show.	10.00 – 15.00
Snoopy's Band.	10.00 – 15.00
Snoopy, Spike, and the Cat Next Door.	10.00 – 15.00
Snoopy's Birthday Party.	10.00 – 15.00
Snoopy Hits the Beach	10.00 – 15.00

Outfits sold separately. Each item has an embroidered patch that reads "The World of Snoopy."

Title	Value
Blue, two-piece warm-up suit, with shoes, #701603.	$25.00 – 35.00
Flying Ace jacket, goggles, and a red scarf, #701601.	30.00 – 40.00
One-piece pajamas and matching nightcap with a dog bone pattern, and a red blanket, #701602.	25.00 – 35.00

Snoopy, 22", his eyes, nose, and mouth move, and he comes with a storybook and cassette, $95.00 – 140.00; Woodstock, 10", he chirps but does not need batteries, $20.00 – 30.00.

Marionettes & Puppets

What could be more fun than interacting with the Peanuts characters through a puppet or marionette?

No less a puppeteer than Snoopy himself regards this as an honorable form of serious theater, as revealed during his incredibly lavish "Pawpet Theater" presentations (with their "cast of thousands").

The plush hand puppets of Snoopy and Woodstock have been favorites in the United States for years. Other countries, such as Japan, feature hand puppets of other characters, including Spike.

The height of luxury for Peanuts marionette fans is the store display used to advertise the Pelham Snoopy, Charlie Brown, and Woodstock marionettes made in England. They're on stage and dance when plugged in. As a condition of sale, each boxed Pelham puppet came with the written words, "This puppet may not be used for commercial purposes without written consent from Pelham Puppets."

Prices are based on excellent to mint condition. There should be no scratches or marks. Clothing should be intact, not torn or faded. Tags should be attached. Sizes are approximate.

• Marionettes •

Pelham, late 1970s

Charlie Brown wears his red shirt with black zigzag, orange shoes, and cap, 8", #7993, in box, $75.00 – 125.00; without box, $60.00 – 100.00; Snoopy, 8½", #8001, in box, $85.00 – 140.00; without box, $50.00 – 90.00; Woodstock, 8", #8002, in box, $45.00 – 80.00; without box, $30.00 – 65.00.

Snoopy wears a red shirt and blue jeans, 24", #9007, $320.00 – 390.00.

Store display, Woodstock, Snoopy, and Charlie Brown dance when electrical plug is connected, 21" high, #8004, $375.00 – 520.00.

Marimo Craft Co. Ltd. (distributed for Determined Productions), late 1980s

Snoopy, wooden, 6"; Charlie Brown wears a yellow shirt with black zigzag, black shoes, and green cloth cap, wooden, 7" tall; $60.00 – 85.00 each.

• Finger Puppets •

Determined Productions/Ideal (distributed for Determined Productions)

Peanuts Show Time Finger Puppets. Snoopy, Charlie Brown, Peppermint Patty, Linus, Lucy, and Woodstock, #5379-3, 1975, in box, $30.00 – 43.00; without box, $3.00 – 18.00; Peppermint Patty, Snoopy Flying Ace, Snoopy businessman, Snoopy sitting, Lucy, Charlie Brown, Woodstock, and Linus, early 1990s, in box, $15.00 – 30.00; without box, $10.00 – 15.00.

• Hand Puppets •

Determined Productions

Not Pictured
Woodstock, velveteen with yarn feathers, 6",
early 1970s. . . . .$15.00 – 20.00

Applause "Pawpets"

Not Pictured
Snoopy sleeve puppet, 12", #36021,
1990. . . . .$18.00 – 24.00
Woodstock, chirps, 10", #06018, 1990. . .16.00 – 22.00

Snoopy wears "HEE HEE HA HA" shirt, body puppet, 13", #15815, 1990, $25.00 – 35.00; Woodstock wears a red shirt with chirp marks, chirps, 11", sleeve puppet, #15816, 1990, $18.00 – 28.00.

Figurines

Bobbing Head Figurals (Nodders or Bobbleheads)

These figurals with moving heads are increasingly popular with collectors. We've also included some Snoopy figurals on springs.

• Lego •

Papier-mâché, issued in 1959, standing from 5¼" to 5¾" tall

The German company, Lego, produced the first six Peanuts nodders that are a must with serious collectors. They are very delicate and tend toward fine-line cracking. The names of the characters, which appear on each nodder, also tend to come off. The phrase "of the Peanuts comic strip" appears beneath each name. Because of their date of issue, 1959, they depict earlier incarnations of the characters, and not many items do this.

Prices are based on mint to near-mint condition. There should be no lines, no cracking, no flaking or missing paint. The name should appear clearly, with no missing letters. The spring action should be in good working order.

Charlie Brown, $75.00 – 110.00; Snoopy, $90.00 – 125.00; Linus, $65.00 – 100.00.

Lucy; Schroeder; Pig Pen; $65.00 – 100.00 each.

• Determined Productions •

Papier-mâché, issued in 1976, standing approximately 4" tall

There should be no lines, cracking, flaking, or missing paint. The spring action should be in good working order.

Snoopy, as Santa Claus, stands; Snoopy sits dressed as the World War I Flying Ace, $30.00 – 40.00 each; Snoopy sits, $20.00 – 30.00 each.

Lucy stands, wearing red dress; Woodstock stands, hold-

ing a flower, $20.00 – 30.00 each; Snoopy as Joe Cool, stands, $20.00 – 30.00; Charlie Brown stands, wearing a blue baseball cap and his traditional orange shirt, $25.00 – 35.00.

Baseball Set

Each baseball cap is green. Figures are high-gloss ceramic and stand approximately 4½" to 5" tall. Comes boxed, but the box does not affect the value. Prices are based on mint condition, with no cracks or chips. The spring action should be in good working order. Japan, 1989.

Snoopy with baseball mitt; Charlie Brown with baseball mitt; Woodstock holds baseball bat; $40.00 – 52.00 each.

Peppermint Patty with baseball bat; Schroeder as catcher; Lucy with baseball bat; $40.00 – 52.00 each.

• Quantasia, Inc. •

A plastic Snoopy stands on a spring and bounces. Each comes in a box, which does not affect the value. All pieces should be intact. The spring action should be in good working order. Japan, mid 1980s.

Snoopy, as a tennis player, holds a racket, #SNS 780, $15.00 – 25.00; Snoopy, dressed in traditional Japanese clothing, holds a fan, the Lucite base has a sticker captioned "World's Greatest," #SNS 780, $18.00 – 30.00; Snoopy wears swimming trucks, holds a surfboard, the Lucite base has a sticker captioned "World's Greatest," #SNS 780, $15.00 – 25.00; Snoopy sits, wearing movable sunglasses, the Lucite base has a sticker captioned "Joe Cool," #SNS 980, $12.00 – 22.00.

Solid Bronze

Crafted by respected artisan Stan Palowski, these five limited-edition figures were presented in a wooden box lined with velvet. Each statue included its own wooden base and came with a certificate of authenticity. 7,500 sets issued worldwide, International Trading Technology. Approx. 2" – 3" tall with base, 1992.

"Friends," Snoopy and Woodstock roast hot dogs over a campfire; "Sharing," Snoopy and Woodstock enjoy an ice cream cone and hot dog, as well as other goodies; "Snow Buddies," Snoopy holds ski poles and Woodstock rides on his ski cap; "Dreaming," Woodstock sleeps in his nest, and Snoopy leans against the tree trunk; "Admiration," Snoopy and Woodstock sit on his doghouse; set in box, $425.00 – 600.00.

Crystal

While some crystal, for example, blown glass figures produced by Swarovski for Silver Deer, remains very delicate, pieces in the leaded crystal category are quite substantial.

Although a favorite with collectors, this category can be quite expensive, so each piece is especially treasured.

Value is based on mint condition with no scratches or chips. Always examine a potential purchase carefully.

• Determined Productions, Inc. •

Because the figurines were handblown, the same product number may include differences in size.

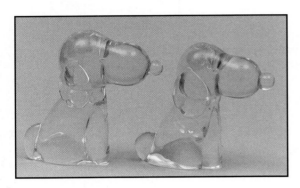

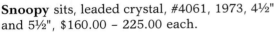

Snoopy sits, copyright information is etched at the bottom, 4½" tall, FM Konstglas for Determined Productions, Inc., 1972, $250.00 – 325.00.

Snoopy sits, leaded crystal, #4061, 1973, 4½" and 5½", $160.00 – 225.00 each.

• Sasaki Glass •

Snoopy wears a hat, unleaded crystal, 3½" tall, #LA96002, mid to late 1980s; Snoopy holds a briefcase with one hand, unleaded crystal, 3" tall, #LA96003, mid to late 1980s; Snoopy lead down, his tail sticks up, unleaded crystal, 3¾" long, #LA96001, mid to late 1980s; $35.00 – 50.00 each.

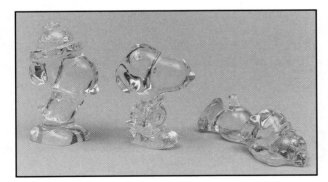

• Marcolin Art-Crystal •

Leaded glass, handmade in Sweden, 1986

Snoopy sits, a red ribbon is tied around his neck, 6½" tall, limited edition of 1,000, $175.00 – 290.00.

Snoopy sits, a red ribbon is tied around his neck, 4¾" tall, $90.00 – 150.00; Snoopy reclines on his tummy, a red ribbon is tied around his neck, 6½" long, $120.00 – 200.00; Snoopy sits, his head bows down and a red ribbon is tied around his neck, 4¾" tall, $90.00 – 150.00.

• Silver Deer •

1990s.

"Spike," Spike wears a gold filigree-like hat and stands next to a decorated cactus, 2½" x 2½" x 3¼", #93146, $75.00 – 120.00.

"Good Grief!", Snoopy sits on an obelisk, ¾" x ¾" x 1⅞", #01974, $40.00 – 60.00; "Snoopy with Heart," Snoopy in a walking stance, wears a red heart on the left side of his chest, 1⅛" tall, #00131, $50.00 – 70.00.

"Joe Cool Ski," Snoopy wears black sunglasses, holds his ski poles and stands on his skis, 2" dia. x 1⅛", #02020, $90.00 – 140.00.

"Literary Ace," Snoopy sits at his gold typewriter and types, "It was a dark and stormy night," 1½" x 1½" x 1⅝", #02810, $95.00 – 145.00.

"Snoopy's Suppertime," Snoopy sits with several dog dishes, limited edition of 5,000, hand etched with sequential number, 3" x 2" x 2¼", #01973, $120.00 – 175.00.

"Joe Cool Jammin'," Snoopy wears sunglasses and holds drumsticks, his drums are gold-colored metal, 3" dia. x 1¹⁵⁄₁₆", #02319, $100.00 – 150.00.

 # Gold

• Tse Siu Luen Jewelry •

Mar Lok Shan designed these figures. He is reknowned in the world of Peanuts collecting because he has designed many figurines throughout the years. The hollow, pure gold figures come with a wooden base and plastic cover for display, 1996.

Snoopy, 1½", $275.00 – 325.00; Woodstock, ¾", $225.00 – 285.00.

Lead

The French company Pixi began producing Snoopy figures in 1991, which, alas, were only available in France.

We are listing their first products: small, painted figures, each in a limited edition of 3,000. A certificate number accompanies each piece.

Snoopy reclines on his doghouse, 2" tall; Snoopy rides a green motor scooter, Woodstock sits on the back, 1⅞" tall; $60.00 – 85.00 each. Snoopy wears a blue shirt and red and blue cap, he holds a pillow, 1½" tall, $50.00 – 75.00; Snoopy drives a yellow convertible, 1½" tall, $70.00 – 95.00.

Porcelain & Ceramic

Porcelain is actually a finer material than ceramic, but for the purposes of this guide, they will be combined into one category.

This remains one of the most highly prized categories of collecting, whether the figures are small or large. The two standout companies are Willitts and Determined Productions (Japan).

Condition should be as close to mint as possible, no chips or missing paint. While it is fine to have the box, it really doesn't affect the value of these lovely pieces.

• Determined Productions •

Tumbling Series, ceramic, five poses of Snoopy performing a somersault, 1½" to 2¾", #1316-2, 1980, $18.00 – 22.00 each.

The following little figurines are prototypes and are very tiny, mid 1970s.

Articulated Snoopy, ceramic, Snoopy's legs and arms move, 12", 1982, $260.00 – 335.00.

Snoopy's ears stick out as he drives a green and yellow convertible car, 1½", $50.00 – 65.00.

Belle reclines in a bathtub filled with colorful bubbles, 1¼", $40.00 – 50.00; Woodstock stands in his nest, these are two separate pieces, 1¼", $40.00 – 50.00 set of two.

• Determined Productions K.K. (Japan) •

Snoopy Persona Series

Ceramic, each approx. 2" – 2⅛" tall, 1992

Snoopy stands, he wears a blue hat and carries a briefcase in one hand, #DP-357; Joe Cool stands with his arms folded, he wears sunglasses, #DP-358; Snoopy sits in front of a typewriter, #DP-359; Snoopy sits, #DP-360; Snoopy sits, he hugs Woodstock, #DP-361; $20.00 – 25.00 each. Snoopy stands and holds a blue dog dish in his mouth, #DP-362, $18.00 – 23.00; Snoopy stands as if walking, #DP-363, $20.00 – 25.00; Flying Ace stands, he wears an aviator helmet and goggles, #DP-364, $22.00 – 27.00.

Snoopy dressed in Happi coat, this figurine is open in the back and allows for a disk to be inserted to catch mosquitoes. There were various color combinations, 9½", 1983, $175.00 – 250.00.

Snoopy sits and holds a shoe brush in one hand, in front of him is a wooden box with a ceramic shoe on top, inside the box is a polishing cloth, shoe brush, and shoe polish, 10¼", 1990, $165.00 – 240.00; Snoopy holds a shoe in one hand, he wears a denim apron that holds a shoe brush and shoe polish, 9¼", 1990, $150.00 – 225.00.

Musician Series

Ceramic, each approx. 7½" – 8" tall, 1993

Snoopy wears a black top hat and formal jacket and carries a red baton, $60.00 – 95.00; Lucy wears an orange dress and plays the bass; Linus wears a blue shirt with dark blue stripes and plays a trumpet; Charlie Brown wears a red shirt with black zigzag, he plays a violin; Sally wears a pink dress dotted with dark pink and plays a drum; $45.00 – 80.00 each.

• Willitts •

This lighted snowfall with Snoopy as Count Dracula inside is a winner. The only problem is the water tends to contaminate, making it next to impossible to find Snoopy without some discoloration. Requires two AA batteries, 5", #7906, 1987, $60.00 – 80.00.

Baseball Series, porcelain, each approx. 2" tall, 1988

Charlie Brown wears a mitt and holds a baseball, #8126; Schroeder wears catcher's gear, #8128; Linus holds his blanket and sucks his thumb, #8129; $18.00 – 23.00 each. Snoopy holds a baseball bat over one shoulder, Woodstock sits on his cap, #8127, $22.00 – 30.00; Peppermint Patty wears a mitt, #8130; Lucy wears a mitt on one hand, #8125; $18.00 – 25.00 each. The set also came with a baseball field made from hardwood, 10" wide x 20¾" deep x 1" tall, #8627, field with six figures, $170.00 – 198.00.

Sports Series, porcelain, each approx. 2" tall, 1989

Lucy sits and holds a football, #9467, $14.00 – 18.00. Snoopy wears a hockey uniform and holds a hockey stick, #9468; Snoopy holds a basketball, #9469; Snoopy wears a tennis visor and holds a racket, #9470; Snoopy wears a cap and gets ready to swing his golf club, #9471; Snoopy has a soccer ball beside his feet, #9476; $16.00 – 20.00 each.

Springtime Series, porcelain, each approx. 2½" tall, #400290, 1990

Snoopy as a bunny, he holds a basket with Woodstock in it; Snoopy wears a blue hat with pink band and holds flowers behind his back; Snoopy as a bunny, he holds a large decorated egg; $20.00 – 25.00 each.

Snoopy Sweethearts Series, porcelain, each approx. 2", #40590, 1990

"I'm Yours," "Be Mine," "I Love You," Snoopy holds a large red heart; $12.00 – 18.00 each.

Christmas Pageant Series, porcelain, approx. 1¾" x 2¼" tall, 1990

Charlie Brown as Joseph, #9692; Lucy as Mary, #9691; Schroeder as a shepherd, he plays his piano with Woodstock sitting on top, #9695; Baby Jesus in the manger, #9689; $20.00 – 30.00 each. Snoopy as a shepherd, #9690, $35.00 – 45.00; Linus as a shepherd, #9693, $20.00 – 30.00; Sally as a shepherd, #9694, $20.00 – 30.00; Pop-Up Creche with seven figures, $225.00 – 350.00.

Not Pictured
Musical Wooden Creche, accompanied the
    seven figures, also sold separately,
        #440390. . . . .$50.00 – 75.00
Pop-up Creche #9912, accompanies the
    seven figures . . . . .15.00 – 25.00

Celebration Miniature Series, porcelain, approx. 2½" tall, 1990

These figures were also part of the design of Willitts' 40th Anniversary Signature Birthday Music Box #19005.

Marcie wears a party hat and holds a balloon, #19012; Schroeder wears a party hat and plays his piano, #19008; Linus wears a party hat and holds a balloon, #19013; Sally holds a gift, #19010; $15.00 – 25.00 each. Snoopy wears a party hat and holds a gift, #19006, $20.00 – 30.00; Charlie Brown wears a party hat and holds a cake with candle on it, #19007, $18.00 – 28.00; Lucy wears a party hat and holds a balloon, #19009; Peppermint Patty wears a party hat and holds a balloon, #19011; $15.00 – 25.00 each.

General, ceramic, 1989

"World Famous Author," Snoopy sits and types, 3½", #9311; "Best Friends," Snoopy hugs Woodstock, 4", #9312; "The Good Life," Snoopy reclines in his dog dish, #9313; $14.00 – 22.00 each. "Flying Ace," Flying Ace sits, he wears helmet, goggles, and a red scarf, 4", #9314, $16.00 – 24.00.

Yoshitoku Co. Ltd. (Japan)

Not Pictured
Girls Day Set, porcelain, 1" x 2¾", #182102, 1991. Snoopy, Belle,
    Sally, Lucy, Peppermint Patty, Schroeder, Linus, Franklin,
    Charlie Brown, Marcie, Olaf, Spike, and three birds dressed in
    formal Japanese attire, seven lacquered boards, and various
    accessories, including lanterns. . . . .$450.00 – 625.00

PVC Figures

Small, charming PVC figures are an easy way to collect without overwhelming the storage — or lack thereof — in your home or office.

In the early 1980s, Determined Productions began its first line of "Fun Figures," 2½" tall PVC play figures that depicted Snoopy in many of his well-known poses or activities. About a year thereafter, more designs were released; the rest is collecting history. These figures have caught on with collectors around the world who seek those final few figures to make up a complete set. That's the fun part of collecting — you're never really finished.

Applause became the PVC licensee in 1989 and added quite a bit to the scene. Their figures are interesting because they come in small sets with themes such as Christmas or Halloween. That still holds true today. Sunkisses Ltd. made a short but mighty contribution in the mid 1990s (not listed), and Whitman's Candies produced figures which are snapped up as soon as they arrive at the market (not listed). Color variations are significant as are figures that belong to a series.

Figures in Europe by Comic Spain and Schleich (not included) are two other companies which produced these small nuggets of fun.

Figures should be in excellent condition with no paint missing or scuff marks.

• Determined Productions •

1981

Snoopy holds a tennis racket and wears a blue tennis visor, yellow top, and green shorts, $12.00 – 20.00; Snoopy holds a basketball in one paw, he wears brown pants and blue tank top with "2," $14.00 – 22.00; Snoopy runs, he wears a red top with "1" on it, blue pants, yellow visor with red trim; Snoopy kicks a soccer ball, he wears a blue and red outfit; $12.00 – 20.00 each.

Snoopy skis, he wears a purple turtleneck sweater, yellow pants, and holds red ski poles; Snoopy roller skates, he wears a blue top and yellow pants and holds a blue suitcase; Snoopy holds a candlestick, he wears a red nightshirt and cap; $12.00 – 20.00 each. Snoopy rides a racing bike with red wheels, he wears a yellow top, green shorts, and yellow and green cap, $14.00 – 22.00.

Snoopy holds a magnifying glass, he is Sherlock Holmes with green cap and blue jacket, $14.00 – 22.00; the WWI Flying Ace wears brown helmet with goggles, green jacket, and a very large mustache, $12.00 – 22.00; Snoopy holds a suitcase, wears purple tank top, his supper dish is on his head and Woodstock is on his nose, $12.00 – 20.00; Snoopy in a disco dance pose, he wears an orange jacket, yellow shirt, and black pants, $14.00 – 22.00.

Olympic Sports, 1984

Snoopy as a fencer; Snoopy jumps the hurdle, he wears a yellow tank top and green shorts; Snoopy in a red kayak, he's wearing a yellow helmet and holding the paddle; Snoopy in a yellow scull, he's holding the oars; $15.00 – 25.00 each.

Snoopy and Woodstock ride in a silver bobsled; Snoopy as a speed skater, he wears a blue running suit; Snoopy as a skier, he wears white top over red sweater, black pants, yellow hat, and ski goggles; Snoopy as a hockey player, he wears red and blue uniform with yellow hat and holds a hockey stick; $15.00 – 25.00 each.

Snoopy as a weight lifter, he wears a green outfit with brown belt; Snoopy as a shot put player, he wears a yellow top and green shorts and holds shot put in one hand; Snoopy as a diver, he wears red swimming trunks and is ready to jump off the block; $15.00 – 25.00 each. Snoopy holds a javelin, he wears red tank top and yellow shorts, $35.00 – 50.00 each. Because of the sharp point on the javelin, the production of this figure was very limited, and it was eventually recalled.

• Applause •

1989

Snoopy brushes his teeth with a green toothbrush, his collar and slippers are blue, and he holds a light orange towel over one arm, #15922; Snoopy is a bowler, he holds the ball in one hand and wears a yellow top and blue shorts, #15923; Snoopy wears silver astronaut suit and helmet, he holds a pink moon rock and light blue bag, #15914; the WWI Flying Ace holds one arm forward with his index finger pointed up, his helmet is brown, and his red scarf sticks out in back, #15924; Belle is a nurse, she wears a green nursing uniform and cap, and holds a syringe in one hand, #15920; Snoopy is a runner, he wears blue shirt with "1" on it, black pants, and yellow and blue visor hat, #15921; $8.00 – 10.00 each.

Snoopy wears a white chef cap with blue band, he holds a pink frosted triple-layer cake decorated with cherries, #19519; Snoopy lies on his doghouse roof, the doghouse is hollow, the doorway is trimmed with blue, #15917; Snoopy holds a large red heart, one hand cups his chin, #15916; Snoopy holds a lasso, his cowboy hat is pale yellow, and he wears a red knotted kerchief around his neck, blue overalls, and a light blue long-sleeved shirt, #15913; $8.00 – 10.00 each.

Snoopy as a groom, wears black formal jacket, pink vest, dark pink bowtie, gray pants, and gray top hat with pink band, #15918; Belle, as a bride, wears pink wedding dress and hat and holds flowers, #15919; $15.00 – 25.00 each.

Irish Figure Series, 1990

Snoopy wears a green cap and a long-sleeved yellow sweater trimmed in red with a three-leaf clover in the middle, he waves the Irish flag in one hand; Snoopy holds a pot of gold that contains Woodstock, they both wear traditional Irish caps with buckles at the band, Snoopy is completely clothed in green suit and shoes; Snoopy wears a green suit and hat and holds several four-leaf clovers; $18.00 – 25.00 each.

Graduation Cap Series, 1990

Snoopy wears a red cap with yellow tassel. He stands by three books, yellow, blue, and red, his red shirt has the caption "Class of Cool"; Snoopy stands with his arms out, he wears a blue cap and gown and holds his diploma in one hand, his gown opens enough to reveal pink and yellow trunks and orange shirt with the caption "I'm Out of Here!"; Snoopy wears a blue gown and cap with yellow tassel, he straightens his bowtie as Woodstock lies against his back, caption on back of Snoopy's robe is "Kick Me"; Snoopy wears red cap and gown, he stands in front of a blue podium and holds a piece of paper; $15.00 – 22.00 each.

Halloween Series, 1990

Snoopy is dressed as Count Dracula, the inside of his cape reads "Happy Halloween"; Snoopy pops up from a pumpkin, he wears a purple shirt with "Boo!" on it; Snoopy is dressed as a red devil, he holds a large pumpkin with Woodstock on it; Lucy is a witch in a blue costume and orange cap, she rides a broom; $25.00 – 35.00 each.

Christmas Series, 1990

Charlie Brown is dressed in a blue coat, red scarf, and a cap with green tassel ball, he holds a stack of gifts; Snoopy wears a red sweater and cap, he carries a Christmas tree laden with birds; Lucy wears a red dress and leans on a red package tied with green ribbon, Woodstock is on her head; Linus sits and sucks his thumb as he holds his red blanket, a string of Christmas lights is over him; $15.00 – 22.00 each.

Snoopy 40th Anniversary Collection

Boxed set with figures of Snoopy dressed in formal jacket with red shirt and bowtie; sits and hugs Woodstock; as Joe Cool, wearing blue turtleneck and black pants with yellow design; and as the WWI Flying Ace, wearing bomber jacket, red scarf, and brown helmet, #19587, 1990, in box, $25.00 – 40.00 set.

Comics Spain (Europe), early 1990s

Snoopy rides a sled, he wears red cap with green band and tassel, there are two gifts on the sled; Snoopy wears green sweater and cap as he skis, he holds red poles; $12.00 – 20.00 each.

Snoopy as an English gentleman, he wears a black bowler hat and jacket with blue shirt and red tie, in one hand he carries a suitcase, in the other an umbrella; Snoopy wears a green shirt and a brown hat with green band, he holds a camera in both hands; Snoopy is a pilot with helmet and goggles, he wears a scarf and holds a flight journal; $12.00 – 20.00 each.

Snoopy leans against a barstool, he's wearing a green print shirt and rosy-hued sunglasses, he sips a lemonade; Snoopy plays the bass, he wears a purple jacket and a red bowtie; Snoopy sings into a microphone, he wears a purple jacket, pink shirt, and black tie; Snoopy plays a green and purple concertina, he wears a red cap and jacket, and blue pants; $12.00 – 20.00 each.

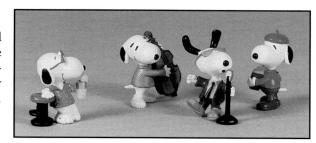

Snoopy dressed as a Beaglescout, he holds a walking stick; Snoopy holds a pink and green surfboard, he wears blue swimming trunks; Snoopy wears a red, full-length swimsuit as well as swimming goggles and snorkel; $12.00 – 20.00 each.

Snoopy is dressed in purple nightshirt and cap, he holds a candlestick in one hand and a pink teddy bear in the other; Snoopy's head is on his pillow, he's asleep, he wears a blue sleeping cap, Woodstock also is asleep on the pillow; Snoopy leans against a rock and holds Woodstock on one foot; $12.00 – 20.00 each.

Snoopy rollerskates and wears headphones, his shirt is red; Snoopy holds a red tennis racket, his tennis outfit is green; Snoopy rides a green skateboard, he wears a pink tank top with purple pants; Snoopy rides a red skateboard, he wears a yellow tank top and green pants; $12.00 – 20.00 each.

Figurescenes by Determined

These 18 Figurescenes represent some of the very best work Determined produced in the 1970s. Colorful, appealing, yet somewhat pragmatic, each scene perfectly conveyed each character's persona. One of the most popular was the first to be released: Linus and Sally holding hands above the familiar phrase, "Love is walking hand in hand." This one simple sentence, sweet and succinct, said it all.

Each scene rests on green felt and was produced in, but not always sold with, a box. The box shows the front and back of the figure. Height is anywhere from 4½" to 6".

Condition of the scene you purchase or own is extremely important. The papier-mâché material is vulnerable to chips; the paper caption easily tears or rips. Prices represent the statue in excellent-mint condition with or without the box: no nicks, chips, or missing paint; paper caption in its entirery with no corners missing. A couple of the scenes have attachments, such as the poles to Lucy's psychiatrist stand or the sign holding Woodstock's question mark. Make sure the candle and mug are affixed to the scene with Snoopy sitting at the table.

To demonstrate just how much these have appreciated, most originally sold for $1.50.

"Happiness is having someone to lean on," Charlie Brown and Snoopy lean against one another, #760, 1971, $15.00 – 20.00; "Love is walking hand in hand," Linus and Sally hold hands, #761, 1970, $15.00 – 25.00; "I look forward to the day when I'll understand men," Schroeder plays his piano while Lucy leans on it, #762, 1971, $50.00 – 70.00.

"I'm allergic to morning," Snoopy, bleary-eyed, lies on his doghouse roof, #763, 1971, $10.00 – 20.00; "I've developed a new philosophy — I only dread one day at a time," Charlie Brown and Linus sit on a bench, #766, 1971, $55.00 – 65.00; "My secretary isn't worth anything before coffee break," Woodstock types as Snoopy sits behind him, #767, 1971, $40.00 – 55.00.

"Bleah!", Lucy stands and sticks out her tongue, #768, 1971, $30.00 – 40.00; "Even my anxieties have anxieties," Charlie Brown sits in front of Lucy's psychiatric stand, #769, 1971, $60.00 – 85.00; "I'm thinking of you," Linus sits under a tree, sucks his thumb, and holds his blanket, #770, 1971, $35.00 – 50.00; "It's hero time," Snoopy stands proud, showing his chest and Hero badge, #771, 1971, $35.00 – 50.00.

"Look out — I'm going to be crabby all day," Lucy stands, wears a hot pink dress, her eyebrows are furrowed and she has a very determined expression, #772, 1971, $30.00 – 45.00; "Perhaps some dark-haired lass will share my table," Snoopy the World War I Flying Ace sits at a cloth-covered table, a bottle with a candle and a cup are on top of the table, #773, 1971, $55.00 – 85.00; "He's a nice guy but I don't know where he stands," Woodstock holds a paper sign with a question mark on it, Snoopy sits and looks on, #775, 1971, $35.00 – 50.00.

"America, you're beautiful," Snoopy stands proudly, wears an Uncle Sam hat, #776, 1971, $35.00 – 50.00; "To know me is to love me," Linus stands and holds red blanket, #777, 1971, $30.00 – 42.00; "I made 120 decisions today...all of them wrong," Charlie Brown stands, showing his side view, he wears a baseball cap and glove, #778, 1971, $35.00 – 50.00; "Joe Cool," Snoopy stands with arms folded, wears sunglasses and orange turtleneck, #779, 1972, $35.00 – 45.00.

"How can we lose when we're so sincere?" Linus, Schroeder, Charlie Brown, Snoopy, and Lucy stand or sit, each wearing baseball gear, #790, 1971, $150.00 – 225.00.

Housewares

 ## Ceramic Bath Accessories

A very popular category indeed, particularly for collectors who concentrate on ceramic and porcelain items. Prices are based on excellent condition, no cracks or fine lines, missing paint or chips. They should retain their original gloss.

• Determined Productions, Inc. •

Snoopy Soap Boxes

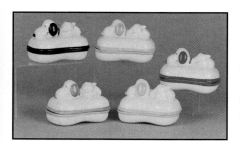

White with color trim. Two-dimensional Snoopy reclines on a lift-off lid, 4¼" x 3", 1979. Blue, #8421; Yellow, #8423; Black, #8422; Pink, #8424; Red, #8425; $32.00 – 45.00 each.

Snoopy Bubble Tub, lift-off lid is Snoopy's upper body, surrounded by pastel-colored bubbles; a bubble rests on Snoopy's nose, white tub with pastel green and yellow trim, 4" x 2⅜" x 4¼", #8458, 1979; "Bubble Bath," Snoopy Bubble Bucket, lift-off lid is Snoopy's upper body surrounded by pastel-colored bubbles, yellow pail trimmed in brown and white, 5¼" tall x 3" wide, #8453, 1979; $35.00 – 50.00 each.

Snoopy soap dish, a three-dimensional Snoopy sits by a white soap dish, 6½" x 2½" x 3¾", #8459, 1979, $25.00 – 37.00; Snoopy soap dispenser, Snoopy sits with one paw touching his face, 5½", DP-350, Japan, mid 1990s, $20.00 – 28.00; Snoopy soap dish, Snoopy reclines inside a white oblong-shaped dish, 5¼" x 3½" x 1¾", Japan, 1970s; $25.00 – 35.00 each.

• Saturday Knight, Inc. •

Blue and white with Snoopy and Woodstock, 1993, soap dish with three-dimensional Woodstock on the rim, 5½" x 4" x 1⅛", #00200, $15.00 – 24.00; Toothbrush holder, 3", #00220, $10.00 – 14.00; Lotion dispenser, 5⅜", #00230, $15.00 – 24.00; Tumbler, #00210, $10.00 – 14.00.

Candy Dishes

What better way to offer guests some candy than by placing the goodies in a Peanuts candy dish? Although these dishes could be used for jewelry or trinkets, for the sake of categorizing, we'll call them candy dishes.

Prices are based on excellent to mint condition: no chips, hairline cracks, or missing paint. The lid should seat securely.

• Determined Productions, Inc. •

Snoopy and Woodstock recline on a blue ribbon which ties a white gift box, 4¼" x 4¼" x 6", #8821, 1978, $75.00 – 120.00.

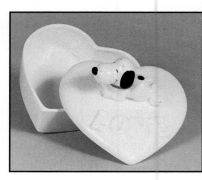

"Love," a three-dimensional Snoopy leans on his elbows, the dish is heart-shaped, 6" x 6" x 4", #8483, 1978, $85.00 – 120.00.

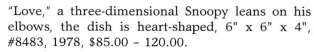

Snoopy reclines on the top portion of a peanut, which is the lift-off lid, 7¾" x 4" x 5¼", #8920, 1979, $65.00 – 105.00.

A three-dimensional Snoopy sits on several envelopes which are tied with an orange bow, Snoopy holds an envelope in his hands, 5" x 4" x 5¾", late 1970s, $70.00 – 110.00.

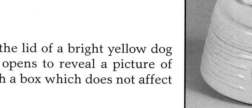

"Snoopy — Hooray for Suppertime," a dog bone rests on the lid of a bright yellow dog dish, a label in front has a picture of Snoopy, lift-off lid opens to reveal a picture of Snoopy with his ears sticking way up. This dish comes with a box which does not affect the value, 2¾" x 5½" dia., Japan, 1982, $60.00 – 90.00.

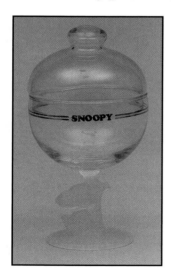

• Sasaki Glass •

"Snoopy," the frosted stem of the dish is Snoopy leaning against a tree trunk, the container has two gold lines going around the circumference, lift-off lid is plain glass with knob, 7½", Japan, #T106-4892, mid 1980s, $75.00 – 105.00.

Clocks

Snoopy is very concerned with a clock ... his *stomach* clock. When it goes off, it's time to eat. A clock is a must for those of us in the day-to-day world: going to work, keeping appointments, making sure we don't miss our favorite television shows. Naturally, a Peanuts clock helps the time pass more pleasantly.

Remember, always test battery-operated clocks to ensure they work. Have batteries handy. Value is based on the clock's being in good condition, with no scratches or missing paint and in working order. The alarm must function.

Clocks are assumed to be mint-in-the-box unless otherwise noted.

• Table Alarm Clocks •

Blessing (for Determined)

These wind-up alarm clocks, made by Blessing in West Germany, are highly prized by collectors, especially in good working condition. They have metal casing and alarm bells. The faces have bright colors which were representative of the times: some bright yellow or hot pink. They came in two sizes. There were no boxes.

Snoopy dances on the face of the clock, his arms are the hands, the background has smaller drawing of Charlie Brown, Lucy, and Linus, plastic and metal casing, metal legs, brass bells, clear plastic face cover, 10¾" tall x 8" dia., 1972: red face, blue case, #3552; yellow face, orange case, #3553; black face, white case, #3554; $95.00 – 130.00 each. Snoopy dances on the face of the clock, his arms are the hands, plastic and metal casing, metal legs, brass bells (unless noted), clear plastic face cover, 5⅛" tall x 3½" dia., 1972: blue face, orange case, #3531; black face, chrome case and bells, #3532; red face, blue case, #3533; hot pink face, green case, #3534; yellow face, red case, #3535; $35.00 – 50.00 each.

Determined

Snoopy & Charlie Brown Talking Alarm Clock (by Janex for Determined), two-dimensional figures of Charlie Brown and Snoopy snoozing, the alarm rings with the sound of Charlie Brown's voice saying, "Hey Snoopy; wake up, good friend of mine, happiness is being on time," black letters against yellow background, orange plastic casing, clear plastic face, battery operated, 6¾" tall, #8002, 1974; in box, $115.00 – 142.00; no box, $75.00 – 110.00.

Equity

Finding one of these clocks in its original box is a real bonus; these Equity clocks have become highly collectible. Each was issued in the early 1980s and is wind-up unless otherwise noted.

Snoopy holds a tennis racket in one hand, the tennis ball is the second hand, silver trim, white metal casing, clear plastic face cover, 4⅛" dia., #590, $50.00 – 65.00.

Snoopy and Woodstock play football, Snoopy holds the football in one hand, Woodstock is the second hand, orange numbers against light green background, silver trim, white metal casing, clear plastic face cover, 4⅛" dia., #595, $50.00 – 65.00; Snoopy reclines on his doghouse, caption, "I'm allergic to morning," yellow numbers against light green background, yellow alarm bells, silver trim, white metal casing, clear plastic face cover, 4⅛" dia., #596, $55.00 – 70.00.

Snoopy and Woodstock dance in front of a rainbow, white numbers against dark blue background, white metal casing, clear plastic face cover, 4⅛" dia., #598, $35.00 – 45.00; Snoopy performs his Pawpet Theater, two birds participate, white numbers against red/brown background, white metal, clear plastic face cover, 4¼" tall, 3⅜" wide, #599, $50.00 – 65.00.

The Flying Ace sits on his doghouse, Woodstock flies nearby, white numbers against orange background, white plastic case (which is also a travel alarm clock), battery operated, 2⅝" tall, 3" wide, #SN811, $38.00 – 47.00; Snoopy and Woodstock ride a skateboard, white numbers against red background, orange circle around Snoopy and Woodstock, gold tone trim, clear plastic face cover, 3¼" dia., #SN891, $35.00 – 45.00.

Snoopy holds a baseball bat in one hand, the baseball is the second hand, white numbers, orange background, inside design is a baseball diamond, silver trim, white metal casing, clear plastic face cover, 4⅛" dia., $70.00 – 95.00; Snoopy holds a butterfly net in one paw, butterfly is second hand, white numbers against blue background, silver trim, white metal casing, clear plastic face cover, $50.00 – 65.00.

Not Pictured
Snoopy holds a lap flag, Woodstock, in a car, is the second hand, white numbers against red background,
    white metal casing, clear plastic face cover, 4⅛" dia., #592 . . . .$65.00 – 80.00
Snoopy and Woodstock dance, caption, "Live it up a little," blue numbers against yellow background, design is
    highlighted in white circle along with red and blue stripes, blue alarm bells, silver trim, white metal housing,
    clear plastic face cover, 4⅛" dia. . . . . .55.00 – 70.00

Citizen

Snoopy sits at his typewriter, green numbers, white background, yellow heart-shaped housing and alarm bells, battery operated, 4¾", #QHB5032-BS, mid to late 1980s, $18.00 – 22.00.

Snoopy and Woodstock hold umbrellas, light blue numbers against white background, blue plastic casing and alarm bells, battery operated, 4¾", #QHB5024-CS, mid to late 1980s, $18.00 – 22.00.

Woodstock paints a picture of a flower but Snoopy, flexing his muscles, thinks the picture is of him, blue trim, white plastic housing, clear plastic face cover, battery operated, Japan, 4" tall, 4¾" wide, #QKB5016-3, 1984, $18.00 – 22.00; Snoopy kicks a soccer ball, pink numbers against white background, pink plastic housing, clear plastic face cover, battery operated, Japan, 3" tall, 3½" wide, #QKB5027-AO, mid to late 1980s, $12.00 – 14.00.

Snoopy leans on his elbows, a glass with a straw is nearby, black numbers against white background, highlighted by various colors, white plastic casing with red alarm bar, battery operated, Japan, 3⅝", the plain box does not affect value, #QHB-5018, mid to late 1980s, $15.00 – 22.00.

Snoopy holds a tennis racket in one hand, the face of the racket is the face of the clock, Woodstock is perched on Snoopy's other hand, alarm is a voice that tells Snoopy to wake up (in Japanese), plastic, clear plastic face cover, blue trim, Japan, battery operated, 8" tall, #4RE490-003, mid to late 1980s; with box $75.00 – 105.00, no box $60.00 – 80.00.

Faces of Snoopy, Schroeder, Lucy, Charlie Brown, Franklin, Eudora, Woodstock, Linus, Sally, Spike, Marcie, and Peppermint Patty replace the numbers usually on a clock, white background, silver metal casing, battery operated, Japan, 4¾" tall, 3½" dia., the plain box does not affect the value, #QAB-5071, 1988, $45.00 – 55.00; Snoopy, Olaf, and Woodstock stand next to each other, black numbers against pale pink background, red plastic casing, battery operated, Japan, 4¼" tall, 4⅛" dia., the box does not affect the value, #QAB-5098, 1990, $30.00 – 42.00.

Snoopy, Woodstock, and Charlie Brown wear top hats and bowties, caption, "Peanuts Anniversary," issued in conjunction with the 40th anniversary of the Peanuts strip, small 40th anniversary booklet included, gold metal casing and alarm bells, Japan, 6½" tall, 4⅛" dia., #QHB-5112, 1990, $68.00 – 75.00.

Snoopy wears a preppy plaid jacket, Woodstock is nearby, caption, "Snoopy," black numbers against pale cream background, metal trim, legs, and alarm bells, red plastic casing, clear plastic face, 17½" tall, 12" dia., #QHB-5054, mid to late 1980s, $110.00 – 150.00.

Armitron

Sitting plush Snoopy houses a clock in his stomach, battery operated, 8¾", #900/55, 1989, $27.00 – 37.00.

Trousslier

Not Pictured
Snoopy hugs Woodstock, wooden cut-out stands on black plastic base, the clock face is white metal with black numbers, battery operated, France, 8" tall, #3351, 1991, the plain box does not affect the value. . . .$32.00 – 42.00

• Wall Clocks •

The variety in this category is impressive, thanks to a seemingly endless supply from Japan. The listings below barely scratch the surface. Each is battery operated.

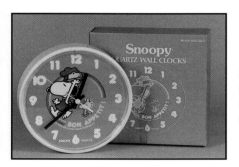

Equity

Chef Snoopy holds up a cake he has just baked, Woodstock walks behind him, caption, "Bon Appetit," white numbers against light orange background, white casing, and clear plastic face, 7¼" dia., #602-25Q, early 1980s; with box, $55.00 – 68.00; no box, $35.00 – 48.00.

Citizen

Cuckoo clock, Snoopy plays golf while Woodstock waits his turn, Woodstock is the cuckoo bird who comes out of his nest, pendulum caption, "Snoopy," black numbers against green grass face, plastic casing with two-dimensional cut-outs of Snoopy, 16" tall from top to bottom of pendulum, Japan, #QHS-2159-1, 1983, $175.00 – 260.00.

Cuckoo clock, Snoopy walks by a house, he carries his business satchel, Woodstock follows, Woodstock is the cuckoo bird who comes out of his house, pendulum caption, "Snoopy," black numbers against white face, plastic casing with two-dimensional cut-outs of Snoopy and Woodstock, 16" tall from top to bottom of pendulum, Japan, #QHS-2040, 1983, $175.00 – 260.00.

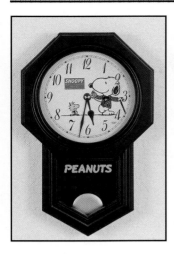

Pendulum clock, Snoopy wears a brown plaid jacket and green bow tie, he leans on a cane and holds a stopwatch while timing Woodstock, caption, "Snoopy World Famous Beagle," black numbers against cream background, plastic casing with wooden back insert, Japan, 13" tall, #QH2457-1, mid 1980s, $95.00 – 135.00.

Pendulum clock, Woodstock is the top portion of the pendulum, Snoopy on a unicycle with a ball is the lower portion, they're on a plastic rod and rock up and down as the clock ticks, the face has a small black outline picture of Lucy, Linus, Charlie Brown, Peppermint Patty, and Sally, caption, "Snoopy," green numbers against white background, pink plastic casing, clear plastic face cover, Japan, 9½" dia., #QA-2266, early to mid 1980s, $65.00 – 90.00.

Pendulum clock, Snoopy and Charlie Brown talk to each other on the telephone, they are the pendulum on a plastic rod that rocks back and forth as the clock ticks, the face has a small black outline picture of Lucy, Linus, Charlie Brown, Peppermint Patty, and Sally, caption: "Snoopy," green numbers against white background, green plastic casing, clear plastic face cover, Japan, 9½" dia., #QA2305-2, early to mid 1980s, $65.00 – 90.00.

Heart shape, Snoopy's smiling face, outlined in red, dark blue numbers against white face, red plastic heart-shaped casing, clear plastic face cover, Japan, 8½" tall, 10" wide, #QH2455-1, mid 1980s, $30.00 – 45.00.

Snoopy listens to music on his headphones as he rollerblades, yellow numbers against blue background, pink plastic casing, clear plastic face cover, Japan, 9½" dia., #QA2295-1, mid 1980s, $25.00 – 35.00.

Snoopy hugs Woodstock, luggage is nearby, white numbers against red background, white plastic casing, clear plastic face cover, Japan, 9½" dia., #QA2148, mid 1980s, $25.00 – 35.00.

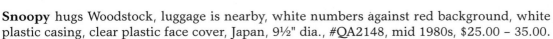

Coasters

While serving the practical purpose of protecting furniture and countertops, Peanuts coasters lend a festive air to any gathering.

At first Hallmark produced the paper coasters. More recently, other countries — notably Japan — entered the field with metal and porcelain coasters.

• Hallmark •

12 – 16 coasters per package

Snoopy and Woodstock dance in front of a red circle bordered by a denim-like edge (Ambassador Division of Hallmark), 3¼" dia., #73CO118J, 1970s, $3.00 – 4.00; Snoopy on top of a brightly colored orange and hot pink balloon (Ambassador Division of Hallmark), 3¼" dia., #50CO60M, early 1970s, $6.00 – 9.00; Halloween, Snoopy jumps up in a pumpkin, 3¼" dia., #39HC0144, early 1970s, $10.00 – 14.00.

"Drinks are on the house!", Christmas, Snoopy and Woodstock stand on Snoopy's decorated doghouse and quaff a root beer, 3¼" with scalloped edges, #50XCO233, $5.00 – 6.00; Valentine's Day, Snoopy holds a heart with the words, "Be Mine," 3¼" dia., #75VC012, mid 1970s, $6.00 – 8.00.

Not Pictured
Christmas, Woodstock wears a green knit cap
and balances a large candy cane on his nose,
3¼" x 3¼", 75XC046, early 1980s. . . .$5.00 – 6.00

• Determined Productions •

During the mid to late 1980s, Determined (Japan) produced coaster sets that matched metal trays. The sets were sold separately, each with six coasters with a different theme. Approximate size 3¹⁄₁₆" x 3¹⁄₁₆".

Snoopy, Woodstock, Charlie Brown, Linus, Lucy, and Sally each hold some food, blue trim with white background, names of various foods printed on the background, $14.00 – 20.00.

Snoopy sits on either one or two strawberries, red trim, white background, two each of three designs, $14.00 – 20.00.

The upper half of Snoopy, Peppermint Patty, Sally, Linus, Charlie Brown, and full view of Woodstock, eating or getting ready to eat, blue trim with either white, red, blue, green, or yellow background, $16.00 – 22.00.

Not Pictured
Snoopy and Woodstock with fruit, red
background. . . . .$14.00 – 20.00

Ceramic

Snoopy's face wears a different expression on each coaster, this set of five was accompanied by a little gold metal stand to house the coasters when not in use, white trim with different solid color background, approx. 3½" x 3½", #FN-52, mid 1980s, $35.00 – 57.00.

Cork

Outline of Snoopy's face in green, he's wearing a green polka-dot bowtie, irregular shape, #Y30252-250, 1987, $2.00 – 3.00.

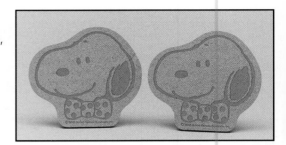

A wooden Chef Snoopy holds onto a woven basket filled with six cork coasters with Woodstock, Snoopy stands 5" tall, #SNW-11, mid 1980s, $75.00 – 110.00.

• Limited Editions •

Made exclusively for "Redwood Empire Ice Arena, Santa Rosa, CA," Snoopy wears a red bowtie and black jacket as he ice skates, plastic coated, cork back, set of four, 1989, $20.00 – 30.00.

"**Woodstock** Open," Woodstock swings his golf club, made for the golf tournament held each year, plastic coated, cork back, set of four, late 1980s, $20.00 – 30.00.

• Willitts Designs •

Metal set of six identical coasters with Snoopy and Woodstock dancing in the snow, comes in a metal box with the same design on the cover, a matching metal tray was sold separately, #7861, 1987, $15.00 – 23.00.

Cookie Cutters

• Hallmark •

Each of the cutters listed is plastic and was sold in the United States. The first few digits of a Hallmark item number reflect the original purchase price, i.e., 150PF7-2 means the package sold for $1.50. Hallmark cutters have skyrocketed because cookie cutter collectors are so persistent, the rising prices have impacted Peanuts fans. But while a die-hard cookie cutter collector must have each cutter in every distinct color, Peanuts collections are, for the most part, content with one of each ... except for ambitious folks who actually use them to bake cookies (imagine that!). Those collectors usually want a second set for the archive.

Set of four Snoopy cutters: astronaut, lying on his home, World War I Flying Ace, dancing, each set could have a different color cutter such as red, orange, green, and blue, #150PF7-2, mint in package, $90.00 – 110.00, without package, $75.00 – 90.00; Snoopy on top of his home, this is larger than the cutter in the preceding set, #150PF7-2, #75PF102-3, mint in package, $10.00 – 15.00; without package, $8.00 – 12.00.

Set of two red heart cutters, Charlie Brown with hands clasped, surrounded by hearts, Snoopy sits and thinks a heart, #75VPF102-3, mint in package, $40.00 – 60.00, without package, $30.00 – 40.00.

Set of four, Charlie Brown, Lucy, Linus, and a sitting Snoopy, #150PF974, 1971, mint in package, $90.00 – 100.00, without package, $80.00 – 90.00.

Set of four Christmas cutters, Charlie Brown, Snoopy with ornament hanging from his collar, Linus with outstretched arms, Lucy holding package, each set could have a different color cutter, white, blue, red, or green, #150XPF384, mint in package (also released under Hallmark's Ambassador Division, product #150XPF9G). $60.00 – 85.00, without package, $35.00 – 45.00.

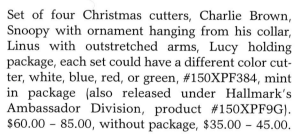

Set of two, Snoopy "What's Cookin'" and Joe Cool "Hi, Sweetie!" these cutters came in either white or yellow, #75PF96-6, mint in package, $30.00 – 40.00, without package, $25.00 – 35.00.

Snoopy lying on top of pumpkin, #75HPF14-6, 1974, mint in package, $150.00 – 200.00, without package, $95.00 – 150.00.

• Caketown •

These cutters were sold in Japan, but U.S. collectors managed to acquire quite a few. The cutters came in either pink or white plastic. Late 1980s.

Snoopy's face, #K-207; side view of Woodstock, #K-208; Charlie Brown's face, #K-209; Lucy's face, #K-210; mint in package, $10.00 – 15.00 each, without package, $8.00 – 13.00 each.

Snoopy holding large flower, #K-287; Snoopy lying inside star, #K-288; mint in package, $10.00 – 15.00 each; without package, $8.00 – 13.00 each.

Set of two cutters for making sandwich-type cookies with filling, one has Snoopy's face while the other imprints the back of his head, #K-289, mint in package, $17.00 – 22.00; without package, $15.00 – 20.00; set of four bearing playing card suits: diamond, club, heart, and spade, #K-371, mint in package, $20.00 – 24.00; without package, $18.00 – 20.00.

Not Pictured
Set of six in various shapes in a case: heart, star, crescent, circle, triangle, and crimped-edge circle, Snoopy and Woodstock plastic imprints are included, in this way each cookie could reflect either character, #K-372. . . . . .in case, $30.00 – 35.00

Cake Pans

Each pan was made of aluminum and came with a plastic design to put on top of the baked cake. A paper insert inside the pan, covering the plastic, should also be included, 1986.

Charlie Brown cake pan, Charlie Brown wears a baseball cap, #2106-1317, $25.00 – 40.00; Snoopy cake pan, the Flying Ace, #1821-1319, $35.00 – 48.00.

Cookie Jars

This category needs no introduction since cookie jars are a uniquely American keepsake. Remember Andy Warhol's extensive collection? We see cookie jars as an integral part of most kitchens. It is, therefore, quite appropriate that Snoopy, who has scarfed several chocolate chip cookies at one sitting, has made his presence known in kitchens through several designs of cookie jars.

The best-known is the McCoy jar with Snoopy lying on the top of his doghouse. It is ceramic with a plain, unglazed finish. The two "chef" cookie jars continue to grow in popularity due to their luster and beauty, plus the fact that Snoopy doesn't often appear as a chef.

Value is based on excellent to mint condition with no chips, missing paint, or cracks. The lid should seat securely. All cookie jars listed are ceramic unless otherwise noted.

• McCoy •

Snoopy relaxes on top of his doghouse, unfinished ceramic, no glaze, 11", $155.00 – 255.00.

• Determined Productions •

Snoopy Chef, hat lifts off, large, 11" high, #8480, late 1970s, $160.00 – 265.00; Snoopy Chef, hat lifts off, small, 7½" high, late 1977, $50.00 – 85.00.

• Con Agra •

Snoopy "Pet Snack" jar, Snoopy's upper half, surrounded by chocolate chip cookies lifts off, Stoneware, 13" high, 1981, in box, $150.00 – 250.00, without box, $140.00 – 240.00.

• Anchor Hocking Corporation •

Snoopy sits and scarfs cookies, caption on reverse, "I Love Cookies!", glass, 9½" high, #3100/346, late 1980s, in box, $70.00 – 95.00, without box, $50.00 – 65.00.

• Willitts Designs •

Snoopy sits and munches chocolate chip cookies, Woodstock is perched on Snoopy's blue cap, ceramic, 14½", #45018, 1990, in box, $95.00 – 145.00, without box, $65.00 – 110.00.

• Benjamin & Medwin •

1994

Snoopy the Flying Ace, 11½", #98501, in box, $35.00 – 50.00, without box, $30.00 – 40.00; Snoopy sits and wears a red bow, 11", #98001, in box, $30.00 – 40.00, without box, $25.00 – 35.00.

Snoopy Doghouse, 10½", #98101, in box, $35.00 – 50.00, without box, $30.00 – 40.00; Woodstock holds a flower, 11½", #98301, in box, $50.00 – 75.00, without box, $40.00 – 60.00.

Lucy wears a yellow dress, 11½" tall, #98401, in box, $50.00 – 75.00, without box, $40.00 – 60.00; Charlie Brown wears a baseball hat, 11½", #98201, in box, $50.00 – 75.00, without box, $40.00 – 60.00.

Cups, Mugs, Chili or Soup Bowls, and Steins

This category could go on for days. To maintain our sanity, however, we're just showing a sampling of what was out there: something of the interesting and diverse items which fall into this broad category.

Most designs pictured here are from the 1970s, a period popular with collectors when this category was quite active.

Japan also produced wonderful teacups, cups, and mugs, which became available in the early 1980s. For the sake of brevity, we'll just list a few samples of these.

While the Determined Productions entry is the most prolific and probably most desired, it must be pointed out that Applause and Willitts also contributed quite a bit in the late 1980s and early 1990s.

Values are based on absolutely pristine items: no chips, missing paint, or caffeine stains. Unless indicated, each item is made from ceramic. All measurements indicate height.

• Cups & Mugs •

Determined

Oval "patch" design. An oval-shaped design is the background for the picture and the caption. Some were produced for Zappetini, a California floral supplier in the mid 1970s, 3⅛".

"My Serve!", Snoopy wears a tennis visor and holds his tennis racket, the design is repeated on the back, $10.00 – 14.00; "Curse You, Red Baron," Snoopy as the World War I Flying Ace; "Raw Strength & Courage," Snoopy flexes his arm; "It's Hero Time," Snoopy shows off the ribbon pinned on his chest; "Come Dance With Me Baby," Snoopy does his happy dance; "Joe Cool," Snoopy stands, arms folded, wearing sunglasses; "World Famous Ski Champion," Snoopy sails through the air on his skis; $10.00 – 14.00 each.

Wraparound Sports Series

Snoopy and Woodstock participate in a given sport depicted in three panels.

Jogging, #1262, $6.00 – 8.00; Baseball, #164, $8.00 – 10.00; Tennis, $1265; Soccer, #1263; $6.00 – 8.00 each.

Initial Series

While Japan boasts a series of cups with initials on them as well, we'll concentrate on the series produced for the U.S. market in 1977. All feature Snoopy, stand 3½" tall, and are available in initials A through Z, with the exception of I, O, Q, U, V, X, and Y. The letters are large, with Snoopy next to them in various poses. Samples are pictured.

Location Mugs

Snoopy travels in the right circles, and he travels all over the country. He decided to commemorate each visit with a new mug design, 3½".

"San Francisco," Snoopy and several bird friends go down the hill in a cable car, #2159; California, Snoopy and Woodstock spend a day at the beach with surfboard and scuba gear, #2160; "Los Angeles," Snoopy and Woodstock ride in a convertible toward Venice for a day at the beach, #2158; $10.00 – 12.00 each.

"Philadelphia," Lucy, Charlie Brown, Woodstock, and Snoopy make the first Stars and Stripes flag, $10.00 – 12.00; "New Jersey," Snoopy announces the winner of the "Ms. Atlantic City Boardwalk" as Miss New Jersey, none other than Lucy Van Pelt, #2167, $10.00 – 14.00; "Florida," Snoopy and Woodstock lounge on beachchairs in the sun, #2166; "New Orleans," Snoopy is dressed as a devil, his bird friends also wear various costumes, ready for Mardi Gras; "Chicago," Snoopy's ears stick straight up as he looks at Woodstock, who is being blown against the Chicago skyline, #1263; $10.00 – 12.00 each.

"**Texas,**" Snoopy uses his lasso to spell out "Texas," and Woodstock uses his to form a star shape, #2168; "Washington, D.C.," Professor Snoopy takes a flock of bird students to see the White House, #2161; "Massachusetts," Snoopy and Woodstock dine on a huge lobster, #2165, $10.00 – 12.00 each.

"**New York City,**" Snoopy and Woodstock are dressed up and wearing top hats as they walk, a New York City evening skyline is in the background; "New York," Snoopy and Woodstock look through their binoculars at the Statue of Liberty which looks just like Snoopy, #2162; New York City, Snoopy and Woodstock are dressed up and wearing top hats for a night on the town, #1331; "New York," Snoopy hugs Woodstock in front of a large apple; $10.00 – 12.00 each.

Stack Mugs

These two mugs have a three-dimensional figure of Snoopy as the handle. Snoopy's name is written all over the mug portion. Japan, series #83ST-1. 3⅛". Mid 1980s.

Pink; Blue; $20.00 – 32.00 each.

Halloween

"Great Pumpkin Country," trick or treaters are Lucy, Woodstock, Charlie Brown, and Snoopy, 3½", late 1970s, #2156, $14.00 – 22.00; Linus and Snoopy in the pumpkin patch, the reverse side explains about the Great Pumpkin, a three-dimensional Snoopy is on the handle and peers into the cup, Japan, #94143-3, 3¼", 1989; Snoopy takes on different disguises in honor of Halloween, orange pumpkins complete the design, a three-dimensional Snoopy dressed as a witch peers over the rim of the cup, #72360-6, Japan, 4½", 1989; $20.00 – 32.00 each.

Birthday Cups

"Happy birthday to you," Snoopy sits by a birthday cake with one lit candle, Woodstock is on the cake, and they're both singing, 3½", #1305(A), 1979, $8.00 – 10.00; Snoopy is the engineer for a train with passengers Peppermint Patty, Sally, Lucy, Charlie Brown, Schroeder, and Linus, the steam spells out "Happy Birthday," by Determined for The Dupont Collection — a matching birthday plate was issued, 3½", 1976, $10.00 – 14.00; "Happy Birthday," Belle, Woodstock, Spike, Lucy, Charlie Brown, and Snoopy all sit around a festive birthday table, #1305(B), 3½", 1979, $10.00 – 14.00.

Raised Design

Snoopy, his home, and the sunflower portion of the plants are raised, #1194, 3¾", 1977, $14.00 – 18.00.

General

Plain white cup with three-dimensional figure of Snoopy lying on handle, #1582, 3¼", 1977, $22.00 – 34.00; "Beagles are my favorite people!" Spike, Snoopy, and Belle, 3½", 1982, $10.00 – 14.00.

Snoopy hugs Woodstock against a large white heart background, 3½", 1977; Snoopy hugs Woodstock against a large red heart background, 3½", 1977; $8.00 – 10.00 each.

Snoopy appears in various costumes: chef, Joe Cool, cowpoke, and pirate, Woodstock wears an article of clothing complimentary to Snoopy's costume, #1223, 3½", 1977, $10.00 – 14.00.

Woodstock as a stork flies to deliver a blanket holding "baby" Snoopy, #1229, 3¼", 1977, $10.00 – 12.00.

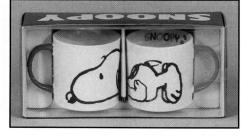

Set of two mugs, each with Snoopy on his tummy, one handle is blue, the other is red, 3", Japan, #71748-7, 1980s, $20.00 – 30.00.

• Soda Mugs •

Soda fountain attendant Snoopy prepares some treats for Woodstock, #1214, 5¼", 1977, $22.00 – 33.00; Snoopy holds blue, red, and yellow-colored balloons, Woodstock holds a single red balloon on the reverse, 5", 1977, $20.00 – 30.00.

• Soup Mugs/Chili Bowls •

"Superstar!", Joe Cool stands in front of a large yellow star trimmed with a red border, #1227, 3½", 1977, $14.00 – 24.00.

Snoopy in various poses by flowers and butterflies, #1184, 2½", 1977, $20.00 – 30.00; "Come and Get It," Snoopy as a cowboy is joined by several bird friends, Spike is the cook, #1769, 2½", mid 1970s, $22.00 – 32.00; Snoopy appears in costumes of different countries, such as Spain and Holland, #1770, 2½", 1977, $18.00 – 28.00.

• Specialty Drinks •

These are unusually shaped vessels bearing Snoopy's image.

"To the bunny slope!", Apres-ski mug, Snoopy carries his skis over one shoulder, Woodstock follows him, #1249, 5⅝", 1977, $14.00 – 22.00; Cappuccino cup and saucer, Woodstock brings flowers to Snoopy who sits with his arms oustretched, no design on saucer, #1196, 2¾", 1977, $20.00 – 32.00.

Cup for baby, Woodstock "stork" delivers "baby" Snoopy in a pale orange and white polka-dot blanket, 2¼", 1977, $10.00 – 14.00; Cup for baby, Woodstock "stork" delivers "baby" Snoopy in a pink blanket, 2¼", early 1980s, $8.00 – 10.00.

"Peanuts World Famous Baseball Team," set of tea cups, Peppermint Patty, Snoopy, Woodstock, Charlie Brown, and Lucy wear green baseball caps, #DP-150-180, 1989, in box, $60.00 – 75.00; no box, $45.00 – 60.00.

• Steins •

"Girls and root beer are not the answer," Flying Ace sits at a table with a red and white checkered cloth, 5", #1216, 1977, $15.00 – 27.00; Snoopy and Woodstock play tennis, golf, skiing, and baseball, #1224, 3", 1977, $13.00 – 24.00.

"Actually, we Joe Cools are scared to death of chicks," Joe Cool wears red turtleneck and sunglasses, Woodstock also wears sunglasses, they're both standing on a green lawn, #1225, 5", 1977; "Actually, we Joe Cools are scared to death of chicks," Joe Cool wears orange turtleneck and sunglasses, he stands in front of a rainbow, #1226, 5", 1977; $14.00 – 26.00 each.

Snoopy's name is spelled out in bright yellow and orange letters, above the letters Snoopy appears as Joe Cool and the Flying Ace, 4⅞", 1977, $18.00 – 28.00; Snoopy wears a fake fur coat, porkpie hat, and carries a "Rah" banner on a pole, Woodstock follows him, #1252, 4¼", 1977, $14.00 – 20.00.

Snoopy and Woodstock dancing design all around stein, 4⅜", #1253, 1977, $14.00 – 20.00; "Girls and root beer are not the answer," the Flying Ace sits at a table with a red and white checkered cloth, 4½", #1924, 1979, $15.00 – 27.00.

Plain white stein with a three-dimensional figure of Snoopy as the handle, 4", #1583, 1977, $20.00 – 32.00.

"Here's Joe Cool hanging around on a Saturday afternoon...no wheels, man!", Joe Cool and Woodstock stand against the bricks of a school building, 4½", #1932, 1979, $14.00 – 26.00; "Joe Cool never eats in the campus cafeteria!", Joe Cool sits at a table with a root beer, 4⅞", #1933, 1979, $14.00 – 24.00.

• Anchor Hocking – Fire-King •

Cups and Mugs/General

These cups have a milky white appearance and are quite heavy. They only recently received serious attention from collectors and are considered a "late bloomer." The cups with an "F" on the bottom or with the words "Fire-King" are from the mid to late 1960s. The remainder of the cups are from the 1970s, 4".

Black, white, and red drawings of Linus, Snoopy, Lucy, and Charlie Brown wrap around the cup; "At times life is pure joy!", Snoopy and Woodstock dance; $6.00 – 8.00 each.

"How nice...they're playing the Skater's Waltz," Snoopy listens to music on his headphones as he rollerskates; "Pedal power," Snoopy as a bicycle racer; "It's great to be an expert," Snoopy skateboards; $6.00 – 8.00 each.

"I feel strangely confident today," Charlie Brown dances and Snoopy watches him; "Snoopy, Come Home," Snoopy wears his dog dish on his head and carries a hobo pack over a shoulder as Woodstock walks behind him; "Curse You, Red Baron!", Snoopy as the World War I Flying Ace sits on his doghouse; $6.00 – 8.00 each.

"I'm not worth a thing before coffee break!", Snoopy sits and looks unhappy, Woodstock brings him a cup of coffee; "I hate it when it snows on my French toast!", it's snowing, and Snoopy frowns as he wears his gold nightcap and sits next to his supper dish; Snoopy dreams of popsicles, oranges, lollipops, and ice cream cones, all colored orange, a matching bowl was issued; $6.00 – 8.00 each.

Not Pictured
"I think I'm allergic to morning," Snoopy reclines on the roof of his home. . . . .$6.00 – 8.00
"This has been a good day!", Woodstock leans against Snoopy, who has
      outstretched arms. . . . . .6.00 – 8.00
"Keeping fit is hard work," Snoopy's tongue hangs out as he jogs. . . . . .6.00 – 8.00

Presidential Collector Series

These four cups are colored in red, white, yellow, and blue against a milky white background. Each is numbered either 1, 2, 3, or 4, 4", 1980.

#1, "Back the beagle," Snoopy's upper half, holds his Uncle Sam hat; #2, "Vote for the American Beagle," Snoopy's face, Woodstock acts as an eagle; #3, "Put Snoopy in the White House," Snoopy wears an Uncle Sam hat and sits on his doghouse roof; #4, "The people's choice," Snoopy's upper half, wears a red, white, and blue bowtie; $10.00 – 14.00 each.

Anchor Hocking — Taylor International Division

These four cups are made from stoneware and stand 3¼" tall. A similar series was available in the United Kingdom, but with some slight differences. While the rose on the petite four in the U.S. was colored red, it is pink on the U.K. issue. The designs in the U.S. were pictured on one side (listed and pictured), while the U.K. set has the picture on both the front and back.

Snoopy leans against a petite four topped by a rose; Snoopy sits by a cup filled with hot chocolate topped with marshmallows; Snoopy sits by a large slice of cherry pie; Joe Cool leans against a chocolate-covered donut; $10.00 – 14.00.

Willitts

Each cup is made of stoneware.

Halloween, Snoopy wears a cape and has a mask over his eyes, he and Woodstock enjoy their trick-or-treat candy in the pumpkin patch, 3¾", 1987, $10.00 – 14.00.

40th Anniversary, Snoopy's upper half, he waves one paw, background design is blue squares with different character faces, the design wraps around the cup, 40th Anniversary logo appears on bottom, #19018, 3⅜", 1990; 40th Anniversary, Snoopy's upper half, he waves one paw, background design is red squares with different character faces, this design wraps around the cup, 40th Anniversay logo appears on bottom, #19019, 3⅜", 1990; $6.00 – 8.00 each.

Applause

Figural face mug, Woodstock as a Beaglescout, 4", #36124, 1992; Figural face mug, Snoopy as the World War I Flying Ace, 3½", #36123, 1992; $12.00 – 16.00 each.

Dish Sets

Not too many sets of dishes were available in the United States, but collectors soon learned about tableware available in Japan. Those few sets available in the United States are quite beautiful. The Determined Production/ Iroquis China set is particularly desirable, and finding it in the original box is a plus.

Many Japanese pieces added a little extra something to enhance the designs, such as a little picture inside a drinking cup, or an image on the bottom of the plate. These little touches added charm and collectibility. Many times, though, these items were not packed in sets —

meaning one box — but rather could be purchased piece by piece, as you would a real table setting. We also thought it would be fun to picture some tea sets. For the sake of brevity, only a sampling in a particular pattern will be shown.

We're including children's sets here that are made of breakable materials, such as porcelain, ceramic, or ironstone.

Prices are based on excellent to mint condition. There should be no chips, missing paint, or missing pieces. Some of the boxes add to the value.

• Coloroll •

Tea Time Set, Snoopy as a vulture in a tree is the design for the teapot and the four accompanying tea mugs, caption, "I'm allergic to morning," the plain box without graphics does not enhance the value, England, 1980s, $125.00 – 175.00.

• Determined Productions, Inc. •

"Peanuts 3-Piece China Set," Lucy, Schroeder, Charlie Brown, Snoopy, and Linus are pictured on the plate, the design is blue, gold, and red, the bowl has Snoopy dancing and the cup has the names of the characters printed by the rim, made by Iroquois China, #341, 1968, in box, $90.00 – 120.00; no box, $65.00 – 95.00.

"3-Piece Children's Set," plate, bowl, and cup, Snoopy raises his cup at the dinner table, #SN-1800, made for Familiar, a children's department store in Japan, but imported for the U.S. as well, 1986, in box, $50.00 – 75.00; no box, $30.00 – 45.00.

Tea pot with two cups, pink design with blue drawings of Snoopy all around the tea pot and cups, Japan, #80177-1, 1985, in box, $60.00 – 90.00; no box, $40.00 – 50.00.

Tea pot with two cups, Snoopy holds some carrots, Woodstock is nearby, Reverse: Snoopy shows Woodstock the menu on the tea pot, the cups depict Snoopy holding a large bowl of food for Woodstock, while the box does not carry any graphics, it does have Snoopy's name all around as the design, Japan, #DP-32, 1986, in box, $50.00 – 75.00; no box, $30.00 – 45.00.

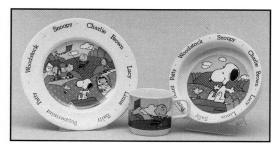

Three-piece set, plate, cup, and bowl, plate design has Linus, Sally, Charlie Brown, Peppermint Patty, Linus, Snoopy, and Woodstock outdoors in various activities such as jumping rope and flying a kite, bowl is Snoopy and Woodstock sitting on the doghouse, cup has Charlie Brown, Lucy, Snoopy, and Woodstock, Another Determined Production by Johnson Bros., made in England, late 1970s, in box, $55.00 – 80.00; no box, $40.00 – 60.00.

Pastel design. Small design of the characters against white background, Japan, 1984, (there is also a bud vase that goes with this pattern, shown in the "Bud Vases" section). The plain box without graphics does not enhance the value.

Cup and saucer, saucer has drawings of Snoopy dining, rim caption, "Snoopy and His Friends," Woodstock and tableware are also part of the rim design. Cup: Sally, Snoopy, and Peppermint Patty make a sandwich, #HI-42, $35.00 – 47.00; Candy pot, lift-off cover has figure of Snoopy lying down, pot (bowl) has Marcie and Snoopy sitting at a meal, #HI-41, $65.00 – 85.00; Plate, Lucy, Linus, and Snoopy dine as they sit at a table, rim caption, "Snoopy and His Friends," Woodstock and food are also part of the rim design, #HI-44, $35.00 – 47.00; mug, Charlie Brown pours cereal into a bowl, Snoopy sits near him at the table, #HI-43, $18.00 – 28.00.

Sushi set. Small pictures of Snoopy and Woodstock against a blue design. Snoopy is dressed in Japanese attire, Japan, mid 1980s.

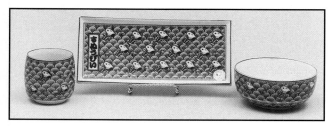

Tea cup, #DP-42, $15.00 – 24.00; plate, #DP-45, $45.00 – 60.00; bowl, #DP-41, $15.00 – 24.00.

Won Ton set, Snoopy is dressed in Chinese attire, blue Asian design along with black writing against white background, consists of small plate, small sauce bowl, spoon, and large won ton soup bowl, #DP-38, 1986, $130.00 – 185.00.

A separate spice and sauce set for condiments was available to go with the above set, 1986, $30.00 – 45.00.

Snoopy Fan Club design. Snoopy plays baseball; fans Sally, Marbles, Spike, Belle, Woodstock, Lucy, Charlie Brown, Linus, and Marcie cheer him on. The boxes carry the same graphics. Japan, mid 1980s.

Rice bowl, #28399-1; teacup, #28402-5; in box, $14.00 – 22.00 each; no box, $10.00 – 18.00 each. Mug, #28390-8, in box, $12.00 – 20.00; no box, 10.00 – 16.00.

"Dear Snoopy." Snoopy reads a letter. "Dear Snoopy, This is your ol' brother, Spike, writing from the desert...Wish you were here." A little red mailbox appears on each piece. Light brown background with dark brown trim. Red and white highlights. The boxes carry the same graphics, 1987.

Cup, #28439-4, in box, $12.00 – 20.00; no box, $10.00 – 18.00; Small plate, #48390-7; Bowl, #28437-8; in box, $15.00 – 25.00 each; no box, $12.00 – 20.00 each.

Sports cup and saucer sets. Snoopy appears dressed for a sport. The saucer is plain except for a thin design and "Snoopy" trim. Each design is quite ornate. Japan, 1991.

Snoopy basketball, blue and gold design, #90N 15-4, $47.00 – 62.00.

Snoopy golf, green and gold design, #90N 15-3, $47.00 – 62.00.

40th Anniversary pattern, Snoopy wears a vest and dinner jacket and holds a baton, the background has several pastel-colored stripes against white background, Japan, Determined Productions, Inc./Sanrio Co., Ltd., 1990. Saucer and cup, in box, $28.00 – 42.00; no box, $24.00 – 36.00.

• Taylor Smith & Taylor (a division of Anchor Hocking) •

Not Pictured

"Snoopy & The Peanuts Gang 3-pc. Snoopy Kiddie Ironstone set," Sally, Lucy, Schroeder, Peppermint Patty, Linus, and Snoopy are in the center design of the plate and bowl, the words "Supper" and "Suppertime" are repeated around the design. The cups show the characters standing, #C5011/630, mid to late 1970s. . . . . .in box, $60.00 – 80.00
no box, 40.00 – 60.00

Drinking Glasses

Everybody needs drinking glasses, which makes it easier for collectors to justify these items. Many sets of Peanuts glasses have been produced: short, medium, and tall. For the sake of space, we have pictured just a few.

Anchor Hocking is the leading producer of Peanuts glasses in the United States; in Japan, it's Determined and Sasaki.

Value is based on excellent condition with no scratches, chips, or cracks. All colors should be bright.

• Anchor Hocking •

Unless noted, all glasses came with cardboard packaging which does not include any graphics. The packaging does not affect value much, but you can add a few dollars if it is included.

Juice/Rocks (many times used for beverages with ice)

Juice: Snoopy and Woodstock with an ice cream sundae, reverse side is Snoopy with cookies, set of four, 6.75 oz., Anchor Hocking #2147, 1970s, $22.00 – 28.00 set; Rocks: "My ambition is to be too smart for my own good!", wrap-around design of Snoopy as a school teacher, his students are Peppermint Patty, Linus, Marcie, and several birds, set of four, 9 oz., Anchor Hocking, #3178-CF, 1986, $24.00 – 32.00 set.

Beverage

Wrap-around design of Snoopy, Linus, and Woodstock watching Violet and Sally turn a jump rope for Lucy, set of four, 12.5 oz., in a plastic holder, Anchor Hocking, $28.00 – 36.00 set.

Snoopy and Woodstock with a large hamburger and bag of french fries, reverse side is Snoopy and birds with hot dog, set of four, 12 oz., Anchor Hocking #2152, 1970s; "Never underestimate the effects of a pretty face!", Lucy is on Schroeder's piano, both he and Snoopy aren't too pleased with her, balance of wrap-around design is Sally and Linus sitting on sofa, Peppermint Patty and Charlie Brown dancing, and Woodstock shooting Cupid's arrow, set of four, 12.5 oz., Anchor Hocking, #3172-CF, 1986; $24.00 – 32.00 each set.

Iced Tea

Set of four, Snoopy shows Woodstock his dish of spaghetti, reverse side is Chef Snoopy holding a huge submarine sandwich while Woodstock holds an olive, set of four, 16.05 oz., Anchor Hocking, #2156, late 1970s, $24.00 – 32.00 set.

• Determined Productions for Cassidy's/Canada •

"Life is too short not to live it up a little!", Snoopy and Woodstock dance, set of four, 10 oz., cardboard packing has small graphic of Snoopy, 1970s, $24.00 – 32.00 set.

• Sasaki Glass/Determined Productions, Inc., Japan •

These glasses are more interesting than those available in the United States. The designs are more intricate, and the shapes more varied.

Juice

"40 Years of Happiness," wrap-around design of formal Snoopy, Lucy, Charlie Brown, Sally, Olaf, and birds; wrap-around design of Snoopy, Peppermint Patty, Lucy, Linus, Spike, and birds wearing party hats, pedestal, #M49-1238, 1990, $25.00 – 35.00.

"40 Years of Happiness," each glass has a different character on it: Charlie Brown, Lucy, Snoopy, Linus, or Sally; above each is a smaller picture of Snoopy, Woodstock, Olaf, Spike, or Marbles. The reverse has a small picture of Snoopy and birds riding in a dog dish, with the caption "Since 1950" written above, #M49-1826, 1990, $38.00 – 60.00.

Beverage

"**Snoopy** & His Friends," Charlie Brown holds paper airplane, the glass is tinted light green, "Lucy Van Pelt," Lucy stands, the glass is tinted pink, a cloud design is on each glass. Set of two, #M49-1088, 1989, $14.00 – 22.00.

"**Snoopy**," pink tint, Snoopy walks and holds a sleeping Woodstock; green tint, Snoopy peers into Woodstock's nest as he sleeps, V-shaped, #M49-1221, 1989; $28.00 – 40.00.

Champagne

"Snoopy," the frosted pedestal is made to look like a tree trunk, Snoopy leans against it, the clear glass top has two bands of gold, set of two, #M49-1284, mid 1980s, $65.00 – 90.00.

Commemorative

These tumblers, in two different sizes, were issued in conjunction with the Tsukuba Expo '85 in Japan, 1985. Each came boxed, but in this case, the box does not affect the value, since these glasses are very difficult to obtain. There are four to the series.

Snoopy, Woodstock, Lucy, Charlie Brown, Sally, and Linus are astronauts afloat in space, #3057486A, 4¾", $30.00 – 40.00; Snoopy the astronaut holds a blue star while Woodstock sits nearby, 4½", #3057485A; Snoopy sits on top of a jet-plane while Woodstock is nearby, #3057485B, 4½"; $25.00 – 35.00 each.

 # Lamps & Nightlights

This is a diverse category, and we've endeavored to give a wide sampling of the styles available from the United States, Europe, and Japan. Some of the lamps also serve as nightlights, but we've chosen to separate those that function solely as such.

Value is based on excellent condition: no scratches and no frayed cords. The item must be in working condition. The box does not necessarily affect the value, although some boxes do have great graphics. The Snoopy figures on the lamps by Nuova Linea Zero tend toward yellowing, and this must be taken into consideration when evaluating this series. It is next to impossible to purchase a white Snoopy.

• Lamps •

C. N. Burman Co.

Snoopy lamp, Snoopy stands, his arms are folded, he wears a red bowtie with white polka dots, shade is white with red trim, 14", #6B3290, 1987, $40.00 – 55.00; Snoopy desk lamp, Snoopy sits on a book and types, he wears a green bowtie, the lamp is similar to a gooseneck style, 10", #6D3292, 1987, $55.00 – 70.00.

Gladys Goose

Plastic figure of Snoopy sitting, with bulb housed inside, 17", #H395F, 1984, $40.00 – 50.00.

Glory Co., Ltd. (Japan)

Snoopy sits and hugs Woodstock atop a globe, at the push of a button the light changes color and also flashes strobe-like, 10¾", #SNL 5000, 1990, $75.00 – 95.00; 40th Anniversary Lamp, clear plastic bubble reveals globe inside which spins both clockwise and counterclockwise, various characters hold balloons, wave, etc., in honor of the 40th anniversary of Peanuts, 9½", #PNR 5000, 1990, $55.00 – 75.00.

Kamco

Plain white molded wooden base topped by shade with sleeping Peppermint Patty, Charlie Brown, Woodstock, Snoopy, Linus, and Lucy, Schroeder plays his piano, 15½" with shade, 1970s, $35.00 – 55.00.

Wooden cut-outs of Snoopy reclining on top of his doghouse, Lucy at her psychiatrist booth, and Charlie Brown receiving Lucy's advice, 18" with shade, 1970s, $125.00 – 155.00.

White milk glass globe, Snoopy and Woodstock sit on the doghouse, surrounded by hearts, 15½", 1970s, $85.00 – 105.00; Hurricane style, with white milk glass, Snoopy dances among the flowers, 11", 1970s, $95.00 – 125.00.

Nuova Linea Zero (Italy, distributed in Europe and Japan)

These special lamps feature excellent depictions of Snoopy. The company has taken one pose and dressed Snoopy in different personae, of which a few are pictured here. The lamps are wired for European electrical outlets.

Each could come several ways with the same design: a plastic or glass globe cover, or a fabric. Each stands approx. 16½" tall without the globe or shade. Mid to late 1980s.

Snoopy as a tennis player, wears a yellow cap and shirt and holds a tennis racket in one hand, #401, $140.00 – 225.00.

Snoopy as a proper English gentleman, wears a dinner jacket, maroon vest, top hat, and bowtie, and carries an umbrella in one hand, #387; Snoopy as a dandy, wears a blue plaid jacket with yellow vest and bowler hat, and carries a cane in one hand, #386; $170.00 – 200.00 each.

Snoopy as Sherlock Holmes, dressed in the traditional hound's-tooth apparel, holding a magnifying glass in one hand, #388; Snoopy as an English Bobby, wears a hat with "Metropolitan Police" decal, a coat, and holds a red and white stop sign in one hand, #389; $170.00 – 200.00 each.

The following lamps by Nuova are somewhat plain. Each is approx. 10½", mid to late 1980s.

Snoopy sits in front of his doghouse and hugs Woodstock, $50.00 – 70.00; Snoopy stands in front of a Miami Beach cabana wearing swimming trunks; Snoopy stands in front of his doghouse holding a tennis racket; $25.00 – 45.00 each.

Nursery Originals

Snoopy holds three balloons, Woodstock carries felt flowers, various characters decorate the shade, #120-365, 18", early 1980s, $80.00 – 105.00.

Snoopy and Woodstock sit in front of a rainbow, various characters decorate the shade (also came with only Woodstock on the shade), #110-360, 17", mid 1980s, $45.00 – 60.00.

Toybox (Japan)

"**Snoopy** Lighted Figurine," Snoopy sits, his mouth opens for the light, 7¼", #TC-461, early to mid 1980s, $85.00 – 120.00.

• Nightlights •

Determined Productions, Inc. (Japan)

"**Snoopy** Mascot Lamp," Snoopy sits, hugging Woodstock, 6¼", #40081-5, early to mid 1980s, $20.00 – 35.00.

Hallmark

"**Snoopy's** Doghouse," decorative lamp, Snoopy sleeps on top of his doghouse, 6½", #QHD361-2, early 1980s, $65.00 – 95.00; Snoopy stands, he wears a blue bowler hat and red bowtie, and carries a red briefcase, plugs in wall, 5½", Japan, #79113-0, 1984, $20.00 – 35.00; "Snoopy Fireman," Snoopy stands on a stage-like red stand, he wears a firehat which when turned, lights up, battery operated, 7½", Hallmark/AMIE, Japan, 1985, $35.00 – 47.00.

Kato Kogei (Japan)

"**Snoopy** Ceramic Figurine Light," two-dimensional side view of Snoopy, #83K-29, 6¼", 1985, $55.00 – 75.00.

Quantasia/Glory Co., Ltd. (Japan)

"**Charlie Brown:** Baseball Team Manager," Charlie Brown wears brown baseball cap and mitt and sits on top of a large baseball, was also available with red hat and glove, plastic, 7¾", #CBL 2900, late 1980s, $95.00 – 140.00.

Willitts Designs

Snoopy sits and hugs Woodstock, porcelain, 5½", #8122, 1990, $25.00 – 45.00; Linus sits, sucks his thumb, and holds his blanket, porcelain, 7¼", #45024, 1990, $65.00 – 80.00.

• Light Bulbs •

Snoopy lights up our life in more than one way, in the two light bulbs produced by Marimo Craft for Butterfly Originals in Japan. The design lights up in two colors with a neon effect. They're not your basic everyday lights — each contains Snoopy and his name.

Snoopy Charm Light, Snoopy raises his top hat, #SN 040(A); Snoopy Charm Light, Snoopy sits on a shooting star, #SN-040(B); $30.00 – 45.00 each.

Pillows

This section is by no means complete but gives merely a sample of the available pillows. Values reflect a mint-excellent condition pillow with no tears. All colors should be vibrant with no fading. Original tags should be included.

• Simon Simple •

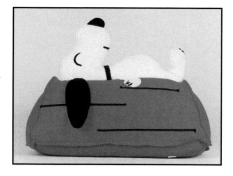

Felt Snoopy lying on top of his doghouse, late 1960s, $23.00 – 32.00.

• Determined Productions, Inc. •

Not Pictured
Cloth Snoopy lying on top of his home, irregular
    shape, #5961, early 1970s. . . . .$18.00 – 30.00.

Round cloth, stuffed. These are known as "Peanuts Patch Pillows" because they match the cloth patches also issued by Determined. Approx. 14" dia., late 1960s - early 1970s.

Not Pictured

"The Mad Punter," Snoopy kicks football, orange background, green lettering and piping, #0661. . . . . .$18.00 – 25.00

"Tennis Anyone?" Snoopy holds a tennis racket, blue background, gold lettering and piping, #0666. . . . .18.00 – 25.00

"World's Crabbiest Female," Lucy wears a green dress, hot pink background, orange lettering and piping, #0667. .18.00 – 25.00

"Ice is Nice," Snoopy ice skates and wears a red ski cap and scarf, blue background, gold lettering and piping, #0668. . . . . .18.00 – 25.00

"You're Away," Snoopy wears a golf cap and leans against golf club, gold background, green lettering and piping. .18.00 – 25.00

"Jamming," Snoopy rollerskates and wears a blue helmet and a green scarf, red background, green lettering and piping, #0670. . . . . .18.00 – 25.00

"World Famous Ski Champion," Snoopy is on skis, he wears a red ski cap and scarf, green background, gold lettering and piping, #0671. . . . . .18.00 – 25.00

"Joe Cool," Snoopy as Joe Cool, blue background, gold lettering and piping. . . . . .18.00 – 25.00

"To Know Me is to Love Me," Linus wears red and green striped shirt, holds red blanket, gold background, green lettering, #0662, $18.00 – 25.00.

"Strike," Snoopy holds bowling ball, green background, gold lettering and piping, #0663, $18.00 – 25.00.

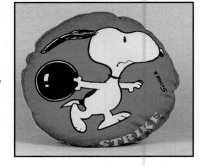

"It's Hero Time," Snoopy stands proudly, blue background, gold lettering and piping, #0664, $20.00 – 32.00.

"Come Dance with Me Baby," Snoopy does his dance of joy, orange background, green lettering and piping, #0665, $20.00 – 32.00.

Square pillows made of sweatshirt material. Each pillow is a solid color background with black drawing, lettering, and piping. While a color is indicated here, the pillows came in assorted colors. Approx. 17" square.

Not Pictured

"Security is Having Someone to Lean On," Charlie Brown and Snoopy lean against each other,
    #591-05. . . . .$18.00 – 25.00
"I Suppose I'll Just Have to Sleep in the Guest Room..." Linus lies on top of Snoopy's doghouse,
    Snoopy's head stick out of his doorway, gold background, #591-14. . . . . .18.00 – 25.00
"Happiness is a Warm Puppy," Lucy hugs Snoopy very tightly, hot pink background, #591-01. . . . . .25.00 – 35.00
"It's Nice to Get Home to Your Own Bed," Snoopy lies on top of his doghouse, red background. . . . . . .18.00 – 25.00
"I'm Allergic to Morning," Snoopy, bleary eyed, lies on top of his doghouse, hot pink background. . . . . .18.00 – 25.00
"The Moon is Made of American Cheese," Snoopy is an astronaut who has landed on the moon,
    orange background. . . . . .50.00 – 75.00

"Security is Knowing You're Not Alone," Linus kneels and prays by his bed, orange background, #591-08, $18.00 – 25.00.

"Love is Tickling," Sally tickles Linus, gold background, #591-03, $18.00 – 30.00.

Smaller square pillows made of sweatshirt material, approx. 14". Each pillow is a solid color background with black drawing, lettering, and piping.

Not Pictured

"I Love My Home," Snoopy lies on top of his doghouse roof, Woodstock sits on Snoopy's tummy,
    gold background. . . . .$10.00 – 14.00
"I'm Allergic to Morning," Snoopy looks tired as he sits on top of his doghouse, blue background. . . . . .10.00 – 14.00
"Live It Up a Little!", Snoopy does his dance of joy, red background. . . . . .10.00 – 14.00
"I'm Not Perfect, But I'm Pretty Perfect!", Snoopy stands and wears a Magna Cum Laude badge,
    green background. . . . . .10.00 – 14.00

• Determined Productions K.K., Japan •

Round, cloth, Snoopy's face, he wears a Santa cap, the bow on his collar is real ribbon with felt "mistletoe," #86-3302676, 1986, $35.00 – 45.00.

"Stay in Shape," square, cloth, Snoopy sits and watches as Woodstock and his friends splash in Snoopy's waterdish, blue background, green lettering, reverse side: Snoopy watches as Woodstock and his friend ride a bicycle built for two, "Keep Trim," #D-OS-6603, mid 1980s, $15.00 – 18.00.

Irregular shape, velveteen, Snoopy holds an ice cream cone with several different flavors, comes in pink or blue background, made by Osaka Nishikawa, mid 1980s, $20.00 – 30.00.

Irregular shape, cloth. Sally dressed in typical Bavarian women's clothing, mid 1980s; Snoopy dressed in typical Bavarian men's clothing, mid 1980s; $15.00 – 22.00 each.

 # Ceramic Planters and Vases

This is where a very serious Peanuts collector's attention turns: the all-important category of ceramics. It was Determined Productions (again!) out of San Francisco, California, which first created the wonderful designs that have captured our imaginations, collector's cravings, and bank accounts. Serious collectors wish to own each and every one of these planters and vases.

Determined later manufactured planters and vases for fans in Japan. When the collectors elsewhere learned of this great merchandise, they made special trips to visit Japan; not just to soak up the centuries of culture, but to buy bags full of Peanuts goodies.

It began in 1977 when the Wm. Zappettini Co., under Determined Productions, produced many beautiful ceramic items bearing the likenesses of Peanuts characters. The line included cups, mugs, and steins, which appear elsewhere in this book, and also the planters and vases we cherish today.

Prices are based on mint (never used) condition. If a saucer accompanied the planter, it, too, should be in mint condition. The design should not have any scratches or missing paint. Be certain to examine Snoopy's collar; the red paint tends to come off. There should be no chips.

All items were made by Determined Productions, Inc., with the exception of the Willitts vase, which is indicated. Dimension refers to height.

• Mini Vases (1977) •

Each is approx. 2½".

Charlie Brown, Series #1295; Snoopy sits and sniffs a pink flower, 2¼", #1294; Linus, Series #1295; Peppermint Patty, Series #1295; Lucy, Series #1295; $14.00 – 20.00 each.

Snoopy sits between two tulips and hugs Woodstock; Snoopy wears Hawaiian lei and kisses Woodstock; Snoopy sits in front of a rainbow, his arms are outstretched; $14.00 – 20.00 each.

Snoopy Series

Each vase is captioned "Snoopy" and has a wire handle, 2½" to 3½", 1977.

Canister, Snoopy stands on his name beneath an arch of roses; Cauldron, Snoopy reclines on his name and holds a yellow flower; Kettle, Snoopy admires several yellow flowers; $14.00 – 20.00 each.

Pitcher, Snoopy reclines on his doghouse, two yellow sunflowers are near-by; Water pail, Snoopy leans to touch a single yellow flower; Vase, Snoopy stands next to a large red tulip; $14.00 – 20.00 each.

• Bud Vases •

Snoopy holds strings attached to several red, yellow, and blue balloons, 6½", #1124, 1977, $28.00 – 42.00; "This Has Been a Good Day," Snoopy reclines on his doghouse, Woodstock is asleep in his nest which is on Snoopy's tummy, 5", #1128, 1977, $22.00 – 32.00; "How nice," Snoopy holds a red flower while Woodstock holds several, 7⅝", #1281, 1977, $40.00 – 55.00.

Snoopy holds a flower to his nose, design is yellow oval trimmed in green with tiny pink flowers, 7", #1277, late 1970s; "I Hate Not Having a Lapel," Snoopy sits and appears forlorn, Woodstock flies nearby, 6½", late 1970s; $28.00 – 42.00 each. "Snoopy and His Friends from The World Famous Comic Strip by Charles M. Schulz," Woodstock, Sally, and Charlie Brown watch Snoopy arrange flowers in a vase (This item came packaged in a box with several of the characters on it. It also has matching tableware pictured in the Tableware section.), 7⅞", Japan, #HI46, 1984, no box, $45.00 – 55.00; in box, $55.00 – 70.00.

"Snoopy," Snoopy wears a blue baseball cap and swings his bat, 6¼", late 1970s; "Snoopy," Snoopy wears a Pawpet on each hand and on his tail, 6¼", late 1970s; $55.00 – 70.00 each.

• Cylindrical Vases •

"All Girls Look Forward to Their First Kiss!" Snoopy kisses Sally, 5½", #1218, 1977; "Love is Walking Hand in Hand," Linus and Sally walk as they hold hands, 5½", #1573, 1977; $40.00 – 50.00 each. "Love is What It's All About," Snoopy watches two birds kiss, 5½", late 1970s, $45.00 – 55.00.

"All Right, Who Planted the Flower?!", a big flower towers over Snoopy as he reclines on the roof of his doghouse, Woodstock nearby holds a flower, 8¾", #1283, 1977, $55.00 – 80.00; "It's Hard to Feel Sorry for Yourself When You're Happy!", Snoopy kicks up his heels as he reclines on his doghouse, 7", late 1970s, $35.00 – 45.00.

• Planters with Saucers •

Each of these pots has a draining hole and is accompanied by a plain white draining dish. 1977.

"Surprise a Friend With a Hug!", Snoopy hugs Woodstock tightly, hearts and flowers are all around, 3¼", #1195, $28.00 – 40.00; "Woodstock is Really into Flowers!", Snoopy stands in his garden and Woodstock stands on a packet of seeds, 3¼", #1208, $45.00 – 55.00.

A figure of Snoopy climbs on the side of a plain white pot, 3", #1198, $35.00 – 45.00; a figure of Snoopy holds onto the rim of a plain, white pot 4¼", #1199, $45.00 – 55.00.

Planter Dishes

Each has an unusual shape.

Eight-sided dish, alternate panels of Snoopy with flowers, Woodstock appears with Snoopy in three of the panels, the remaining panels are plain white, 2¼", #1197, 1977; Eight-sided dish, alternate panels show Snoopy with a large flower, seated Woodstock appears on the remaining panels, 2¼", #1525, 1977; $25.00 – 37.00 each.

"I'm Not Perfect, But I'm Pretty Perfect!", Snoopy displays a ribbon that says "Great," Woodstock holds a red flower, 1¾", late 1970s; Snoopy sits surrounded by several yellow, red, and orange flowers as well as a butterfly, the sun shines in the background, 1¾", late 1970s; $25.00 – 37.00 each.

Doghouse Planters

Snoopy's Doghouse Planter. These were available in three sizes.

6¼", #1111, $25.00 – 30.00; 7¾", #1103, $35.00 – 50.00; 4¾", #1113, $15.00 – 20.00.

Planters with a Baby Theme

Florists loved carrying these planters, which made it easy for their arrangements to appeal to the heartstrings of proud new parents, 1977.

Baby boot, Snoopy with Woodstock, who is in a baby buggy, pink laces with blue trim, 3½", #1290(A); Baby boot, Snoopy with Woodstock, who is in a baby buggy, blue laces with pink trim, 3½", #1290(B); $40.00 – 52.00 each.

Baby block, Snoopy appears with each of the letters A, B, C, and D. Woodstock is in one of the panels with Snoopy, 3", #1291, $20.00 – 35.00; Drum, several poses of Snoopy with Woodstock, 3¼", #1292, $25.00 – 40.00.

Cradle, Snoopy in a polka-dot blanket is carried by Woodstock to several of his bird friends (Some of these planters did not carry the cloud pattern on the front.), 4¼", #1293, $35.00 – 45.00.

Figural

Snoopy sits, the rear portion of his body is the opening for the plant, 5", #1118, 1977, $35.00 – 45.00.

Snoopy wears his dog dish on his head and carries a suitcase, Woodstock sits on Snoopy's nose, 1977: 7½", #1101, $25.00 – 35.00; 4½", #1102, $18.00 – 30.00.

Snoopy leans next to a barrel, 4¼", 1977: "SNOOPY" is written in black letters, #1115; "SNOOPY" is written in raised white letters, #1116; $25.00 – 35.00 each; "SNOOPY" is written in black letters, #1105, 6¾", $45.00 – 60.00.

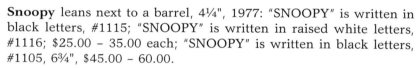

Snoopy wears a Hero badge with ribbon, 7", #1127, 1977, $50.00 – 70.00.

Snoopy sits and hugs Woodstock next to a brown woven basket, 7¼", Japan, early 1990s, $75.00 – 135.00.

Snoopy stands and holds Woodstock in one arm next to a cylindrical vase, 7¾", Japan, early 1990s, $60.00 – 90.00.

Heart-Shaped

"Love," red with a figure of Snoopy reclining near the opening (This vase was issued in different hues of red, from bright red as pictured to a very dark shade; sometimes the word "LOVE" also was painted red instead of white.), 4½", #1572, 1977, $28.00 – 42.00; Snoopy grins and holds his hands together, little white hearts are nearby, red with two-dimensional figure of Snoopy, 3¾", late 1970s, $35.00 – 45.00.

Snoopy holds an envelope with a heart on it, the background is a large red heart and an opening for a plant or flowers, 5", late 1970s, $45.00 – 60.00.

Snoopy smells a yellow rose as Woodstock looks on, has pedestal legs, late 1970s, 3", $25.00 – 42.00; Snoopy holds a bouquet of flowers while Woodstock peers down from the top of the heart, 4", #1530, 1977, $40.00 – 50.00.

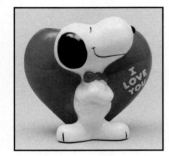

"I Love You," Snoopy stands in front of the heart planter, 5", Willitts, #8132, 1988, in box, $35.00 – 42.00; no box, $28.00 – 35.00.

Christmas Theme

Santa Snoopy stands next to a chimney bearing a Christmas wreath, 7¼", #1106, 1977, $85.00 – 125.00; "Merry Christmas," Santa Snoopy stands next to a small barrel, 4½", #1117, 1977, $40.00 – 50.00.

Santa Snoopy rides in front of his sleigh, Woodstock rides in the back, 4½", #1529, 1977, $50.00 – 65.00; Santa Snoopy sits next to an empty gift sack, Woodstock is in front of the sack, 3¼", 1977, $40.00 – 50.00.

Miscellaneous

Half circle, Snoopy as a vaudeville entertainer tips his hat and presents Woodstock with a bouquet of flowers, 4¼", #1212, 1977; Half circle, a raised Joe Cool stands with his arms folded, the background is a rainbow-colored arc, 4¼", late 1970s, $45.00 – 60.00 each.

Figures of Snoopy and Woodstock sit in front of Snoopy's house, 5", late 1970s, $45.00 – 65.00.

"Ah! Here it is! A Beagle's Blooming Garden Guide!", book-shaped, Snoopy looks at his book-shelves," 3½", #1278, 1977, $45.00 – 55.00.

Star-shaped, Snoopy wearing a Hero badge in front of a yellow star vase, 4¼", #1126, 1977, $30.00 – 40.00; Bucket, several poses of Snoopy and Woodstock dancing on the word "FLOWER," a wire for the basket should be included (but is not pictured here), 4¾", #1209, 1977, $30.00 – 40.00.

Boot, raised design of Snoopy as a cowboy, Woodstock wearing a feather headband, 4½", early 1980s; Snoopy peers over his U.S. mail-box, Woodstock stands at one side, 3¼", #1528, 1977; $35.00 – 45.00 each.

Bathtub, Linus, Schroeder, Lucy, Charlie Brown, Franklin, Sally, Pepper-mint Patty, and Woodstock hold up "Have a Nice Day! Everyone" signs, 2½", early 1980s, $25.00 – 35.00; Milk can, Snoopy and Woodstock relax in a pile of hay, 4¼", mid 1970s, $35.00 – 45.00.

Block, Snoopy with a large piece of fruit on the four sides: watermelon, pineapple, strawberry, and banana, 3", #1763, 1977, $30.00 – 45.00; Bag with handles, Snoopy holds a green flag with a heart on it, several birds surround him, 4¾", mid 1970s, $35.00 – 50.00.

Pitcher, Snoopy hides a bouquet of flowers to surprise Woodstock, 4", #1297, 1977, $26.00 – 38.00; Watering can, Woodstock watches Snoopy pour water on his flowers, three metal and wooden garden utensils accompany this planter, 3", #1119, 1977, $38.00 – 48.00.

Watering can, Woodstock presents Snoopy with several flowers, 4½", mid 1970s, $35.00 – 48.00.

Baskets

Snoopy holds a pink flower and stands next to a white basket with a handle, 4", mid 1970s, $50.00 – 70.00; Woodstock peers into a white basket with a handle, 4¼", mid 1970s, $45.00 – 65.00.

Snoopy reclines on top of the handle of a woven white basket, 5¾", #1120, 1977, $35.00 – 47.00.

Berry basket, front and back carry different pictures of Snoopy in his garden with Woodstock, 3½", #1210, 1977; Berry basket, the front pictures Snoopy with a flower cart, the sides each have small flowers, the back is Woodstock holding a bouquet of red and yellow flowers, 3½", #1122, 1977; $45.00 – 60.00 each.

Pots

Set of three graduated sizes, #1190, 1977

Snoopy hugs Woodstock, hearts are in the background, 3¼"; Snoopy and Woodstock hold flowers, 2¼"; Snoopy and Woodstock dance among flowers and butterflies, 2"; $65.00 – 85.00 set of three.

Not Pictured
Raised design of Snoopy with a sunflower bending over him, 3¾", #1194, 1977. . . . .$30.00 – 38.00

 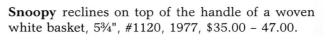

Glass Planters/Vases by Anchor Hocking

Anchor Hocking's most notable contribution to Peanuts collectibles comes in the shape of large, clear glasses. While the manufacturer referred to them as "Giant Coolers" in their catalogs, collectors prefer to call them glass planters or vases. Their shape is unique because they appear to be on pedestals. Spanning a variety of themes, the glasses were an inexpensive yet expressive means of turning a flower vase into a gift. They were issued in the late 1970s.

Each glass/vase is approximately 6½" tall.

Santa Snoopy hands candy cane to Woodstock, $12.00 – 18.00; Banner design, with Charlie Brown, Lucy, Snoopy, and Linus, the names are printed with a caption appropriate to each persona, $10.00 – 12.00; Snoopy is dressed in shorts and top with a band around his head, he's ready for a workout, along with birds, "We Superstars Stay in Shape," $10.00 – 12.00; Snoopy tosses flowers from his basket, Woodstock is nearby, "Love Drives Me Crazy," $12.00 – 14.00; Snoopy wears top hat and formal jacket and hands bouquet of flowers to Woodstock, "To You, My Special Friend!", $10.00 – 12.00.

"Baby" Snoopy is delivered by "stork" Woodstock and several birds, "Congratulations," $12.00 – 14.00; Lucy, Snoopy, and Peppermint Patty admire "baby" Woodstock in his cradle, "What a Cutie!", $12.00 – 14.00; Cowboy Snoopy looks like he doesn't feel very well, Woodstock flies overhead, "Nothing's As Easy As It Looks," $10.00 – 12.00; Snoopy shows off his bandaged foot, "Get Well Soon!", $10.00 – 12.00; Woodstock presents flowers to Snoopy, "How nice!", $12.00 – 14.00.

Birds Harriet and Bill touch noses, a heart is between them, "Love," $12.00 – 14.00; Charlie Brown, Snoopy, Sally, Lucy, Linus, Snoopy, and Woodstock laugh, "Ha Ha Hee Hee," $10.00 – 12.00; Snoopy sits and hugs Woodstock, "Somebody Cares!"; Snoopy holds lots of envelopes, Woodstock is near, "Happy Birthday"; Woodstock and Snoopy wear party hats, a birthday cake is between them, "Happy Birthday"; $12.00 – 14.00 each.

Snoopy wears a Western-style hat, red kerchief, and plays his guitar, along with Woodstock, who plays his fiddle, "There's a Little Bit of Country in All of Us," $10.00 – 12.00.

Radios

Value is based on mint in the box with some wear on the box allowed due to aging. All parts should be included, and the radio should be in working order.

When the box has been missing for a long time, the radio's plastic may be discolored. The radios are more valuable without the discoloration.

Each radio is battery operated.

Snoopy Sing-A-Long Radio, two-dimensional plastic Snoopy is the tuner for the radio by pointing to the stations, microphone included which can be used to sing along with the tunes or a P.A. system, Another Determined Production, 7¼" x 1½" x 6¾", #457, 1977, in box, $70.00 – 105.00; no box, $40.00 – 65.00; Snoopy Doghouse Radio, Snoopy is the handle for the doghouse-shaped radio, earphone included, Another Determined Production, 4" x 4" x 6¾", #354, mid 1970s, in box, $45.00 – 60.00; no box, $30.00 – 45.00; Snoopy, Woodstock, Charlie Brown Radio, paper cover on plastic two-dimensional radio, Charlie Brown, Snoopy, and Woodstock sit close to one another, carry strap and earphone included, Determined Productions (H.K.) Ltd., 5" x 1¼" x 6¾", #353, mid 1970s, in box, $25.00 – 40.00; no box, $15.00 – 25.00.

Snoopy Hi-Fi Radio, two-dimensional plastic Snoopy wears headphones and stands next to his radio, Another Determined Production, 8¼" x 2⅝" x 7½", #405, 1977, in box, $75.00 – 105.00; no box, $50.00 – 70.00; Snoopy AM Portable Radio, a two-dimensional plastic figure of Snoopy sitting, carry strap included, Concept 2000 (a Mattel company), 5" x 1¼" x 6¾", #351, late 1970s, in box, $25.00 – 40.00; no box, $15.00 – 25.00; Snoopy Bank Radio, two-dimensional plastic Snoopy strikes a disco pose, a nickel or quarter activates radio, Concept 2000 (a Mattel company), 4¾" x 1⅝" x 6½", #4442, late 1970s, in box, $65.00 – 90.00; no box, $35.00 – 50.00.

Snoopy Spaceship AM Radio, three-dimensional plastic spaceship with astronauts Snoopy and Woodstock, Concept 2000 (a Mattel company/Another Determined Production), 8¼" x 6¾" x 5", #4443, late 1970s, in box, $125.00 – 175.00; no box, $75.00 – 105.00.

Snoopy Plush Radio, Snoopy sits, the battery is housed in a zippered compartment in his back, Determined Toy, 8" tall, #8819, 1983, in box, $35.00 – 45.00; no box, $20.00 – 28.00; "Flashbeagle," Snoopy AM Headphone Radio, plastic radio with drawing of Snoopy dancing, headphones and belt clip included, Justin Products, Inc., 3⅝" x 1¼" x 3⅝", #DP 1562, 1984, in box, $25.00 – 35.00; no box, $20.00 – 30.00.

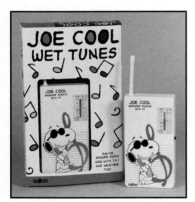

Joe Cool Wet Tunes, AM & FM shower radio with TV and weather channels, plastic, Snoopy Joe Cool holds towel and backbrush and wears sunglasses, Salton Maxim Housewares, Inc., 3¾" x 1" x 7½", #WT-11, 1992, in box, $12.00 – 20.00; no box, $5.00 – 12.00.

Tableware & Kitchen Accessories

• Salt & Pepper Sets •

Chef Snoopy has an "S" on his apron, Chef Woodstock sits on the pepper shaker, ceramic, salt 4¼", pepper 3", Determined Productions, #8830, late 1970s, $38.00 – 50.00; Figures of Snoopy and Charlie Brown sitting, ceramic, salt 2¾", pepper 2", Japan, Determined Productions, Inc., #DP-378, early 1990s, $25.00 – 35.00; Figures of Charlie Brown and Lucy with a blue sofa, 4", Willitts Designs, #45021, 1990, $45.00 – 60.00; Figures of Snoopy sitting, holding either an "S" or "P," ceramic, 2", Japan, Determined Productions, #DP20900, mid 1980s, $30.00 – 40.00.

Snoopy, cupping his chin with his hands, is the salt shaker, his dog dish with bone, is the pepper, bone caption, "To Snoopy," title on box, "Spice Set," Snoopy: 3½", dog dish: 1¼", Japan, Another Determined Production, #EH-58 early to mid 1980s, $30.00 – 45.00.

• Egg Cups •

Chef Snoopy egg cup, ceramic, 4", Determined Productions, #1567, late 1970s, $25.00 – 34.00; Figure of Snoopy holds an egg cup behind him, ceramic, 3", accompanied by a chocolate egg, Kinnerton Confectionery, late 1980s; "Good Morning," hourglass-shaped, Snoopy and Woodstock lean against each other, ceramic, United Kingdom, accompanied by a chocolate egg, 2½", Kinnerton Confectionery, late 1980s; $8.00 – 12.00 each.

"Good Morning," hourglass-shaped, Snoopy holds Woodstock, ceramic, United Kingdom, accompanied by a chocolate egg, 2½", Kinnerton Confectionery, late 1980s, $8.00 – 12.00.

• Jam & Mustard Jars/Lemon Juicers/Butter Dishes •

Snoopy sits on top of jam jar, ceramic, 3½", Determined Productions, #8490, 1977, $28.00 – 42.00; chef Woodstock sits on top of a mustard jar, ceramic, 2½", Determined Productions, #8480, 1977, $25.00 – 38.00. Lemon Juicer: figure of Snoopy sits by the reamer, caption, "Snoopy," ceramic, 1¾" x 3" dia., Japan, Another Determined Production, #SNH-10, mid 1980s, $24.00 – 36.00. Butter dish: Snoopy reclines on the cover of the dish, plate is bordered in black, ceramic, 4" tall x 3½" wide x 8" long, cover caption, "Snoopy," Japan, Another Determined Production, mid 1980s, $35.00 – 47.00.

• Cream Pitcher/Sugar Bowls •

Two-dimensional Linus sits on a blue chair with a handle, 4½", Willitts, #45020, 1990, $24.00 – 35.00. Sugar Bowl: Snoopy holds a cookie and sits on a blue ottoman, cover lifts off to reveal inside of the bowl, 4", Willitts Designs, #45026, 1990, $25.00 – 37.00.

• Pie Plates •

"My Compliments To The Chef!", Snoopy shows his supper dish to Chef Charlie Brown, ceramic, edges are crimped, 7½" dia., United Kingdom, Another Determined Production, 1980s, $65.00 – 95.00.

Not Pictured

"Bon Appetit!", Snoopy sits at a picnic table, Chef Woodstock flies nearby, ceramic, edges are crimped, 7½" dia., United Kingdom, Another Determined Production, 1980s; "I'm in No Mood for Supper Guests," Snoopy sits and wears a puzzled expression while Woodstock chirps, ceramic, edges are crimped, 7½" dia., United Kingdom, Another Determined Production, 1980s. . . . .$50.00 – 95.00

• Bottle & Can Openers •

Wood figure of Snoopy sits on a bench, bench caption, "Snoopy," two barrels are near him, their bottom portions are either a bottle or can opener, 5¼", Japan, Another Determined Production, #SNW-07, mid 1980s; Wood figure of Chef Snoopy stands by a toaster, two slices of bread actually are a bottle or can opener, 5½", Japan, Another Determined Production, mid 1980s; $75.00 – 110.00 each.

• Ice Bucket •

Snoopy and birds dance in front of red, orange, yellow, green, and blue background, vinyl with plastic handle, 9", Sheldon Ware, 1979, $120.00 – 150.00.

Music Boxes

Anri (Wood)

Obtaining some of these carved musicals is the pinnacle of success for a dedicated Peanuts collector. They tend to be elusive and, therefore, are even more cherished.

Small allowances can be made regarding condition; if a small flower is chipped, for example, it might be repaired or replaced with parts from another Anri music box.

Dates indicated are stamped on the musical. These items revolve, and the measurements refer to height.

The Flying Ace holds a baton, his helmet, barbed wire, a portion of a wall and tree are nearby, mushrooms are on the lawn, 4¼", tune, "Pack Up Your Troubles," #819-010, 1968, $85.00 – 125.00; The Flying Ace holds a baton, his helmet, barbed wire, a portion of a wall and tree are nearby, mushrooms are on the lawn, 4¼", "It's a Long Way to Tipperary," #819-020, 1968, $85.00 – 125.00; Schroeder plays his piano on which rests Beethoven's bust, a bird sits on the floor, 4½", tune "Leitmotiv Kaiserkonzert," #819-030, 1968, $125.00 – 175.00; Linus holds his blanket, Snoopy lurks nearby, mushrooms are on the lawn, 5¼", tune, "Release Me," #819-040, 1968, $145.00 – 190.00.

Charlie Brown holds a baseball bat, birds and mushrooms are on the lawn, Charlie Brown revolves, but the base does not, 6¼", tune, "Take Me Out to the Ball Game," #819-060, 1968, $190.00 – 225.00; Lucy stands behind her psychiatrist's booth, a bird sits on the counter, mushrooms are on the lawn, 6¾", tune, "Try to Remember," #819-400, 1968, $175.00 – 260.00.

Lucy stands behind her psychiatrist's booth and dispenses advice to Charlie Brown, bird and mushrooms are on the lawn, 8½", tune, "Try to Remember," #819-200, 1968, $290.00 – 375.00.

Lucy and Snoopy look at a bird sitting on the roof of a small house, mushrooms are on the lawn, 3", tune, "Close to You," #81971, 1972; Linus, Snoopy, and a bird stand near a small house, mushrooms are on the lawn, 3¼", tune, "What the World Needs Now is Love," #81972, 1972; Lucy and Charlie Brown stand near a tall mushroom, smaller mushrooms dot the lawn, 5", tune, "Rose Garden," #81973, 1972; $155.00 – 210.00 each. Snoopy's face looks upward at a large mushroom, a bird sits on a nearby house, mushrooms are on the lawn, 4¼", tune, "Yellow Bird," #81970, 1972, $145.00 – 200.00; Schroeder plays his piano, a bird sits on top of it, a large mushroom is nearby, other mushrooms are on the lawn, 5", tune, "Emperor," #81974, 1972, $135.00 – 190.00.

Lucy stands, mushrooms are on the lawn, 5¼", tune, "Love Story," #81981, 1972; Charlie Brown stands and holds a baseball bat, mushrooms are on the lawn, 5¼", tune, "Take Me Out to the Ballgame," #81983; Linus holds his blanket, mushrooms are on the lawn, 5¼", tune, "Close to You," #81982, 1972; $155.00 – 195.00 each.

Not Pictured

Snoopy wears an orange and white stocking cap, he ice skates, the top of the base is edged with white paint intended to resemble snow (because this paint tends to crack and wear off, it is next to impossible to find this musical in mint condition), mushrooms and a snow-laden tree complete the design, 5", tune, "The Skater's Waltz," #819-050, 1970. . . . .$125.00 – 170.00

Snoopy wears gloves and holds a hockey stick, a hockey puck, mushrooms, and a bird complete the design, 5", tune, "My Way," #819-070, 1971. . . . . .125.00 – 170.00

• Jewelry/Trinket Boxes •

6½" x 4¼" x 1¾". The inside bottom of the box is lined with velvet; the music mechanism shows through plastic, 1971.

Linus waits in the pumpkin patch, inside Snoopy dances as Schroeder plays the piano, tune, "Who Can I Turn To?" #33905/1; Snoopy kisses Lucy, inside Snoopy sits on his doghouse, Woodstock flies upside down, tune "Honey," #33905/3; $150.00 – 195.00 each.

Snoopy sits on his doghouse, Woodstock flies upside down, inside Charlie Brown scratches Snoopy's head, tune, "Yellow Bird," #33905/4, $135.00 – 175.00; Charlie Brown scratches Snoopy's head, inside Peppermint Patty strikes a baseball pose, Snoopy wears a baseball cap and mitt, tune, "Raindrops Keep Fallin' on My Head," #33905/5, $150.00 – 195.00.

Not Pictured

Schroeder plays his piano, Snoopy dances, tune, "I Could Have Danced All Night," #33905/2. . . . . .$150.00 – 195.00

Peppermint Patty holds a baseball bat and get ready to swing, Snoopy wears a baseball cap and mitt, tune, "Take Me Out to the Ball Game," #33905/6. . . . . .150.00 – 195.00

• Three-Dimensional Pictures •

7¾" x 1½" x 8½". These musicals are quite lovely and make an excuse for placing a Peanuts character on the wall. A three-dimensional fence and other little touches add to the picture's depth. A knob at the bottom front is turned for the music. 1971.

Linus waits in the pumpkin patch, tune, "Who Can I Turn To?" #72393/1, $260.00 – 330.00.

Schroeder plays his piano, Snoopy dances, tune, "I Could Have Danced All Night," #72393/2, $260.00 – 330.00.

Snoopy kisses Lucy, tune, "Honey," #72393/3, $260.00 – 330.00.

Snoopy is on his doghouse, Woodstock flies upside down, tune, "Yellow Bird," #72393/4, $260.00 – 330.00.

Charlie Brown scratches Snoopy's head, tune, "Love Makes the World Go Round," #72393/5, $260.00 – 330.00.

Not Pictured
Peppermint Patty holds a baseball bat and gets ready to swing, Snoopy wears a baseball cap and mitt, tune, "Take Me Out to the Ball Game," #72393/6. . . . .$260.00 – 330.00

Aviva Enterprises, Inc. (Ceramic)

Tunes may vary. These musicals revolve unless otherwise noted.

• Series 100000 •

These do not revolve, 1973.

Snoopy is on one bended knee, holding a bouquet of flowers, the base is decorated with hearts, 4¾", tune, "Somewhere My Love"; Snoopy reclines on his doghouse, Woodstock stands on Snoopy's tummy, the base is decorated with flowers (door may be black or brown, as shown in photo), 5", tune, "Fur Elise"; $40.00 – 55.00 each.

Snoopy lies on top of a podium with the letters LOVE on its sides, Woodstock sits on Snoopy's tummy, base is decorated with hearts (colors of the letters may vary), 5", tune, "Love Story"; Snoopy lies on top of a podium with the letters LOVE on its sides, Woodstock sits on Snoopy's tummy, base is decorated with flowers (colors of the letters may vary), 5", tune, "Love Story"; Snoopy wears a party hat and holds cake with one candle, the base is decorated with "Happy Birthday" and musical notes (colors of cake and Snoopy's hat may vary), 5½", tune, "Happy Birthday"; Snoopy wears a party hat and holds cake with one candle, plain base (colors of cake and Snoopy's hat may vary), 5½", tune, "Happy Birthday"; $40.00 – 55.00 each.

Snoopy holds Woodstock, they are bundled up in a blanket, Snoopy holds a pennant with the caption "Rah," the base is decorated with college pennants, 4¾", tune, "Raindrops Keep Fallin' on My Head"; Snoopy is bundled up in winterwear, he stands on skis and holds poles (color of Snoopy's clothing may vary), base caption, "Ski Love," 5", tune, "Edelweiss"; Snoopy is bundled up in winterwear, he stands on skis and holds poles (color of Snoopy's clothing may vary), plain base, 5", tune, "Edelweiss"; $40.00 – 55.00 each.

• Series 100020 •

1974

Snoopy wears a nightcap and reclines in a quarter moon, Woodstock is at the top of the moon, 5½", tune, "The Impossible Dream," $60.00 – 80.00; a tree trunk is arched over Snoopy who sits on a swing that can move back and forth manually, Woodstock is in his nest at the top of a trunk, 6", tune "Yellow Bird," $65.00 – 85.00; Snoopy wears a dog dish on his head and carries a red hobo pack on a stick over his shoulder, Woodstock stands beside him, 5", tune, "Born Free," $55.00 – 75.00.

• General •

Snoopy wears a black top hat with a red band and red bowtie and carries a cane over one arm, 8", revolves, tune, "Happy Days Are Here Again" (or "Pennies from Heaven"). Note: Musical came boxed in Styrofoam with a cardboard slipcover that bears its picture, #213, 1979, $85.00 – 110.00.

Snoopy reclines on his doghouse, Woodstock is on his tummy, the roof lifts off, and the bottom portion may serve as a place for candy or trinkets, 7½", tune, "The Candy Man," #214, 1979; Snoopy sits on top of a heart, he holds Woodstock, base caption, "Love," bottom portion caption, "and Kisses," top portion lifts off to reveal a place for candy or trinkets, 6½", tune, "Love Makes the World Go Round," #215, 1979; $85.00 – 110.00 each.

Snoopy wears a pink tennis visor and holds a tennis racket, Woodstock sits on the racket, 5½", tune, "Lara's Theme," 1982, $60.00 – 85.00; Snoopy and Woodstock rollerskate, Snoopy wears headphones, pink base, 5", tune "Love Story," #212001, 1982; Snoopy sits and holds a heart, Woodstock sits on Snoopy's doghouse, 4¾", tune, "Let's Fall in Love," #MB-2800, 1982; $65.00 – 90.00 each.

Aviva Enterprises, Inc./Sanyo (Lucite)

The lid of these boxes opens to reveal a mirror and a velvet-lined space to store jewelry or trinkets. While the musical itself does not revolve, the outside design does.

Two of the styles were available in the United States; all three were available in Japan, 3¾" dia., 1982.

"Have a Nice Day," lid design: Snoopy rides a carousel horse, Woodstock holds a star, side design: Snoopy, Woodstock, Charlie Brown, Marcie, Linus, Lucy, and Schroeder ride carousel horses, blue background, tune, "Lara's Theme," #211001; "Snoopy," lid design: Snoopy is a music conductor, Woodstock plays the violin, side design: Linus, Snoopy, Woodstock, Sally, Marcie, Charlie Brown, Schroeder, and Lucy play musical instruments, pink background, tune, "Music Box Dancer," #211002; $60.00 – 75.00 each. "Snoopy in New York," lid design: Snoopy and Woodstock walk along with the New York skyline in the background, side design: Marcie, Peppermint Patty, Sally, Linus, Charlie Brown, Snoopy, and several birds walk with New York skyline in the background, the inside of the box is not lined with velvet, it is clear and the musical works are revealed, clear brown background, tune, "Music Box Dancer" (tunes may vary), #092080, $90.00 – 115.00.

Glory, Japan (Ceramic)

The following musicals were made for the Japanese market, but some managed to reach the United States where collectors quickly snapped them up.

"Snoopy," Snoopy stands on a green mound, his paw is on his mouth, 4½", tune, "Somewhere Over the Rainbow," #SNO(T), 1990, $25.00 – 32.00.

"40 Years of Happiness," Snoopy wears a black jacket and red bowtie, he stands on a podium which revolves on a black base, 7¾", tune, "When You Wish Upon a Star," 1990; "40 Years of Happiness," Snoopy wears a red jacket and blue bowtie, he stands on a podium which revolves on a blue base, 7¾", tune, "When You Wish Upon a Star," 1990; $120.00 – 160.00 each.

Snoopy swings back and forth from a tree, Woodstock sits on top of the tree trunk, 7½", tune, "Somewhere Over the Rainbow," 1991, $190.00 – 220.00.

• Miniature Blue and Gold Series •

Base captioned in gold, "Snoopy," 3½", #SNO(C), 1990.

Snoopy as a circus master, points with a baton, tune, "Blue Danube;" Snoopy wears a long blue jacket open in the front while holding a baton, tune, "Rhapsody in Blue;" Snoopy wears a blue jacket and shoes, he holds a hat with one hand and a baton with the other, tune, "Fur Elise;" $35.00 – 48.00 each.

• Character Series •

Each character stands on a white base captioned with his/her name; the base revolves. Tunes are unknown to author, 1991.

Charlie Brown, 4½", #SN2000; Lucy Van Pelt stands with her arms outstretched, 4½", #SN2201; Snoopy hugs Woodstock, 4½", #SN2202; Sally Brown wears a pink dress, 4½", #SN2203; $45.00 – 55.00 each.

Snoopy and Woodstock as Beaglescouts, 4½", #SN2500; Snoopy and Woodstock sit facing each other, 4", #SN2501; $45.00 – 55.00 each.

Quantasia (Ceramic)

"Love is Sharing," Snoopy types while Woodstock sits on the typewriter, pink base, 5", tune, "Yesterday," #C-164-033, 1984, $80.00 – 105.00; Snoopy holds Woodstock and sits on large red heart base, 5", tune, "Maiden's Prayer," #MB2200, 1984, $50.00 – 75.00.

Snoopy plays the bass, Woodstock plays a trumpet, the red base has raised music notes, 5¾", tune, "Feelings," #MB3300, 1984, $80.00 – 105.00; Snoopy holds a trumpet in one hand while leaning on a black musical note, the pink base has raised musical notes, 5¾", tune, "Swan Lake," #MB2200, 1984, $70.00 – 95.00; Snoopy hides flowers behind his back, Woodstock sits in a tree, 6", tune, "My Way," #MB3300, 1984, $70.00 – 95.00.

• Quantasia/Glory (Japan) •

Telephone Rests

A blue base features Snoopy's face, Woodstock appears on the back, the base is decorated with white and blue flowers, 5", tune, "Edelweiss," #A2782, 1986, $75.00 – 95.00; "Snoopy," Snoopy and Woodstock sit on a pink telephone with a gold phone rest, 5", tune, "Somewhere Over the Rainbow," #009415, 1986; Snoopy and Woodstock sit on a blue telephone with a gold phone rest, Snoopy holds the phone, 5", tune, "You Light Up My Life," #A2784 1986; $90.00 – 120.00 each.

Miniature Pink Base Series #SNM1480

Revolves, 3½", 1986

Snoopy sits and holds Woodstock with one arm, a blue bow is around his neck, tune, "The Star Spangled Banner," #A2763; Snoopy holds a tambourine, tune, "You Are My Sunshine," #A2762; Snoopy holds a strawberry, tune, "Do, a Deer," #A2761; $35.00 – 48.00 each.

 # Quantasia/Glory Co., Ltd., Japan

• Metal •

These small music boxes have lids which, when opened, reveal a velvet-lined space for jewelry or trinkets. The musicals are metal with very unusual ornate designs. The lids are plastic.

Value is based on excellent condition. The velvet lining should be intact and the tune should be heard clearly.

"Snoopy," Snoopy's face is surrounded by tiny flowers on this heart-shaped box, tune, "Love Story," 2", #SNM2500(A); "Snoopy," Snoopy's face is surrounded by tiny flowers on this chest-shaped box, tune, "Love Story," 2", #SNM2500(B); $30.00 – 40.00 each.

Because they are metal, these boxes don't damage very easily.

They share the same item number, so we have identified them as "A" and "B."

• Plastic •

Although made from plastic, these musicals are quite unique and charming.

Value is based on excellent condition; all necessary parts must be present. There should be no cracks or chips, and the music should be heard clearly.

"Snoopy," Snoopy and three birds sit on circus balls and twirl as the music plays, clear plastic dome on top of red base dotted with gold stars, tune, "Shall We Dance?" 6½", #SNO 3800, mid to late 1980s, $90.00 – 130.00.

"Snoopy," pink dresser with one pull-out drawer, the mirror on top turns over to reveal a picture of Woodstock sitting on Snoopy, tune, "Feelings," 4¾", #SNM 1300, mid to late 1980s, $35.00 – 45.00.

"Snoopy Music Box,"** music plays when the drawer is opened, a plush Snoopy wearing a felt helmet, goggles, and scarf moves his head around, tune, "Memories," 7", #SNO 3900, mid to late 1980s, $90.00 – 140.00.

• Wood •

Quantasia/Glory Co. Ltd., Japan, produced several musicals which became highly prized after American collectors learned of their existence.

Value is based on excellent condition: no splinters, chips, or missing paint. The music should be heard clearly. Moving parts should be intact and working.

Jewelry/Trinket Boxes

The lid opens to reveal a picture of Woodstock on the inside lid, the interior has room for jewelry or trinkets. Because these boxes share the same series number, we added an "A" and "B" to differentiate between the two, 5", mid to late 1980s.

"Snoopy," Snoopy and Woodstock lean against one another, natural, light-color wood with wine-colored flowers and a green leaf border, tune, "Music Box Dancer," #SN 1580(A); "Snoopy with his best friend," Snoopy looks at Woodstock, cream color with pink flowers and a green leaf border, tune, "Music Box Dancer," #SN 1580(B); $55.00 – 70.00 each.

Wind-Up Boxes

These do not have a lid or any other function. Because they share the same series number, we added an "A" and "B" to differentiate the two, 1¼", mid to late 1980s.

Woodstock reclines against Snoopy who holds a pink gift box tied with red ribbon, tune, "Feelings," SNM980(A); Snoopy holds some flowers, the musical looks like it is a gift tied with a ribbon and a gift tag, tune, "Love Story," #SNM980(B); $25.00 – 35.00 each.

Wall Hanging Boxes

Mid 1980s

"Flashbeagle," Peppermint Patty moves up and down, Snoopy moves back and forth, tune, "Fur Elise," 8½", #SN-10, $125.00 – 175.00.

"Flashbeagle," Snoopy moves back and forth, tune, "Fur Elise," 8¼", #SN-11, $125.00 – 175.00.

Schmid

• Ceramic •

Peanuts collectors always get excited about Schmid; it's a collector's dream to own each and every Schmid musical ever made. The ceramics are favored due to their high-gloss finish and clever depictions of the characters. Some of the boxes are animated, which delights fans even more.

We doubt you would pass up a musical because of a missing box. Most Schmid music boxes were quite plain,

with the exception of the two "baby" musicals, which carry a picture of the item inside; but here again, this doesn't really affect the price.

Value is based on excellent to mint condition. There should be no chips or missing paint. Animated parts should work properly. The music must play fairly clearly, although a slightly tinny sound is acceptable.

30th Anniversary Limited Edition/"For Mother" Series

30th Anniversary Limited Edition (15,000 numbered sequentially), Snoopy wears a party hat and stands on an unwrapped gift box, Charlie Brown sits, 6¼", #289-090, 1980, $65.00 – 95.00. "For Mother" Series (certificate of authenticity included): First Limited Edition (10,000 numbered sequentially), "Mission For Mom," the Flying Ace pilots his doghouse amid some clouds, "MOM" is written on the clouds, tune, "It's a Small World," 7½", #289-021, 1981, $85.00 – 110.00; Second Limited Edition (10,000 numbered sequentially), "Which Way to Mother," Snoopy and Woodstock look at directional signs written in various languages, all mean "Mother," tune, "Edelweiss," 7½", #289-021, 1982, $95.00 – 125.00.

Annual Limited Edition Series

Certificate of authenticity included. With the exception of "Flyin' Tamer Snoopy," which has a wooden base, all the music boxes rotate on separate plastic bases; 15,000 sequentially numbered produced of each.

First Limited Edition, "Peanuts in Concert," Schroeder plays the piano, Snoopy is a circus ringmaster, tune, "Beethoven Piano Concerto," 6", #289-030, 1983, $130.00 – 175.00; Second Limited Edition, "Snoopy and the Beaglescouts," Snoopy is the Beaglescout master with two bird scouts, tune, "I Whistle a Happy Tune," 6½", #289-051, 1984, $130.00 – 175.00; Third Limited Edition, "Clown Capers," Snoopy, Sally, Charlie Brown, Lucy, Schroeder, Peppermint Patty, Marcie, and Woodstock are dressed as clowns and ride in an old-style

open car, tune, "Be a Clown," 5½", #289-052, 1985, $150.00 – 210.00; Fourth Limited Edition, "Flyin' Tamer Snoopy," Snoopy is a circus ringmaster, Woodstock wears a lion's mane, tune, "Pussycat, Pussycat," 6", #289-053, 1986, $130.00 – 175.00.

General

Linus and Snoopy wear baseball caps, composition material, low-gloss finish, tune, "Take Me Out to the Ballgame," 6¼", #278-551, 1974; Snoopy and Charlie Brown stand close, composition material, low-gloss finish, tune, "It's a Small World," 6¾", #278-552, 1974; Snoopy kisses Lucy, composition material, low-gloss finish, tune, "Close to You," 6", #278-553, 1974; $110.00 – 140.00.

Woodstock sits, tune, "Just the Way You Are," 6½", #253-725, 1985, $110.00 – 140.00; Snoopy sits, tune, "I'd Like to Teach the World to Sing," 12", #253-700, 1984, $275.00 – 330.00; Snoopy sits, tune, "When the Saints Go Marching In," 5¾", #253-704, 1984, $140.00 – 170.00.

Charlie Brown sits, wears red shirt with black zigzag, and black pants, tune, "Somebody Loves Me," 12", #253-702, 1984, $275.00 – 330.00; Charlie Brown sits, tune, "Somebody Loves Me," 6", #253-705, 1984, $140.00 – 170.00.

Lucy sits, her dress is blue, tune, "My Favorite Things," 12", #253-701, 1984, $275.00 – 330.00; Lucy sits, her dress is blue, 1984, tune, "Everybody Loves Someone," 5¾", #253-703, 1984, $140.00 – 170.00.

Snoopy lies on his doghouse, four birds stand on the grass, Snoopy's house turns independently, tune, "Oh, What a Beautiful Morning," 7", #253-708, 1984, $125.00 – 155.00; Snoopy and Woodstock ride on a seesaw, Woodstock holds a balloon, tune, "Playmates," 5¾", #253-709, 1984, $145.00 – 175.00; Snoopy lies on his doghouse, tune, "Home Sweet Home," #253-734, 1985, $60.00 – 90.00.

Snoopy as a bunny, dressed in light blue, holds an Easter basket, a ribbon is around his neck, tune, "Easter Parade," 7¼", 281-010, 1985, $140.00 – 160.00; Snoopy sits, his ears are pink and his pink-trimmed bib reads "Baby," tune, "Brahms Lullaby," 5", #281-016, 1985; Snoopy sits, his ears are blue and his blue-trimmed bib reads "Baby," tune, "Brahms Lullaby," 5", #281-017, 1985; $55.00 – 80.00 each.

Snoopy sits, he's dressed in a sailor suit and holds a toy boat, tune, "Anchors Aweigh," 5½", #253-727, 1985, $120.00 – 155.00; Flying Ace Snoopy pilots his red airplane, the propeller turns around, tune, "Around the World in 80 Days," 5", #253-729, 1985, $125.00 – 190.00.

Snoopy wears a party hat and holds two ballons, tune, "Up, Up, and Away," 7¾", #253-730, 1985, $110.00 – 145.00; Snoopy and Woodstock wear purple straw-type hats, Snoopy is poised at the piano, Woodstock twirls on top of the piano, tune, "The Entertainer," 5¼", #253-732, 1985, $135.00 - 180.00.

Snoopy is a clown, he moves up and down in a drum, Woodstock sits on the rim, does not revolve, tune, "Put on a Happy Face," 7½", #253-733, 1985; Snoopy is a clown, he moves up and down in a box decorated with stars, tune, "Be a Clown," 6¾", #265-751, 1985; $145.00 – 180.00 each.

Joe Cool wears green shirt and leprechaun hat in honor of St. Patrick's Day, caption of shirt, "Joe Cool," tune, "With a Little Bit of Luck," 7¼", #281-011, 1985, $90.00 – 120.00; Lucy wears a blue dress and roller skates, tune, "Playmates," 7", #281-018, 1985, $95.00 – 125.00; Charlie Brown wears a baseball mitt and is positioned to catch a ball, tune, "School Days," 6½", #281-019, 1985, $95.00 – 125.00.

Snoopy sits, he's dressed as a train engineer and holds a toy train in his hand, tune, "I've Been Working on the Railroad," 6", #253-728, 1985, $120.00 – 155.00; Snoopy is dressed in a nightshirt and cap, he holds a teddy bear, tune, "My Favorite Things," 6½", #253-726, 1985, $150.00 – 190.00.

Snoopy stands by a flower cart with an umbrella, Woodstock spins around independently, tune, "Younger Than Springtime," 7¾", #253-707, 1984, $160.00 – 210.00; Snoopy wears a straw hat and artist's smock, he paints a self-portrait, tune, "I Whistle a Happy Tune," 6", #293-000, 1986, $150.00 – 190.00.

Snoopy wears a nightshirt and cap, he sits on a swing, which moves back and forth and is suspended from a crescent moon, tune, "Twinkle, Twinkle Little Star," 7½", #281-020, 1985, $170.00 – 225.00.

Miniature Series

4", 1974

Snoopy lies on his doghouse, tune, "It's a Small World," #253-012, 1971, $125.00 – 165.00; Snoopy kisses Lucy, tune, "Try to Remember," #253-010, 1971, $140.00 – 180.00; Lucy stands, she wears a blue dress, tune, "My Way," #253-014, 1971; Charlie Brown stands, he has a baseball mitt on one hand and holds a ball in the other, tune, "The Impossible Dream," #253-013, 1971; Schroeder sits at his piano, tune, "I'd Like to Teach the World to Sing," #253-015, 1971; Linus stands, he holds his blanket and sucks his thumb, tune, "Tie a Yellow Ribbon," #253-016, 1971; $120.00 – 160.00 each.

Not Pictured
Woodstock, tune, "Snow Bird," #253-011, 1971. . . . .$120.00 – 160.00

Savings Bank Series

Characters' faces. The coin is inserted inside the top slot to start the music, 5" x 4½", 1971.

Snoopy, tune, "Superstar," #278-040, $120.00 – 150.00; Linus, tune, "If I Were a Rich Man," #278-043; Lucy, tune, "Second Hand Rose," #278-042; Charlie Brown, tune, "I'd Like to Teach the World to Sing," #278-041; $110.00 – 130.00 each.

Mug Series

The music plays when the key underneath the cup is turned, 4¼", 1971.

Snoopy, tune "Fly Me to the Moon," #276-787, $40.00 – 70.00; Lucy, tune, "Honey," #276-788; Charlie Brown, tune, "Take Me Out to the Ball Game," #276-789; $40.00 – 60.00 each.

• Ice Bucket •

This wonderful and special musical is quite difficult to find. It's been seen in either blue or green, but there may even be more colors. There's a non-musical version as well (#276-934).

8⅛"h, 8" dia., tune, "Love Story," #276-935, 1973, $275.00 – 350.00.

• Wooden •

Schmid musicals are highly desired by serious collectors. The graphics are colorful, and they have a quality that is just downright irresistible.

Value is based on excellent condition, with no chips or missing paint. The music should be bright and clear. The two biplanes have wheels, and there are strings between their wings.

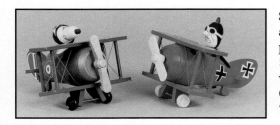

Snoopy flies his green biplane with six red, white, and blue decals, there are strings between the wings and the plane has wheels, 5¼", turn the propeller to hear the tune, "When the Saints Go Marching In," #276-759, 1970, $140.00 – 195.00; the Red Baron flies his red biplane with six black and white decals, there are strings between the wings and the plane has wheels, 6¾" x 8" x 5¼", turn the propeller to hear the tune, "Auf Wiedersehn," #276-763, 1968, $70.00 – 125.00.

Snoopy moves up and down on his doghouse roof, which has a bull's-eye decal on each side, 5¾", tune, "Both Sides Now," #277-352, 1973, $150.00 – 185.00; the Flying Ace sits on his doghouse wearing a felt helmet and goggles with a red ribbon scarf, a red, white, and blue bull's-eye decal is on each side of the roof, 8¼", revolves, tune, "Over There," #276-762, 1968, $85.00 – 125.00; Astronaut Snoopy sits on his white doghouse with an American flag decal on each side of the roof, he wears a plastic helmet over his head and a red ribbon scarf, revolves, 4¼" x 3¾" x 8", tune, "Fly Me to the Moon," #276-764, 1969, $90.00 – 125.00.

Snoopy peers over the roof of this doghouse bank, push his tail and Woodstock comes out to receive a coin, 6", tune, "Raindrops Keep Fallin' on My Head," #276-761, 1970, $140.00 – 195.00; Ferris wheel and bank, Lucy, Charlie Brown, Woodstock, Peppermint Patty, Linus, and Franklin ride a Ferris wheel, the wheel turns when a coin is inserted in the slot, 6½", tune, "Spinning Wheel," #277-408, 1972, $225.00 – 290.00; Musical doghouse and bank, when a coin is inserted in the slot on the roof, Snoopy moves in the doorway of his house and the music plays, Woodstock sits on the roof, 6½", tune, "We've Only Just Begun," #277-353, 1973, $160.00 – 205.00.

Jewelry/Trinket Boxes

The lid opens to reveal the musical mechanism covered in plastic, as well as a small area for jewelry or trinkets, 4¼" x 3" x 2", 1970.

Charlie Brown scratches Snoopy's head and asks Linus, "Who else do you know who's (sic) dog has just been promoted to 'Head Beagle'?", tune, "Camelot," #277-421, $110.00 – 145.00; Schroeder plays a piano, Frieda and Lucy lean against it, Lucy asks, "Do you like Beethoven?", tune, "Emperor Concerto," #277-420, $115.00 – 140.00; Patty, Franklin, Linus, Sally, and Snoopy line up for movie tickets, Sally says to Linus, "You know what I'm doing, Linus? I'm pretending that you're taking me to the movies," Linus replies, "Well, I'm NOT! We just happen to be standing in the same line!", tune, "Who Can I Turn To?," #277-427, $125.00 – 160.00.

Not Pictured
Schroeder, Lucy, Charlie Brown, Patty, Linus, and Snoopy stand on a baseball mound, they're wearing
   sports gear, tune, "Take Me Out to the Ball Game," #277-426. . . . .$125.00 – 160.00

Not Pictured, continued...

Sally and Linus watch a balloon fly skyward, Sally tells the balloon, "Go balloon! Carry your message
of love," tune, "What the World Needs Now," #277-428. . . . .$115.00 – 140.00
Snoopy and Woodstock hold umbrellas as the rain pours, tune, "Raindrops Keep Fallin' on
My Head," #277-429. . . . . .120.00 – 145.00
Snoopy and Woodstock stand in front of the American flag, caption, "America, You're Beautiful,"
tune, "God Bless America," #277-430. . . . . .120.00 – 145.00

Cube

Pictures on five sides, 4" x 3¾". There are usually five different pictures on this musical, but don't be surprised if you find one with two of the same picture. Check to make sure each picture is firmly affixed to the cube. Felt covers the four bottom corners, 1972.

Snoopy engages in different sports, such as golfing, etc., tune, "Superstar," #277-350, $135.00 – 170.00.

Schroeder plays a piano as Snoopy dances, Woodstock flies upside down, Peppermint Patty and Snoopy play base-ball, Charlie Brown scratches Snoopy's head, Snoopy kiss-es Lucy, tune, "I'd Like to Teach the World to Sing," #277-351, $135.00 – 170.00.

Willitts Designs

• Ceramic •

Many of these come in boxes with a picture of the musical. Because the items are relatively recent, there's a good chance you'll find the musical in its box. No collec-tor will turn down a musical because it lacks a box.

Measurement refers to height, unless otherwise noted. Most of these musicals do not revolve; we indicate those that do.

Value is based on excellent to mint condition with no chips, cracks, or missing paint. The tune should play clearly.

The Flying Ace sits on top of his doghouse, the propeller revolves and starts the music, 7", tune, "It's a Long Way to Tipperary," #8106, 1988, $40.00 – 60.00; Lucy leans on Schroeder's piano, 4", tune, "Fur Elise," #8102, 1989, $65.00 – 90.00; Snoopy walks, Woodstock sleeps in his nest atop Snoopy's head, 7¾", tune, "Beautiful Dreamer," #9303, 1989, $35.00 – 47.00.

Snoopy hugs Woodstock, they stand on a blue base captioned "Puppy Love," 6", tune, "Puppy Love," #9304, 1989, $35.00 – 47.00; Snoopy reclines in his red dog dish, 4½", tune, "I'm Sitting on Top of the World," #9305, 1989, $32.00 – 45.00; Snoopy sits on a lavender-colored dictionary as he types, 5", tune, "Nine to Five," #9306, 1989, $55.00 – 65.00.

The Flying Ace sits on billowy clouds, 5½", tune, "It's a Long Way to Tipperary," #9307, 1989, $35.00 – 47.00; Snoopy peers down from atop his doghouse, caption over door "Superbeagle," side caption, "Snoopy," 5¼", tune, "Home, Sweet Home," #9308, 1989, $40.00 – 52.00; Joe Cool leans against his school books with an apple on the top book, caption on base "Joe Scholar," 6", #9309, tune, "Chariots of Fire," #9309, 1989, $45.00 – 65.00.

Beaglescout Snoopy wears a backpack, he walks on grass dotted with flowers, caption on base "Beaglescout," 6½", tune, "Climb Every Mountain," #9310, 1989, $55.00 – 65.00; Easter Beagle wears pink bunny ears, in his basket Woodstock wears blue bunny ears, grass is dotted with flowers and Easter eggs, 6½", tune, "Peter Cottontail," #40001, 1990, $60.00 – 80.00.

Charlie Brown tries to get a red kite airborne, it has green ribbons as its tail, he stands on grass, the base is decorated with small red kites, 7", tune, "Anchors Aweigh," #45001, 1990, $55.00 – 70.00; Sally wears a pink sleeper and holds a sleeping Snoopy under her arm, she walks on a base of billowy clouds, 7½", tune, "Rock a Bye Baby," #45002, 1990, $45.00 – 60.00.

Lucy sits on the grass and holds a football, waiting for someone to kick it, white base caption "Trust Me," 6½", tune, "The Impossible Dream," #45004, 1990, $40.00 – 50.00; Joe Cool stands beside a surfboard, Woodstock sits on top of the board, caption on blue base "Joe Surfer," 7½", tune, "Feelin' Groovy," #45003, 1990, $50.00 – 75.00.

Snoopy wears a blue helmet, he and Woodstock ride a red rollerboard with yellow wheels, the board rotates, 7", tune, "Spinning Wheel," #45008, 1990, $60.00 – 90.00; Snoopy wears an engineer's cap, he reclines on top of a locomotive, 7" long, tune, "Chattanooga Choo-Choo," #45030, 1991, $45.00 – 60.00.

Sports Series, 1989

Snoopy wears a red and white soccer uniform, he prepares to kick a soccer ball, 5½", tune, "Who Can I Turn To?", #9577, $40.00 – 55.00; Snoopy holds a baseball bat and wears a red baseball cap, Woodstock sits on the brim, 7", tune, "Take Me Out to the Ball Game," #9578, $50.00 – 65.00. Snoopy wears a blue tennis visor and holds a tennis racket, 6¼", tune, "In the Good Old Summer Time," #9579; Snoopy holds a hockey stick and wears a red, white, and blue hockey uniform, 6", tune, "Looks Like We Made It," #9580; Snoopy holds a basketball and wears a blue and yellow uniform, 6", tune, "Luck Be a Lady," #9581; $40.00 – 55.00 each. Snoopy the golfer wears a green turtleneck and yellow cap, 5¾", tune, "I Say a Little Prayer," #9582, $45.00 – 60.00.

Convertible Cars

Snoopy drives a red and white Corvette, Woodstock sits on the front hood, license plate caption, "Cool," 10½" long, tune, "Puppy Love," #8105, 1988; Snoopy drives a blue Thunderbird, Woodstock sits on the rear tire, license plate caption, "2 Cool," 10½" long, tune, "Don't Be Cruel," #9360, 1989; $195.00 – 260.00 each.

40th Anniversary

The Peanuts 40th anniversary logo is imprinted on these dated musicals, 1990.

Snoopy wears a red bowtie in this glass snowdome which sits on a ceramic base that depicts the faces of Snoopy, Peppermint Patty, Sally, Lucy, Charlie Brown, Woodstock, and Linus, 5½", tune, "Everything is Beautiful," #19004, $45.00 – 65.00.

Charlie Brown drives a red Volkswagen, its passengers are Lucy, Sally, and Linus, Snoopy reclines on the folded convertible top in the back, and Woodstock sits on the front hood, license plate caption, "1950," 9" long, tune, "King of the Road," #19016, $210.00 – 290.00; Charlie Brown, Snoopy, and Woodstock sit on a red and white sofa with a blue cushion, they wear bowties, 4½", tune, "You Are the Sunshine of My Life," #19014, $90.00 – 130.00.

40th Anniversary Limited Edition, 1,500 numbered sequentially

"40 Years of Happiness," party-goers Charlie Brown, Snoopy, Sally, Linus, Peppermint Patty, Marcie, Schroeder at his piano, and Lucy decorate the first layer of a two-tier birthday cake, Woodstock appears on the circular decoration which bears Charles M. Schulz's signature and a few words about the Peanuts characters, revolves, 7" tall x 6¼" dia., tune, "Love Makes the World Go Round," #19005, 1990, $275.00 – 350.00.

Carousel Horse Series

Snoopy rides a carousel horse that moves up and down, he holds an ice cream cone, Woodstock sits on top of the pole, painted and decorated hardwood base, 10¼" tall, tune, "Loveliest Night of the Year," #7858, 1988, $175.00 – 225.00.

Snoopy, Charlie Brown, Lucy, and Linus ride carousel horses that revolve on a wooden base, the horses move up and down, 9" tall, 6¼" dia., tune, "Tales from the Vienna Woods," #8113, 1988, $275.00 – 350.00.

Peanuts Playland Carousel

The following musicals have an inlaid disk with Snoopy's picture on it. Blue wood base. Be certain each blue wooden leg is included, 1989.

Linus rides a carousel horse that moves up and down, the canopy above him is decorated with Woodstock's likeness and revolves, 10", tune, "In the Good Old Summertime," #9556, $135.00 – 170.00; Snoopy rides a carousel horse which moves up and down against a backdrop of a musical band organ, birds appear on the backdrop, 7", tune, "The Loveliest Night of the Year," #9794, $105.00 – 140.00; Linus and Lucy ride carousel horses that move up and down, 5¾", tune, "Edelweiss," #9558, $85.00 – 130.00.

Linus rides a carousel horse that moves up and down, 4¾", tune, "The Loveliest Night of the Year," #9562; Lucy rides a carousel horse that moves up and down, 4¾", tune, "Carousel Waltz," #9561; Charlie Brown rised a carousel horse that moves up and down, 4¾", tune, "Tales from the Vienna Woods," #9563; $45.00 – 60.00 each. Snoopy rides a carousel horse that moves up and down, 4¾", tune, "When the Saints Go Marching In," #9564, $65.00 – 80.00.

Musicals – Special Editions

To celebrate the 40th anniversary of Peanuts, United Media K.K. (Japan) issued 500 sequentially numbered music boxes. These were given only to Peanuts licensees and some of the staff at United Media and Creative Associates.

"40 Years of Happiness," wooden box, 11¾" x 8" x 4", opens to reveal a mirror on the inside lid, housed inside are bone china figures of Snoopy and his doghouse, Charlie Brown, Sally, Peppermint Patty, Linus, Marcie, Lucy, and Schroeder with his piano, a metal plaque on the front side shows Snoopy hugging Charlie Brown, tune, "Schroeder" by Vince Guaraldi, 1990, $1,100.00 – 1,600.00.

One of the premier music boxes comes from Japan. When American collectors learned of this musical, many made arrangements with friends in Japan, or even made the trip themselves. It's that special.

"Peanuts Merry-Go-Round," porcelain figures of Snoopy, Charlie Brown, Lucy, Linus, and Sally sit on carousel horses, the horses move up and down and revolve while lights flash and music plays, merry-go-round is metal, battery operated, two music tapes are included, octagon shape, 9½" wide, 9½" deep, 14½" tall, Yoshitoku Co. Ltd./Determined Productions, #38001, 1993, $650.00 – 775.00.

"96 Ana Ski Tour," Snoopy stands on a snowboard, this resin musical was available only in Japan on a limited basis to Ana Ski Package customers, 5½" tall, tune, unknown, $250.00 – 325.00.

"Beaglefest July 1993," the Peanuts Collector Club logo of Snoopy reading his newsletter while Woodstock sits in front of him is the focus of this resin musical in honor of Beaglefest, only 500 were produced. Marian Wolff, a Peanuts Collector Club member and music box aficionado, coordinated the project with Willitts Designs from start to finish, 4" tall, tune, "Memories," 1993, $80.00 – 120.00.

Seasonal

Christmas Bells

How better to ring in the festive Christmas season than with a Peanuts bell? As collectors scramble for items made from ceramic or porcelain, these remain all-time favorites. While the bells came in boxes, the boxes really don't affect the value except perhaps to add a few dollars.

Prices are based on excellent to mint condition with no chips or missing paint. The clapper should be intact.

• Schmid •

Not part of a series. Each is a limited edition in a box.

Snoopy lies on his house where he has hung many Christmas stockings, Woodstock stands on a tree nearby, green-tipped handle, 6", 1973, $60.00 – 85.00.

"Perfect Performance," Snoopy ice skates, caption inside bell, 1982, $40.00 – 50.00.

Limited Edition Series

Each is 5¾" tall and comes in a box.

"Christmas 1975," first in the series, Snoopy lies on his doghouse, Woodstock dressed as Santa Claus stands on Snoopy's nose, $35.00 – 50.00. "Christmas 1976," second in the series, Snoopy looks up at Woodstock, who is in his nest admiring a tiny Christmas tree; "Christmas 1977," third in the series, Snoopy lies on top of his home which is decorated with strings of Christmas lights, #279-028; "Christmas 1978," final in the series, Santa Snoopy stands in front of a fireplace, Woodstock is in one of the Christmas stockings; $30.00 – 45.00 each.

Signature Series

Each is a limited edition in a box.

"Waiting for Santa," second in the series (the first celebrates Mother's Day and is not a Christmas theme), Snoopy looks at a tree laden with Christmas stockings, Woodstock sleeps in his nest, 1980, #279-325, $30.00 – 45.00.

• Willitts •

Signature Collection

Limited editions, limited to production exclusively in the year they are dated. Each comes in a box with a certificate of authenticity.

"Christmas 1987," first Limited Edition, Snoopy peers over his doghouse roof, his house, which is the body of the bell, has snow and a Christmas wreath on it, Woodstock wears a Santa hat and sits on Snoopy, dog bone chime, 4¾" tall, #7706, $45.00 – 50.00; "Christmas 1988," second Limited Edition, handle is Snoopy, dressed in top hat, scarf, and top coat, he stands on the bell which bears a design of Snoopy and birds by a lamppost, 5" tall, #8429; "Christmas 1989," third Limited Edition, the handle is Snoopy, clad in knit ski cap and sweater, he carries a Christmas tree, the figure stands on top of a bell that shows Snoopy pulling Woodstock on a sled, 5" tall, #9356; "Christmas 1991," fifth and final Limited Edition, Snoopy and Charlie Brown are led in a sleigh by Woodstock, 5" tall, #44029; $30.00 – 45.00 each.

Not Pictured

"Christmas 1990," fourth Limited Edition, Snoopy wears a Santa cap and sits on his house-shaped bell which is decorated with a string of Christmas lights and snow, 5" tall, #44002 (may not have been issued to the general public). . .$75.00 – 120.00

Determined

Handle is figure of Snoopy as Santa Claus standing on a plain white bell with mistletoe and berry trim around the edge, 4½" tall, Japan, 1987, $20.00 – 35.00.

 # Christmas Glassware

While this category is based solely on items from Japan, their unique appeal makes them quite beloved by collectors who focus on seasonal treasures. What follows is the merest sampling to whet your appetite.

Prices are based on excellent-mint condition in the box. Each box has color graphics.

Beverage Glasses. "Merry Christmas," set of two frosted glasses: Snoopy reclines on his decorated doghouse with a nest full of birds sitting on his stomach as Linus and Sally look on; Eudora, Charlie Brown, Spike, Schroeder, and Marcie watch Snoopy and Woodstock decorate a Christmas tree, Sasaki Glass/Determined Productions, Inc., #M49-1252, 1988, $25.00 – 40.00.

Jar with cork lid: Snoopy, Lucy, and Charlie Brown are snowmen, stars in background, frosted glass, Sasaki Glass/Determined Productions, Inc., #DX147-H038, 1988, $50.00 – 65.00. Goblet: "Merry Christmas," Snoopy and Charlie Brown admire a Christmas tree, gold rim, Sasaki Glass/Determined Productions, Inc., #DX147-H039, late 1980s, $15.00 – 24.00. Treasure box: heart-shaped container with Snoopy placing a star on a Christmas tree, Sasaki Glass/Determined Productions, Inc., #DX100-5195, 1988, $35.00 – 50.00. Soda Glass (V-shaped): "Merry Christmas," Snoopy reclines inside a Christmas wreath, gold rim, Sasaki Glass/Determined Productions, Inc., #DX98-5193, 1988, $15.00 – 24.00. Vase: Santa Snoopy and Woodstock gaze at the moon and stars, boot shape, gold rim, Sasaki Glass/Determined Productions, Inc., #DX4-5184, 1988, $12.00 – 22.00.

Juice Glasses: "Snoopy," set of two, three pictures of Snoopy holding a symbol of the Christmas season, Determined Productions, Inc., #34067-7, 1989, $12.00 – 20.00.

Christmas Cups, Mugs, and Steins

Collectors love anything having to do with Christmas. All items are ceramic and were available in the U.S. unless otherwise noted. The dimension indicates height.

Value is based on mint, unused condition. There should be no chips or paint missing from the design. Lettering should be clear and legible.

• Manufacturer Unknown •

"Macy's Parade 1987," Snoopy dressed as an ice skater is the featured balloon in the parade (originally came with hard candy inside the cup), 3¾", 1987, $7.00 – 10.00.

• Determined •

Cups & Mugs

"Noel" (produced by Anchor Hocking/Fire-King), red and green with Snoopy holding a large Christmas wreath and Woodstock pulling its red ribbon, a matching bowl was issued, $6.00 – 9.00. "Merry Christmas 1976," Linus, Charlie Brown, Woodstock, Peppermint Patty, Snoopy, and Lucy have symbols of Christmas in their hands (Another Determined Production for Joy's, Inc.), 3½", 1976; "Merry

Christmas 1977," Lucy, Snoopy in a Santa cap, Woodstock in his nest, Sally with a teddy bear, and Charlie Brown with a large candy cane (Another Determined Production for the Dupont Collection Ltd.), 3½", 1977; Santa Snoopy just left some presents down a chimney of a house as he pilots his red airplane, Charlie Brown's face appears in the window, 3½"; $12.00 – 20.00 each.

Snoopy wears a red nightgown and cap as he is awakened by Santa Woodstock who is delivering some gifts, 3½", $12.00 – 20.00. Lucy holds gifts and a Christmas stocking, Woodstock is perched in his nest on top of the tree, Snoopy is in a gift box just unwrapped by Charlie Brown, 3½", #1304, 1980; Snoopy carries and unwraps a big gift, Woodstock watches as the gift finally reveals a nest with a tree inside it, Woodstock is in the nest, 3½", #1215, 1977; Snoopy and Woodstock sleep next to a fireplace decorated with Christmas stockings and a wreath, the entire design is circled by a large wreath, 3½", #1221, 1975; $10.00 – 15.00 each.

Set of two mugs with Snoopy wearing a red (green) Santa cap and peering out of a red (green) Christmas wreath, Japan, 3⅜", mid 1980s, $20.00 – 30.00.

Marcie, Linus, Peppermint Patty, Sally, Charlie Brown, Snoopy, and Lucy flank a Christmas tree topped by Woodstock, accompanied by a lift-off lid with a three-dimensional sitting Snoopy as Santa, captions on the lid, "Snoopy" and "Merry Christmas," Japan, 3⅜", #34065-1, 1988; Charlie Brown holds a wreath, Schroeder holds a cupcake, Lucy wears a party hat, Snoopy places a star on the tree, Linus holds a tree branch, and Sally has a stocking in her hands, accompanied by a lift-off lid with a two-dimensional raised design of Snoopy's face in the middle of a Christmas wreath, caption on lid, "Snoopy on Christmas Day," Japan, 3⅜", #03436-3, 1989; $16.00 – 24.00 each.

Two scenes, Snoopy holds a gift over his head for Woodstock who is in his nest, Woodstock snuggles on the arm of a large snowman, blue handle, Japan, 3⅜", #87N/144-1, 1980s, $12.00 – 18.00; two scenes, Snoopy and Woodstock flank a decorated Christmas tree, Snoopy holds a bell in one hand, reverse has birds by the fireplace with gifts, pink handle, Japan, 3⅜", #87N/144-2, late 1980s, $16.00 – 24.00.

Set of two mini mugs with the same caption, "A friend can be a few snowflakes that you put together," Snoopy holds hands with a snowman, Snoopy leads his friend (the snowman) by a blue scarf connecting them, blue and red trim, 2⅛", Japan, #27534-5, late 1980s, $10.00 – 20.00.

Steins

Each of the following has the date printed as part of the design. Each is ceramic and stands 3⅞".

"Merry Christmas 1975," Snoopy is on his house holding the reins to Woodstock, Charlie Brown, Linus, and Lucy walk by singing, 1975, $38.00 – 45.00; "Merry Christmas 1976," Snoopy rides in a sleigh as Woodstock guides it, several wrapped packages are nearby, 1976, $28.00 – 33.00; "Merry Christmas 1977," Snoopy receives help from Woodstock in decorating their Christmas tree, Charlie Brown admires their work, $20.00 – 30.00.

"Merry Christmas 1978," Snoopy Santa Claus, Charlie Brown, and Woodstock are by the fireplace with Christmas stockings, wreath, gifts, and Christmas tree; "Merry Christmas 1979," Snoopy sits in the middle of a large Christmas wreath decorated with red berries and a large red bow; "Merry Christmas 1980," it's snowing and Snoopy is on top of his doghouse wearing a Santa cap and holding a large yellow box tied with green ribbon, Woodstock is flying in some mistletoe to Snoopy; $20.00 – 30.00 each.

"Merry Christmas 1981," Snoopy as Rudolph the red-nosed reindeer, Peppermint Patty, Schroeder, Marcie, Sally, Linus, Lucy, and Charlie Brown wear reindeer antlers, they're all ready to pull Santa Woodstock on his sled; "Merry Christmas 1982," Snoopy and Woodstock decorate their Christmas tree with several red bows, Lucy looks at Charlie Brown who holds the platter of turkey, Woodstock stands in front of the fireplace; "Merry Christmas 1983," Santa Snoopy prepares to pack his gifts, his bird elves assist in wrapping presents and making toys; $20.00 – 30.00 each.

• Willitts •

Mugs

Each is made from stoneware. Although the mugs came boxed, neither the absence nor the presence of boxes influences the value.

"Have a Cool Yule," four-piece set, Santa Snoopy is the handle of each, all are the same design, 3½", #7865, 1987, in box, $25.00 – 40.00.

Snoopy rides a sleigh guided by Woodstock, 3½", #8444, 1988; Snoopy wears a green and red ski cap as he skis, Woodstock sits on the tassel of Snoopy's cap, 3½", #44035; "Peace on Earth," repeating pattern of Snoopy as Santa Claus sitting on top of globe, Woodstock stands on Snoopy's foot, 3½", #44036; $6.00 – 8.00 each.

Christmas (Winter) Music Boxes

• Glory Co., Ltd. •

Only a few Christmas/Winter musicals came from Japan. Although packaged in a box, this container does not affect the value one way or another. There should be no paper tears on the cardboard musical, and Snoopy should move freely when the music is played. The ceramic musical should have no chips or missing paint, and Snoopy should move back and forth inside the door. The light should work.

A round cardboard box houses Santa Snoopy who moves around when the music is played, 3½" dia., tune "Jingle Bells," #SNO(C), 1990, $25.00 – 42.00.

Snoopy moves in and out of a house that lights up by an electrical plug, 6¾" tall, tune, "Santa Claus is Coming to Town," 1991, $220.00 – 275.00.

• Schmid •

Products with a Christmas theme are perennial favorites, and Schmid musicals pretty much top the list of "must haves." The musicals listed below are treasures. Collectors not able to obtain these musicals when first released have hunted for them ever since. All Schmid Christmas musicals are figural.

Prices are based on mint condition; the plain packing box is superfluous. There should be no chips, nicks, or missing paint. All have a very high-gloss ceramic finish. The tunes should be fairly clear, but be advised: the music may sound tinny in older musicals.

Schmid began its series of Limited Edition Christmas musicals in 1980, and they quickly caught on with fans.

Limited Editions

Each is ceramic and revolves on a plastic base. 15,000 numbered sequentially of each were issued.

First Limited Edition, "Waiting for Santa," Snoopy looks up at Woodstock in his nest, red, yellow, and green stockings hang in Woodstock's tree, 8¾" tall, tune, "Oh Christmas Tree," #289-000, 1980 (This is a particularly delicate musical; inspect the branches for any cracks or breaks.), $170.00 – 235.00. Second Limited Edition, "A Christmas Wish," Snoopy sleeps on his doghouse which is covered with Christmas stockings, 7" tall, tune, "Silent Night," #289-001, 1981; Third Limited Edition, "Perfect Performance," Snoopy ice skates, he wears a red and yellow knit scarf and ski cap, 7½" tall, tune, "Skater's Waltz," #289-002, 1982; $135.00 – 195.00 each.

Non-Limited Editions

Each is ceramic and rotates on a plastic or metal base unless indicated.

Snoopy, Belle, and Woodstock twirl independently as they ice skate, 4¼" tall, tune, "Skater's Waltz," #253-706, 1984, $175.00 – 245.00; Snoopy on green skis, rocks back and forth, Woodstock is on a sled, 5½", tune, "Let it Snow," #253-720, 1984, $125.00 – 170.00; Snoopy sits, wearing a green and red scarf and knit cap, next to him is a green package tied with a red bow with the word "Joy" on it, 4¾" tall, tune, "We Wish You a Merry Christmas," #253-721, 1984, $75.00 – 115.00.

Lucy wears a green dress, angel wings, and a halo, she holds a red songbook, 6", tune, "Silent Night," #253-722, 1984, $135.00 – 190.00; Santa Snoopy moves up and down in a snow-laden chimney (this musical does not revolve), 8" tall, tune, "Up On the Housetop," #253-723, 1984, $175.00 – 250.00.

Charlie Brown, Snoopy, Sally, Woodstock, Linus, and Lucy stand around a large tree, they move counterclockwise as the tree moves clockwise, 7¾" tall, tune, "Joy to the World," #253-724, 1984, $325.00 – 425.00.

Snoopy and Woodstock sit on a sled which moves up and down as the box rotates, 5¾" tall, tune, "Winter Wonderland," #417-000, 1985, $125.00 – 180.00; Charlie Brown sits next to a red box tied with a white ribbon, the card reads "To Charlie Brown," 5¼" tall, tune, "Joy to the World," #417-001, 1985, $90.00 – 125.00; Snoopy gets ready to place a star on top of a tall Christmas tree, he stands on Lucy, who stands on poor ol' Charlie Brown, 7" tall, tune, "We Wish You a Merry Christmas," #417-004, 1986, $175.00 – 240.00.

Santa Snoopy stands in front of his house and holds a wrapped gift, Woodstock wears a Santa hat and sits on Snoopy's decorated doghouse, 6¼" tall, tune, "Deck the Halls," #417-005, 1986, $125.00 – 180.00; Santa Snoopy holds his pack and peers down at Woodstock, who has opened a red package, Woodstock twirls around independently (this musical does not revolve), 4½" tall, tune, "Here Comes Santa Claus," #418-001, 1985, $110.00 – 160.00.

Snoopy wears a cap and scarf as he looks upon a Christmas tree decorated with birds, Woodstock sits on top and revolves independently, this musical wasn't officially released, but a few of them "escaped," 7" tall, tune, "Oh Christmas Tree," 1986, $275.00 – 450.00.

• Willitts Designs •

Some of the musicals have moving parts while others revolve.

Snoopy wears a red, green, and white stocking cap, he sits and watches Woodstock ice skate on the ice in his supper dish, Woodstock revolves, ceramic, 4½" tall, tune, "Love Makes the World Go Round," #7845, 1987, in box, $55.00 – 70.00; without box, $50.00 – 65.00; Snoopy wears a Santa hat and red turtleneck sweater captioned "Joe Cool," he stands next to a large yellow star, porcelain snow on pine base, 5" tall, does not revolve, tune, "Let It Snow," #7850, 1987, in box, $45.00 – 60.00; without box $40.00 – 55.00.

Snoopy throws a snowball at two birds wearing stocking caps, the birds move up and down in an igloo, ceramic, 6¼" tall, tune, "Let It Snow," #7867, 1987, in box, $95.00 – 160.00, without box, $90.00 – 155.00.

Snoopy ice skates back and forth for an appreciative Woodstock perched on a snowman's hat, ceramic, 4" tall, tune, "Skater's Waltz," #7897, 1987, in box, $65.00 – 80.00; without box $60.00 – 75.00.

Linus, Snoopy, Charlie Brown, and Lucy ride revolving carousel horses, snow on plastic base, 6" tall, tune, "Carousel Waltz," #8111, 1988, in box, $75.00 – 95.00; without box, $60.00 – 70.00.

Musical Motion Water Scope, Lucy, Snoopy, and Charlie Brown revolve in a winter scene, resin, 8" tall, tune, "Skater's Waltz," #8131, 1988; Lucy, Snoopy, and Charlie Brown revolve around a Christmas tree topped by Woodstock, ceramic, 6" tall, tune, "Skater's Waltz," #8436, 1988; in box, $75.00 – 105.00 each; without box, $70.00 – 100.00 each.

Snoopy wears a knit cap and rests on his doghouse roof, Woodstock rests on top of a green ribbon which decorates the side of Snoopy's roof, ceramic, 5½" tall, does not revolve, tune, "We Wish You a Merry Christmas," #8437, 1989, in box, $50.00 – 65.00; without box, $45.00 – 60.00; Snoopy, Lucy, and Charlie Brown wear ice skates and revolve around glass votive candleholder, ceramic, 4½" tall, tune, "Let It Snow," #8622, 1988, in box, $75.00 – 105.00; without box, $70.00 – 100.00; Snoopy wears a blue turtleneck sweater and stands next to a large snowman with a cap and scarf, ceramic, 5⅛" tall, does not revolve, tune, "Let It Snow," #9684, 1989, in box, $65.00 – 75.00; without box, $60.00 – 70.00; Snoopy and Woodstock wear knit caps as they ride downhill on a sled, ceramic, 6" tall, does not revolve, tune, "Winter Wonderland," #9685, 1989, in box, $50.00 – 85.00; without box, $45.00 – 80.00.

Santa Snoopy sits and holds a large sack of presents, ceramic, 4¾" tall, does not revolve, tune, "Jolly Old St. Nicholas," #9687, 1989, in box, $43.00 – 53.00; without box, $38.00 – 45.00; Snoopy wears knit cap and holds Woodstock while sitting on the roof of his house, the roof has a string of Christmas lights, does not revolve, ceramic, 7" tall, tune, "Jingle Bells," #9686, 1989, in box, $50.00 – 85.00; without box, $45.00 – 80.00; Snoopy wears knit cap and scarf as he sings a Christmas carol for Woodstock, ceramic, 5¾" tall, does not rotate, tune, "Joy to the World," #9688, 1989, in box, $45.00 – 65.00; without box, $40.00 – 60.00.

Snoopy and Woodstock wear Santa hats as they hug one another, does not revolve, ceramic, 6" tall, tune, "White Christmas," #44010, 1990, in box, $40.00 – 55.00; without box, $35.00 – 50.00; Snoopy gets ready to place an ornament on a Christmas tree that has Woodstock on top, ceramic, 6½" tall, does not revolve, tune, "Joy to the World," #44007, 1990, in box, $75.00 – 105.00; without box, $70.00 – 100.00; Snoopy is a Santa snowman wearing a Santa cap, ceramic, 6¾" tall, does not revolve, tune, "Have Yourself a Merry Little Christmas," #44008, 1990, in box, $40.00 – 55.00; without box, $35.00 – 50.00.

Santa Snoopy sits and peers at a globe of the world while Woodstock sits in a little train car which revolves around the base, plastic, 6" tall, tune, "Santa Claus is Coming to Town," #44024, 1990, in box, $90.00 – 110.00; without box, $85.00 – 105.00.

Not Pictured
Creche with revolving star, includes porcelain figures of Snoopy, Linus, Lucy, Charlie Brown, Sally, Schroeder (with Woodstock), and baby Jesus, wood, 10½" wide x 5" deep x 8" tall, tune, "O Little Town of Bethlehem," #440290, 1990 (see photo in Figurines – Ceramic & Porcelain) . . . .$275.00 – 425.00

Musical Plastic Snowfalls with Revolving Figures, 5½" tall

Snoopy decorates a Christmas tree while Woodstock flies above, tune, "We Wish You a Merry Christmas," #9594, 1989; Snoopy rides in a sleigh led by Woodstock, tune, "Jingle Bells," #9595, 1989; Snoopy and Woodstock play ice hockey, tune, "Let it Snow," #9596, 1989; in box, $70.00 – 95.00 each; without box, $65.00 – 90.00 each.

Musical Snowfalls on Porcelain Bases, 5½" tall

These do not revolve.

Snoopy wears a knit cap and rests on top of his snow-laden house, tune, "Beautiful Dreamer," #8110, 1988; Snoopy wears knit cap and ice skates, tune, "Skater's Waltz," #8441, 1988; in box, $50.00 – 65.00 each; without box, $45.00 – 60.00 each.

• Signature Collection •

Each Signature Collection music box comes with a certificate of authenticity, and production was limited to the year of issue. The first Signature Snowfall musical was offered in 1988. All have the year printed as part of the design.

First Limited Edition, Snoopy peers over doghouse rooftop to watch Woodstock, who sits on a decorated Christmas tree which revolves, ceramic, 5" tall, tune, "We Wish You A Merry Christmas," #7704, 1987; Second Limited Edition, Snoopy in top hat, stands next to revolving lamplight with Woodstock, ceramic, 7" tall, tune, "God Rest Ye Merry Gentlemen," #8428, 1988; in box, $75.00 – 90.00 each; without box, $65.00 – 70.00 each. Third Limited Edition, Snoopy and Woodstock are dressed in winter clothing, Snoopy carries a Christmas tree over one shoulder while pulling Woodstock on a sled with the other hand, does not revolve, ceramic, 6" tall, tune, "Oh Tannenbaum," #9351, 1989, in box, $70.00 – 85.00; without box, $65.00 – 80.00.

Sixth Limited Edition, Snoopy wears Santa cap and watches Woodstock decorate the little Christmas tree on his doghouse roof, does not revolve, resin, 6" tall, tune, "Winter Wonderland," #44041, 1992, in box, $70.00 – 85.00; without box, $65.00 – 80.00.

Not Pictured
Fourth Limited Edition, Snoopy sits on his decorated doghouse, he holds onto Woodstock who acts as a reindeer, does not revolve, ceramic, 7¾" tall, tune, "Up on the Housetop," #44006, 1990. . . . . .in box, $70.00 – 85.00
. . . . .without box, 65.00 – 80.00
Fifth Limited Edition, Charlie Brown, Snoopy, and Woodstock share a ride on a red sled, does not revolve, resin, 5¼" tall, tune, "Jingle Bell Rock," #44028, 1991. . . .in box, 70.00 – 85.00
. . . . .without box, 65.00 – 80.00

Snowfalls

5½" tall. They do not revolve.

First Limited Edition, Snoopy in top hat stands next to a lamplight, tune, "We Wish You a Merry Christmas," #8442, 1988; Second Limited Edition, Snoopy carries a Christmas tree over one shoulder, tune, "Santa Claus is Coming to Town," #9352, 1989; in box, $45.00 – 55.00 each; without box, $40.00 – 50.00 each.

Third Limited Edition, Snoopy sits on his decorated doghouse, tune, "Up On the Housetop," #44005, 1990; Fourth Limited Edition, Charlie Brown, Snoopy, and Woodstock share a ride on a red sled, tune, "We Wish You a Merry Christmas," #44030, 1991; in box, $45.00 – 55.00 each; without box, $40.00 – 50.00 each.

Christmas Ornaments

• Danbury Mint •

Series of 12 three-dimensional plastic Christmas ornaments

Issued 1991 – 1992, this 12-piece series was popular with fans, particularly those who collect all the characters because their collections were enriched by Sally, Peppermint Patty, and the rarely-seen Marcie, Spike, and Pig Pen.

In addition to the usual copyright information, each ornament carries "© 1990 MBI."

Ornaments should be in pristine condition with no marks, chips, or discoloration. They were mailed in a plain box, which does not add to the value in any way.

The ornaments were sold as a complete series with the recipient receiving them every month or two. The value given here is for a complete 12-piece set. A plain red box in which to store the ornaments was provided once the series was complete. This container is of no consequence to the value of the set.

Value of 12-piece set in mint condition: $300.00 – 350.00.

Lucy wears a Santa cap and holds a clump of mistletoe; Linus as Santa holds his blanket in one hand and a package in the other; Pig Pen is wrapped up in a string of Christmas lights.

Snoopy pops out of a wrapped package with a gift tag inscribed, "Don't Open Until Christmas;" Charlie Brown is all wrapped up in Christmas ribbon and wrapping paper.

Peppermint Patty sleeps at her school desk, a book, "The Story of Christmas," is on top of her head; Schroeder plays his piano, it has a Christmas tree on it and is decorated with holly; Marcie holds a banner with the words "Merry Christmas" on it.

Snoopy as Joe Cool leans against his house, which is decorated with a string of Christmas lights, Woodstock, also wearing sunglasses, sits on the roof.

Woodstock holds a huge Christmas ornament ball; Spike's head is part of the decorations on a Christmas cactus; Sally sits and writes a letter to "Dear Santa."

• Determined •

Determined's Christmas ornaments, particularly their figurines and bells, are highly prized treasures which are becoming more and more difficult to locate.

In the late 1970s and very early 1980s, high-end department stores, such as Bullock's on the West Coast, would decorate trees with various ceramic ornaments. Imagine the smiles of weary shoppers greeted by such a display ... Snoopy to the rescue!

Some of the figurines were a bit rough; the finish was not glossy, and they didn't have the detail we've come to expect from Determined. But this rarely dampens the zeal of ardent collectors who one day hope to own every Peanuts ornament ever made.

The Musician, International, Adventurer, Farmer, Bicentennial, and Junk Food series are the crème de la crème. Their high-gloss captures the light, with perfectly-sculpted faces making Christmas — or any time, for that matter — the happiest time of the year.

Most ornaments were made in the likenesses of Snoopy, Woodstock, and Charlie Brown and his friends. Loyal fans of the less popular Spike and Belle (Snoopy's brother and sister) will find a few representations of both, notably in the Western series.

Some ornaments are extremely scarce. The International series, with 12 basic ornaments, also includes many unusual extras. Some, such as Snoopy dressed as an English king or an Arab, were released only in Europe. Once in awhile you may get lucky, and find an ornament with a Hawaiian theme, such as Snoopy in hula attire. Others, notably the Farmer series, just aren't around. People who have them won't let go, and who can blame them!

The flat ceramic ornaments are unique and they, too, are very much desired by collectors. While they're not quite as popular as the three-dimensional figures, they have all the markings of a wonderful collectible. They maintain the same high standard found in Determined's best figurals, only as two-dimensionals.

While Determined's ceramic ornaments are very much in demand, the wooden ornaments are not nearly as avidly sought. Some collectors like to have all the ornaments, and it's a good idea to pick them up when you can, but the wooden ornaments will never make the same ranks as the ceramic ones. One good thing, though: they won't break if they fall from your Christmas tree!

A few unbreakable satin balls were issued. Each is quite colorful, and each carries a holiday caption. While these were sold boxed, not having the box does not detract greatly from their value.

Determined stopped producing ornaments in 1982, but they went out in style; the Junk Food series and dated 1982 ornaments were hallmarks of this company's creativity. Sadly, many landed in stores which purchased items for pennies on the dollar, and collectors never saw them.

Determined's bells reflect the same attention to artistic detail. Made in three sizes — micro, mini, and standard — these colorful ornaments feature carefully painted scenes, sometimes accompanied by a wise or witty caption.

Prices are based on mint condition. There should be no scratches or chips. The bottom label on the figurines should be glued firmly to the base. Lettering should be legible, and the original cord should be intact.

Unless otherwise noted, ornaments did not come packaged. Each was sold individually and not as a series or group.

• Ceramic Three-Dimensional •

Each is approx. 2½" to 3¼" tall.

Figural Christmas theme

Six in the series, Series #1028, 1975

Snoopy carries a red gift pack over one shoulder, #1031; Charlie Brown carries a white box tied with red ribbon, #1064; Lucy holds mistletoe, #1065; Linus holds a small Christmas tree, #1066; Snoopy holds a red and green Christmas stocking, #1067; Woodstock wears a Santa hat, #1068; $25.00 – 35.00 each.

Snoopy & Woodstock Christmas

Six in the series, Series #1029, 1975

Snoopy holds a Christmas tree over one shoulder, #1032; Snoopy holds a large Christmas wreath in front of him, #1033; Snoopy stands and holds a large candy cane, #1034; Santa Snoopy rings Christmas bells, #1035; Snoopy lies on a white package tied with red ribbon, #1036; Woodstock sits on a red package tied with green ribbon, #1037; $25.00 – 35.00 each.

Snoopy Sports

Six in the original series, with an addition (surfer), Series #1080, 1975

Snoopy golfer, #1081; Snoopy skier, #1082; Snoopy carries a football and wears helmet, #1083, $35.00 – 48.00 each; Snoopy baseball player, #1084, $40.00 – 52.00; Snoopy Olympic runner, #1085; Snoopy tennis player, #1086; Snoopy surfer, #1152 (this ornament is not officially a part of the #1080 series, but because it is sports-related, we include it); $35.00 – 48.00 each.

Snoopy Adventurer Series

Six in the series, Series #1140, 1975

Snoopy as a clown, #1141; Snoopy as Robin Hood, #1142; Snoopy as a bandit, #1143; Snoopy as a Native American, #1144; Snoopy as Davy Crockett, #1146; Snoopy as Sherlock Holmes, #1145; $45.00 – 65.00 each.

Bicentennial

Three in the series, Series #1099, 1975

Snoopy with a drum, #1096; Snoopy holding a paper American flag, #1097; Snoopy wearing an Uncle Sam hat, #1098; $65.00 – 80.00 each.

Peanuts Musicians

Six in the series, Series #1700, 1976

Front row: Charlie Brown plays a drum, #1701; Peppermint Patty plays a guitar, #1702; Lucy plays a trumpet, #1703; back row: Linus plays a saxophone, #1704; Schroeder plays a piano, #1705; Snoopy plays the bass violin, #1706; $40.00 – 50.00 each.

Cable Car Series

Four in the series, Series #1330

Snoopy kicks up his heels on a red cable car, #1335; Snoopy wears a Santa hat, sits on a green cable car, #1336; $32.00 – 45.00 each. Woodstock sits on top of red cable car, #1337; Woodstock wears a Santa hat, sits on a green cable car, #1338; $28.00 – 41.00 each.

International Snoopy

Twelve in the series released in the United States, Series #8860

Snoopy as a Spanish bullfighter, #8861; Snoopy as a Mexican wearing traditional sombrero and serape, #8862; Snoopy as a Bavarian German holding root beer stein, #8863; Snoopy as a British Palace Guard, #8864; Snoopy as a French painter wearing a red beret and holding a palette, #8865; Snoopy as a Scottish bagpipe player, #8866; $45.00 – 57.00 each.

Snoopy as an Italian gondolier, #8867; Snoopy wearing a traditional Japanese kimono, #8868; Snoopy as an East Indian in a turban, #8873; Snoopy as a Scandinavian Viking, #8878; Snoopy dressed in Transylvanian top hat and formal cape, #8879; Snoopy as a British gentleman in black bowler and bowtie, with umbrella, #8880; $45.00 – 57.00 each.

The following ornaments were available in Europe and were produced by a sub-licensee for Determined.

Snoopy wears a green French beret and pink scarf with green dots; Snoopy as a British king, wears a cape and crown, #8882; Snoopy, as a Dutchman, holds a yellow tulip and wears wooden shoes, #8875; $200.00 – 275.00 each.

Snoopy as a Roman soldier, #8874; Snoopy dressed in a Chinese blue robe and red hat; Snoopy as an Arab, in traditional burnoose; $200.00 – 275.00 each.

Snoopy wears a white judo robe tied with a black sash; Snoopy dressed to go on a safari, wears a jacket and pith helmet; Snoopy dressed as a Greek with a black blouse and red cap; Snoopy wears a hula skirt and a large red flower on his head; $200.00 – 275.00 each.

The following ornaments are Snoopy in occupation or hobby attire.

Snoopy as a vaudeville performer; Snoopy as a Beaglescout master; $200.00 – 275.00 each.

Snoopy as a construction worker; Snoopy as a sheriff with green vest; Snoopy as a lifeguard; Snoopy, as a graduate, wears a black cap and gown and holds diploma in one hand; $200.00 – 275.00 each.

Not Pictured

Snoopy as a surgeon wears coat, cap, mask, and stethoscope around his neck. . . . .$200.00 – 275.00
Snoopy as a fireman wears a red hat, and holds an axe with both hands. . . . . .200.00 – 275.00
Snoopy as a bus driver wears a blue uniform and cap. . . . . .200.00 – 275.00
Snoopy as a movie director sits in a director's chair, he wears a red cap and holds a megaphone in
    one hand. . . . . .200.00 – 275.00
Snoopy as an astronaut holds his helmet. . . . . .200.00 – 275.00
Snoopy as a businessman wears a black jacket with blue tie and holds a briefcase. . . . . .200.00 – 275.00
Snoopy as Superman. . . . . .200.00 – 275.00
Snoopy wears a blue jogging outfit. . . . . .200.00 – 275.00

General Series

Six in the series, Series #1897

Belle wears a pink dress dotted with dark pink, and holds a yellow flower; Snoopy, on roller skates, wears a red shirt captioned with "7," and tennis visor; Snoopy reclines on a rainbow; the Flying Ace sits; Spike wears his standard blue overalls and brown hat; Woodstock sits in his nest; $24.00 – 36.00 each.

Red Santa Cap Series

Six in the series, Series #1896

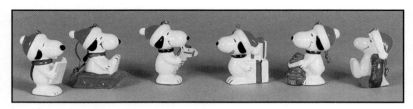

Snoopy holds a yellow songbook with holly design; Snoopy sits on a red sled and wears Santa hat; Snoopy rides a stick horse with red stripes, he wears a Santa hat; Snoopy stands in front of two white boxes, one tied with green ribbon, the other with red ribbon; Snoopy stands behind a decorated Christmas tree; Woodstock sits in a Christmas wreath; $24.00 – 36.00 each.

Snoopy & Woodstock Vehicles

Six in the series, Series #1315, 1979

Snoopy in a steam-engine locomotive; Woodstock in a fire engine; Snoopy in a motorboat with a Christmas tree; Woodstock on a motorcycle; Snoopy in a blue convertible, decorated with a Christmas wreath; the Flying Ace in a red airplane, holding a gift sack; $32.00 – 38.00 each.

Western

Six in the series, Series #1901

Spike wears a ten-gallon hat and blue chaps; Snoopy rides a hobby horse; Belle wears a pink and red outfit with green holster; Snoopy as a sheriff; Snoopy sits on a rock and plays guitar; Woodstock sits on a blue cowboy boot; $24.00 – 36.00 each.

Dated 1977 — Dupont Collection

Series #1850. Boxed in red and white, with clear plastic in front to view the ornament. Four in the series. These ornaments were available at discount houses in the early 1980s and sold for pennies on the dollar.

Snoopy sits and holds a candy cane, "Merry Christmas," #1851; Snoopy sits and holds a poinsettia, "Merry Christmas," #1852; Snoopy lies on his doghouse, with a wreath on the side of the roof, "Merry Christmas," #1853; Snoopy hugs Woodstock, each wears a stocking cap, #1854; without box, $12.00 – 22.00 each, in box, $15.00 – 25.00 each.

Dated 1978

Six in the series. An additional two, the sleigh and wreath, are pictured but not considered a formal part of the series.

Snoopy rides in a sleigh, "Merry Christmas"; Snoopy lies on Christmas wreath with large red bow, "Happy Holidays"; Snoopy poses on a red and green drum, "Merry Christmas"; Santa Snoopy is halfway in a chimney, carrying a sack full of gifts, "Merry Christmas"; $40.00 – 52.00 each.

Snoopy lies on the word "NOEL;" Woodstock holds a large green box with white dots and red ribbon, "Merry Christmas;" Snoopy holds a candy cane "North Pole" sign, "Merry Christmas;" Snoopy wears angel wings, halo, and red robe, "Merry Christmas;" $40.00 – 52.00 each.

Dated 1979

Series #1370, six in the series, some are duplicate designs of 1977 and 1978.

Not Pictured

Snoopy sits and holds a candy cane, "Merry Christmas," #1371. . . . .$40.00 – 52.00
Snoopy lies on his doghouse, a wreath is on the side of the roof, "Merry Christmas," #1372. . . . . .40.00 – 52.00
Snoopy sits and hugs Woodstock, each wears a stocking cap, "Merry Christmas," #1373. . . . . .40.00 – 52.00
Snoopy lies on large Christmas wreath with red bow, "Happy Holidays," #1374. . . . . .40.00 – 52.00
Santa Snoopy is halfway in a chimney, carrying a sack full of gifts, "Merry Christmas," #1375. . . . . . . .40.00 – 52.00
Woodstock holds a large green box with white dots and red ribbon, "Merry Christmas," #1376. . . . . . . .40.00 – 52.00

Merry Christmas — Dated 1980

Series #1998, six in the series

Snoopy and Woodstock, dressed warmly as they carol out-side; Woodstock stands inside a red and green boot; Woodstock sits on a star; Santa Snoopy holds a Christmas stocking; Snoopy stands inside a green and red Christmas boot, he hugs Wood-stock; Snoopy reclines on a half moon; $24.00 – 32.00 each.

Dated 1981

Series #1895, six in the series

Snoopy sits on a green package tied with red ribbon, "Happy Holidays;" Woodstock rides in a red sleigh, he wears a Santa hat, "Noel;" Snoopy as Santa in front of his gift sack, Woodstock peeks out from the sack, "Merry Christmas;" Woodstock as Santa holds a candy cane, "Joy;" Snoopy in front of a candy cane, "Noel;" Snoopy sits and wears Santa cap, holds a large green ornament; $14.00 – 22.00 each.

Dated 1982

Series #1906, six in the series

Belle wears a red winter coat trimmed in faux white fur as she car-ols, "Noel;" Peppermint Patty wears a green coat and hat and holds a gingerbread cookie, "Noel;" Woodstock stands next to a snowman, "Seasons Greetings;" Spike wears a green, red, and yellow court jester's outfit, "Merry Christmas;" Charlie Brown wears a red winter coat trimmed in white faux fur, he holds a gift, "Seasons Greetings;" Snoopy wears a Santa hat and rides on a reindeer, "Merry Christ-mas;" $22.00 – 32.00 each.

Junk Food Series

Series #1905, six in the series, 1985

Snoopy lies on top of a hamburger sandwich bun; Snoopy with french fries; Snoopy lies on top of a hot dog sand-wich; Snoopy holds a large root beer cup; Snoopy sits on a piece of berry pie; Snoopy sits against a large chocolate ice cream cone; $38.00 – 48.00 each.

Mascots

Each character's head is rather large in proportion to his/her body. Each has a very glossy finish. While each may have come in a red and white box, the top price pre-vails with or without the box because they are extremely hard to locate, 1970s.

Charlie Brown wears a baseball cap and his orange shirt with black zigzag, $95.00 – 140.00; Snoopy sits, $110.00 – 170.00; Sally wears a pink dress with ribbon in her hair, $95.00 – 140.00; Linus wears his traditional green and blue striped shirt, holds a red blanket, and sucks his thumb, $95.00 – 140.00.

Lucy smiles and wears a pink dress (dress color variations include lavender); $95.00 – 140.00.

Not Pictured
Peppermint Patty wears her traditional green shirt and brown sandals . .$95.00 – 140.00

Farmer Series

This is a series which wasn't issued to the general public, but some very fortunate collectors have managed to accumulate them through dedication and just plain luck, 1970s.

Sally holds carrots, $170.00 – 250.00; Snoopy wears blue overalls and red neckerchief with blue dots, $190.00 – 270.00; Peppermint Patty holds a shovel, $170.00 – 250.00.

Not Pictured
Charlie Brown holds a rake. . . . .$170.00 – 250.00
Lucy wears a red kerchief over her head and carries a basket under one arm. . . . .170.00 – 250.00
Linus holds eggs. . . . . .170.00 – 250.00

• Flat Ceramic •

Series #1322, hand-painted, six in the series

Snoopy as an angel; Snoopy carries a decorated Christmas tree; $20.00 – 26.00 each. Woodstock as an angel, holds green package with red ribbon, $22.00 – 38.00. Woodstock sits on red letters which spell "NOEL;" Snoopy lies on a Christmas wreath with red bow at the top; Santa Snoopy is halfway in the chimney with his sack; $20.00 – 26.00 each.

Series #1720, hand-painted, six in the series

Not Pictured
Snoopy holds a green package with red bow and Woodstock on top of it, #1721. . . . . .$20.00 – 26.00
Snoopy sits and holds a nest containing Woodstock and a Christmas tree, #1722. . . . .22.00 – 28.00
Santa Snoopy with arms outstretched, #1723. . . . . .22.00 – 28.00
Snoopy leaps as he holds a candy cane, #1724. . . . . .18.00 – 22.00
Snoopy wears a knit ski cap and hugs Woodstock, #1725. . . . . .20.00 – 26.00
Woodstock sits on a large red package tied with a green bow, #1726. . . . . .22.00 – 28.00

• Plastic •

The following ornaments are believed to have been produced for consumers outside the United States. Even though they are made of plastic, they are not that easy to obtain. Approx. 2¼" tall, 1970s.

Snoopy reclines on the roof of his doghouse; Snoopy wears a red badge with a blue ribbon; Lucy wears a red dress and holds a bouquet of flowers; Charlie Brown wears his traditional red shirt with black zigzag; Linus licks his ice cream cone; Woodstock stands; $25.00 – 40.00 each.

• Crochet •

Each was packaged in clear plastic with a green cardboard header and white lettering, 3" tall.

Not Pictured
Hand crocheted Snoopy, #0817. . . . .$6.00 – 10.00
in pkg., 12.00 – 14.00
Hand crocheted Woodstock, #0816. . . . . . .5.00 – 8.00
in pkg., 8.00 – 12.00

• Wooden •

Snoopy flat Christmas ornaments, dated 1977, 12 in series

Design painted on wood. Each came packaged in clear plastic with a red and white cardboard header. Prices are comparatively low because a discount warehouse bought a huge supply of these ornaments and sold them at a very low price in the early 1980s.

Not Pictured
"Happy Holidays 1977," Snoopy sits next to large green, yellow, and red ornaments. . . . .$4.00 – 6.00
in pkg., 6.00 – 8.00
"Merry Christmas 1977," Snoopy sits inside a large Christmas wreath. . . . . .4.00 – 6.00
in pkg., 6.00 – 8.00
"1977 Happy Holidays," Snoopy dances in front of a large red Christmas bell trimmed at the bottom
with pine and pinecones. . . . . .4.00 – 6.00
in pkg., 6.00 – 8.00
"Noel 1977," Snoopy sits in front of a large yellow star with gifts at each side. . . . . .4.00 – 6.00
in pkg., 6.00 – 8.00
"Merry Christmas 1977," Snoopy sits and hugs Woodstock in front of a large red heart decorated with
sprigs of holly. . . . . .4.00 – 6.00
in pkg., 6.00 – 8.00
"Noel 1977," Snoopy stands in front of a large yellow snowflake, he wears a red stocking cap with
green trim. . . . . .4.00 – 6.00
in pkg., 6.00 – 8.00
"Happy Holidays 1977," Snoopy stands in front of a large decorated Christmas tree. . . . . .4.00 – 6.00
in pkg., 6.00 – 8.00
"Merry Christmas 1977," Snoopy in a red brick chimney, with a Santa pack over one shoulder. . . . . .4.00 – 6.00
in pkg., 6.00 – 8.00
"Merry Christmas 1977," Snoopy lies on top of his red and yellow home which is decorated with
Christmas stockings. . . . . .4.00 – 6.00
in pkg., 6.00 – 8.00
"Noel 1977," Snoopy holds a green and white package just about his size, tied with red ribbon. . . . . .4.00 – 6.00
in pkg., 6.00 – 8.00
"Happy Holidays 1977," Snoopy examines the caption of a large red, yellow, and green ball-shaped
ornament. . . . . .4.00 – 6.00
in pkg., 6.00 – 8.00
"Noel 1977," Snoopy reclines on a red and yellow striped candy cane. . . . . .4.00 – 6.00
in pkg., 6.00 – 8.00

Series #8608, 12 in the series

Wooden string ornaments. Design painted on wood. The packaging, which was simply a clear plastic bag with a red and white header, will add a couple of dollars to the value.

Not Pictured
Charlie Brown holds a green package tied with red ribbon. . . . .$6.00 – 8.00
Linus holds a green package tied with red ribbon. . . . . .6.00 – 8.00
Lucy holds a small green package tied with red ribbon. . . . . .6.00 – 8.00
Peppermint Patty sits and unwraps a red package tied with green ribbon. . . . . .6.00 – 8.00

Sally holds a large green package tied with red ribbon. . . . . .6.00 – 8.00
Snoopy smiles, sits, and holds a red package tied with green ribbon. . . . . .6.00 – 8.00
Snoopy wears a Santa cap and collar made from holly. . . . . .6.00 – 8.00
Snoopy's face and paws stick out from a green and red striped Christmas stocking. . . . . . .6.00 – 8.00
Snoopy sits among three packages with green and red wrappings. . . . . .6.00 – 8.00
Snoopy, wearing green stocking cap, sleeps on the roof of his home which is decorated with
    a string of Christmas lights. . . . . .6.00 – 8.00
Woodstock's sleeping face sticks out of a green and red Christmas stocking. . . . . .6.00 – 8.00
Woodstock holds a green package tied with red ribbon. . . . . .6.00 – 8.00

Peanuts String Toy Ornaments

Six to the series, wooden with painted design. Pulling a red string makes these ornaments move their arms and legs. Package is clear plastic with a red cardboard header.

Not Pictured
Snoopy wears a sheriff's outfit with a gold badge on his chest. . . . .$8.00 – 10.00
                                                                      in pkg., 10.00 – 12.00
Snoopy as an angel. . . . . .8.00 – 10.00
                                                                      in pkg., 10.00 – 12.00
Snoopy as Santa. . . . . .8.00 – 10.00
                                                                      in pkg., 10.00 – 12.00
Snoopy as the Flying Ace. . . . . .8.00 – 10.00
                                                                      in pkg., 10.00 – 12.00
Snoopy as Joe Cool. . . . . .8.00 – 10.00
                                                                      in pkg., 10.00 – 12.00
Woodstock, dressed warmly, wearing ice skates. . . . . .8.00 – 10.00
                                                                      in pkg., 10.00 – 12.00

Peanuts Christmas Ornaments

Six to the series, wooden with painted design. Jointed to enable arms and legs to move. Packaged in clear plastic with red cardboard header.

Snoopy as a Christmas caroller; Snoopy as a court jester; Snoopy wears a nightshirt and cap, holds a candy cane; Snoopy as a chef; Snoopy as a park ranger dressed in green and yellow outfit; Snoopy as a drum major; no package, $5.00 – 7.00 each; in package, $8.00 – 10.00 each.

• Ceramic Bells •

Series #1347

2¾" high, 2½" dia., six in series, did not come packaged

"O.K.! Who's the decorator?", Charlie Brown observes Woodstock decorating Snoopy and his house with Christmas lights; "Woodstock makes great root beer egg nog," Snoopy, Charlie Brown, and Woodstock indulging in root beer egg nog; "This is a happy time of year!", Sally and Snoopy with wrapped gifts; $25.00 – 32.00 each.

"Someone thought Woodstock was a Christmas goose!", Woodstock is upset and tells Snoopy; "I never take any chances!", Snoopy sleeps on the roof of his house which is decorated with Christmas stockings, Woodstock looks up at Snoopy; "O Christmas Tree," Peppermint Patty, Schroeder, Snoopy, and Lucy in front of a Christmas tree; $25.00 – 32.00 each.

Series #1345

Mini-bells, 1½" high x 1½" dia., six in series, did not come packaged

Lucy smiles as Snoopy stands beneath some mistletoe; Schroeder plays piano for Snoopy, the Christmas tree is nearby; Snoopy stands by Linus who sits, sleeps, and sucks his thumb; Snoopy and Peppermint Patty hold hands, Snoopy holds sign which reads "JOY!"; Snoopy wears a nightcap, sits and hugs Woodstock; Snoopy and Charlie Brown dance to "Jingle Bells"; $12.00 – 16.00 each.

Series #1945

Micro-Mini bells, 1" high x 1" dia., six in series, did not come packaged

Articulated Santa Snoopy, ceramic, 3½", 1982, $85.00 – 130.00.

Charlie Brown holds a candy cane and Snoopy wears Santa cap; Snoopy sleeps on top of his home decorated with a string of Christmas lights; Lucy with Santa Snoopy; Snoopy and Woodstock bring home a large Christmas tree; Snoopy lifts a nest which holds Woodstock and his Christmas tree; Snoopy with three packages; $5.00 – 8.00 each.

Satin Ornament

Box is green with white writing and red trim, 1982

"Season's Greetings," Santa Snoopy supervises his Woodstock elves in his toyshop, orange background; "Happy Holidays," Snoopy and his Woodstock friends enjoy a traditional Christmas day feast, red background; "Merry Christmas 1982," Lucy, Chralie Brown, Sally, Linus, Peppermint Patty, and birds sing Christmas carols, blue background; $14.00 – 18.00 each, in box, $18.00 – 24.00 each.

• Christmas Wreaths •

While the two largest "Snoopy hugging Woodstock wreaths" listed were not designed as ornaments, we thought this would be the appropriate place to list them. The largest wreath is the most difficult to find and is considered one of the premier items for a Peanuts collection.

Not Pictured
6½", #1716-8. . . . . .50.00 – 90.00
3", #1719-9. . . . . .35.00 – 50.00

Snoopy hugging Woodstock, 12", #1715-7, $450.00 – 600.00

• Hallmark/Ambassador Ornaments •

You really can't go wrong when purchasing a Hallmark ornament in excellent to mint condition (although you should consider holding out for an ornament in its original container). Hallmark collectors are legion, and Hallmark ornaments are among the most popular cross-collectibles.

All ornaments are by Hallmark unless otherwise noted, and all prices are based on mint condition. Some satin ornaments came housed in a very desirable dog-house-shaped box, and it should be noted that full value presupposes the existence of an original container and that its price-tag (where applicable) has not been removed. Specific names given to a particular ornament are indicated, i.e., "Hitting the Ice," but this does not happen often. The original price can be deciphered from the first three or four digits of the product number, i.e., 250QX162-2 would mean the original price was $2.50.

Glass Ornaments

Set of two housed in doghouse-shaped box: 1. Snoopy and Peppermint Patty ice skate, Linus throws a snowball, Charlie Brown stands next to a snowman, Woodstock makes a snowball; 2. "Snoopy Claus" rides his sleigh, Woodstock and the other birds act as reindeer, #400QC163-5, 1977; $90.00 – 115.00. Two panels: Charlie Brown tells Sally and Snoopy, "A watched stocking never fills"; second panel: Lucy wishes Schroeder, "Merry Christmas," #250QX162-2, 1977, $35.00 – 48.00.

"Sing a Song of Christmas Joy," dated 1985, Keepsake ornament, Snoopy leads a chorus of Woodstock and his friends in song, #475QX266-5, 1985, $32.00 – 45.00; "Merry Christmas," dated 1986, Keepsake ornament, Snoopy, Woodstock, and several birds ice skate, #475QX276-6, 1986, $30.00 – 37.00; Dated 1987, Snoopy and several birds use the supper dish as a sled, several other birds play in the snow, everyone wears sunglasses, #475QX281-9, $28.00 – 35.00.

"Where friendship goes, happiness follows!", dated 1988, "Snoopy Claus" rides in a sled led by three birds dressed as reindeer, "Christmas 1988," #475QX280-1, $28.00 – 35.00; "A Charlie Brown Christmas," dated 1989, Patty, Violet, Lucy, Frieda, Linus, Shermy, Pig Pen, Schroeder, Sally, Snoopy, and Charlie Brown recreate a scene for the 25th anniversary of the television special "A Charlie Brown Christmas," "Christmas...Season of Love," "A Charlie Brown Christmas Television Special Happy 25th Anniversary 1965 – 1989," #475QX276-5, $23.00 – 30.00; "Christmas is the merriest, lightest, jolliest, brightest, happiest time of the year!", dated 1990, a joyous Christmas scene as Schroeder plays the piano for Marcie, Peppermint Patty, Snoopy, Charlie Brown, Lucy, Sally, Linus, Pig Pen, and Woodstock, who dance in celebration, #475QX223-3, $28.00 – 32.00.

"It's the time of the year for sharing good cheer," dated 1991, Snoopy, Linus, Peppermint Patty, Marcie, Franklin, Lucy, Charlie Brown, and Sally flank Snoopy's decorated home, #500QX225-7; "...Behold, I bring you good tidings of great joy which shall be to all people," dated 1992, Marcie, Peppermint Patty, Linus, Charlie Brown, Lucy, Franklin, Schroeder, Snoopy, and several birds in nativity scene, "Christmas 1992," #500QX224-4; $26.00 – 30.00 each.

Dated 1993, Snoopy, Woodstock, Sally, Linus, and Charlie Brown wish us "Merry Christmas" in different languages, "Frohliche Weihnachten," "Buon Natale," "Feliz Navidad," and "Joyeux Noel," #500QX207-2, $22.00 – 26.00; Personalized ornament, the Hallmark stores accepted inscriptions and sent the ornament in a box that read "Personalized for You," Woodstock, Lucy, Linus, Snoopy Claus, and Charlie Brown flank a white banner that carries the personlized message, #900X604-5, 1993, $18.00 – 22.00.

Satin Ornaments

Dated 1977, Charlie Brown, Lucy, Snoopy, Woodstock, and Linus with a Christmas tree, #350QX135-5, $45.00 – 58.00; "The Sounds of Christmas," dated 1978, Snoopy, Woodstock and several birds work in Santa's toyshop, #350QX206-3, $42.00 – 55.00; "The Sounds of Christmas," dated 1978, Charlie Brown, Marcie, Linus, Pig Pen, Schroeder, Lucy, Snoopy, Sally, Peppermint Patty, and Woodstock sing, the wreath carries the date, "Joy To the World," #350QX205-6, $48.00 – 60.00.

"Time to Trim," dated 1979, "Snoopy Claus" hands several birds candy canes to decorate the Christmas tree, "Merry Christmas 1979," #350QX202-7, $25.00 – 32.00; "Grandson," dated 1979, Tree-Trimmer Collection, Snoopy and Woodstock ride downhill in a sled, "GRANDSON...A special someone whose merry ways bring extra joy to the holidays," "Christmas 1979," #350QX210-7, $20.00 – 25.00; Dated 1980, Tree-Trimmer Collection, Snoopy, Woodstock, and several birds portray scenes from the Christmas song, "The Twelve Days of Christmas: Four Colly Birds... Three French Hens... Two Turtle Doves... and a Partridge in a Pear Tree! Christmas 1980," #400QX216-1, $28.00 – 35.00.

"Merry Christmas," dated 1980, the Holiday House Collection, Ambassador (a division of Hallmark), Peppermint Patty, Linus, Sally, Lucy, Snoopy, Charlie Brown, and Woodstock ice skate, "1980," #398QX 10H; "Deck the halls with boughs of holly..." dated 1981, Keepsake Ornament, Snoopy and several birds wear Santa hats and sing as they decorate with holly, "Christmas 1981," #450QX803-5; $25.00 – 32.00 each. "Christmas 1982," dated 1982, Keepsake Ornament, Snoopy as Santa rides in back of special bicycle with eight birds wearing reindeer antlers, #450QX200-6, $20.00 – 25.00.

"May the joy of the season warm every heart!", dated 1983, Keepsake Ornament, three panels, Snoopy and Woodstock by fireplace, "Christmas 1982," #450QX212-7, $20.00 – 25.00; Dated 1984, Keepsake Ornament, Snoopy and snowmen hold a "Merry Christmas" banner, Woodstock appears in a different scene with Snoopy, #450QX252-1, $22.00 – 28.00.

Not Pictured
Dated 1978, Snoopy and Woodstock bring
    a tree home, #250QX204-3. . . . . . .$48.00 – 60.00
"Have a delightful Christmas," 1978, Charlie
    Brown is wrapped in Christmas lights,
    #250QX203-6. . . . . .35.00 – 45.00

Panoramic Ball Ornaments

A three-dimensional scene appears within each ball.

"Ice-Hockey Holiday," dated 1979, Snoopy and Woodstock play ice hockey (Note: Nowhere on the original box is "Panorama Ball Ornament" indicated. This box reads "Tree-Trimmer Collection." The subsequent four ornaments in the series read "Panorama Ball."), first in the series, #800XQ141-9, $125.00 – 140.00.

"Snoopy Ski Holiday," dated 1980, Snoopy skis and Woodstock rides in Snoopy's supper dish, second in the series, #900QX154-1; "Snoopy & Friends," dated 1981, Snoopy rides a sled being pulled by Woodstock and friends, a snowman resembling Snoopy is in the background, third in the series, #1200QX436-2; $90.00 – 110.00 each.

"Snoopy & Friends," dated 1982, Snoopy rides his sled, it is led by Woodstock and his friends, they appear to be on the chimney of a home, fourth in the series, #1300QX480-3, $80.00 – 100.00; "Snoopy," dated 1983, Snoopy is dressed as Santa, nearby is a large sack filled with toys, Woodstock holds the dated banner, fifth and final in the series, #1300QX416-9, $75.00 – 90.00.

Keepsake Ornaments — Magic

Each of these ornaments has some motion, lights, or music.

Dated 1991, Snoopy and Woodstock cuddle up in a Christmas stocking, fire in the fireplace flickers, first in the series, #1800QLX7229, $42.00 – 62.00. Dated 1992, Snoopy and Woodstock wrap themselves in a blanket on top of Snoopy's house, keeping warm in the snow, lights blink in a Christmas wreath, second in the series, #1800QLX721-4; Dated 1993, Snoopy and Woodstock admire their Christmas tree, decorated with little Woodstock-shaped ornaments, the lights on the tree blink, third in the series, #1800QLX715-5; $38.00 – 58.00 each.

Not Pictured

Dated 1994, Snoopy and Woodstock sing Christmas carols under a lamppost, the light in the post flickers, fourth in the series, #2000QLX740-6. . . . .$34.00 – 44.00

Dated 1995, Snoopy ice skates in front of Woodstock, fifth and final in this series, #2450QLX7277. . . . .34.00 – 44.00

Dated 1996, Schroeder plays his piano as Lucy leans on it, the music played is "Linus and Lucy," #1850QLX7394. . . . . .22.00 – 28.00

Dated 1997, Snoopy as Santa, his house is his sleigh and his reindeer are birds, they're on top of a house on which they spin, #QLX7475. . . . . .22.00 – 28.00

Keepsake Ornaments, Snoopy and Woodstock Series, three-dimensional

Snoopy and Woodstock stand on a pair of red skis, #750QX439-1, 1984, $40.00 – 48.00; Snoopy holds a hockey stick, and Woodstock sits on the puck, #750QX491-5, 1985, $30.00 – 38.00; Snoopy and Woodstock sit on a snow disk, ready to slide downhill, #800QX438-3, 1986, $28.00 – 34.00; Snoopy stands next to Christmas tree, Woodstock is the tree topper ornament, #725QX472-9, 1987, $28.00 – 34.00; Snoopy and Woodstock perch in a red and white knit Christmas stocking along with a large ribbon-tied bone, #600QX474-1, 1988, $24.00 – 32.00.

Snoopy and Woodstock wear top hats and hold candy canes, #675QX433-2, 1989; Snoopy hugs Woodstock, each wears a knit cap, #675QX472-3, 1990; Dated 1991, Snoopy and Woodstock share a pizza, #675QX519-7; $22.00 – 30.00 each. Dated 1992, Snoopy ice skates, with Woodstock hanging onto his cap, #875QX595-4, $20.00 – 28.00.

Keepsake Ornaments, three-dimensional

Dated 1996, "A Tree for Snoopy," Snoopy pulls a sled with a Christmas tree on it, #895QX5507, $14.00 – 18.00; Dated 1996, miniature, "A Tree for Woodstock," Woodstock pulls a sled with a Christmas tree on it, #575QXM4767, $10.00 – 14.00.

The Peanuts Gang Collector Series

Four ornaments in the series; there is no Snoopy ornament, which surprised collectors. Ornaments are numbered in order listed below.

Dated 1993, Charlie Brown stands next to a snowman which looks exactly like him, first in the series, #975QX531-5; Dated 1994, Lucy holds a football inscribed "For Charlie Brown," second in the series, #995QX520-3 (Christmas tree only prop); Dated 1995, Linus rides a sled, third in the series, #995QX5059; $15.00 – 22.00 each. Dated 1996, Sally holds a "Dear Santa" letter, fourth and final in the series, #995QX5381, $13.00 – 17.00.

Reach Program

Four ornaments with a stand. Issued in 1996 to celebrate the 30th anniversary of the animated classic television special, "A Charlie Brown Christmas." The ornaments cost $3.95 with any Hallmark purchase.

Base with Woodstock in a tree, the four ornaments fit into slots, $35.00 – 40.00; Charlie Brown stands with outstretched arms, one hand holds a handbell, #QRP4207; Lucy wears a purple coat and holds a candy cane, #QRP4209; Linus wears a blue coat, his hands are in the pockets, #QRP4217; Snoopy wears a Dickens-style top hat and red shirt, with a green neck scarf, #QRP4219; $15.00 – 22.00 each.

• Silvestri •

Each item has a thin gold cord and comes boxed unless otherwise noted. All were issued in 1990.

Ornaments are made of resin unless otherwise noted.

Top price is based on mint-in-the-box figures. Inspect each ornament closely for hairline cracks.

Prices are also given for individual figures out of the box.

Note: It may be difficult to locate the copyright information on these ornaments. Some have a loosely affixed paper tag; others have the information on the ornament, but due to coloration, it is difficult to read. Still others seem to be missing the information. The boxes do carry the copyright information, but the actual item should be the holder.

Series #30010

Set of three: Lucy in a Santa outfit holds a package; Santa Snoopy with a gift pack stuffed with dog bones over shoulder; Charlie Brown wears a red cap decorated as a Christmas tree; $35.00 – 45.00 each, out of box, $10.00 – 15.00 each.

Series #30012

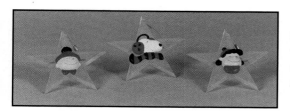

Set of three: Clear plastic stars with the faces of Charlie Brown, who wears a red cap with green ball on top; Snoopy, who wears red and green ear muffs and scarf; Lucy, who wears a red cap with green pompon and red scarf; $25.00 – 32.00 each, out of box, $6.00 – 8.00 each.

Series #30013

"Winter Peanuts" figurines, packaged individually

Linus wears a red coat, red winter cap with green pompon, and holds a green or gray shovel to clear the snow (this figurine resembles Charlie Brown quite a bit); Snoopy wears a red bow and hugs Charlie Brown, who wears a red coat, green scarf and red ear muffs with a sprig of holly on each ear; $18.00 – 25.00 each, out of box $12.00 – 15.00 each. Snoopy wears a green Christmas wreath decorated with red berries and red bow, $10.00 – 12.00, out of box, $8.00 – 10.00.

Series #30014

"Peanuts Light Covers" figural, set of two. Backed on cardboard with clear plastic covering the figural light covers.

Not Pictured
Snoopy and Woodstock sit wearing red Dickens-style hat and red scarves, Snoopy
    holds a large green gift package, he wears a red and green winter cap. . . . .$8.00 – 12.00 each
                                       out of box, 5.00 – 7.00 each

Series #30015

"Peanuts in Stocking" figural series of four. Each character is in a stocking with head sticking out.

        Not Pictured
        Lucy holds a candy cane. . . . .$15.00 – 18.00
                           out of box, 10.00 – 12.00
        Sally holds Christmas wish list. . . . . . . .15.00 – 18.00
                           out of box, 10.00 – 12.00
        Snoopy and Woodstock. . . . . .18.00 – 22.00
                           out of box, 15.00 – 18.00
        Linus. . . . . .15.00 – 18.00
                           out of box, 10.00 – 12.00

Series #30017

"Nightgown Peanuts" figurines, packaged individually

Charlie Brown wears green robe with red trim and red cap with green ball at its end, he holds a cup of hot chocolate; Lucy looks her most angelic in a white nightgown and red nightcap, she's holding her teddy bear; Sally wears a red nightgown, white nightcap and holds a large yellow star; in box, $18.00 – 22.00 each; out of box, $15.00 – 18.00 each. Snoopy wears a red nightshirt and a green and red night cap and holds a candleholder with a red candle on it; in box, $20.00 – 25.00; out of box, $18.00 – 22.00.

Series #30019

"Peanuts Waterglobe Ornaments," did not come boxed

Each ornament is topped by a holly design. The waterglobe itself houses a figurine of one character. Shake the globe to start a snowstorm.

Lucy smiles, wears a green dress, and holds a candy cane; Charlie Brown wears an orange shirt with black zigzag and black pants, holds wreath; $24.00 – 30.00 each.

Snoopy Santa stands; Woodstock reclines on a candy cane; $24.00 – 30.00 each.

Series #30021

"First Peanuts Christmas Bell"

The figures are housed on a clear glass bell with gold lettering, "Baby's 1st Christmas." A gold cord and clear ball at the end of it rings the bell. These ornaments were featured in Silvestri's catalog but never released to the general public. They are extremely difficult to locate. They did not come packaged.

Linus sits, wears green pajamas, sucks thumb, and holds red blanket; Lucy stands and wears red pajamas; $40.00 – 60.00 each.

Series #30503

"Peanuts on Glass Bell"

A gold cord holds each of the figures housed in a clear glass bell, topped by three sprigs of holly. These are extremely difficult to locate. They did not come packaged.

Woodstock reclines on a candy cane, $40.00 – 60.00.

Not Pictured
Snoopy stands and wears a Santa hat. . . .$50.00 – 65.00

Series #4362
"Snoopy Mistletoe Ornaments"

Set of three, wooden with painted design. Each has the characters placed under mistletoe; each is captioned "Mistletoe" at the bottom of the design. Did not come packaged.

Not Pictured
Snoopy and Woodstock wear Santa hats and hug. . . . .$3.00 – 5.00
Snoopy wears red nightcap and kisses Lucy, who wears red ear muffs. . . .3.00 – 5.00
Snoopy hugs Charlie Brown. . . . . .3.00 – 5.00

Series #4363
"Snoopy Doghouse Ornaments"
Set of three, wooden with painted design. Did not come packaged.

Snoopy lies on top of his green house and birds are on top of Snoopy's scarf; Snoopy lies on his wreath-adorned home as Woodstock lies on his tummy; Snoopy hugs Woodstock on the roof of his green home decorated with yellow and red Christmas lights; $4.00 – 6.00 each.

Series #4364
"Snoopy Personalized Ornaments"
Set of three, wooden with painted design. Did not come packaged.

Schroeder plays piano as Lucy leans on it, musical staff above wrapped with Christmas lights; Snoopy stands close to snowman and Woodstock sits on snowman's green hat; Charlie Brown and Snoopy each wear winter caps and hold shovels; $3.00 – 5.00 each.

Series #4365
"Palm Tree Snoopy"

Figural Joe Cool Snoopy wears sunglasses, red shirt with green holly design, arms are folded, he stands under palm tree decorated with Christmas lights, Woodstock sits on top of the tree also wearing sunglasses, $20.00 – 25.00, out of box $18.00 – 22.00.

Series #4366
"Peanuts Skaters" figurines, packaged individually

Except for Snoopy, each character wears Santa cap and ice skates. Linus wears green top, red pants, and mittens; Charlie Brown sits, wears red shirt and green pants; Lucy wears red top with white fur trim and green skating skirt; $15.00 – 20.00 each, out of box $13.00 – 15.00 each. Snoopy wears a red and green muffler, his Dickens-style hat has a sprig of holly in its band, $18.00 – 23.00, out of box $15.00 – 20.00.

Sally holds an apple; Charlie Brown holds an empty box; Linus holds a yellow star; Lucy holds a doll, $15.00 – 20.00 each; out of box, $13.00 – 15.00 each.

Series #4367
"Peanuts Transportation"

Each figure comes in its own box.

Snoopy and Woodstock wear red and green winter caps. They ride in Snoopy's red supper dish, $18.00 – 22.00; out of box, $14.00 – 18.00.

Snoopy wears Santa suit as he shows off his skateboard skills, the board is green with white trim, red wheels, $15.00 – 18.00; out of box; $11.00 – 15.00.

Series #4369
"Peanuts Frame Ornaments"

Each frame is white with room to insert a photograph.

Not Pictured

Charlie Brown sits next to the frame, he wears traditional yellow zigzag shirt, black pants, red
ribbon trim on top of frame as well as a sprig of holly. . . . .$10.00 – 12.00
out of box, 8.00 – 10.00
Linus looks up toward snowman's face at the top of the frame. . . . . .10.00 – 12.00
out of box, 8.00 – 10.00
Snoopy and Woodstock each wear Dickens-style top hats, red ribbon trim on top of the frame as
well as a sprig of holly. . . . . .12.00 – 14.00
out of box, 10.00 – 12.00
Snoopy looks toward the sky through binoculars, red ribbon trim on top of the frame as well as
a sprig of holly. . . . . .10.00 – 12.00
out of box, 8.00 – 10.00

Series #4373
"Snoopy/Linus Toboggan"

Figural Linus and Snoopy, each wearing Santa caps, Woodstock is at the helm of the toboggan, $20.00 – 30.00; out of box, $15.00 – 25.00.

• Japan •

The United States is not the only country to place the Peanuts gang on pedestals (or Christmas trees) during the holiday season. A few ornaments were available in Japan, most notably in the 1980s. Some from the United States, by Applause, crept into Japanese product catalogs.

Some of the ornaments may have been available at Familiar Dept. Stores or through Sanrio, but Determined is the main licensee.

Prices are based on mint condition: no chips, nicks or missing parts. Dimension refers to height.

Ceramic, three-dimensional

Set of three, 2", 1984.

Small Santa Snoopy holds a Christmas wreath and stands on top of bell shape, 2", #61902-7, 1990; small Santa Snoopy stands on a bell and holds his gift sack, 2", #62139-1, 1990; $25.00 – 35.00 each.

Charlie Brown wears a baseball hat and mitt; Snoopy stands with his arms close to his body; Lucy wears a red dress; $55.00 – 70.00 set of three.

Plastic, two-dimensional

Flat with picture on front and greeting on the reverse. Cream background, 3¼", Series #587478, 1986.

Charlie Brown holds a red package; Sally holds a green package tied with red ribbon; $6.00 – 8.00 each. Snoopy holds a dog bone tied with red ribbon, given to him by Woodstock, $8.00 – 10.00. Lucy holds a green package tied with red ribbon; Schroeder holds a red and white striped gift tied with green ribbon; $6.00 – 8.00 each.

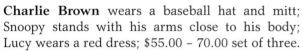

Not Pictured
Linus holds a brightly colored gift box. . . .$6.00 – 8.00

Figural, flocked

Snoopy holds ski poles and stands on green wooden skies, 2½", 1988, #E1816(A), 1987; Snoopy sits on red wooden sled, 2", 1988, #E1816(B), 1987; $40.00 – 55.00 each.

Satin cloth, stuffed

Each shape is irregular, approx. 2¾", Series #740369, 1988.

Santa Snoopy holds a white giftpack over shoulder; "Merry Christmas," Santa Snoopy's face is the main ornament on the Christmas tree; "Snoopy," Santa Snoopy holds several gifts; "Merry Christmas," Santa Snoopy tips his hat, star-shaped; Santa Snoopy rests against his giftpack; $8.00 – 10.00 each.

Christmas Plates

Prices on these ceramic, porcelain, or glass plates are based on mint-in-the-box, even if the box does not bear graphics. There should be no nicks or chips; the lettering and drawing should be bright and clear. The box should not show signs of wear.

Plates which have a date as part of the design are so indicated. Unless otherwise noted, plates were available for purchase in the U.S.A.

• Determined •

"Merry Christmas," Charlie Brown, Lucy, Linus, Peppermint Patty, Schroeder, Snoopy, and birds engaged in activities in front of a Christmas tree, 9½" dia., mid 1970s, $35.00 – 45.00.

"O' Christmas Tree..." Peppermint Patty and Linus decorate a Christmas tree, Lucy brings a gift while Woodstock, Snoopy, and Charlie Brown dance to Christmas music played by Schroeder. (This plate came in a plain box, and its absence should not affect the plate's value.) 9" dia., the plate was produced for Joy's, Inc., Chicago, Illinois, #1588, 1976, $40.00 – 60.00.

Snoopy on Christmas Day

Linus, Sally, Snoopy, Lucy, Woodstock, Charlie Brown, and Schroeder join hands to form a ring around their decorated Christmas tree, 7½" dia., Japan, #03447-9, 1989, $45.00 – 55.00; Charlie Brown, Linus, Sally, Snoopy, and Lucy appear in the center of a Christmas wreath, 7½" dia., Japan, #61926-4, 7½", 1990, $40.00 – 50.00.

• Franklin Mint •

"Merry Christmas, Charlie Brown," Snoopy as Santa takes center stage, he is surrounded by merrymakers: Lucy, Linus, Charlie Brown, Peppermint Patty, and several birds, gold trim, limited edition, porcelain, 8" dia., plate did not come in box, packed in Styrofoam container, 1994, $80.00 – 100.00.

• Noritake •

Snoopy sits in a Christmas boot and hands a gift to Woodstock, the border is green with red and gold. (This plate also had matching tableware pieces, but we are listing the plates only.) 10½" dia., Japan, #87N/140, early 1990s, $75.00 – 105.00; Snoopy sits in a Christmas boot and hands a gift to Woodstock, the border is green with red and gold (This plate also had matching tableware pieces, but we are listing the plates only.) 7½" dia., Japan, #90N/4, early 1990s, $25.00 – 35.00.

Winter and Christmas scenes feature Charlie Brown and Sally; Snoopy with birds; and Linus and Lucy. (This plate also had matching tableware pieces, but we are listing the largest plate only.) 10½" dia., Japan, #87N/140, 1989, $175.00 – 225.00.

• Sasaki •

Each plate is made of glass, 10¾" dia., Japan.

"Merry Christmas 1989," Santa Snoopy and Woodstock appear inside a decorated wreath, $90.00 – 140.00.

"Merry Christmas 1996," Santa Snoopy has several bird helpers to decorate his Christmas tree, #57301-H757, 1996, $58.00 – 70.00.

Not Pictured
"Merry Christmas 1997," Santa Woodstock and Snoopy walk along with holly leaves
above them and gifts nearby. . . . .$58.00 – 70.00

• Schmid •

Each plate is 7½" dia.

1972, "Snoopy Guides the Sleigh," Snoopy holds the reins of his sleigh and guides Woodstock, who acts as a reindeer, first edition, $30.00 – 40.00; 1973, "Christmas Eve at the Doghouse," Snoopy sleeps on top of his yellow doghouse, Woodstock sleeps on top of a plain Christmas tree, second edition, $140.00 – 210.00.

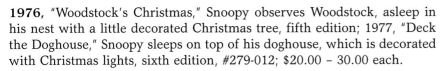

1974, "Christmas Eve at the Fireplace," Snoopy and Woodstock sleep in front of their fireplace, Christmas stockings hang from the mantel, candles burn and a Christmas wreath is on the wall, there are many wrapped packages, third edition, $45.00 – 70.00; 1975, "Woodstock, Santa Claus," Woodstock, dressed as Santa, and stands on Snoopy's nose while he sleeps on the roof of his doghouse, fourth edition, $20.00 – 30.00.

1976, "Woodstock's Christmas," Snoopy observes Woodstock, asleep in his nest with a little decorated Christmas tree, fifth edition; 1977, "Deck the Doghouse," Snoopy sleeps on top of his doghouse, which is decorated with Christmas lights, sixth edition, #279-012; $20.00 – 30.00 each.

1978, "Filling the Stockings," Santa Snoopy looks concerned as he finds Woodstock sitting in a Christmas stocking hanging on top of the fireplace, seventh edition, #279-014; 1979, "Christmas at Hand," Snoopy, on his doghouse roof, performs a Christmas play with hand Pawpets, eighth edition, 15,000 issued, #279-016; $25.00 – 35.00 each.

1980, "Waiting for Santa," Snoopy looks up at Woodstock asleep in his nest, the tree housing the nest is decorated with stockings, ninth edition, 15,000 issued, #279-320, $35.00 – 45.00; **1981,** "A Christmas Wish," Snoopy sleeps on top of his doghouse completely covered in colorful Christmas stockings, tenth edition, 15,000 issued, #279-321, $20.00 – 30.00.

1982, "Perfect Performance," Snoopy etches out the greeting, "Merry" as he ice skates, eleventh edition, #279-322, $35.00 – 45.00.

• Willitts •

Christmas Signature Collection

Collectors accustomed to a yearly plate from Schmid became quite sad when that company discontinued the license. After a lapse of five years, collectors were once again excited about the prospect of annual Christmas plates. Now, several years later, collectors really appreciate Willitts' efforts. Locating these plates is a challenge to newer collectors.

A certificate of authenticity accompanied each limited edition Christmas plate. The descriptions below are quoted from the back of each plate. Each plate is 7½" in diameter and made of porcelain.

1987, "What a song WOODSTOCK brings in his bird-speak carolings! SNOOPY listening from above offers coaching — and his love," first edition, #7705, $35.00 – 45.00; **1988,** "Snoopy and his yuletide friends are caroling for a reason, they're bearing tidings of great joy in this merriest of seasons!," second edition, #8445, $32.00 – 42.00.

1989, "They're bringing home the Christmas tree — what a joyful holiday sight! With a little love and tinsel it will soon light up the night!", third edition, #9354; **1990,** "All dressed up in Christmas lights SNOOPY'S doghouse scales the heights with WOODSTOCK proudly flying high, holiday wishes fill the sky!", fourth edition, #44001; $32.00 – 42.00 each.

1991, "Sledding down a snowy hill, these jolly friends won't take a spill, with SNOOPY in the driver's seat their holiday joy is quite complete!", fifth edition, #44027; **1992,** "SNOOPY and WOODSTOCK know the perfect gift to last throughout the year, as they deck the halls they wish for you: Good friends, good times, good cheer!", sixth and final edition, #44037; $35.00 – 45.00 each.

Christmas Stocking Holders

• Hallmark/Holidays Products, Inc. •

"Snoopy Stocking Hanger"

Snoopy and Woodstock ride a red sled, the price on this hanger varies since it was issued for several years. It comes housed in a cardboard box or in a cardboard box with a cellophane front, Hallmark, #QHD816-3, 1970s (with cardboard box), 1980s (with cellophane front), in box, $40.00 – 52.00; no box, $34.00 – 42.00; Snoopy hugs Woodstock, both are on Snoopy's doghouse, which is decorated with a mistletoe wreath, the lights twinkle, #XSH3117, 1995, in box, $25.00 – 35.00; no box, $10.00 – 18.00. Holiday Products, Inc.; Snoopy sits with a couple of packages, his candy cane serves as the stocking hanger, comes in cardboard backed blister-card, date of issue late 1980s, with or without box, $5.00 – 10.00.

Stationery

Bookends

It's natural for a Peanuts fan to want at least one pair of bookends, if only to hold the books in his or her collection! Bookends aren't that common, so when you find a set in good condition, you have something that is both decorative and useful.

Although the most popular bookends are made of ceramic, don't dismiss those made from other materials.

The sets made by Leatherlines, while lightweight, reflect the Peanuts characters in their older incarnations.

The value is based on excellent to mint condition. If ceramic, there should be no chips or missing paint, all colors should be bright. Other bookends should have no rips or tears in the material. Finding the box is great, but values here reflect the bookends alone.

• Leatherlines •

Usually one background shade and a black drawing, although the pair of Flying Ace bookends have a white background with red and black drawings. Mid to late 1960s.

Charlie Brown flies a kite; Lucy holds a balloon as Snoopy sits nearby, $25.00 – 45.00.

Not Pictured
The Flying Ace on top of his doghouse,
 "This time I've got you, Red Baron!
 This time you're mine!" . . . .$30.00 – 50.00

• Butterfly •

Ceramic (with the exception of the heart pair, which is a type of rubberized material) and figural.

These are the most popular. Issued in the mid 1970s to very early 1980s.

Snoopy and Charlie Brown at the door, 100CPBE-002, $150.00 – 210.00.

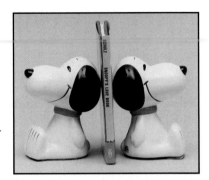

Snoopy sits, wears a red collar, #1301, $60.00 – 75.00.

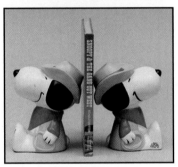

Western Snoopy, #1305, $80.00 – 95.00.

Rain slicker Snoopy, #1320, $75.00 – 90.00.

Not Pictured
Baseball player Snoopy, #1322. . . . .$80.00 – 100.00
Flying Ace Snoopy, #1323. . . . . .90.00 – 105.00

• Willitts •

Snoopy and Woodstock on a train, ceramic, #45029, 1990, $50.00 – 65.00.

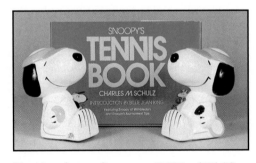

Tennis player Snoopy, #1321, $75.00 – 90.00.

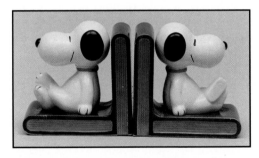

Snoopy sits on and against a brown book, #1391, $110.00 – 160.00.

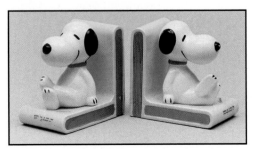

Snoopy sits on and against a yellow book, #1392, $110.00 – 160.00.

Snoopy and Woodstock sit against a large red heart, #700 1303, $25.00 – 40.00.

• Bumper Stickers •

This form of displaying one's likes or dislikes was highly popular during the 1960s and early 1970s. We've included just a sampling of what was available. All were by Hallmark, which carried the worldwide license for bumper stickers. Many of the stickers listed here (with the exception of those with political messages) were available in Europe and Mexico.

The first two or three digits of the Hallmark number indicate the original retail price, i.e., 75HD 117-5 means the bumper sticker sold for 75 cents.

Prices are based on mint, unused condition with no bent corners and self-adhesive intact.

Pack of Two: "Win With Charlie Brown" and "Let's Elect Linus," Charlie Brown stands in his classic pose with a kite, Linus sits in a classic pose with his blanket, #60KF 1-1, mid 1960s, $6.00 – 8.00.

"Golf is a Great Game...No Matter How You Slice It!", Snoopy knocks a golf ball away, #75HD 117-5, late 1960s, $2.00 – 4.00.

"Support Your Local Tennis Bum," Joe Cool holds a tennis racket and bounces a tennis ball, #75HD 228-2, late 1960s, $2.00 – 4.00.

"Get in the Spirit of '76," Snoopy wears a tri-cornered hat, #75HD119-7, 1976, $5.00 – 7.00.

"If You Don't Vote Don't Crab!", Lucy instructs the voting public, #100HD124-1, mid 1970s, $3.00 – 5.00.

"Happy Birthday, America!", Snoopy wears a tri-cornered hat and holds a pole with an American flag and Woodstock, #100HD119-6, mid 1970s, $5.00 – 7.00.

"Clean Up Government!", side view of Pig Pen walking in a cloud of dust, #100HD124-2, mid 1970s, $3.00 – 5.00.

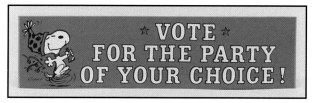

"Vote for the Party of Your Choice!", Snoopy wears a party hat and holds a party favor, Hallmark #100HD124-5, mid 1970s, $3.00 – 5.00.

Calendars

Much of the Peanuts merchandise legacy began with a simple calendar. It was Determined Productions' very first Peanuts product, and it was released at the end of 1961. The first several calendars in this series did not feature Peanuts characters on the cover. From then on, Determined continued to make licensing history with its innovative use of the Peanuts characters in everyday items.

This section covers the ordinary to the unusual, the Peanuts way to keep track of time. Prices are based on mint, unused condition. Covers should be crisp with no marks or dog-eared edges.

• Determined Productions, Inc. •

"Peanuts, A Date Book with Charlie Brown, Lucy, Schroeder, Snoopy, Linus, Pig Pen, Violet, and Frieda for 1962," monthly calendar with pictures of older, obscure characters such as Frieda, Violet, and Patty plus a great picture of Snoopy on all four legs, spiral bound at top, 1962, $35.00 – 50.00.

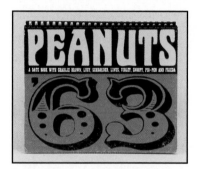

"Peanuts, A Date Book with Charlie Brown, Lucy, Schroeder, Linus, Violet, Snoopy, Pig Pen, and Freida," monthly calendar with pictures of older characters such as Patty, Frieda, and Shermy, as well as a picture of the gang on a baseball mound, spiral bound at top, 1963, $15.00 – 25.00.

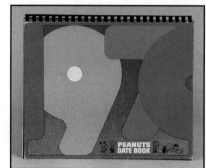

"1970 Peanuts Date Book," cover: small drawings of Snoopy, Charlie Brown, Linus, Schroeder, and Lucy appear at the bottom, monthly calendar, each month with a different picture, spiral bound at top, 1970, $10.00 – 20.00.

"**Snoopy** 1978 Week by Week," cover: Snoopy and Woodstock look at one another, each week features a different picture, spiral bound at side, 1978, $8.00 – 12.00.

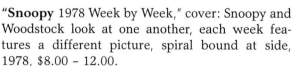

"Snoopy 1980 Fun Fact Calendar," cover: Snoopy and Woodstock visit an amusement park, several characters can be seen riding a roller coaster in the background, monthly calendar, each page has pictures and interesting facts, stapled inside cover, 1980; "Snoopy 1981 Fun Fact Calendar," cover: Snoopy and Woodstock as drum majors lead the Peanuts parade of band members, monthly calendar, each page has pictures and interesting facts, stapled inside cover, 1981; $10.00 – 14.00 each.

"Snoopy 1983 Week by Week," cover: Snoopy, surrounded by several bird friends, each week features a different picture, spiral bound at side, 1983, $8.00 – 15.00.

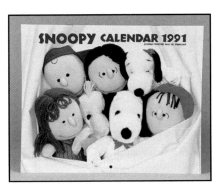

"**Snoopy** Calendar 1991," cover: plush dolls of Peppermint Patty, Charlie Brown, Lucy, Belle, Woodstock, Snoopy, and Linus, monthly calendar, the pictures inside are all plush dolls in various scenes, stapled inside cover, Determined Productions for Familiar, a chain of children's department stores in Japan, #740881, 1991, $15.00 – 22.00.

"**Snoopy** Metal Perpetual Calendar," a circular metal disk labeled with the months, days, and dates, and a pointer to mark them, design is the faces of Charlie Brown, Peppermint Patty, Linus, Snoopy, Sally, and Lucy surrounding Snoopy carrying his dog dish, Woodstock is on one of the pointers, blue background, distributed by Sanyel Import Co., Ltd. in Japan, #SP 123-A, mid 1980s; "Snoopy Metal Perpetual Calendar," a circular metal disk labeled with the months, days and dates, and a pointer to mark them, design is Snoopy's face against red background, Woodstock wears a Beaglescout cap and is on one of the pointers, distributed by Sanyel Import Co., Ltd. in Japan, #SP 123-B, mid 1980s; $30.00 – 45.00 each.

• Hallmark/Ambassador •

"The Family Sticker Calendar," 17 months: 9/84 – 1/86, cover: Snoopy sits on a blue sofa with several birds all around, while each calendar page is plain and lacks an accompanying picture, two pages of small Peanuts stickers may be used to mark doctor appointments, anniversaries, parties, football games, etc., spiral bound at top, #650HC 215-4, $5.00 – 8.00.

"The Peanuts Coping Calendar 1985," monthly calendar, each drawing is accompanied by a bit of advice, spiral bound at top, Ambassador, #AC 540 H, 1985, $4.00 – 6.00.

"Peanuts 1988 Desk Calendar," daily calendar, each page features a cartoon, pages are glued to a cardboard stand, comes boxed, #HC6787, 1988, $8.00 – 14.00.

• Harry N. Abrams Inc. (A Times Mirror Company) •

"Snoopy Around the World 1991 Calendar," cover: Snoopy and Belle, dressed in fashionable clothing by French designer Angelo Tarlazzi, the background is Egypt, monthly calendar, each page has plush dolls dressed by world-famous designers such as Chanel, Bob Mackie, and Mary McFadden, various world locations are the backgrounds, stapled inside cover, 1991, $12.00 – 18.00.

• Sparkler Books (an imprint of Pharos Book, a Scripps Howard Company) •

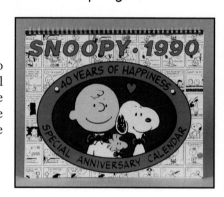

"40 Years of Happiness Special Anniversary Calendar," cover: 40th anniversary logo of Charlie Brown, Snoopy, and Woodstock wearing red bowties inside an oval design, monthly calendar, each month features a picture and information on the dates on which special Peanuts events took place, such as when characters made their debut, initial broadcast of specials and when Apollo 10 blasted off to the moon, spiral bound at top, ISBN 0-88687-428, 1990, $12.00 – 18.00.

• Manufacturer Unknown •

"Snoopy & Woodstock '87 Calendar," cover: Snoopy holds a sign with "87" on it, Woodstock holds the "R" in calendar, monthly calendar, tear the bottom portion of each page off, and a new bottom portion appears, using the same top portion of Snoopy, made to hang on the wall, Japan, 1987, $6.00 – 10.00.

Diaries

Many people grew up counting on Snoopy as their best friend, telling him all their secrets, and a Snoopy diary was the perfect way to record the day's personal news.

Value is based on mint condition, with the lock and key or combination lock intact and working.

"Happiness is having secrets!" Snoopy covers his mouth with his paws, multi-color dot background, combination lock, Hallmark, #RA3617, early 1990s, $7.00 – 11.00; "Diary," Snoopy and Woodstock jump over a rainbow design, lock and key, Determined, ISBN #0-925696-24-X, 1970s; "Diary," Snoopy hugs Woodstock inside a heart, lock and key, Determined Productions, Inc., ISBN #0-915696-24-X, 1970s; $8.00 – 12.00 each.

"Keep Out!", Lucy makes it clear no one is allowed to view her diary, Hallmark, #RA3809, 1989, $16.00 – 22.00; "No Snooping Allowed!", Snoopy makes an entry into his diary while a group of birds tries to see what he's writing, combination lock, Hallmark, #RA3814, 1989, $18.00 – 25.00.

"Peanuts Free Diary," Snoopy hugs Woodstock, smaller images of Spike, Linus, Lucy, Marcie, Peppermint Patty, Sally, and Charlie Brown, no lock, Japan, Determined Productions, Inc., Japan, #64400-5, 1988, $8.00 – 12.00; "Snoopy Dear Diary," Snoopy stands, he raises one of his feet, lock and key, Determined Productions, Inc., Japan, #08065-9, 1988, $9.00 – 14.00; "Snoopy Diary," Sally holds a diary, Snoopy and Charlie Brown are nearby, free diary with no lock or key, Japan, Determined Productions, Inc., Japan, #ISBN4-07-918264-3, 1987, $15.00 – 25.00.

 # Keychains

Plastic, rubber, metal, leather, wood and brass...all these materials, and more, have been used to make the common, everyday keychain.

If you fancy Snoopy in a particular pose, you'll probably find it. Even those who love more sophisticated items should be happy with Japanese keychains, which incorporate music or light.

While we could go on and on with this category, a small sampling should suffice.

Value is based on mint condition, with keyring opening still intact and not broken. If the keychain was packaged, packaging does not add to the product's value.

Snoopy as an archer, leather, Aviva, 1970s, $2.00 – 4.00; Snoopy with his dog dish on his head, he carries a knapsack, vinyl, Aviva Enterprises, Inc./Hollywood Accessories, 1970s, $4.00 – 6.00; Snoopy Bicentennial, 1776 – 1976, he wears a tri-cornered hat and holds a bell in one hand, wood, Aviva, 1975, $4.00 – 6.00; Snoopy wearing a large cowboy hat, strums his guitar, picture moves to show the action of Snoopy playing, plastic, Aviva, 1971, $5.00 – 7.00.

The Flying Ace, brass, Aviva Enterprises, Inc., 1970s, $5.00 – 7.00; "40 Years of Happiness," metal, Japan, Glory Co., Ltd., 1990, $12.00 – 15.00; L.A. Rams, cloisonne, Quantasia, mid to late 1980s, $7.00 – 9.00; Snoopy and Woodstock sit close together, cloisonne, Quantasia, mid 1980s, $4.00 – 6.00.

Snoopy drives on twisty Lombard Street in San Francisco, plastic, Quantasia, mid 1980s, $4.00 – 6.00; Snoopy sits with several birds, plastic, Monogram Products, Inc., 1990, $2.00 – 3.00; Snoopy wears traditional Japanese attire, Japan, Quantasia, late 1980s, $4.00 – 6.00.

Snoopy reclines on doghouse, Japan, Determined Productions/Takara mid 1980s, press the "O" in Snoopy to play the music, tune, "The Sting," $15.00 – 28.00; Lighted two-dimensional figure of Snoopy holding Woodstock, battery operated, Japan, manufacturer unknown, late 1980s or early 1990s, $12.00 – 22.00.

Not Pictured
Japan, Determined Productions/Takara, mid 1980s, Snoopy holds a tennis ball, press the ball to play the music, tune, "The Sting." $15.00   – 28.00

Paperweights

All these paperweights feature Snoopy, and many of the older ones still are fairly easy to find. It's finding them in good condition which sometimes is a bit difficult!

This is an interesting category for serious collectors who appreciate minor distinctions in certain items. A case in point is the Butterfly ceramic Joe Cool paperweight; the sweater color can be red or blue (we've assigned A or B to the different colors).

Values are based on mint condition: no chips or missing paint.

While many came in boxes — and it would be nice to have the box — it shouldn't affect the price that much, but we'll indicate the value with and without a box.

Dimension is height, unless noted.

• Butterfly Originals •

Snoopy sits on a yellow base, he wears a blue cap and holds a red baseball, ceramic, 3¾", #PW001, mid to late 1970s, in box, $20.00 – 30.00; no box, $17.00 – 27.00; Snoopy sits in a chair, his legs are crossed, ceramic, 3", #PW002, mid to late 1970s, in box, $38.00 – 48.00; no box, $35.00 – 45.00; Snoopy sits on a red heart base and types, ceramic, 3½", #PW003, mid to late 1970s, in box, $20.00 – 30.00; no box, $17.00 – 27.00; Snoopy holds Woodstock and both sit in his dog dish, ceramic, 3⅛", #PW004, mid to late 1970s, in box, $18.00 – 25.00; no box, $15.00 – 22.00; Snoopy wears a red cap and backpack as he climbs a rock, ceramic, 3¾", #PW005, mid to late 1970s, in box, $32.00 – 42.00; no box, $29.00 – 39.00.

Snoopy lies on his tummy, his arms hold his face off the ground, 4¼" long, ceramic, #1004, 1979; Snoopy lies face up, ceramic, 4½" long, #1005, 1979; Snoopy lies face down, ceramic, 4½" long, #1007, 1979, in box, $18.00 – 23.00 each; no box, $15.00 – 20.00 each; Snoopy sits, Woodstock is in his lap, 3¼", ceramic, #1009, 1979, in box, $18.00 – 28.00 each; no box, $15.00 – 25.00 each.

Joe Cool's head rests on a rock, he wears green sunglasses and a red shirt with "Joe Cool" on it, ceramic, 3½" long, #1008A, 1979, in box, $24.00 – 34.00; no box, $21.00 – 31.00; Joe Cool's head rests on a rock, he wears green sunglasses and a blue shirt with "Joe Cool" on it, ceramic, 3½" long, #10008B, 1979, in box, $27.00 – 37.00; no box, $24.00 – 34.00.

Snoopy sits, "Hat Series"

Ceramic, approx. 3¼", 1982

Snoopy wears a yellow rain slicker and hat and holds an umbrella, #1020; Snoopy wears a blue tennis visor and a blue and white striped shirt, he holds a tennis ball in one hand and a tennis racket in the other, #1021; in box, $24.00 – 34.00 each; no box, $21.00 – 31.00 each. Snoopy wears a red and white striped baseball uniform and a red cap, he holds a baseball in one hand and a bat in the other, #1022, in box, $28.00 – 38.00; no box, $25.00 – 35.00; Snoopy wears a blue helmet with goggles, he holds Woodstock on his lap, #1023, in box, $32.00 – 40.00; no box, $25.00 – 35.00.

Glass

The design is etched from the bottom of the glass.
In this particular series, the box is desirable and adds to the value, ⅝", 1979.

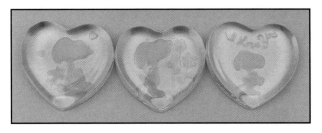

Snoopy and Woodstock sit back to back, heart shape, #1801; Snoopy sniffs flowers, heart-shaped, #1802; "I Love You," Snoopy holds a heart, heart shaped, #1804; in box, $40.00 – 55.00 each; no box, $35.00 – 48.00 each.

"Friends," Woodstock brings a flower to Snoopy, heart-shaped, #1805; Snoopy with five birds, round, #1803; in box, $40.00 – 55.00 each; no box, $35.00 – 48.00 each.

Base is flat with green felt, rounded dome, 3" dia., 1970s.

Snoopy throws a football to Woodstock; Snoopy gets ready to hit a tennis ball; Snoopy lies on his doghouse; Snoopy hugs Woodstock; in box, $25.00 – 35.00 each; no box, $20.00 – 30.00 each.

• Determined Productions •

Stippled glass, two-dimensional figures, 1979

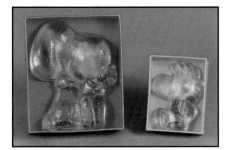

Snoopy holds a flower, 4½", #8572, in box, $20.00 – 28.00; no box, $15.00 – 24.00; Woodstock, 3", #8576, in box, $12.00 – 17.00; no box, $8.00 – 11.00.

• Leonard Silver •

Gold tone, silverplated Snoopy, sitting, 3½", #9677, 1980, $35.00 – 50.00.

Hallmark Centerpieces

Countless dinner and party settings have been enhanced by Hallmark's cheerful, brightly colored centerpiece settings. For collecting purposes, however, these cardboard and tissue creations must remain unopened and in their original packages; if they've been punched out and assembled, collectible value is all but lost (once the bottle has been uncorked, we can't get the genie back inside!). The package and contents should be crisp without dog-eared edges or sun-faded colors. Most are long out of print, but some are still available at standard retail prices.

• Valentine's Day/Easter •

"**Snoopy's** Heart," Snoopy reclines on a honeycomb heart, Charlie Brown, Linus, and Lucy are nearby, #150VCP3-1, early 1970s; "Peanuts Valentine Celebration," Lucy covers her eyes as she watches Snoopy staff her psychiatric booth, Woodstocks line up because "The Kisser is IN," #175VCP1-2, mid 1970s; $10.00 – 14.00 each. "Easter Beagle-Mobile," cardboard car hauls little baskets, each with a honeycomb egg, Snoopy is the driver and two Woodstocks are passengers, #350EHM3251-6, late 1970s, $8.00 – 10.00.

• Christmas/Party •

"Peanuts Holiday Trimmings Centerpiece," Snoopy and Woodstock decorate Snoopy's house for Christmas, #250XHD801-6, late 1970s; "Peanuts Express Card Holder," Snoopy is the train's engineer, locomotive and car serve as containers for Christmas cards, #250XCH46-6, late 1970s; $8.00 – 10.00 each. "Snoopy Christmas," Snoopy and Woodstock are on top of Snoopy's house decorating a little honeycomb Christmas tree, #275XCP17-1, early 1980s, $10.00 – 12.00.

"**Snoopy** 'n Friends," Christmas decoration, Snoopy decorates large honeycomb Christmas tree, Woodstock as an angel serves as the tree topper, 350XHB632-3, early 1980s, $10.00 – 12.00. "Hallmark Plans-a-Party Centerpiece" featuring a Peanuts comic-strip character, honeycomb Snoopy holds "Happy Birthday" pennant as he lies on top of house, #125CP9-3, 1964; "Snoopy and the Red Baron," Flying Ace Snoopy sits on his bullet-riddled house, #150CP97-5, 1969; $15.00 – 22.00 each.

"Super Snoopy Centerpiece," football player Snoopy watches Woodstock kick honeycomb football, #150CP102-9, 1973, $6.00 – 8.00; Snoopy centerpiece, a honeycomb Snoopy lies on the roof of his doghouse, Woodstock stands on Snoopy's tummy, #165CP97, 1973, $10.00 – 12.00; Snoopy centerpiece, Snoopy as World War I Flying Ace and Woodstock wearing infantry helmet walk on honeycomb grass, #175CP97-2, 1973, $15.00 – 22.00.

"Peanuts Rainbow Party" centerpiece, Snoopy leads Peppermint Patty, Charlie Brown, and the gang as he walks under a rainbow, Woodstock holds balloons, #175CP1160-2, 1977, also released under Ambassador product, #298CP120J, late 1970s; Snoopy's Party Centerpiece, Snoopy and Woodstock perform on top of Snoopy's roof, Linus, Lucy, and Charlie Brown comment on the entertainment, also released under the Ambassador Division, #200CP97-4, 1970s, $8.00 – 12.00; "Carnival Capers," Snoopy, Charlie Brown, Linus, Lucy, and birds ride a "Happy Birthday" Ferris wheel, #300CP117-4, early 1980s, $8.00 – 10.00.

"Peanuts Happy Birthday Centerpiece," Schroeder plays piano for birds, Charlie Brown, Sally, and Snoopy, honeycomb birthday cake is on Schroeder's piano, #350CP277-8, late 1970s, $8.00 – 10.00. Ambassador: "Party with Peanuts," Schroeder plays piano for Woodstock and Snoopy, who is dancing, #189CP1181J, 1970s, $6.00 – 8.00.

Not Pictured
"Snoopy and Friends," Snoopy dances on top of his doghouse, Lucy, Charlie Brown (with a bird on
    his head), and Linus stand in front of the house, #150CP60J, mid to late 1960s. . . . .$12.00 – 15.00

 # Hallmark Party Invitations

This category belongs to the Missouri-based company, which throughout the years has produced dozens of various invitations. We've listed some of the more interesting examples, many of which have a seasonal theme.

Packages in black, white, and red represent older bits of Hallmark memorabilia. For several years, these three colors were the primary focus of Hallmark's Peanuts designs.

Invitations should appear mint in the original package, with the original price clearly shown. The cello-wrap should not be torn, and all invitations (normally eight unless otherwise indicated) should be intact.

"Let's get together..." Snoopy sits on his doghouse as a bird flies by, #60PM 97-7, late 1960s, $6.00 – 10.00; "Admit one for birthday fun!", Birthday, Snoopy hits a tall carnival striker as Woodstock sits on the bell, #150PM1174, 1980, $4.00 – 5.00; "Barbecue," Chef Snoopy uses a bone against his dog dish to call everyone to dinner, #75PM 12-9, 1970s, $5.00 – 7.00; "An overnight party!", slumber party, several birds are at Snoopy's house while he sleeps on his roof, #100PM 492-2, 1970s, $4.00 – 5.00.

Snoopy as the World War I Flying Ace pilots his bullet riddled Sopwith Camel house with smoke coming out of it, package contains five invitations, made for distribution in Mexico, 1980, $5.00 – 7.00; "Hooray! A party!", Charlie Brown and Snoopy dance for joy, Ambassador Division of Hallmark, #PM 118, early 1980s, $3.00 – 5.00; "It's party time!", Peppermint Patty and Snoopy are dressed up and dance along with Woodstock, #75PM 97-4, mid 1970s, $5.00 – 7.00; "A birthday party!", Snoopy holds three balloons and Woodstock blows a noise maker, #150PM2778, 1980s, $2.00 – 4.00.

"**Snoopy** Invitation Card," Snoopy, Lucy, Linus, Charlie Brown, Sally, Peppermint Patty, and several birds gather in a very festive atmosphere, Hallmark, Japan division, #80 HC-9, 1983, $3.00 – 5.00.

• Seasonal •

"It's a Party! It's a Party! It's a Party!", Valentine's Day, Snoopy holds a heart trimmed with lace, #60VIN 32, late 1960s, $6.00 – 10.00; "Ah, here it is...A Valentine party invitation!", Valentine's Day, Snoopy stands on Charlie Brown's legs to get into the mailbox, #60VIN2-5, late 1960s, $8.00 – 12.00.

"You're invited," graduation, Snoopy wears a graduation mortarboard and carries a diploma in one hand, he and Woodstock dance, #60GIN1-1, 1970s; "A graduation party!", Snoopy spells out words on a blackboard, #G19 39, early 1980s; $3.00 – 5.00 each.

"Join us at the Pumpkin Patch," Halloween, Linus and Snoopy are in the pumpkin patch, #60HIN 14-4, mid 1970s, $8.00 – 12.00; "Yikes!", Halloween, Snoopy is scared by the costumes worn by a couple of birds, #HIN34-3, late 1980s, $5.00 – 7.00.

Not Pictured
"Witch way's the party?", Halloween, Snoopy and Woodstock ride on a broom, #240HIN782, 1989. . . . .$2.00 – 4.00.

Napkins

This category could go on and on, so we've listed only a few of the older designs, all of which are beverage napkins.

Condition is based on mint in the box, with all napkins present. Very minor wear of the box is acceptable due to the products' age.

Cover of box: Charlie Brown and Snoopy, nearby are Violet, Patty, Schroeder playing the piano, Lucy, and Linus sucking his thumb, 36 napkins, each with a different design, monogram of California, date 1950s or early 1960s, $27.00 – 37.00. Cover of box: Charlie Brown stands with his arms outstretched, background shows the four available designs, "Good Grief Peanuts Beverage Napkins," four different designs, 36 total, Hallmark, #100NK9-3, late 1960s; Cover: World War I Flying Ace Snoopy sits on top of his bullet-riddled house, smoke emanates from it, Snoopy and the Red Baron, four different designs, 32 total, caption, "Rats!", Hallmark, #100NK97-5, early 1970s; Cover: World War I Flying Ace Snoopy, caption, "A Distinguished Combat Hero!" Snoopy for President, four different designs, 32 total, Hallmark, #100NP97-2, early 1970s; Cover: Snoopy dances, "Good Grief Peanuts Beverage Napkins," four different designs, 36 total, background shows the four available designs, Hallmark, #100NK97-1, late 1960s; $20.00 – 30.00 each.

Hallmark Party Favors & Accessories

Whether used for party favors, decorations or gifts, Hallmark products often were the life of the party. One had only to walk into a Hallmark store to find everything needed for a *real* party! Many of these items catapulted an innocent person into the throes of Peanuts collecting... how can such goodies be resisted?

We've listed a bit of this and that to provide an idea of what was produced.

Value is based on mint in the package, with no package wear (in other words, they've not been used).

Snoopy Super Sipper, clear straw with Snoopy's face, #39PF98-3, late 1960s, $6.00 – 10.00; Peanuts Telephone Dial Plate, plastic plate with pictures of Snoopy, Charlie Brown, Lucy, and Linus, #100HD3-7, late 1960s, $8.00 – 14.00.

Peanuts Erasers, two-dimensional figures of Charlie Brown, Lucy, and Snoopy, #50M999-3, late 1960s, $15.00 – 22.00.

Snoopy Door Plate, Snoopy reclines on his doghouse with Woodstock on his tummy, includes self-sticking letters to personalize, #175PF407-5, mid 1970s, $5.00 – 8.00; Snoopy Party Picks, 12 sticks with Snoopy on top of each, early 1970s, $6.00 – 9.00.

Not Pictured

"VAROOM!" Peanuts License Plate, plastic plate with Snoopy on his doghouse, includes self-adhesive letters to personalize, mid 1970s. . . . .$3.00 – 4.00

"Property of," Snoopy license plate, Snoopy and Woodstock ride a unicycle, includes self-adhesive letters to personalize, Ambassador Division of Hallmark, #125PF245, mid 1970s. . . . . .3.00 – 4.00

Snoopy Jump Rope, the handles are figures of Snoopy dancing, late 1960s. . . . .$12.00 – 24.00

Snoopy Nut Cups, four each of the Flying Ace and Woodstock sitting on Snoopy's bullet-riddled doghouse, #75NC97-2, early 1970s. . . . . .12.00 – 26.00

Snoopy's Party Nut Cups, Snoopy hugs Woodstock on his doghouse roof, the cups also serve as name tags, #75NC97-4, mid 1970s. . . . . .8.00 – 14.00

Peanuts Rainbow Party Nut Cups, Woodstock flies on the cup portion, a rainbow forms the handle, and a cloud serves as the name tags, #85NC116-2, mid 1970s. . . . . .6.00 – 10.00

Pin the Ears on Snoopy, game with Snoopy poster and ears, #150HD97-7, early 1970s. . . . . .20.00 – 35.00

Crepe Paper Streamers, Woodstock and birds wear party hats in repeated design, 2¾" x 10 yds, #HS592-7, early 1980s. . . . . .4.00 – 8.00

Snoopy Super Service, four each of plastic forks and spoons, with Snoopy at the top of the handle, #100PW96-7, early 1970s. . . . . .10.00 – 18.00

"Happy Birthday to You!", Peanuts Birthday Party Hats, four paper hats with Lucy, Schroeder, Snoopy, Sally, and birds, #PF277-8, early 1980s. . . . . .6.00 – 12.00

Peanuts Party Games, eight different games in notepad form, cover: Sally, Schroeder, Lucy, and Charlie Brown lift Snoopy, who has Woodstock in his dog dish, #100PB97-4, 1972. . . . . .20.00 – 32.00

Peanuts Party Games, eight different games in notepad form, cover: Schroeder plays the piano for Snoopy and Woodstock, rainbow background, #200PB 116-2, mid 1970s. .14.00 – 20.00

"Hooray for Birthdays!", Peanuts Cake Decoration, 23 candy pieces with paper centerpiece, Charlie Brown and Snoopy dance, Ambassador Division of Hallmark, #169PCD752J, 1970s. . . . . .10.00 – 16.00

"Hail! Hail! The Gang's All Here!", Peanuts Cake Decoration, 12 candy pieces with paper centerpiece, Sally, Schroeder, Lucy, and Charlie Brown lift Snoopy, Woodstock is in his dog dish, #150PCD97-4, 1970s. . . . . .14.00 – 18.00

Snoopy Flashlight, figure of Joe Cool, wearing red turtleneck and sunglasses, #250PF117-1, mid 1970s, $25.00 – 35.00; Woodstock Whistle, three-dimensional plastic Woodstock, #100PF101-8, mid 1970s, $12.00 – 20.00; Snoopy Whistle, three-dimensional plastic Snoopy, holding his supper dish behind his back, #100PF119-2, mid 1970s, $24.00 – 34.00.

Peanuts Desk Set, this would make a great gift for the birthday girl or boy, includes three plastic desk accessories: Linus stapler, Charlie Brown tape dispenser, and Snoopy letter opener, Springbok Division of Hallmark, #DSK 1201, early 1970s, $65.00 – 95.00.

Great Pumpkin Honeycomb Party Favors, two each of Snoopy and Linus, with fold-out pumpkin, #100HPF4-9, mid 1970s, $12.00 – 18.00; Snoopy and Woodstock Honeycomb Party Favors, two different designs of Snoopy and Woodstock, #100PF99-8, mid 1970s, $8.00 – 12.00.

Charlie Brown's Runaway Kite Glider, styrofoam glider to assemble, #125PF300-2, mid 1970s, $8.00 – 10.00; Snoopy's Flying Ace Glider, styrofoam glider to assemble, #125PF121-3, mid 1970s, $10.00 – 15.00; Woodstock's Flying Leaf Glider, styrofoam glider to assemble, mid 1970s, #125PF121-4, $6.00 – 8.00.

Peanuts Doodle Board, design with Woodstock, Charlie Brown, and Lucy looking at Snoopy drawing, lift-up slate erases whatever is drawn or written, the back has additional games, #100PF375-2, early 1970s, $8.00 – 14.00; Snoopy's Doodle Board, rainbow design with Charlie Brown, Woodstock, Snoopy, Peppermint Patty, and Lucy, lift-up slate erases whatever is drawn or written: the back has three different games, #100PF122-7, mid 1970s, $4.00 – 6.00.

Peanuts Blowouts, four paper whistles, each with a face of Linus, Lucy, Snoopy, or Charlie Brown, late 1960s, $24.00 – 38.00.

Peanuts Vinyl Visors, four adjustable visors with Snoopy and birds, #395PF117-4, early 1980s, $8.00 – 12.00.

Daisy Hill Puppies Party Pack, includes 8 sign holders and 8 treat cups featuring Snoopy, Belle, Marbles, Olaf, Andy, and Spike, #CPN2720, 1994, $10.00 – 20.00.

Plastic Cups

Given today's environmental consciousness, it's no wonder we now lament items we used capriciously and threw away. Fortunately, some people prized their Hallmark plastic cups with Peanuts characters!

The value is based on mint-in-the-box condition, although a small amount of wear on the box is acceptable.

"I'm available for a party," Snoopy's Plastic Party Glasses, set of four, top left glass description: Snoopy holds a bright pink and orange balloon, Ambassador Division of Hallmark, #125DC60M, late 1960s, $14.00 – 23.00; Peanuts Pak of Plastic Party Glasses, one character appears on each glass with a caption: Snoopy springs up and down, Linus holds his blanket, Lucy looks crabby, and Charlie Brown holds his baseball bat over one shoulder, Ambassador Division of Hallmark, #125DC60K, late 1960s, $18.00 – 30.00; "First beagle on the moon," Snoopy the Super Star Plastic Party Glasses, Snoopy in four different poses, including an astronaut, #125DC97-8, late 1960s, $18.00 – 30.00; Snoopy and the Red Baron Plastic Party Glasses, four pictures and captions with Snoopy as the Flying Ace, #125DC97-5, late 1960s, $18.00 – 30.00.

Hallmark Press-Out Decorations

These decorations were an easy and inexpensive way to carry out a theme for a party or season. Several designs were printed in each book. The book should be intact

with no missing pages. It's acceptable to have a small bit of wear on the cover, due to the age.

• General •

"Peanuts Barbecue Party Signs," Snoopy, Marcie, Peppermint Patty, Linus, Lucy, and Charlie Brown with various captions, #100HD12-9, 1975, $12.00 – 18.00; "Snoopy Home Decorations," Snoopy as the WWI Flying Ace, #100HD97-3, 1971, $14.00 – 20.00; "Peanuts Home Decoration Book," Snoopy looks down from the roof of his doghouse, Woodstock sits on him and chirps, #100HD97-5, 1968, $12.00 – 18.00.

"America, You're Beautiful!", Snoopy holds the American flag, Woodstock stands on top of flag pole with other birds following, #100HD 97-6, late 1960s, $14.00 – 20.00. "Peanuts Football Press-Out Decorations," Snoopy and Woodstock wear red football helmets, #125HD253-3, 1977; "Peanuts Fall Decorations," Snoopy and Woodstock jump into a pile of autumn leaves, #HM995-6, 1982; $6.00 – 8.00 each.

• School •

"Back-to-School Home Decoration Book," Woodstock rests on top of large red apple, #100HD190-5, 1976, $10.00 – 14.00. "Congratulations are in Order!", A tower of birds gives graduate Snoopy congratulatory greetings, #125GHD250-2, 1981; "Peanuts Graduation Home Decoration Book," Graduate Snoopy looks at "Good Times Ahead" directional sign, #125GHD 252-3, early 1980s; $6.00 – 8.00 each.

"Four Score and Seven Thousand Hours to go Until Vacation..." Snoopy is dressed as Abraham Lincoln, #150HD251-1, 1981, $8.00 – 10.00. "Hats Off to Grads!" Snoopy and Woodstock toss their mortarboards, #GHM250-7, 1983; "I Get a Kick out of School!" Snoopy, Woodstock, and several birds with soccer ball, #HFM996-2, 1985; $6.00 – 8.00 each.

• Valentine's Day •

"There's Nothing More Romantic than a Pizza-Scented Valentine!", Snoopy holds a Valentine, #125VHD250-7, 1979, $8.00 – 12.00. "Happy Valentine's Day," Snoopy places a valentine in Woodstock's nest, #125VHD251-3, 1978; "Peanuts Valentine Decorations," Snoopy paints a Valentine's Day greeting on a heart for Woodstock and his friends, #VHM66-3, 1982; $6.00 – 10.00 each.

"Happy Valentine's Day!", Hanging Decoration: Snoopy holds a valentine while Woodstock and many other birds hold cards, #VHD202-6, 1982, $10.00 – 14.00.

• St. Patrick's Day/Easter •

St. Patrick's Day: "Peanuts St. Patrick's Day Decorations," Snoopy sleeps on the roof of his doghouse while Woodstock and fellow leprechauns paint "Happy St. Patrick's Day!" on its side, #SHM69-3, 1982; "If Your Irish Heart is Happy, Let Your Irish Feet Show It!" Snoopy and Woodstock with a pot of gold, #SHM69-6, 1986; $6.00 – 10.00 each. Easter: "Snoopy Home Decoration Book," Snoopy sleeps while an Easter egg is on his nose, Woodstock sits on his tummy, #100EHD 16-9, 1975, $10.00 – 14.00.

"Easter Parade," Snoopy rides an Easter basket on wheels pulled by Woodstock and another bird, #125EHD252-1, 1980; "Peanuts Easter Decorations," Snoopy holds an Easter basket full of eggs and gives one to Woodstock, #EHM608-3, 1982; $10.00 – 14.00 each.

• Halloween/Thanksgiving •

Halloween: "Snoopy and Woodstock Halloween Decorations," Snoopy and Woodstock ride a witch's broomstick, #HHM782, 1989; Thanksgiving: "Peanuts Thanksgiving Home Decoration Book," Charlie Brown and Snoopy admire their Thanksgiving turkey, 1976; $8.00 – 12.00 each.

• Christmas •

"Peanuts Christmas Home Decoration Book," Snoopy's face appears in middle of Christmas wreath, #100XHD28-4, 1976, $16.00 – 22.00. "Peanuts Christmas Press-Out Decorations," Snoopy lies on top of his doghouse which is trimmed with Christmas decorations, Woodstock pulls a "Season's Greetings" banner, #125XHD251-9, 1979; "Christmas Puts a Carol in Your Heart!" Woodstocks sing carols for Snoopy, #XHD843-5, early 1980s; $10.00 – 14.00.

"Christmas with Peanuts," Santa Snoopy holds a gift sack, Woodstock sits inside a Christmas stocking, #XHM850-7, 1983; "Peanuts Holiday Decorations, press-out decorations of the gang in winter poses, #275XHD772-9, early 1980s; $10.00 – 14.00 each.

Photo Albums & Cases

Hallmark reigns supreme in this category. They produced photo albums for Peanuts fans in the United States, Europe, and Japan.

Albums should be in mint condition. While it's nice to own the box, it's usually not necessary. Exceptions are made if the box has graphics of the characters. The album cover should be without marks, smudges, or tears, and the inside should be clear of any added materials.

When Hallmark first produced the albums, drawings were included inside, sometimes of more obscure characters such as Violet and Frieda. You'll notice the drawings on the older albums are red, white, and black, the colors Hallmark first used on products. As the years went by, only the album cover bore any Peanuts characters. The exception are those albums produced for the Japanese market; they often had novelties inside, such as a pop-up scene.

"Don't you just love school?", Charlie Brown raises his hand as he sits by his school desk, nine pages of drawings, red background, 4¼" x 3¾", #250PHA 106-1, 1967, $22.00 – 40.00; "It was a great trip!", Snoopy holds his hobo pack on a stick over his shoulder, nine pages of drawings, red background, 4¼" x 3¾", #250PHA 108-1, 1967, $22.00 – 30.00.

Not Pictured
"Want to see my pictures?", Linus stands and wears his camera on a strap around his neck. 11 pages of drawings, white background, 4¼" x 3¾", #250PHA 105-1, 1967. $28.00 – 35.00

"Watch the birdie!", Snoopy gets ready to operate his camera, Woodstock is the birdie, yellow background, 6½" x 9¾", 1973, $18.00 – 28.00.

"Oggi mi sono svegliato con un pensiero meraviglioso...", Snoopy lies on top of his doghouse, 9¾" x 11½", Hallmark/Virca, Italy, mid 1980s, $14.00 – 28.00.

Snoopy rides a skateboard, Woodstock stands on top of Snoopy's head, green background with white border, 10" x 12", Coutts Hallmark, Canada, #PHA653-3, mid 1980s, $16.00 – 22.00.

Sally, Charlie Brown, Lucy, and Snoopy all pose for the camera, "Cheese!!", each page has a small picture of Snoopy and Woodstock, Japan, blue background, 7½" x 7⅛", #83827-6, 1985, $8.00 – 14.00.

Five albums in a cardboard case, Peppermint Patty, Schroeder, Snoopy, Lucy, and Woodstock all listen to Charlie Brown who stands on the baseball mound, each album has a different picture, blue and white background, case is 2¼" x 6", Hallmark/Kokuyo, Japan, #SNL30-7, late 1980s, $20.00 – 32.00.

Five albums in a cardboard case, Marcie, Peppermint Patty, Linus, and Lucy watch Snoopy as he holds a baseball bat in one hand and Woodstock carries the baseball in his mouth, each album has a different picture on it, background is residential street, case is 11⅜" x 8⅜", Hallmark/Kokuyo, Japan, #SNL1-10, late 1980s, $40.00 – 55.00.

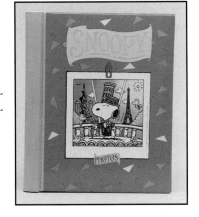

Snoopy and bird buddies in front of several famous landmarks such as the Statue of Liberty, Leaning Tower of Pisa and Eiffel Tower, Italy, red background with multi-color confetti design, 9¾" x 11½", late 1980s, $12.00 – 25.00.

Party scene with Woodstock, Snoopy, Linus, Peppermint Patty, Sally, Schroeder, and Lucy, lots of packages are near Snoopy's doghouse, inside cover folds open to reveal a table laden with food and a large cake, each page is decorated with small pictures of Snoopy, pink background, 12½" x 13", Hallmark/Kokuyo, Japan, #7-SN14-2, 1990, in box, $65.00 – 80.00; no box, $50.00 – 65.00.

"Smack," Snoopy kisses an unwilling Lucy, "Snoopy has a special place in the hearts of his friends, that playful, fun-loving, intelligent beagle shows an affection for his friends that is almost human," each page is decorated with small pictures of Snoopy, Hallmark/Kokuyo, Japan, green background, 13" x 13", #7-SN11-4, 1990, in box, $38.00 – 50.00; no box, $32.00 – 44.00.

"Look inside!", Snoopy holds a camera, Woodstock is nearby, case holds fold-out plastic photo holders, white background with varied color dots, 3⅜" x 4⅛", #PHA1106, 1991; "Lookin' good!", Snoopy's upper half, his arms are open and his ears stand up, purple, red, blue, and hot pink background, 3⅜" x 4⅛", #PHA1007, 1992; $4.00 – 7.00 each.

Not Pictured

"Don't you just love school?", Charlie Brown raises his hand as he sits by his school desk, nine pages
of drawing, red background, 4¼" x 3¾", #250PHA 106-1, 1967. . . . .$22.00 – 40.00
Snoopy and Woodstock enjoy pictures of themselves while sitting on a lawn, blue sky background,
5⅞" x 4⅝", #PHA 401-0, 1982. . . . . .15.00 – 22.00
Five albums in a cardboard case, Snoopy looks at Woodstock, each album has a different picture on it,
background is light blue with darker blue trim on one side, case is 7⅝" x 10½", Hallmark/Kokuyo,
Japan, #SNE1-1, late 1980s. . . . . .25.00 – 32.00

Picture Frames

This category has everything, from the most basic to the whimsical and sophisticated. Frames are made from all sorts of materials: wood, ceramic, metal, and plastic. We've mentioned a few of each.

Value is based on mint condition, with or without the box. Mesaurements refer to height unless otherwise noted.

• Wood •

A hot air balloon carrying Woodstock sports a "Snoopy" banner as Charlie Brown and Snoopy look skyward, a portion is cut out for the picture, and pencil cup is attached to the rear of the frame, 3⅜" x 3½" x 4¼", Japan, Tombow-Sugar/Butterfly Originals, #SD N01, Mid 1980s, $23.00 – 31.00; "Friendships are meant to be shared...", a two-dimensional Snoopy on a spring moves up and down, there are also two-dimensional cut-out figures of Woodstock and Charlie Brown who holds a bouquet of flowers, 4¼", Japan, Butterfly Originals, mid 1980s, $28.00 – 38.00.

A plastic figure of Snoopy holds a bouquet of flowers for Harriet and Bill, on their wedding day, 4½", Japan, Butterfly Originals/Glory Co., Ltd., late 1980s, $32.00 – 40.00.

Two-dimensional figures of Woodstock and Snoopy stand next to a gumball machine with two places for photos, 12", Japan, Idol Co., Ltd./Phoenix Corporation, Ltd., mid 1990s, $25.00 – 38.00.

• Metal •

"A Real Star," Snoopy in a triumphant pose by a star with a circle cut out for a picture, 4½", Burnes of Boston, early 1980s; "A friend is someone you can lean on," Snoopy and Woodstock lean against the opening providing for a picture, 3", Burnes of Boston, 1985; $20.00 – 30.00 each.

"**Snoopy,**" Snoopy reclines on top of his name, the letters "O" have openings to insert a picture, enamel painted, 3" x 7¼", Butterfly Originals, #3935, 1979, $35.00 – 42.00; "**Love,**" Snoopy reclines on the word itself, a kick-stand functions as an easel, enamel painted, 3¼" x 5⅝", Butterfly Originals, 1979, $30.00 – 37.00.

"**Is it Friday yet?!!**" Snoopy sits on his doghouse and furiously types, 6", Hallmark Frames, 1985; "**Thinking of You...**" Snoopy leans on a tree stump, 6", Hallmark Frames, #PP3019, 1985; $10.00 - 17.00 each.

Snoopy sits and hugs Woodstock, the cover is a laminated picture on metal backing, bi-fold opens up to display a picture on each side, 3⅔", Hallmark, #1000PP3051, 1984, $20.00 – 30.00.

• Ceramic •

Snoopy sits, he holds a clear acrylic frame, 7½", Japan, Pocket House, #SS-525-350, late 1980s, $75.00 – 95.00.

Charlie Brown sits next to a baseball that holds a clear acrylic frame, baseball caption, "Charlie Brown," 5¾", Japan, Butterfly Originals/ Glory Co., Ltd., #CBP 2400, 1989, $50.00 – 65.00.

Charlie Brown sits on a brown baseball glove, which holds an acrylic frame, glove caption "Charlie Brown," 6", Japan, Butterfly Originals/Glory Co., Ltd., #CB2000, 1989, $50.00 – 65.00.

Baseball Figures

Each character wears a baseball cap and holds a baseball glove or ball while sitting next to a ceramic heart, with an opening for a photo. 4¾", Japan, Determined Productions, Inc., 1993.

Peppermint Patty holds a bat, #SW-32, $35.00 – 55.00. Snoopy wears a baseball glove, #SW-31; Charlie Brown wears a baseball glove, #SW-33; $40.00 – 60.00 each.

"**Snoopy and Linus Van Pelt,**" faces of Linus and Snoopy and a scene with them tugging at Linus' blanket, 4¾", Japanese manufacturer not known, #79734-1, 1993, $22.00 – 34.00.

• Plastic •

Plain frame with a gold, two-dimensional metal figure of Snoopy hugging Woodstock, which is also a pin that helps the frame stand, 4", Japan, Phoenix Corp., #SNF(G), 1990, $15.00 – 20.00.

"Perfect, Like Me!", Lucy wears a pink dress, 3¾", Burnes of Boston, early 1984, $10.00 – 14.00; "To the Greatest," Snoopy holds a mug of root beer, 3¾", Burnes of Boston, 1984, $13.00 – 16.00; Snoopy unwraps a gift box with an opening for a circular picture, Woodstock flies above the box, 2¾", Butterfly Originals, Japan, late 1980s, $8.00 – 12.00; "My friend," Woodstock and Lucy flank the inserted picture, Snoopy holds the frame, 2½", Butterfly Originals, Japan, late 1980s, $10.00 – 14.00.

 # Playing Cards by Hallmark

A mint deck of cards includes a gold seal of Snoopy lying on his doghouse. The seal should be intact and not broken. Prices reflect mint condition in the box with mint slipcover (if applicable). All decks come in a cardboard box unless otherwise noted.

Decks were released in the USA, unless otherwise noted. (Many boxed cards from Japan are teamed up with Nintendo.) The first two digits of the item numbers reflect the original retail price; for example, the first deck below sold for 75 cents (applies to cards for sale in the United States).

• Mini Size •

Item No.	Description	Value
75BC98-1	Charlie Brown stands, 1970	$10.00 – 15.00
75BC97-1	Lucy stands and smiles, 1970	10.00 – 15.00
75BC98-7	Snoopy lies atop his doghouse, 1970	8.00 – 12.00
75BC98-8	Snoopy performs his famous happy dance, 1970	9.00 – 13.00
75BC101-6	Snoopy holds a football, 1972	9.00 – 13.00
75BC101-7	Charlie Brown and Snoopy hug, 1972	9.00 – 13.00
75BC101-8	Snoopy in a faux raccoon coat holds a "RAH" pennant, 1972	9.00 – 13.00
75BC101-9	Snoopy as Joe Cool, 1972	9.00 – 13.00
75BC102-7	Snoopy stands with a hobo pack attached to a stick over his shoulder, 1973	8.00 – 12.00
75BC102-8	Snoopy lies atop his doghouse with a single sunflower overhead, 1973	8.00 – 12.00
75BC103-1	Snoopy gets ready to hit a baseball, 1972	9.00 – 13.00
75BC103-2	Snoopy holds a tennis racket, 1972	9.00 – 13.00
75BC103-4	Snoopy and Woodstock sit very close to one another, 1973	9.00 – 13.00
75BC103-5	Snoopy as a referee, 1973	9.00 – 13.00
75BC104-1	Snoopy gets ready to kick a football, 1973	9.00 – 13.00
75BC104-2	Snoopy carries skis over his shoulder, 1973	9.00 – 13.00
89BC96-6	Snoopy hugs Woodstock, early 1970s	9.00 – 13.00
89BC96-9	Snoopy wears a red and green knitted cap as snow falls, early 1970s	9.00 – 13.00
100BC118-7	Snoopy, surrounded by jelly beans, early 1970s	15.00 – 15.00
100BC118-8	Snoopy blows a bubble with his gum, early 1970s	10.00 – 15.00
100BC121-1	Snoopy and the Beaglescouts, early 1970s	12.00 – 17.00
27950	Snoopy hugs Woodstock (Europe), late 1970s	9.00 – 13.00

Charlie Brown stands, 1970; Lucy stands and smiles, 1970; Snoopy lies atop his doghouse.

Snoopy performs his famous happy dance, 1970; Snoopy holds a football, 1972; Charlie Brown and Snoopy hug, 1972.

Snoopy blows a bubble with his gum, 1970s; Snoopy and the Beaglescouts, early 1970s; Snoopy hugs Woodstock, Europe, late 1970s.

• Regular Size •

Item No.	Description	Value
150BC96-6	Snoopy and Woodstock play cards on the doghouse, 1970	$14.00 – 18.00
125BC99-7	Charlie Brown and Snoopy hug, 1970s	14.00 – 18.00
125BC99-6	Snoopy in a faux raccoon coat holds a "RAH!" pennant, 1970s	12.00 – 16.00
125BC99-5	Snoopy as Joe Cool, 1970s	12.00 – 16.00
45182-7	Plush sitting Snoopy and Woodstock, Japan, 1990, plastic box, cardboard slip cover	15.00 – 22.00
47837-7	Snoopy sits surrounded by Woodstock and several birds, Japan, 1988, plastic box, cardboard slip cover	14.00 – 18.00
31714-4	Snoopy wears a crown, Japan, plastic box, cardboard slip cover, 1986	15.00 – 22.00
SN1009	Two panels each of Snoopy and Woodstock, Japan, plastic box, 1989	14.00 – 18.00
SN1029	Snoopy and Woodstock on rollerboards, Japan, 1992, plastic box	14.00 – 18.00
SN1036	Snoopy hugs Charlie Brown at a bus stop, Japan, 1992, plastic box	14.00 – 18.00
SN1037	Snoopy reads a letter he just took from a mailbox, Japan, 1992, plastic box	14.00 – 18.00
SN1038	Snoopy holds paw to mouth, Woodstock flies in front of him, Japan, 1992, plastic box	14.00 – 18.00
SN1039	Snoopy plays golf, Woodstock holds the flag, Japan, 1992, plastic box	14.00 – 18.00
960JQGC	Snoopy, Woodstock, and another bird, with telescope, Japan, 1990, plastic box	15.00 – 22.00
1000JQGC	Snoopy holds a tennis racket, Japan, 1992, plastic box	14.00 – 18.00
1000JQGC	Snoopy holds a tennis racket, Woodstock sits on a tennis ball, Japan, plastic box	14.00 – 18.00
1000JQGC	Snoopy and Woodstock sit in a restaurant, "He hates to eat at a place where you have to sit at a counter," Japan, plastic box	15.00 – 22.00
	Snoopy hugs Woodstock inside a heart design, Europe	14.00 – 18.00
	Snoopy performing his happy dance inside a diamond shape, Europe	12.00 – 16.00
PC900-5	Snoopy and Woodstock sit inside house made of cards, Europe	14.00 – 18.00

Charlie Brown and Snoopy hug, 1970s; Snoopy in a faux raccoon coat holds a "RAH!" pennant, 1970s; Snoopy as Joe Cool, 1970s.

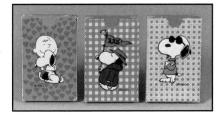

Snoopy hugs Charlie Brown at a bus stop, Japan, 1992, plastic box; Snoopy reads a letter he just took from a mailbox, Japan, 1992, plastic box; Snoopy holds paw to mouth, Woodstock flies in front of him, Japan, 1992, plastic box.

• Card Games •

Item No.	Description	Value
125BC98-1	"Security:" Linus with blanket, sucking thumb, early 1970s	15.00 – 22.00
125BC98-2	"Fussbudget:" Lucy with her big mouth wide open, early 1970s	15.00 – 22.00
125BC98-3	"Snooping Around:" Snoopy as Sherlock Holmes, early 1970s	15.00 – 22.00
125BC99-3	"Rats:" Snoopy as the WWI Flying Ace, sits on his doghouse, early 1970s	15.00 – 22.00
125BC98-5	"Go Fly a Kite:" Charlie Brown with kite, early 1970s	15.00 – 22.00
125BC98-7	"Born Loser:" Charlie Brown on cover, early 1970s	15.00 – 22.00

"Fussbudget," Lucy with her big mouth wide open, early 1970s; Snooping Around, Snoopy as Sherlock Holmes, early 1970s; Rats, Snoopy as the WWI Flying Ace, sits on his doghouse, early 1970s.

• Bridge Sets (two decks) •

Item No.	Description	Value
350BC984-2	"Jolly Jokers," 1. Snoopy as a court jester, 2. Woodstock and friends as jesters, 1970s	$20.00 – 28.00
	"The Ace," 1. Snoopy walks, wears Flying Ace helmet, red scarf, and carries baton, 2. The Flying Ace sits on top of his house, late 1960s	22.00 – 32.00
	"Snoopy," 1. Snoopy watches Woodstock fly, 2. Woodstock stands on Snoopy's tummy, 1970s	20.00 – 28.00
BC981-4	"Peanuts Fancy Shuffling," 1. Snoopy performs, 2. Woodstock and friends perform (both are vaudeville acts)	14.00 – 18.00

"Jolly Jokers," Snoopy as a court jester; Woodstock and friends as jesters, 1970s.

"Playing for Peanuts," Snoopy displays his cards; Woodstock sits in a house made from cards, early 1980s; "Peanuts Rainbow," Snoopy on skates, Woodstock skates, holding a balloon, early 1980s; $18.00 – 26.00 each.

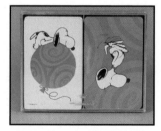

"Snoopy," Snoopy lies on a balloon; Snoopy side view, dancing, $15.00 – 22.00.

• Playing Card Ensembles •

Item No.	Description	Value
450BCE97-4	Two decks (Snoopy and Woodstock with flowers), score pad and pencil, early 1980s	$24.00 – 32.00
450BCE1162	Two decks (Snoopy on skates, Woodstock on skates with balloon), score pad and pencil, early 1980s	22.00 – 30.00
500BCE9803	Two decks (Snoopy displays his cards, Woodstock in house of cards), matching score pad, early 1980s	22.00 – 30.00

Puzzles

This category is wonderfully diverse. Unfortunately, we don't have room to go into the length and breadth of one of our favorite categories. But we must mention one puzzle.

In 1994 the Peanuts Collector Club was contacted by Hallmark's Springbok Division to find a Peanuts collector who could provide enough material for a Peanuts puzzle. No problem. Right near Hallmark's headquarters lived

Pauline Graeber, who is a *very* serious Peanuts collector.

The end result of the collaboration between Hallmark Cards and Pauline Graeber is a colorful puzzle which is a joy to Peanuts collectors and gives the "outside" world a little insight into just what a collector likes.

"Peanuts," 500 pieces, graduated pieces so family members of various ages can work alongside one another, assembled size 20½" x 26¾", #PZL700, 1995, $15.00 – 20.00.

Scrapbooks

There's no better way to hold memories than with a Hallmark scrapbook. The earlier examples are the most interesting, as they carry red, black, and white drawings of the characters, including some not seen today, such as Frieda and 5. These

older items provide a glimpse of how the characters appeared in their earlier incarnations.

Values are based on mint condition, with some allowance for a bit of wear due to the age of the item. Some came in plain boxes and while they're nice to have, they really don't affect the value. There should be no marks or tears inside or outside the scrapbook.

"Snaps, Scraps, and Souvenirs," Lucy and Linus review some of the memorabilia in their scrapbook, each page has drawings, gold burlap background, 11¼" x 9⅛", #400SB10-1, 1967, $55.00 - 75.00.

"The Peanuts Thoughtfulness Album," Snoopy lies on top of a mailbox and watches a bird holding a letter, a page for each month of the year, and pages with pockets to store items, every page has drawings, red background, 8" x 10", 1968, $50.00 – 70.00; Snoopy wears his Flying Ace helmet and scarf, he sits on top of his doghouse, the design appears to be a large decal applied to blue burlap, two pages include drawings, 10" x 12½", #695BK500-1, 1968, $35.00 – 47.00.

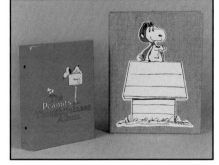

"Scraps," Snoopy sits on top of his doghouse and holds a book, Woodstock looks on, 10⅞" x 9⅛", green background with blue trim and writing, 1972, $18.00 – 22.00; Snoopy wears a tank top with the caption "Super" and a star, white background with multi-color dots, 10⅞" x 12½", #RA6034, 1990; Snoopy's upper body, he holds his arms out and wears a big smile, hot pink, purple, red, and blue background, 12½" x 11", #RA6045, 1992; $15.00 – 20.00 each.

Hallmark Stationery & Greeting Cards

Hallmark certainly gave us a wide variety of designs from which to choose. Because each category — stationery, post cards, stickers, greeting cards, etc. — has a long list of products behind it, a sampling is provided as just a small taste.

Fans of these products are fortunate because many mint copies still are around.

Value is based on excellent in-the-box or in-the-package condition. It is acceptable for the box to show some wear, but the entire contents must be present. The cover of each is described.

• Boxed Stationery •

Each set comes in a cardboard box.

Four panel cartoon strip: Lucy hands Snoopy a letter from Miss Helen Sweetstory, #200ST913-1, early 1970s, $15.00 – 20.00; "Good Grief," Charlie Brown holds his hand to his chin, #125ST, late 1960s, $16.00 – 21.00; Snoopy and Woodstock ride a rollercoaster, #ST352-1, early 1980s, $10.00 – 15.00; the Flying Ace reads a letter, #200ST929-1, 1972, $16.00 – 21.00.

Mailman Snoopy follows his route in the country, #300ST108-8, 1978, $10.00 – 15.00; Snoopy is on top of an open mailbox, #200ST963-1, 1973, $16.00 – 21.00; "Have a Nice Day!", Drum major Snoopy marches with several birds, #250ST951-1, 1973, $12.00 – 17.00; "Watch the Birdie!", Snoopy operates a standing camera while Woodstock holds a "Smile" sign, #250ST465-6, 1976, $10.00 - 15.00.

• Memo Pads •

4" x 6"

"I Need All the Pity I Can Get," Charlie Brown wails on the baseball mound, #50KM 956-8, 1969; "On a beautiful day like this it would be best to stay in bed so you wouldn't get up and spoil it," Charlie Brown and Freida, Ambassador Division of Hallmark, #49M 101K, 1969; "No One Understands Us Crabby People!", Lucy frowns, #39M 400-5, 1967; $3.00 – 4.00 each.

6⅞" x 10"

"It's Good to Have a Friend," Snoopy reclines on his doghouse, a bird stands on Snoopy's tummy, four different designs of paper, #100KF 3-7, 1970s; "Rats," four different designs of paper, #100KM 957-5, 1970s; $5.00 – 8.00 each.

• Boxed Note Cards •

"Quotable Notes by the Peanuts Philosophers," Lucy, Charlie Brown (sitting on a bench eating a sandwich), and Linus are near Snoopy, who sits on his doghouse, #100BM 61-4, late 1960s, $25.00 – 34.00.

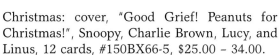

Snoopy sniffs a flower, plastic-trimmed box, late 1960s, $20.00 – 30.00.

• Boxed Greeting Cards •

Valentines: The Flying Ace holds a valentine, box is house-shaped, 18 cards, #100BV2-5, 1973 (re-released in 1977 as #125BV25), $18.00 – 27.00.

Christmas: cover, "Good Grief! Peanuts for Christmas!", Snoopy, Charlie Brown, Lucy, and Linus, 12 cards, #150BX66-5, $25.00 – 34.00.

Christmas: three each of Linus, Snoopy, Charlie Brown, and Lucy holding a symbol of Christmas, #100BX69-3, late 1960s, $25.00 – 34.00.

Mixed assortment: 16 birthday and friendship cards, #450BM965-8, 1977, $15.00 – 22.00.

• Individual Greeting Cards (Christmas) •

Because Christmas is a time highlighted by warm and colorful cards, we thought you'd enjoy seeing a few samples.

"Happiness is Having a Friend Like You...", Snoopy wears a Christmas wreath, #100KXX204-2, mid 1960s, $4.00 – 8.00; "For You!", Charlie Brown has a large gift, open the box, and up pops Snoopy, #110KX202-1, mid 1960s, $4.00 – 6.00.

"Merry Merry Merry Merry Merry Christmas!", Snoopy dances and wears a tag around his neck, oversized greeting card, approximately 24½" accompanied by a cardboard mailing envelope with a picture of Snoopy and a bird on the front, #250X 201-6, late 1960s, $22.00 – 32.00.

"Merry Christmas to someone I'm immensely fond of!", Lucy stands and holds a Christmas greeting. Oversized greeting card, approx. 24½", accompanied by a cardboard mailing envelope with a picture of Snoopy and a bird on the front, #250X 203-6, late 1960s, $14.00 – 25.00.

Not Pictured
"I went to a department store and asked the saleslady to wrap up what she thought was the neatest, cutest gift in the place..." Lucy stands with her hands behind her back, open the card, and Lucy pops out with her arms outstretched, #100KXX204-5, mid 1960s. . . . .$4.00 – 6.00

• Postcards •

"It's good to have a friend," Snoopy reclines on his doghouse, a bird sits on his tummy, 20 different designs, #200KF 1-5, 1970s, $10.00 – 22.00; "Happiness is getting mail at your new address!", Snoopy holds an envelope, pad of 25, identical design, $10.00 – 14.00.

"Each of us has his own calling!", Snoopy reclines on top of his doghouse, #25M 400-7, late 1960s; "I never made a mistake in my life! I thought I did once, but I was wrong," Lucy stands and looks smug, Ambassador Division of Hallmark, #25M 104J, 1968; "People Always Expect More of You When You Have Naturally Curly Hair!", Frieda touches her hair, #25M 400-6, 1968; $1.00 – 2.50 each.

• Seals and Stickers •

Sticker Picture Book, Snoopy and Woodstock are on the doghouse reading a book, includes two pages of stickers to affix to the outlined images, #100HD 100-2, mid 1970s, $10.00 – 14.00; Sticker Coloring Poster, press the stickers onto a poster, Ambassador Division of Hallmark, #APT518LB, mid 1980s.

Packs with multiple sheets of seals or stickers. Valentine, "Smak," Snoopy kisses Lucy, Ambassador Division of Hallmark, #59VSS3E, early 1970s; Halloween, "The Great Pumpkin is a Male Chauvinist!", Lucy holds up sign in the pumpkin patch with Linus nearby, #59HHD49, early 1970s; $3.00 – 4.00 each. St. Patrick's Day, "I'm just loaded with Irish charm!", Lucy expresses herself to Snoopy, who thinks, "Talk about blarney!", #75SSS519, mid 1970s, $2.50 – 3.50; Patriotic, Snoopy and Woodstock against a red, white, and blue background, mid 1970s, $5.50 – 8.00.

"What goes up must come down...except golf scores!", Snoopy plays golf, #59SS1194, 1970s, $3.00 – 4.00; "World's Greatest," Snoopy in his various personae, Springbok Division of Hallmark, #750G113 1D, 1974, $4.00 – 6.00; "Keep those cards and letters coming!", Linus holds a sign, #75KF 11-6, 1970s, $6.00 – 8.00.

"A kiss on the nose does much toward turning aside anger," Snoopy gets ready for a smooch, #50 HD995, 1970s; "If you can't dance, at least do a happy hop!" Snoopy hops, #50 HD997, late 1960s; $3.00 – 4.00 each. "Curse you, Red Baron!", Flying Ace on the roof of his doghouse, each sticker features a different character with a caption, 1960s, $8.00 – 12.00.

• Record and Bookplates •

"Peanuts record and bookplates," first design is Snoopy reading on the roof of his doghouse, "Ex Libris," #100M 400-4, 1968, $8.00 – 12.00; Snoopy and Woodstock on the doghouse, #150HBM29-1, 1972, $6.00 – 10.00; Lucy is at her psychiatrist's booth, Charlie Brown holds a book and looks back at Lucy, 1986, Antioch Publishing, $4.00 – 6.00.

Hallmark Postalettes (Notelettes)

Hallmark came out with this dandy way to get a written message across for busy people who didn't need reams of paper to say what they wanted. You just wrote your message on the fold-up letter, attached the sticker, addressed and stamped the letter, and it was ready for the post office.

This is just a sampling of what was available. Each box came with stickers to seal the letter unless otherwise noted.

The average box size is 5⅝" x 5⅜" and contains 12 to 15 fold-up notes and matching stickers. Prices are based on mint-in-the-box condition with no tears to the cello wrap.

• General Themes •

Snoopy plays his trombone as a flock of birds follow him playing horns, #1505ST522-1, 1973; Snoopy's house, the matching sticker is Snoopy, #150ST539, 1973; $6.00 – 10.00 each. Woodstock is a postal carrier with a letter in his mouth, Snoopy sits by his mailbox, #S150-BM, 1970s, $4.00 – 6.00.

Snoopy wears a sweatsuit and runs against a background of different-colored hills, #ST104-8, 1970s, $4.00 – 6.00; Snoopy sits on his doghouse and reads one of many letters stacked up for him, #ST105-8, 1970s, $5.00 – 7.00. Snoopy and Woodstock run on a soccer field, #ST120-4, 1974; Snoopy plays tennis, his opponent is Molly Volley, #ST182-2, early 1980s; $4.00 – 6.00 each.

Professor Snoopy instructs a class filled with birds, #ST299-6, 1986, $4.00 – 6.00; Snoopy sings as Woodstock plays the organ, comes with sealing wax and handle, #ST3725, mid 1970s, $10.00 – 16.00. Snoopy and Woodstock perform a happy dance against bright strips of blue, red, green, and orange, #ST7377, 1977; Chef Snoopy tosses a pizza crust into the air, Woodstock juggles pepperoni, #ST522-3, 1983; $4.00 – 6.00 each.

French artist Snoopy paints Woodstock's portrait, #ST257-0, 1980, $4.00 – 6.00; Aerobics instructor Snoopy leads a flock of birds in exercise, #ST330-5, $5.00 – 7.00. Lucy perspires as she pedals her stationary bicycle, #ST523-3, mid 1980s; Woodstock, in his nest, reads a letter, Ambassador Division of Hallmark, #ST801R, 1983; $4.00 – 6.00 each.

Beaglescout leader Snoopy roasts some marshmallows for his bird scouts, Ambassador Division of Hallmark, #ST804J, 1984; French painter Snoopy holds his paint palette and stands near an easel, Ambassador Division of Hallmark, #ST805M; $5.00 – 7.00.

Not Pictured
Snoopy types "Hi!" on his typewriter, the background is various calico-type
    prints, self-adhesive flaps, 1970s. . . . .$5.00 – 7.00

• Christmas theme •

Snoopy's Christmas tree is decorated with dog bones, #150NX256-5, $8.00 – 10.00. Snowmen wish Snoopy and Woodstock "Happy Holidays," #200NX358-1; Snoopy and Woodstock wear Dickens-style hats and scarves and sit on the doghouse, #225NXS1-7; $7.00 – 9.00 each. Santa Snoopy hands an envelope to Woodstock who has a Christmas tree in his nest, #225NX53-4, $6.00 – 8.00.

Toys

General

"Speak Up, Charlie Brown," pull the cord housed in a cardboard storybook and hear a story, Mattel, Inc., #4312, 1967, in box, $125.00 – 175.00; no box, $30.00 – 75.00.

"Snoopy See 'N Say," pull the string and the arm on the two-dimensional plastic Snoopy turns to a picture of Charlie Brown, Snoopy, Peppermint Patty, Linus, Pig Pen, Frieda, Sally and Snoopy, Lucy, Schroeder, or Violet and listen to an appropriate phrase, Mattel, Inc., #4864, 1969, in box, $125.00 – 175.00; no box, $30.00 – 75.00.

Head Beagle Megaphone, metal, Snoopy in a director's cap and sunglasses, stands next to Lucy and Charlie Brown, inspired by the 1969 film, "A Boy Named Charlie Brown," this toy comes in several background colors, including green, blue, and red, 1969, $15.00 – 27.00.

Kenner Movie Viewer featuring "Snoopy," hand-held plastic viewer holds movie cassette, one cassette included (see list of available movies under "Battery-Operated Toys" section). Kenner/General Mills Fun Group, Inc., #35900, 1975, in box, $28.00 – 46.00; no box, $20.00 – 32.00; Fisher-Price Movie Viewer featuring "Snoopy Meets the Red Baron," hand-held plastic viewer holds movie cassette (cassette included with scenes from "It's the Great Pumpkin, Charlie Brown"), Fisher-Price Toys, a division of The Quaker Oats Company, #465, 1982, in box, $24.00 – 42.00; no box, $16.00 – 30.00.

"Snoopy's Bubble Blowing Bubble Tub," blow bubbles from the shower pipe over Snoopy's tub, comes with 4oz. bottle of bubble liquid, Chemtoy/Aviva, #121, 1976, in box, $32.00 – 52.00; no box, $18.00 – 28.00; "Snoopy Gyroscope featuring Charlie Brown," Charlie Brown sits on a globe, by pulling the string the toy does tricks, Aviva Toy Company, Inc./Hasbro Industries, Inc., style #400, 1978, in box, $18.00 – 30.00; no box, $15.00 – 27.00; "Snoopy Gyroscope featuring Snoopy," Snoopy sits on a globe, by pulling the string the toy does tricks, Aviva Toy Company, Inc./Hasbro Industries, Inc., style #400, 1978, in box, $20.00 – 32.00; no box, $17.00 – 29.00.

"**Snoopy**-Matic Instant Load Camera," Snoopy is prone on his doghouse-shaped camera, camera strap included, Another Determined Production/Helm Toy Corp, camera is licensed by Eastman Kodak Company, #975, mid to late 1970s, in box, $145.00 – 180.00; no box, $65.00 – 105.00.

Snoopy Camera, shaped like a soda can, the film cartridge acts as the mechanism for the camera to work, camera strap and name tag included, available in red or blue casing, Japan, Tomy for Determined Productions, 1984, in box, $125.00 – 160.00; no box, $45.00 – 85.00.

"**Snoopy** Tell-Time Clock," plastic clock to be taken apart and reassembled, clock runs up to eight hours, Another Determined Production/Concept 2000, #171, late 1970s, in box, $23.00 – 40.00; no box, $17.00 – 22.00; "Snoopy Take Apart Clock," plastic clock with Woodstock pendulum can be taken apart and reassembled, clock ticks and runs for a few hours, Japan, Toybox/Another Determined Production, #TC-433, early 1980s, in box, $20.00 – 32.00; no box, $17.00 – 22.00.

Not Pictured

"Charlie Brown Tell-Time Clock," plastic clock to be taken apart and reassembled, clock runs up to
eight hours, Another Determined Production/Concept 2000, #172, late 1970s. . . . . .in box, $18.00 – 35.00
no box, 12.00 – 18.00

"Woodstock Tell-Time Clock," plastic clock to be taken apart and reassembled, clock runs up to
eight hours, Another Determined Production/Concept 2000, #173, late 1970s. . . . . .in box, $18.00 – 35.00
no box, $12.00 – 18.00

"Snoopy Copter Pull Toy," pull Snoopy by the string and he rolls on the wheels while his ears spin,
Woodstock is along for the ride, Hasbro Preschool/Hasbro Industries, Inc., #82201, 1980s. . . .in box, 10.00 – 14.00
no box, 6.00 – 10.00

Action Figures

These toys are winners, and Mattel's Skediddlers are the real show-stoppers. Collectors spend years seeking toys mint in the box. Many of the graphics are colorful, a great plus when showing off a collection.

Prices are based on mint in the box. Due to the age of some of the toys, a bit of wear on the box is acceptable. There should be no rip or tears on the boxes or cellophane (if applicable).

• Mattel •

Snoopy Jack-in-the-Music Box, Snoopy pops up from inside the box, his head and two paws are made of plastic, his body is white cotton fabric with a red ribbon around his neck, his ears are felt, his nose is painted black, #4745, 1966, in box, $45.00 – 65.00; no box, $10.00 – 30.00.

• Skediddlers •

The figures have a wheel attached to help them walk. Their clothes are cloth and their shoes are part of the figure.

It is very important, if you purchase an unboxed Skediddler, to make sure a working wheel attachment is included.

Snoopy as the Flying Ace with goggles and a red scarf around his neck, #3630, 1968; Charlie Brown wears his yellow shirt with black zigzag and black pants, #3632, 1968; Lucy wears a blue dress, #3631, 1968; Linus wears a red and white striped shirt, black pants, #3634, 1969; in box, $75.00 – 115.00 each; no box, $30.00 – 55.00 each.

Snoopy Skediddler and his Sopwith Camel, a vinyl case opens to reveal the Flying Ace in his camouflaged bi-plane, #4954, 1969, in box, $145.00 – 205.00; no box, $80.00 – 125.00.

Not Pictured
"Club House Set," Charlie Brown, Snoopy, and Lucy, as described
    above, boxed in a set, #3803, 1968. . . . . .in box, $225.00 – 295.00
                                                            no box, 90.00 – 165.00

• Aviva Toy Company/Hasbro Industries, Inc. •

Action Toys starring Snoopy

Each features a plastic Snoopy participating in a sport. Boxes may be red or blue. Some boxes bear the name

Aviva while others cite both Aviva Toy Company and Hasbro, Series #200, 1977.

Snoopy kicks a football, style #740, in box, $25.00 – 40.00; no box, 20.00 – 30.00; Charlie Brown plays baseball, style #200, in box, $35.00 – 45.00; no box, $25.00 – 35.00; Snoopy holds a hockey stick and moves the puck, style #200, in box, $25.00 – 40.00; no box, 20.00 – 30.00.

"**Woodstock** Climbing String," Woodstock's wings and tail move and he chirps, #667, in box, $18.00 – 32.00; no box, $12.00 – 20.00.

"**Woodstock** Flying Trapeze Toy," push the buttons to see Woodstock work the trapeze, #2000, 1979, in box, $8.00 – 13.00; no box, 6.00 – 11.00; Snoopy Flying Trapeze Toy, push the buttons to see Snoopy work the trapeze, #2000, 1979, in box, $10.00 – 15.00; no box, $8.00 – 13.00.

"**Snoopy** Trigger Action Toy," Snoopy's head moves up and down to give the impression he is talking, packaged on card (no box), #70460; "Woodstock Trigger Action Toy," Woodstock's head moves up and down to give the impression he is chirping, packaged on card (no box), #70460; $12.00 – 20.00 each.

• Ideal Toy Corporation •

Push Puppets

Plastic figures stand on a base. Push the underside and the figures move, six different styles, Ideal, 1977.

Snoopy wears formal attire, including black top hat, in box, $50.00 – 70.00; no box, $35.00 – 50.00. Snoopy as the Flying Ace; Charlie Brown as a baseball manager, in box, $60.00 – 80.00 each; no box, $45.00 – 60.00 each. Snoopy as a western sheriff; Snoopy as Joe Cool; Lucy as a nurse; in box, $50.00 – 70.00 each; no box, $35.00 – 50.00 each.

Butterfly Originals/Kutsuwa

Snoopy figure stands next to a metal globe with Woodstock on top, plastic gears turn both Snoopy and the globe (the plastic figures tend to yellow even if stored in original box), Japan, 1985, in box, $175.00 – 275.00; no box, $125.00 – 180.00.

Snoopy and some birds sit at the controls of a spaceship, in front is a globe of the world, which can spin (the plastic figures tend to yellow even if stored in original box), stand is metal, Japan, #20SS, 1985, in box, $175.00 – 275.00; no box, $125.00 – 180.00.

Romper Room/Hasbro Industries, Inc.

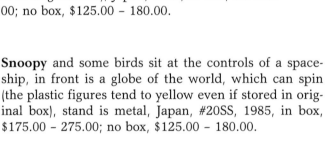

Snoopy Jack-in-the-box, wind the player and Woodstock comes out of his nest, then Snoopy pops out the front door of his house, #820, early 1980s, in box, $20.00 – 28.00; no box, $15.00 – 22.00.

Balance Toys

These unique toys are made from plastic; most have parts that include figures of one or more Peanuts characters.

Values are based on mint in the package with no major tears. If the toy is not in its package, all parts should be included.

• Aviva Toy Company, Inc./Hasbro Industries, Inc. •

Balance Bars. The middle figure balances a character on each end of the metal bar. Packaged either on a blister card or box (both styles pictured), 1979.

Not Pictured

"Charlie Brown Bar," figures of Charlie Brown, Woodstock, and Snoopy, blue plastic base,
#150. . . . . .in package, $27.00 – 42.00
no package, 20.00 – 35.00
"Snoopy Balance Bar," figures of Snoopy, Lucy, and Charlie Brown, blue plastic base, #155. .in package, 27.00 – 42.00
no package, 20.00 – 35.00

Balance toys. One or more characters balance at the end of a wire. Series #555 is blister packed; series #560 is boxed. 1980.

Charlie Brown and Woodstock on skis, in package, $27.00 – 42.00; no package, $20.00 – 35.00; Snoopy and Woodstock scouting, in package, $35.00 – 52.00; no package, $30.00 – 48.00; Snoopy and Woodstock on skis, in package, $27.00 – 42.00; no package, $20.00 – 35.00.

Snoopy & the 5 Balancing Woodstocks, plastic two-dimensional figures, Snoopy attempts to hold five birds, each a different color, #826, 1982, in package, $12.00 – 18.00; no package, $5.00 – 10.00.

Not Pictured

Snoopy biplane. . . . . .in package, $35.00 – 52.00
no package, 30.00 – 48.00
Snoopy and Woodstock on doghouse. . . . . .in package, 27.00 – 42.00
no package, 20.00 – 35.00

Baseballs

When the Wilson Sporting Goods Company produced their Peanuts baseballs in 1969, little did they realize how prized they would become to Peanuts collectors in the years to follow.

Finding an "Official Peanuts League" baseball in its original box is the pinnacle of collecting success!

"Official Peanuts Baseball," black outline drawings of Schroeder, Charlie Brown, Snoopy, Lucy, and Linus decorate the ball, horsehide cover with red stitching, 1969, in box, $125.00 – 190.00; no box, $50.00 – 90.00.

Battery-Operated

Toys always are more valuable when in their original box, even if there is some wear. However, a good toy is a good toy; it's difficult to pass one by if the chance of finding one in a box is quite slim. A case in point is Snoopy the Critic. It's very difficult to locate at all, let alone in its original box. Both the Snoopy Drive-In Movie Theater and Peanuts Mattel-O-Phone came in great boxes, but both toys are so desirable that it would be a shame to pass them up if the box is nowhere to be found.

All toys should be in working condition. There should be no rust in the battery storage compartment. Always have various sized batteries on hand to test such toys so you won't be disappointed after getting it home. Wear is acceptable on the box, depending on the toy's age. All parts should be included, along with the instructions.

"Peanuts Mattel-O-Phone," talking telephone has five discs that provide 40 phone calls with Snoopy's friends Charlie Brown, Linus, Lucy, Pig Pen, Frieda, Violet, Schroeder, Sally, and Peppermint Patty, requires two "D" batteries, Mattel, #4858, 1968, in box, $180.00 – 230.00; no box, $80.00 – 140.00.

"**Snoopy** Drive-In Movie Theater," Snoopy views movies from his convertible, the toy comes with one movie, "Woodstock's Dream House," Requires three "D" batteries, Kenner, #49-16529, 1975, in box, $155.00 – 215.00; no box, $65.00 – 125.00.

Additional movies available but not included with the Drive-In. The movie is the collectible; the box does not influence the value.

1. I'll Be a Dirty Bird!
2. Good Grief!
3. Roll Over, Beethoven!
4. Snoopy's Garage Sale
5. Chow Hound Snoopy
6. Skateboard Olympics
7. Blockhead's Bobble
8. Hang On, Snoopy!
9. The Easter Beagle
10. Sherlock Snoopy
11. Lucy vs. Masked Marvel
12. Curse You, Red Baron!

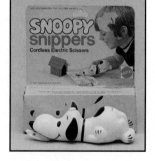

"**Snoopy** Snippers," cordless electric scissors in the shape of Snoopy reclining on his stomach, the bottom of his mouth opens to cut, accompanied by a sheet of Peanuts characters to cut, requires two "AA" batteries, Mattel, #7410, 1975, in box, $38.00 – 47.00; no box, $24.00 – 32.00.

"Chirping Woodstock," Woodstock chirps while he is suspended from a spring, his wings are feathers, requires one 9-volt battery, Another Determined Production, #115, mid 1970s, in box, $27.00 – 37.00; no box, $20.00 – 28.00.

"**Snoopy** the Critic," Snoopy stands on top of his doghouse, Woodstock sits in his nest, the attached microphone amplifies a voice or enables Snoopy to moves his arms to clap, while Woodstock moves up and down, requires two "D" batteries, Aviva Toy Company, Inc./Hasbro Industries, Inc., #222, 1978, in box, $95.00 – 130.00; no box, $50.00 – 90.00.

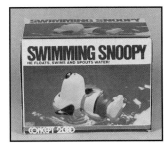

"**Swimming Snoopy,**" Snoopy reclines on his back and floats, swims, and spouts water, requires two "AA" penlite batteries, Concept 2000/Another Determined Production, #106, late 1970s, in box, $32.00 – 47.00; no box, $25.00 – 35.00.

"**Snoopy's** Beagle Bugle," a mini phonograph inside the bugle plays several different bugle calls, plastic figures of Snoopy and Woodstock can be removed or inserted at the top of the bugle, a Child Guidance Toy/Questor Education Products Company, #1730, mid to late 1970s, in box, $75.00 – 115.00; no box, $40.00 – 70.00.

"**Electronic Snoopy** Playmate," press a button on Snoopy as a drum major, as well as other buttons and a knob to activate games, lights, sounds, and music, as well as recording ability, requires 2 "D" batteries and one 9-volt transistor battery, Romper Room/Hasbro Industries, Inc., #830, 1980, in box, $45.00 – 98.00; no box, $30.00 – 60.00.

"**Chirping Woodstock,**" plastic Woodstock has a cord, he performs five different bird calls, requires one 9-volt battery, Aviva Toy Company/Hasbro Industries, Inc., #477, 1980, in box, $27.00 – 37.00; no box, $20.00 – 28.00.

"**Snoopy** Hoola Hoop," Snoopy twirls the hoop around his hips, while standing on a circus podium, two hoops are included, hand-held control unit, requires three "AA" batteries, International Trading Technology, Inc., #888, 1991, in box, $45.00 – 70.00; no box, $35.00 – 50.00; Snoopy Tumbling Toy, Snoopy moves forward and backward in a tumbling action, he holds a hoop in each hand, and Woodstock is in each hoop, requires one "AA" battery, International Trading Technology, Inc., #875, 1991, in box, $40.00 – 65.00; no box, $30.00 – 45.00.

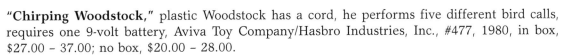

Not Pictured
"Snoopy Battery Powered Pencil Sharpener," Snoopy sits on his doghouse and types on his typewriter,
    insert a pencil in the hole in back of Snoopy to automatically sharpen it, the house sits on a green
    plastic base that has slots to house pencils, caption, "Snoopy Pencil Sharpener," Requires three "D"
    batteries, Kenner/General Mills Fun Group, #3550, 1974. .in box, $27.00 – 40.00
                                                                                                    no box, 18.00 – 25.00

Colorforms

These are comprised of plastic forms which stick to a playboard to make up scenes. All sets are playsets unless otherwise indicated. Prices are based on mint-in-the-box condition with all of the pieces intact. A little booklet from Colorforms should be enclosed.

"Hit the ball, Charlie Brown!", item no. 750, $14.00 – 22.00; "Come home, Snoopy!", item no. 751, $8.00 – 12.00; "How's the weather, Lucy?", item no. 752, $14.00 – 22.00; "Hold that line, Charlie Brown!", item no. 753, $12.00 – 16.00.

"Carry on, Nurse Lucy!", item no. 754, $14.00 – 22.00; "What's on Sale, Snoopy?", item no. 755, $8.00 – 12.00; "Yankee Doodle Snoopy," item no. 756, $12.00 – 16.00; "What's Cooking, Snoopy?", item no, 757, $12.00 – 16.00.

"You're a Pal, Snoopy!", item no. 758, $8.00 – 12.00; "Disco Snoopy," item no. 759, $14.00 – 22.00; "Snoopy & Woodstock," item no. 760, $12.00 – 16.00; "Peanuts Playset," item no. 761, $12.00 – 16.00.

"Snoopy & Belle," item no. 762, $12.00 – 16.00; "Star Snoopy," item no., 2358, $22.00 – 28.00.

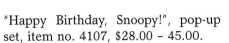

"Happy Birthday, Snoopy!", pop-up set, item no. 4107, $28.00 – 45.00.

"Snoopy's Beaglescouts," three-dimensional set, item no. 4108, $28.00 – 45.00.

"**Snoopy,** You're A Star!" theatre set, item no. 4307, $28.00 – 45.00.

"**Lucy's** Winter Carnival," item no. 7400, $22.00 – 28.00.

"Let's go to the beach, Snoopy!", item no. 7401, $22.00 – 28.00.

"You're A Sport, Snoopy!", item no. 7403, $26.00 – 32.00.

"**Peanuts** Play Set," pre-school set, #8110, $22.00 – 28.00.

 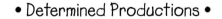

Costumes and Masks

Even if he is considered a loser, parents don't mind dressing up their children as Charlie Brown come trick-or-treat time. After all, Charlie Brown is the most popular of all the round-headed kids on the block.

Prices are based on mint-in-the-box condition with the box or cellophane having no tears (in other words, the items haven't been used). Possibly there will be a price tag that has been removed.

Not Pictured
Official Snoopy costume worn by a small adult during appearances in the 1960s and early 70s, the one listed here was used in various Dolly Madison promotions. . . . .$300.00 – 450.00

• Determined Productions •

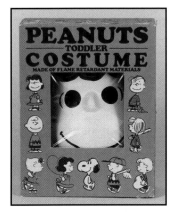

The boxes are orange with green, white, and black pictures of Lucy, Charlie Brown, Sally, Schroeder, Snoopy, Peppermint Patty, Linus, and Woodstock bordering the sides of the box. A partial cello cover reveals the mask. The costumes came in different children's sizes. 1970s.

Lucy, #6310; Charlie Brown, $15.00 – 25.00 each. Snoopy, $20.00 – 30.00.

• Collegeville Flag & Mfg. Co. •

The boxes are blue with Snoopy, Charlie Brown, Lucy, and Woodstock with lots of pumpkins. Early 1980s.

Woodstock, #2462; Charlie Brown, #2463; Lucy, #2464; $10.00 – 15.00 each.

Not Pictured
Snoopy, #2461. . . . .$20.00 – 30.00

• Masks Only •

Not Pictured
Snoopy's head with red top hat and bowtie, Japan, 1989. . . . .$3.00 – 4.00
Snoopy's face, the package includes bags of Halloween candy, Sanrio, #600 866130, Japan, 1989.   .6.00 – 12.00

 # Crafts

Crafts projects are limited only by the talent and imagination of amateur artisans, and many companies have produced products that provide the perfect Peanuts touch. The reward, in the end, is a Peanuts item that can be displayed and treasured. There's much to choose from, so we provided a sampling of different types of crafts.

Value is based on all items' being intact, and in the box. The box for older items (pre-1985) can show a little wear. Be sure the instructions are included.

• Another Determined Production or Determined Productions, Inc./Craft House •

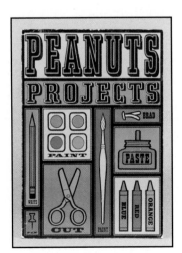

Peanuts Projects, an activity book which requires a pencil, paints, scissors, push-pins, paste, and brads to assemble the various projects, 1963, $35.00 – 50.00.

"Snoopy...The Great Master!" Acrylic Paint-by-Number Set, 6" x 8" panels of Lucy ice skating and Snoopy and Woodstock on a frozen birdbath, six pots of color and brush, #3073, 1976; "Snoopy...The Great Master!" Acrylic Paint by Number Set, 6" x 8" panels of Snoopy and Woodstock on the golf course and Charlie Brown swinging his golf club, six pots of color and brush, #3074, 1976; $8.00 – 12.00 each.

"**Snoopy's** Mini Wood Christmas Ornaments Acrylic Paint-by-Number Set," sandpaper, six pots of paint, wood stain, brush, and gold cord are used to complete 14 different mini Christmas ornaments on mahogany, #3570, 1978, $25.00 – 30.00.

"**Snoopy** Felt Pen Picture Set," four marking pens are used to color six 8" x 10" pictures, #4570, 1979, $10.00 – 14.00.

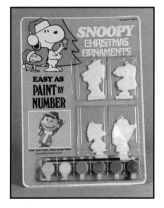

"**Snoopy's** Wood Painting Fast Dry Paint-by-Number," Snoopy, Charlie Brown, and Linus with baseball mitts, caption, "I Can't Stand Showoffs!" #6074, 1976, $10.00 – 14.00.

"**Snoopy's** Wood Painting Christmas Ornaments Acrylic Paint-by-Number Set," sandpaper, six pots of color, wood stain, brush, and gold cord are used to complete 20 different Christmas ornaments on mahogany, #8070, 1977, $25.00 – 40.00.

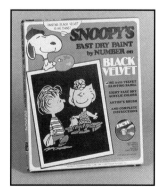

"**Snoopy** Christmas Ornaments," four paint-by-number ornaments completed with a brush and six pots of paint, #8085, 1981, $10.00 – 16.00.

"**Snoopy's** Fast Dry Paint-by-Number on Black Velvet," Linus holds his blanket and walks by Sally who sits on a bench, #8573, 1978, $8.00 – 12.00.

"**Snoopy** Mosaic Crushed Stone Craft Kit," crushed stone and glue complete a picture of Lucy rollerskating, #9572, 1979, $12.00 – 16.00.

"**Snoopy** Mosaic Crushed Stone Craft Kit," crushed stone and glue complete a picture of Charlie Brown holding a baseball bat, #9573, 1979, $12.00 – 16.00.

• Avalon •

"**Snoopy** Sign Mobile," display signs created with the pre-printed paper, stencils, and crayons, #262, 1980, $60.00 – 75.00.

"**Snoopy** Color 'n Recolor Mug Set," crayons are used to color various designs to insert in the two mugs, #741, 1980, $24.00 – 32.00.

"**Snoopy** Color 'n Recolor Mug-Bowl-Place Mat Gift Set," crayons are used to color various designs for the mug, bowl, and place mat, #742, 1980, $60.00 – 75.00.

"**Snoopy** Color 'n Recolor Deluxe Playcloth Set," eight crayons are provided to color a 40" x 36" plastic playcloth, ten stand-up pictures of the gang are included, #943, 1980, $35.00 – 48.00.

• Butterfly •

"**Snoopy** Color Me Cork Board," six crayons complete the corkboard picture of Snoopy, Sally, Charlie Brown, Peppermint Patty, Woodstock, and Linus in an ice cream parlor, #275-7949-6, early 1980s, $8.00 – 14.00.

"**Snoopy** Fantastic Fun Set," contains construction paper, scribble pad, Snoopy Snippers, glue, 16 crayons and one color pencil, Butterfly Originals, Ltd./Plymouth, Inc., #8071, early 1980s, $25.00 – 37.00.

• Craft House •

"Snoopy Big 3 Fast Dry Paint-by-Number," nine pots of paint and brush are used for pictures, Snoopy, Charlie Brown with Woodstock, and Lucy, in baseball-related activities, #2571; "Snoopy Big 3 Fast Dry Paint-by-Number," nine pots of paint and brush are used for pictures of Snoopy and Woodstock involved in sports: tennis, running, and football scenes, #2572; $14.00 – 22.00 each.

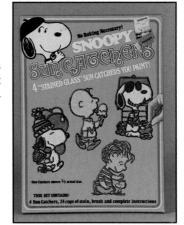

"Snoopy Sun Catchers," 24 cups of color stain and brush are used to complete four different plastic pictures that can be hung in the window to catch the light, #8275, $10.00 – 14.00.

"Snoopy Fun Figures You Paint," paints and brush are used to complete plain white figures of Snoopy as a Native American, Spike strumming a banjo, Snoopy playing guitar and Belle holding a coffee pot, #04801, 1984; "Snoopy Fun Figures You Paint," paints and brush are used to complete plain white figures of Snoopy on roller skates, holding baseball bat, as a scuba diver, and as a sailor, #04802, 1984; $18.00 – 26.00 each.

"Snoopy Fast Dry Paint-by-Number Set," eight pots of color and brush are used to complete a picture of Snoopy fishing in his small sailboat, #13571, 1981, $8.00 – 12.00.

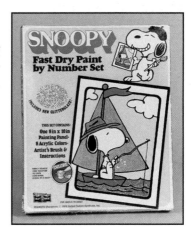

"Snoopy Snap 'n Paint," a plastic hollow figure of Snoopy and Woodstock on the doghouse can be painted with six pots of paint, glitter finish, and a brush, #19121, 1981, $12.00 – 15.00.

"Snoopy Sun Ornaments," plastic, Snoopy kisses Lucy, Linus sucks his thumb and holds blanket, Snoopy hugs Woodstock and cuddles inside a blanket, and Charlie Brown gets ready to swing his golf club, each can be completed with six pots of paint and brush, #40095, 1983, $10.00 – 14.00.

"Snoopy Window Picture," nine different colors of stain and a brush are used to complete a translucent picture of Peppermint Patty kissing Charlie Brown, caption, "Love is accepting a person for what he is," #48062, 1983; "Snoopy Window Picture," nine different colors of stain and a brush are used to complete a translucent picture of Schroeder and Lucy, the outline of the figures and background are raised to give the picture dimension, caption, "Love is not nagging," #48064, 1983; $16.00 – 22.00 each.

• Mattel •

"Super Cartoon-Maker featuring Snoopy and his Peanuts pals," Electric Cartoon-Maker heater, eight ¾-oz. bottles of Plastigoop, cartoon blocks, cooling tray, handle, knife, cartoon dialogue, and other accessories are used to form five two-dimensional figures of Snoopy, Charlie Brown, Linus, Lucy, and Schroeder in 14 poses, #4696, 1969, $140.00 – 170.00.

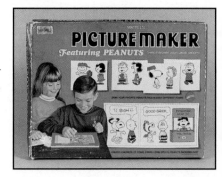

"Picture Maker Featuring Peanuts," a plastic tray becomes a drawing board for templates and paper, to draw various Peanuts characters and dialogue, #4153, 1970, $45.00 – 70.00.

"Plush Point," includes everything needed to make one picture each of Charlie Brown, wearing a baseball glove and cap, and Snoopy, lying down with the thought balloon, "Rats," the background is burlap, #3963, 1971, $20.00 – 32.00.

"Play-Fills," soft clay is used to fill the outlines of three 7½" x 9½" pictures: Lucy, Snoopy, and Charlie Brown, three colored background sheets are included, #8951, 1972, $28.00 – 40.00.

"Peanuts Sculpt-Sure," several different colors of clay and a sculpting tool are provided to sculpt a 12" tall Charlie Brown who wears a baseball cap and mitt, #8956, 1972, $30.00 – 45.00; "Peanuts Sculpt-Sure," several different colors of clay and a sculpting tool are provided to sculpt a 10½" figure of Snoopy as the WWI Flying Ace, #8957, 1972, $40.00 – 65.00.

• Pastime Industries, Inc. •

"**Snoopy** Sticks Bank," wood sticks, cardboard parts, paint, brush, and glue are used to form a bank in the shape of Snoopy's doghouse, #1247, 1988; "Snoopy & Friends Sewing Cards," includes four reusable sewing cards, yarn in assorted colors, plastic sewing frame, and Pop 'N Sticker, #1251, 1988; $10.00 – 15.00 each.

"**Snoopy** Pop 'N Charms," use pop beads and charms to create your own jewelry, #1255, 1988, $10.00 – 15.00.

Not Pictured

"Snoopy & Friends Lace-Ups," vinyl lacing, and Snoopy stick-ons are used to complete pre-cut vinyl
    wallet, change purse, key ring, and pencil holder, #1245, 1987. . . . .$14.00 – 26.00

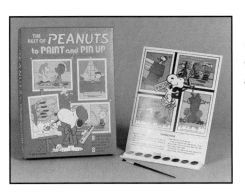

• Saalfield •

"The Best of Peanuts to Paint and Pin Up," eight
9" x 12" scenes to be painted with eight colors
and brush, #6176, early 1970s, $24.00 – 34.00.

"Peanuts Wet the Brush and Bring Out Colors,"
eight 12" x 9" scenes, whose colors appear when colored by a wet brush, early 1970s, $18.00 – 28.00.

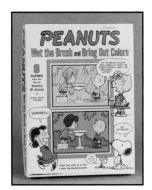

Games

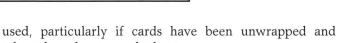

Values are based on mint-in-the-box condition. The
value decreases if it is obvious that the contents have been
used, particularly if cards have been unwrapped and
tokens have been punched out.

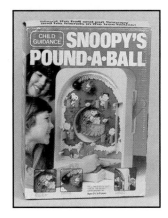

• Child Guidance •

"Snoopy's Pound-A-Ball," non-electrical or
battery-operated pinball machine game,
#51702, 1980, $35.00 – 45.00.

• Colorforms •

"Tell Us A Riddle, Snoopy!", a question and answer game, #2397, 1974,
$35.00 – 45.00.

• Determined Productions •

"The Pursuit of Happiness Game," board
game, #0285, 1965, $38.00 – 52.00.

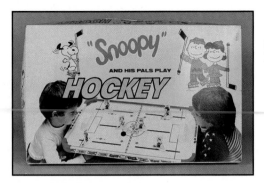

"Snoopy and His Pals Play Hockey," action game using plastic figures of the gang playing ice hockey, Another Determined Production/Munro Games, Inc., #2324, 1972, $150.00 – 190.00.

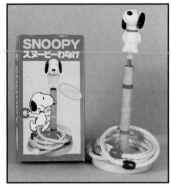

"Snoopy Toss Rings," a figure of Snoopy stands on top of the pole, five rope rings with wooden beads are included, Japan, #STR-35, mid 1980s, $60.00 – 85.00.

• Educa (Ravensburger) •

"Memory Snoopy," memory game, Europe, #3518, 1988, $12.00 – 14.00.

• Gabriel •

"Snoopy Snack Attack," action game, #70345, 1980, $18.00 – 32.00.

• Golden •

"Great Shakes, Charlie Brown," a dice game that matches characters appearing on the game sheets, #4235, 1988, $12.00 – 14.00.

• Hanayama •

"Family Game," a selection of nine different board games, Japan, #101001-06108-2500, mid 1980s, $25.00 – 35.00.

• Hanayama/Determined •

"Super Snoopy Golf Game," board game with three plastic figures of Snoopy as a golfer, Japan, #101001-05037-3600, mid to late 1980s, $40.00 – 55.00.

• Ideal/Determined •

"Can You Catch It, Charlie Brown?", non-electrical and non-battery-operated pinball game, #8282-6, mid 1970s, $53.00 – 70.00.

• Milton Bradley Company/Determined •

"**Snoopy** Come Home Game," board game, #4303, 1972, $12.00 – 15.00; "Snoopy and the Red Baron," skill and action game, #4067, 1970, $30.00 – 48.00.

"Good ol' Charlie Brown Game," board game, #4139, 1972, $28.00 – 40.00.

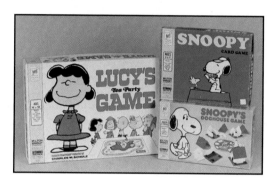

"**Lucy's** Tea Party Game," board game with teapot and saucers, #4129, 1972, $15.00 – 28.00; "Snoopy Card Game," #4425, $4.00 – 8.00; Snoopy's Doghouse Game, spin/board game with three-dimensional doghouses, #4704, 1977, $14.00 – 22.00.

Snoopy's game of Tiddly-winks, a new approach to an old favorite, United Kingdom, #4016, 1980s, $6.00 – 10.00.

• Milton Bradley Company •

"The Snoopy Game," comes with plastic figures of Charlie Brown, Peppermint Patty, Lucy, Linus, and Snoopy on his house, board game, #4413, 1988, $24.00 – 48.00.

• Nintendo of America, Inc. •

"**Snoopy** Game & Watch," battery-operated action game, #SM-91, early 1980s, $45.00 – 60.00; "Snoopy Tennis Game & Watch," battery-operated action game, #SP30, smaller version of SM-91, early 1980s, $20.00 – 30.00.

Not Pictured
"Tabletop Snoopy Game & Watch," largest version of the
Nintendo tennis game, #SM-73, early 1980s. . . . . . .$95.00 – 150.00

• Parker Brothers •

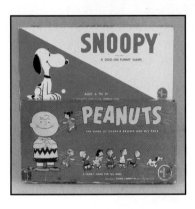

"Charlie Brown's All-Stars," baseball board game, #410, 1974, $28.00 – 40.00.

"Snoopy Dodgem Game," board game with Snoopy's Dodgem car as the main focus, United Kingdom, #8809, late 1970s, $35.00 – 50.00.

• SelRight (Selchow & Righter Co.) •

"Snoopy, A Dog-On Funny Game," board game, the box cover of the game has Snoopy pictured on it as well as the spinner and one disk, #66, 1960, $35.00 – 48.00; "Peanuts: The Game of Charlie Brown and His Pals," board game, #86, $32.00 – 60.00.

• Tsukuda Original •

"Snoopy Family Game," small version of a pinball machine game (not electrical or battery-operated), Japan, #D002071, mid 1980s, $25.00 – 35.00.

 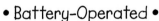 # Grooming Aids

These products were developed to aid parents and entice children into practicing good grooming. Some of the graphics on the boxes are actually more attractive than the toy itself, so it's highly desirable to find the item in its original box.

Value is based on mint in the box. All parts should be included, and toy must work. Some wear on the box is acceptable due to the age of the product.

• Battery-Operated •

"Snoopy Toothbrush," doghouse shape with Snoopy who serves as the handle for a toothbrush, includes two toothbrushes, a comb, brush, Woodstock toothpaste tube winder, two adapters, and dental care booklet, requires two "D" batteries, Kenner Productions/General Mills Fun Group, #30100, 1975; in box, $35.00 – 47.00; no box, 20.00 – 32.00; "Snoopy Doghouse Toothbrush," Woodstock is in his nest at one end of the doghouse-shaped case and Snoopy is on the other end, the house holds the toothbrush, comes with two brushes, Aviva Toy Company/Hasbro Industries, Inc., #300, 1980; in box, $28.00 – 35.00; no box, 20.00 – 30.00; "Snoopy Comb and Brush," a small boat with a sail with Snoopy's name on it, houses a Snoopy figure that holds a comb and brush, requires two "D" batteries, Kenner Products/General Mills Fun Group, #30900, 1975; in box, 35.00 – 47.00; no box, 20.00 – 32.00.

• Non-Battery-Operated •

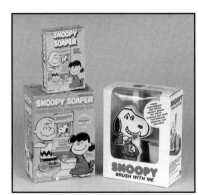

"Snoopy Soaper," Snoopy is the "Clean Hands Inspector," place hand under his soap dispensing station to receive soap, pictured with soap refill box, Kenner Products/General Mills Fun Group, #30700, 1975; in box, $20.00 – 32.00; no box, $10.00 – 15.00; "Snoopy Brush With Me," two-dimensional Snoopy arm moves up and down so he can brush his teeth, a toothbrush, and plastic cup are included, Determined Toy, #5001, early 1980s; in box, $15.00 – 28.00; no box, $8.00 – 14.00.

 # Kaleidoscopes

These cylindrical toys boast Peanuts artwork, which adds to their festivity and colorfulness.

Value assumes the container is in excellent condition with no tears. The eyepiece should lend itself to clear visibility of the designs.

"Peanuts Rainbow Kaleidoscope," Sally, Lucy, Snoopy, Woodstock, Marcie, Charlie Brown, Linus, and Peppermint Patty enjoy a day of outdoor activities, with a large rainbow as the backdrop, Hallmark, #200PF500-2, early to mid 1970s, $12.00 – 18.00; "Snoopy Disco Kaleidorama," Snoopy is dressed for, and dancing to, disco music, Woodstock stands nearby, Determined Productions, #4961, 1979. $15.00 – 23.00.

 # Minis

This little word refers to a big line of products issued by Butterfly Originals in the mid 1970s to early 1980s, mostly for the younger set to enjoy. There are at least 200 to 300 different items, so we'll settle for a sampling here. These are charming little pieces of nostalgia.

Prices are based on the item being in mint condition with all the included parts. Packaging should be intact.

Snoopy Mini Picture Frame, plastic with separate stand, Snoopy hugs Woodstock, #79-3910, $3.00 – 5.00; Mini Telephone Book, fold-out telephone book with mini plastic mascot of Woodstock, #79-0716, $2.00 – 4.00; Snoopy & Woodstock Mini Attache Case, plastic case unsnaps to reveal writing tablet, a pencil is housed at the top of the case, #99-0726, $3.00 – 5.00.

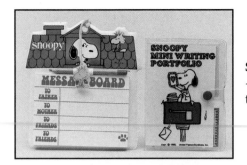

Snoopy Message Board, vinyl-covered board with message pad, #99-0730, $8.00 – 14.00; Snoopy Mini Writing Portfolio, the plastic snap case opens to reveal stationery, envelopes, and a sheet of stickers, #99-0731, $3.00 – 5.00.

Mini Coloring Book, set of three books, #125-0820, $6.00 – 8.00; Snoopy Mini Twin Pack, two little pads of paper and one colored pencil, in a plastic briefcase, #129-0741, $3.00 – 5.00.

Snoopy Mini Index, plastic case pops up to alphabetically list address and phone numbers, #149-1745; Peanuts Roll Call Folder, vinyl-covered notebook with plastic clip of Beaglescout birds opens to reveal a writing pad, #179-0766; $8.00 – 12.00 each.

Peanuts Scribble Board, board in the shape of Snoopy's house, comes with two pieces of chalk and a Snoopy eraser, #200-3401, $8.00 – 14.00.

Snoopy Gift Pack, "Merry Christmas," six crayons, eraser, scribble pad, and three color pencils in a gift box, #219-0779; Snoopy Gift Pack, "Be My Valentine," a memo pad, four colored pencils, eraser, and two plastic hearts in a gift box, #300-0780; $8.00 – 14.00.

Not Pictured

Peanuts Mini Color Pencil Set, plastic carrying case unsnaps to reveal 14 colored pencils and drawing pad, #300-0732. . . . .$8.00 – 14.00

Snoopy Mini Color Pencils, eight colored pencils, each with a picture of Snoopy, packaged in a plastic case, #CN-200 EN0 01. . . . . .4.00 – 6.00

Snoopy Tool Set, plastic pouch holds wrench, pliers, axe, and hammer. . . . . .6.00 – 10.00

Mini Binder, plastic clipboard with picture of Snoopy typing as Woodstock watches, comes with pencil and plastic Woodstock mascot. . . . . .6.00 – 10.00

Model Kits

Make certain all parts are included for a finished, working model. There should be no rust in the battery storage compartment. Test the toy, if possible, before taking it home. If decals are mentioned in the description, be sure they are included. Having the box is highly desirable since it serves as a reference point for the included parts.

All sets are Snap Tite kits by Monogram, Inc., a division of Mattel.

Values are based on mint-in-the-box condition with some wear allowed on the box due to age.

• Battery-Operated •

"**Snoopy** and his Bugatti Race Car," Snoopy sits in his red Bugatti, he wears his Flying Ace helmet with goggles, his head moves back and forth, and the wheels turn, the car sits on a stand, decals are included, #6894, 1970, in box, $80.00 – 135.00; no box, $40.00 – 75.00; "Snoopy is Joe Cool," Snoopy rides his surfboard which goes up and down on waves, he also spins around, #7502, 1973, in box, $60.00 – 85.00; no box, $35.00 – 50.00. "Snoopy and his Motocycle with Woodstock in the Sidecar," the Flying Ace rides his motorcycle with Woodstock in the sidecar, the motorcycle rolls on its wheels, #5902, 1971; "Snoopy and his Sopwith Camel," Snoopy flies his plane which sits on a portion of his doghouse, propeller spins, decals are included, #6779, 1970; in box, $90.00 – 145.00 each; no box, $40.00 – 75.00 each.

• Non-Battery-Operated •

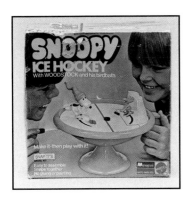

"**Snoopy** Ice Hockey with Woodstock and His Birdbath," a game of hockey takes place between Snoopy and Woodstock, #5696, 1971, in box, $50.00 – 75.00; no box, $15.00 – 30.00.

"**Snoopy** High Wire Act" with Woodstock, assemble Snoopy and his house and have him walk the high wire, a gold Woodstock is included as counterweight, #661, 1972, in box, $35.00 – 50.00; no box, $20.00 – 30.00.

Motorized

This is where the Aviva Toy Company shines. They produced most of the Peanuts vehicle-type toys, and many were wonderfully imaginative, such as Schroeder's piano on wheels, which could be played with like a car. And baseball memorabilia fans and collectors love Charlie Brown and his Mound Buggy. Aviva left Peanuts collectors a legacy of fun.

Value is based on mint-in-the-box condition. Due to age, minor wear of the box is acceptable. There should be no tears, however, on the box or cellophane (if applicable). The toy should move easily on its wheels.

The following series featured Snoopy, Aviva Toy Company/Hasbro, 1976.

Snoopy drives a yellow taxi with a red stripe on the front hood, a decal of Woodstock functions as Snoopy's passenger, #70800-5; Snoopy, in a yellow rain slicker and hat, rows a boat, #70800-2; Snoopy takes a bubble bath and uses a brush on his back, #70800-3; Snoopy plays conductor on a red locomotive with yellow trim, #70800-4; Flying Ace Snoopy sits on the roof of his house, #70800-1; in box, $15.00 – 22.00 each; no box, $8.00 – 13.00 each.

This series put wheels on a item associated with each character, Aviva Toy Company, style #966, 1977.

"Snoopy and his Desk-Mobile," in box, $45.00 – 60.00; no box, $25.00 – 35.00; "Charlie Brown and his Mound Buggy," in box, $50.00 – 65.00; no box, $25.00 – 40.00. "Lucy and her Doctor Booth;" "Linus and his Blanket-Mobile;" "Snoopy and his Doghouse;" "Schroeder and his Piano-Mobile;" in box, $45.00 – 60.00 each; no box, $25.00 – 35.00 each.

Peanuts Motorized Toys, Aviva Toy Company, Hasbro, assortment #500, 1978

Flying Ace Snoopy, in box $18.00 – 25.00, no box $15.00 – 22.00. Charlie Brown wears a baseball cap, his yellow shirt with black zigzag and black pants; Woodstock sits in his nest; in box $15.00 – 22.00 each, no box $8.00 – 13.00 each.

Snoopy Show Boat Motorized Toys, features moving smoke stacks, Aviva Toy Company/Hasbro, assortment #575, 1979

Woodstock stands in front, Charlie Brown and Snoopy sit on top, red boat with white hull; Snoopy and Lucy sit in front, Woodstock sits on top, white boat with blue hull, red wheels; in box, $25.00 – 40.00 each, no box, $15.00 – 23.00 each.

Wheelies

These first were issued by Hasbro Industries, Inc./Aviva Toy Company. Similar editions later were issued by International Trading Technology, with some differences. The section concerns the first release, not the more recent editions. Be sure to look closely for the decals on each vehicle, Series #777, 1979.

Woodstock rides a red scooter, in box, $12.00 – 20.00; no box, $8.00 – 14.00. Snoopy rides a green delivery scooter; Snoopy rides a blue scooter; in box, $15.00 – 22.00 each; no box, $10.00 – 15.00 each. Woodstock rides an orange ice cream scooter, in box, $12.00 – 20.00; no box, $8.00 – 14.00.

Musical & Instruments

What makes a parent more proud than a child who has mastered a musical instrument? Even Professor Harold Hill knew how to take advantage of this parental weakness, and besides, after some practice, these toys will sound great!

Whether from the Chein Company or International Trading Technology, Inc., these instruments make a sweet sound in the world of Peanuts collecting.

Value is based on mint-in-the-box condition. Some wear is acceptable on older boxes, pre 1985. All parts should be included, and the item must work properly.

• Battery-Operated •

Child Guidance/Questor Education Products Co.

"**Schroeder's** Piano with the Peanuts," figures of Lucy, Peppermint Patty, Snoopy, Linus, Schroeder, and Charlie Brown fit into the holes on top of the piano and pop up and down in time to the music, requires one "C" battery, #1701, mid 1970s, in box, $75.00 – 110.00; no box, $35.00 – 50.00.

International Trading Technology, Inc.

"**Schroeder** Piano," blue plastic piano with interchangeable figures of Charlie Brown, Lucy, and Schroeder which move when music is played, comes with microphone, stand, and sheet music, requires three "C" batteries, #777, 1990, in box, $75.00 – 120.00; no box, $50.00 – 80.00; Schroeder piano, black plastic piano with interchangeable figures of Charlie Brown, Lucy, and Schroeder which move when music is played, comes with microphone, stand, and sheet music, (This piano was made exclusively for the cable television shopping channel, QVC, and produced in black to appeal more to the adults who watch the show.) requires three "C" batteries, #777, 1990, in box, $100.00 – 145.00; no box, $75.00 – 120.00.

• Non-Battery Operated •

Chein

"Peanuts Drum," Lucy tells the band members to "Get in step, you BLOCKHEADS!". The band includes 5, Frieda, Linus who beats on a drum with the caption, "Peanuts Marching Band and Good Grief Society," Sally, Pig Pen, and Schroeder playing the piano, Snoopy and Charlie Brown pull up the rear. Two drumsticks and a red and white cord to hold the drum are included, drum rims come in different colors: silver, red, etc., metal, #129, late 1960s, in box, $130.00 – 180.00; no box, $60.00 – 105.00.

"Peanuts Parade Drum," Linus looks through a movie camera to see Charlie Brown stand on the pitcher's mound, balance of the design is Snoopy, Charlie Brown, Linus, Sally, Schroeder, Lucy, Freida, and Pig Pen sitting in director's chairs captioned with their names, two drumsticks, and a red and white cord to hold the drum are included, drum rims come in different colors: silver, red, etc., metal, #1798, 1969, in box, $165.00 – 205.00; no box, $75.00 – 120.00.

Mattel Preschool — Aviva Toy Company, Inc./Hasbro Industries, Inc./Trophy Music Co.

"Snoopy Musical Ge-Tar," includes strings playing and a crank which, when turned, produces a tune, picture: Snoopy sits up in a tree and holds the baseball that Charlie Brown and Lucy are seeking, plastic, #4715, 1972, in box, $45.00 – 75.00; no box, $30.00 – 50.00; "Snoopy Musical Guitar" with moving Snoopy and Woodstock, includes strings for playing and a crank which, when turned, produces a tune, two-dimensional figure of Snoopy moves, as does Woodstock, when tune is played, small figures of Charlie Brown, Snoopy, Woodstock and Lucy are at the end of the guitar, where the strings are tuned, plastic, #444, 1980, in box, $45.00 – 75.00; no box, $30.00 – 50.00. "Snoopy's Harp," metal mouth harp, box caption "featured in the motion picture 'A Boy Named Charlie Brown!'" Instructions inside the box, as there are no graphics on the harp itself, the box must be present, 1969, Trophy Music Co., in box, $12.00 – 20.00.

"Snoopy Play Piano," picture: Snoopy at a podium, leads Schroeder, Lucy, Peppermint Patty, Linus, Sally, and Charlie Brown in a song, a bird holds a triangle and another plays it, Snoopy appears on three of the keys, red background, comes with three plastic legs, a sheet of color dots for the keys and a music booklet, plastic, with metal trim and wooden base, #29-K, mid 1980s; in box, $150.00 – 225.00; no box, $125.00 – 190.00.

Determined Productions, Inc.

"Snoopy and Woodstock Play Piano," picture: Snoopy and Woodstock dance with two other birds, Snoopy appears on three of the keys, red background, comes with three plastic legs, a sheet of color dots for the keys and a music booklet, plastic with metal trim and wooden base, #29K, mid 1980s, in box, $150.00 – 225.00; no box, $125.00 – 190.00.

Not Pictured

Ely Mello-Tone Chime Piano, Schroeder sits at his piano, Lucy leans on the piano and enjoys the melodic tunes Snoopy plays on his violin along with Charlie Brown and Linus, stand approx. 10¾" high, 1962. . . . . .with or without box, $225.00 – 280.00

 # Play Sets

Packaging is all-important in this category, for two reasons: storage for the pieces, and identification of all the parts.

We list a wide variety; the most interesting and more expensive are those with many or unusual accessories, such as "Snoopy Playland," "Snoopy Camping Set," "Deluxe Peanuts Play Set," or "Snoopy Playhouse." The latter reveals the contents of our favorite beagle's home!

• Battery-Operated •

"Snoopy Playland," with Charlie Brown, Snoopy, Woodstock, Linus, Schroeder, and Peppermint Patty, activities include Ferris wheel and swing, Snoopy rides a battery-operated bus, with non-Peanuts passengers, requires one "C" battery, Aviva Toy Company, #888, 1979, $75.00 – 110.00.

"**Snoopy** Medical Kit," includes battery-operated stethoscope, thermometer, three little bottles, three sheets of decals and medical booklet, Japan, #518800, requires one 1.5 volt battery, Takara/Another Determined Production, #518800, 1985, $62.00 – 85.00.

• Non-Battery-Operated •

A Child Guidance Toy/Questor Education Products Company

"**Charlie Brown** Play Bus," with Snoopy, Charlie Brown, Peppermint Patty, Linus, Schroeder, and Lucy, #1681, late 1970s, $45.00 – 60.00; "Charlie Brown Camp Kamp," Charlie Brown, Snoopy, Lucy, and Linus enjoy the full camping experience with canoes, bunk beds, picnic tables, bench, campfire, and bunkhouse, #1683, late 1970s, $60.00 – 85.00; "Snoopy's Swim and Sail Club," Snoopy, Charlie Brown, Lucy, Linus, and Woodstock enjoy boats, water skis, and surfboard, also includes a surf shop, and lifeguard stand, #1710, late 1970s, $55.00 – 85.00.

"**Snoopy's** Good Grief Glider," spring-loaded launcher propels glider plane, #1775, late 1970s; "Snoopy's Stunt Spectacular!", spring-action shooter propels crash-apart cycle to perform stunts, #1750, late 1970s; "Snoopy's Scooter Shooter," Snoopy and Woodstock perform daredevil stunts by using the shooter stunt ramp, #1720, late 1970s; $35.00 – 50.00 each.

"**Snoopy's** Shape Register," cash register with various shapes, a ringing bell and a drawer that opens, #51740, late 1970s, $55.00 – 70.00.

Child Guidance Playthings, Inc./Gabriel Industries, Inc.

"**Snoopy's** Daredevil Flyer," springboard launcher propels Snoopy on a hang-glider, #51748, late 1970s, $35.00 – 50.00.

A.R.C.

"**Snoopy** Floor Care Play Set," includes broom, dust pan, sponge, apron, and sponge mop, #1636, 1986, $15.00 – 22.00.

Romper Room/Hasbro Industries, Inc.

"My Friend Snoopy," pull back Snoopy's arm and he'll roll the bowling ball to knock down the pins, #825, 1980, $40.00 – 75.00; "Stack-Up Snoopy," Snoopy comes in five parts, each fitting onto a pole to turn him into a Beaglescout, #818, 1980, $12.00 – 22.00; "Snoopy's Doghouse," wind-up figures of Snoopy and Woodstock hop around, play inside Snoopy's house, or on an ice cream truck or sip water from the birdbath, #815, 1978, $30.00 – 40.00.

Hasbro Industries, Inc./Aviva Toy Co.

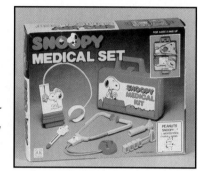

"Snoopy Medical Set," includes medical case, stethoscope, thermometer, blood-measuring gauge, reflex hammer, ostoscope, thorscope and eye chart, #70455, 1980s, $42.00 – 55.00.

Another Determined Production/Helm Toy Corp.

"Deluxe Peanuts Playset," three jointed action dolls: Snoopy, Lucy, and Charlie Brown, along with Lucy's psychiatrist's booth and a stool, #575, 1975, $225.00 – 320.00.

"Snoopy Playhouse," Snoopy's house sits on a mat of grass and is surrounded by a white picket fence, includes pieces of furniture, a piano, and articulated Snoopy and Woodstock, 45 pieces, boxed in a portable carrying case, #120, 1977, $120.00 – 185.00.

"Snoopy and His Doghouse" with Woodstock, includes Snoopy action doll, Woodstock, Snoopy's supper dish, and house, #476, 1975, $55.00 – 70.00; "Snoopy Camping Set," includes Snoopy action figure and boots, log, T-shirt, shorts, pup tent, campfire, backpack, coffee pot, binoculars, coffee mug, camping hat, #900, 1975, $80.00 – 130.00.

Takara/Another Determined Production, Japan

"Snoopy Pochette Room," three styles of small, hand-held-size playsets, each a different-colored house which opens to reveal the various pieces. Included are figures of Snoopy, Woodstock, Charlie Brown, and Lucy, plus additional pieces as indicated, early 1980s.

Tennis, 19 pieces, plus a sheet of decals; School, 19 pieces, plus a sheet of decals; House, 18 pieces, plus a sheet of decals; $20.00 – 35.00 each.

International Trading Technology, Inc.

"**Snoopy** Magnetic Alphabet & Number Board," 40 magnetic tiles and board, #350, 1989, $20.00 – 35.00.

Playskool, Inc. (A Milton Bradley Company)

"**Snoopy** Slugger," baseball cap accompanies plastic oversized baseball bat and ball, #411, late 1970s, $30.00 – 45.00; Snoopy Tennis, tennis visor, plastic racquet, and tennis ball, #415, late 1970s, $26.00 – 38.00.

Knickerbocker Toy Co.

"**Tub Time Snoopy**," Snoopy is jointed and safe to use in water, he comes with a small terry towel monogrammed "Snoopy," and a red bathrobe, #0539NUO, 1979, $22.00 – 32.00; "Snoopy Soft House," cloth house for small Snoopy and Woodstock dolls, accessories include nightclothes for Snoopy, a scarf for Woodstock, easy chair, and sleeping bag, #0573, 1979, $28.00 – 42.00.

"**Snoopy** the Chef," includes 5-inch jointed vinyl Snoopy, chef's hat and apron, stove and sink unit, spoon, frying pan, pot with lid, coffee pot, cake, and figure of Woodstock, Knickerbocker Preschool, #0542, 1979, $45.00 – 60.00; "Snoopy the Astronaut," includes 5-inch jointed vinyl Snoopy, space suit, helmet, moon shoes, camera, life-support system, flag, moon rover vehicle, and a figure of Woodstock, Knickerbocker Preschool/Knickerbocker Toy Co., #0540, 1979, $65.00 – 95.00; "Snoopy the Sport," includes 5-inch jointed vinyl Snoopy, two-piece warm-up suit, two-piece tennis outfit, sneakers, socks, sun visor, tennis tote, two tennis racquets, soccer ball, terry towel, and a figure of Woodstock, Knickerbocker Preschool, #0541, 1979, $35.00 – 50.00.

 # Rubber Figures

Whether used as toys or for display, these figures are a delightful way to enjoy the various Peanuts characters. Value is based on mint-in-the-box condition, and the boxes are worth having because of the great graphics. The figures should not have any scratches or missing paint.

• Child Guidance/Questor Education Products Company •

"Charlie Brown's Back Yard," the Flying Ace joins Charlie Brown and Lucy in the back yard, #1735, late 1970s, in box, $30.00 – 40.00; no box, $18.00 – 24.00; "Charlie Brown's All Stars Dugout," Snoopy, Charlie Brown, and Lucy play baseball, #1736, late 1970s, in box, $35.00 – 50.00; no box, $25.00 – 37.00.

• Another Determined Production •

"Peanuts Stackables," Charlie Brown, Lucy, and Peppermint Patty stand on one another, with Woodstock always on top, 1979, in box, $28.00 – 38.00; no box, $18.00 – 24.00; Snoopy Stackables, three poses of Snoopy which stand on top of each other, 1979, in box, $15.00 – 20.00; no box, $12.00 – 16.00.

• Familiar/Determined Productions •

Daisy Hill Puppies, small figures of Olaf, Andy, Spike, Belle, Snoopy, and Marbles, #740311, early 1990s, in box, $15.00 – 20.00; no box, $12.00 – 16.00.

Spinning Tops

Each top should be in excellent working condition. There should be no scratches or paint missing. The original knob should be included. The box, as with almost all toys, is a plus and adds to the value considerably.

Chein Playthings

"Peanuts Top," multi-color design with encircled faces of Charlie Brown, Snoopy, Linus, and Lucy, #263, 1969, in box, $60.00 – 95.00; no box, $32.00 – 65.00; "Peanuts Musical Top," metal, four pictures: Peppermint Patty sits, Linus sits and sucks his thumb while holding his blanket, Lucy leans on Schroeder's piano while he plays, and Charlie Brown talks to Snoopy, purple and red dots occupy the background, metal, #263, 1972, in box, $50.00 – 85.00; no box, $30.00 – 60.00.

Ohio Art

"Snoopy & the Gang Spinning Top," Snoopy, Woodstock, Lucy, Charlie Brown, Linus, and Peppermint Patty dance around the top rim, caption, "Snoopy & the Gang," metal, #305, mid 1980s, in box, $15.00 – 25.00; no box, $8.00 – 16.00; "Charlie Brown & Snoopy Poppin' Top," Snoopy, Woodstock, Lucy, Charlie Brown, Linus, and Peppermint Patty dance on the inside section of the toy, balls inside move and make a popping noise, metal and plastic, #322, mid 1980s, in box, $18.00 – 32.00; no box, $12.00 – 22.00.

Tea Sets & Kitchen Sets

Youngsters always love to play in the kitchen or have friends over for tea. Imaginations take over, with either real or "pretend" guests.

Tea sets and kitchen sets are sought for many reasons, but primarily because they're usually made of metal. These Peanuts sets are wonderful, filled with color and certain to provide years of enjoyment.

Value assumes that all items are in very good to mint condition. Bear in mind that products made by J. Chein and Company are sought by serious cross-over collectors. It's not easy to find complete sets mint in their original boxes, so you may need to be satisfied with a brightly colored single piece with as few scratches and rust as possible. All letters should be legible. All pieces are metal unless noted.

• J. Chein and Company (Chein Playthings) •

"**Snoopy** Tea Set," eight pieces: two cups and saucers, one tray, one plate with Peanuts characters, and two plastic spoons, #276, 1970, with box, $75.00 – 105.00; no box, $35.00 – 65.00.

"Peanuts Tea Set," 12 pieces: one large tray, three large and three small plates, three cups, and plastic teapot with lid, each plate has the face and name of a Peanuts character, #233, 1969, with box, $195.00 – 255.00, no box, $135.00 – 175.00.

• Ohio Art •

"**Charlie Brown & Snoopy** Set," 14 pieces: two each of large and small plates, two plastic cups, two plastic spoons, forks, and knives, and teapot with lid, #409, 1984, with box, $75.00 – 90.00; no box, $30.00 – 55.00; "Charlie Brown & Snoopy Breakfast Set," 13 pieces: four large and small plates, four plastic cups and one toaster, #452, 1984, with box, $90.00 – 150.00; no box, $40.00 – 70.00; "Charlie Brown & Snoopy Tea Set," 26 pieces: four small and large plates, four plastic cups, one plastic tea pot with lid, four each plastic knives, forks, and spoons, #422, 1984, with box, $75.00 – 125.00; no box, $30.00 – 60.00.

Not Pictured
"**Charlie Brown & Snoopy** 45-Piece Cook 'n Serve Tea Set," four large and small plates, one skillet, three saucepans, one pot, three plastic lids, four plastic tea cups, one plastic teapot with lid, one plastic strainer, one each plastic strainer spoon and measuring spoon, four each plastic napkin rings, knives, forks, spoons, and four paper napkins, the box is cardboard with outline drawings of the pieces included; there are no character graphics, #49-10072, 1984. . . .with box, $110.00 – 155.00 no box, 95.00 – 135.00

• Another Determined Production •

"**Snoopy** Play Kitchen Set," 12 pieces: two-piece oven and stove that holds one toaster, one skillet and pan, one saucepan with cover, one frying pan, one plate, and one each spatula, spoon, and tea cup, Japan, #00128003, 1985, with box, $90.00 – 150.00; no box, $50.00 – 75.00.

• Berwick •

"Snoopy Tea Set," 19 plastic pieces: four large and four small plates, four cups, sugar, creamer, Snoopy on his doghouse lid and teapot, and four coasters, England #013, 1979, with box, $110.00 – 150.00; no box, $65.00 – 90.00.

• Unknown Manufacturer •

"Snoopy Play Kitchen Set," eight pieces: one large and two small plates, two cups, one teapot, and two spoons, Japan, #04028025, early to mid 1980s, with box, $75.00 – 125.00; no box, $40.00 – 65.00.

• Battery-Operated Vehicles •

Snoopy and the gang have done a great deal of travelling, particularly on battery-powered toys.

This section includes some classics. The "Talking Peanuts Bus" is a must for the really serious collector, and the battery-operated toys from Aviva also are keepers. The "Snoopy Family Car" has caught on, and finding it mint in the box has become a real challenge.

If the box is missing, all the parts must be present; carefully inspect the toy to make sure it works. (Many times the battery covers are missing.) Bring batteries with you, in case of a find; you don't want to return home with a non-working toy.

Note: When storing your toys, be sure to remove the batteries to prevent leakage.

• J. Chein & Co. •

"Talking Peanuts Bus," caption, "Happiness is an Annual Outing," Snoopy holds a bunny as he drives the bus, birds, Frieda, Charlie Brown, Lucy, Shermy, Sally, Pig Pen, Schroeder, and Linus are passengers, the gang sings and speaks when the toy is turned on, requires one "D" battery, #261, 1967, in box, $425.00 – 675.00; no box, $250.00 – 395.00.

• Aviva Toy Company, Inc./Hasbro Industries, Inc. •

"**Snoopy** Express Station Set," Snoopy is on the locomotive, Charlie Brown and Woodstock move at the train station, requires one "C" battery, #988, 1977, in box, $85.00 – 135.00; no box, $45.00 – 70.00; "Snoopy 500 Slot Car Racing Set," Snoopy and Charlie Brown compete against one another via handheld controls, requires four "D" batteries, #XL-500, 1977, in box, $65.00 – 105.00; no box, $45.00 – 70.00; "Snoopy Battery-Operated Speedway," four race cars with Snoopy, Woodstock, Charlie Brown, and Lucy race around the track, a starting gate and sign are included, requires one "D" battery, #999, 1976, in box, $110.00 – 185.00; no box, $80.00 – 120.00; "Snoopy Train Set," Schroeder, Charlie Brown, Snoopy, and Woodstock ride different cars, includes a doghouse ticket booth, tunnel, two railroad signs, and one cross track, requires one "C" battery, #3000, 1977, in box, $85.00 – 125.00; no box, $55.00 – 95.00.

"**Snoopy** Racing Car Stickshifter," Snoopy is at the controls of his streamlined racing car, Woodstock sits in his nest near the front wheels, requires four "D" batteries, #2500, 1978, in box, $125.00 – 160.00; no box, $75.00 – 105.00.

"**Snoopy** Formula-1 Racing Car," comes with many decals, and pictures of Snoopy on both sides of the car, produces racing sound, #950, 1978, in box, $145.00 – 205.00; no box, $85.00 – 115.00; Woodstock Formula-1 Racing Car, comes with many decals, and pictures of him on both sides of the car, produces racing sound, #950, 1978, in box, $95.00 – 115.00; no box, $55.00 – 75.00.

"**Snoopy** Family Car," caption, "Snoopy and Friends," Snoopy drives passengers Lucy, Peppermint Patty, and Charlie Brown, Woodstock is the hood ornament on this colorful convertible, car moves and has blinking head lights, 1979, in box, $75.00 – 115.00; no box, $30.00 – 60.00.

"**Snoopy** Radio Controlled Fire Engine with Woodstock Transmitter," Snoopy is the fire engine driver and brings firefighters Woodstock, Lucy, and Charlie Brown, Snoopy, Lucy, and Charlie Brown wear their fire hats, requires 4 "C" size and one 9-volt battery, #988 R/C, 1980, in box, $95.00 – 140.00; no box, $65.00 – 110.00; "Snoopy Radio Controlled Doghouse," Snoopy is on his house and Woodstock is the control unit which steers him, requires four penlite and one 9-volt battery, #980 R/C, 1980, in box, $45.00 – 75.00; no box, $35.00 – 50.00.

• Mattel Preschool/Mattel, Inc. •

"Surfing Snoopy," figures of Snoopy and Woodstock on a battery-operated surfboard, requires one "AA" alkaline battery, #3477, late 1970s, in box, $55.00 – 75.00; no box, $35.00 – 42.00; "Rowing Snoopy," figures of Snoopy and Woodstock, with Snoopy rowing a boat, requires two "AA" alkaline batteries, #3478, late 1970s, in box, $60.00 – 80.00; no box, $40.00 – 52.00; "Snoopy & His Flyin' Doghouse," a joystick controls Charlie Brown, Snoopy flies his bullet-riddled doghouse, a wire connects Charlie Brown to Snoopy, requires 4 "D" batteries, #8263, 1974, in box, $145.00 – 225.00; no box, $80.00 – 115.00.

• Matchbox Toys •

"R.C. Snoopy Skateboard," a one-foot tall rubber and plastic Snoopy rides a brightly colored red, green, and yellow skateboard, the transmitter and antenna signals Snoopy to move (this skateboard was available through the J.C. Penney's catalog but only in a plain cardboard box, the value listed here is for the graphic box), requires eight "AA" penlight batteries and two 9-volt transistor batteries, #9299, 1988, in box, $85.00 – 130.00; no box, $55.00 – 75.00.

• D.C.S. •

"Snoopy's Dream Machine," smaller version of item below, without flashing lights, requires six "AA" penlight batteries, #417-M, 1979, in box, $35.00 – 50.00; no box, $25.00 – 30.00, "Snoopy's Dream Machine," Snoopy and Woodstock fly on the doghouse which has a spinning propeller and flashing lights, the Red Baron in his plane, tries to catch them, requires three "C" batteries and two 9-volt batteries, #417-A, 1979, in box, $95.00 – 145.00; no box, $65.00 – 90.00.

Train Sets

People all over the world love trains, and Snoopy is no exception. He's the focus of many train sets.

Prices are based on very good to mint condition. All pieces should be included, and the train should roll fairly easily. Decals should be intact. With these sets, the box greatly enhances the value.

"Snoopy All-American Express Mechanical Wind-Up Wood Train," three-piece wooden train decorated with red, white, and blue banners, stars, and flags. Decals of Snoopy as the engineer and passengers Charlie Brown, Peppermint Patty, and Woodstock, Snoopy also dances in the last car, Aviva, #1776, 1975, in box, $120.00 – 175.00; no box, $65.00 – 95.00.

"**Snoopy** Mechanical Wind-Up Wood Train," includes six-piece plastic track, "Snoopyville" tunnel, traffic light and railroad crossing sign, three-car wooden train with decals of Snoopy as the engineer, Snoopy dancing, and passengers Charlie Brown, Peppermint Patty and Woodstock, decals appear on both sides of the cars, Aviva Toy Company, #922, 1976, in box, $55.00 – 78.00; no box, $35.00 – 45.00.

"**Snoopy** Express Mechanical Wind-Up Train," three plastic cars with Snoopy as the engineer, Woodstock rides one car while sitting on his nest, on the same car are decals of Snoopy, Charlie Brown, and Peppermint Patty, the final car is shaped like Snoopy's doghouse with Snoopy lying on top, Aviva Toy Company/Hasbro, #70911, 1982, in box, $20.00 – 35.00; no box, $15.00 – 28.00.

Vehicle Sets

Happiness, for any collector, is finding items boxed in a set. There's something particularly exhilarating about such a coup; it literally makes the blood race. These are some examples of the sets produced with Peanuts characters. No batteries were required for any of the vehicles.

It's interesting to note that not all the figures are the same size, even though one set basically contains the same vehicles as another. (Serious collectors love such anomalies.) Additionally, each of the toys was sold individually.

Value is based on mint in the box condition. Due to age, some wear on the box is to be expected; however, it should be intact, and the cello should not be torn.

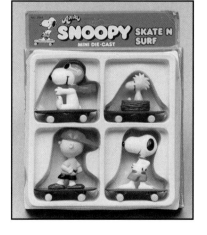

"**Snoopy** Skate N Surf," mini die-cast set consists of two figures of Snoopy and one each of Charlie Brown and Woodstock, all ride on metal skateboards, Aviva Toy Company, #2044, 1976, $36.00 – 48.00.

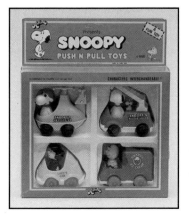

"**Snoopy** Push N Pull Toys," two plastic figures of Snoopy and one each of Lucy and Charlie Brown, each fits in any of four vehicles: Snoopy's Helicopter, Rescue Squad Car, Lucy's Car or Snoopy's Ice Cream Truck, all items are plastic, Aviva Toy Company, assortment #850, 1977, $32.00 – 44.00.

"**Snoopy** Handfuls Mini Die Cast Emergency Set," Snoopy drives a metal fire truck, snorkel, and wrecker, the figures of Snoopy are very small, Hasbro/Aviva Toy Company, assortment #72036, 1980; "Snoopy Handfuls Mini Die Cast Set," three Snoopy figures drive a metal Fun Van, a dune buggy convertible, and a Cat Catcher truck, the figures are very small, Hasbro/Aviva Toy Company, assortment #72036, 1980; $36.00 – 48.00 each.

"**Snoopy** Handfuls Mini Die Cast Set," Woodstock drives an ice cream truck, Snoopy drives a doghouse truck and a U.S. Mail truck, the figures of Snoopy and Woodstock are very small, Hasbro/Aviva Top Company, assortment #72036, 1980, $36.00 – 48.00.

"**Snoopy** Handfuls Mini Die Cast Set," Snoopy drives a metal Cat Catcher truck, Fun Van, and convertible dune buggy, Hasbro Preschool, assortment #72036, 1981; "Snoopy Handfuls Mini Die Cast Set," Snoopy drives metal wrecker, snorkel, and fire trucks, Hasbro Preschool, assortment #72036, 1981; $30.00 – 42.00 each.

"**Snoopy** Push N Pull Toys," set consists of three figures of Snoopy and one each of Charlie Brown, Lucy, and Woodstock, plastic vehicles are mini copter, rescue squad car, ice cream truck, and sports car, the figures can be used in any vehicle, Aviva Toy Company/Hasbro, #70850, 1981, $36.00 – 48.00.

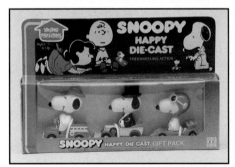

"**Snoopy** Happy Die-Cast Gift Pack," three oversized Snoopy figures in metal cars: fire truck, touring car, and racer, Hasbro Preschool, assortment #72045 C, 1981, $24.00 – 36.00.

"**Snoopy** Mini Die Cast Racing Set," figures of Snoopy, Lucy, and two of Woodstock, each in a brightly colored racing car, Aviva Toy Company/Hasbro, #2038, 1982, $38.00 – 50.00.

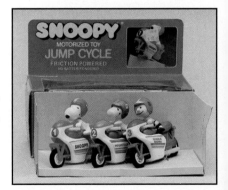

"**Snoopy** Jump Cycle Set," Snoopy, Woodstock and Charlie Brown each ride a plastic, brightly colored motorcycle, International Trading Technology, Inc., #511, 1990, $18.00 – 30.00.

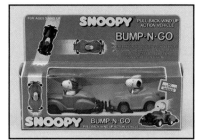

"**Snoopy** Bump-N-Go," plastic red and green cars, each driven by a different Snoopy, International Trading Technology, Inc., #988, 1990, $20.00 – 32.00.

Not Pictured

"Snoopy Die Cast Vehicle Set," Snoopy drives a metal station wagon, fire truck, and tow truck, Hasbro Preschool/Aviva Toy Company, assortment #72229 D, 1982. . . . .$30.00 – 42.00.

 # Other Vehicles

"**Snoopy** Push N' Pull Biplane," figures of the Flying Ace, Snoopy in formal attire, Charlie Brown, and Woodstock fit into the plastic biplane, Aviva Toy Company, Inc./Hasbro Industries, Inc., #70866, 1982, in box, $35.00 – 45.00; no box, $25.00 – 35.00; "Snoopy Deep Diver Submarine," a hand-held squeeze control enables the submarine to dive and surface, Snoopy and Woodstock are included, Knickerbocker Preschool/Knickerbocker Toy Co., Inc., #0553, late 1970s, in box, $48.00 – 62.00; no box, $30.00 – 45.00; "Snoopy Gyro Cycle," the World War I Flying Ace drives his cycle, Charlie

Brown and Woodstock ride on the sidecar portion, Hasbro Industries, Inc./Aviva Toy Company, Inc., #70440, 1982, in box, $38.00 – 47.00; no box, $25.00 – 37.00.

"Operating Charlie Brown and Lucy Handcar," Charlie Brown and Lucy ride a self-propelled handcar, 027 and O gauge, Lionel, #6-18413, 1990, in box $90.00 – 135.00, no box $60.00 – 95.00; Operating Snoopy and Woodstock Handcar, Snoopy and Woodstock ride self-propelled handcar, 027 and O gauge, Lionel, #6-18497, 1990, in box $110.00 – 155.00, no box $75.00 – 110.00.

Not Pictured

"Snoopy Push 'N Pull Locomotive," figures of the Flying Ace, Snoopy in formal attire, Charlie Brown and Woodstock fit into the plastic locomotive, Aviva Toy Company, Inc./ Hasbro Industries, Inc. #70867, 1982. . . . . .in box, $35.00 – 45.00 no box, 25.00 – 35.00

 # Wooden Vehicles

• Aviva Toy Company •

These were produced in 1974. Each has a decal to identify the type of vehicle and another of Snoopy as the driver. Decals appear on both sides. The larger vehicles have wooden wheels; the smaller ones have plastic wheels.

Value is based on mint condition, with no splinters or missing decals. The box should be intact, but a little wear is acceptable due to age.

Large size

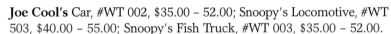

Snoopy's Bug #WT 001, large and small pictured together, $40.00 – 55.00.

Joe Cool's Car, #WT 002, $35.00 – 52.00; Snoopy's Locomotive, #WT 503, $40.00 – 55.00; Snoopy's Fish Truck, #WT 003, $35.00 – 52.00.

Snoopy's Farm Truck, #WT 504; Snoopy's Milk Truck, #WT 505, Snoopy's Gas Truck, #WT 506; $35.00 – 52.00 each.

Not Pictured
Snoopy's Bus, #WT 501. . . . .$40.00 – 55.00
Snoopy's Van, #WT 502. . . . . .35.00 – 52.00
Snoopy's Sedan, #WT 507. . . . . .35.00 – 52.00
Snoopy's Fire Truck, #WT 508. . . . . .40.00 – 55.00

Small size, Series #944

Not Pictured
Snoopy's Bug. . . . .$18.00 – 24.00
Joe Cool's Car. . . . . . . .15.00 – 21.00
Snoopy's Locomotive. . .18.00 – 24.00
Snoopy's Fish Truck. . . .15.00 – 21.00
Snoopy's Sedan. . . . . . .15.00 – 21.00
Snoopy's Milk Truck . . .15.00 – 21.00
Snoopy's Fire Truck . . .18.00 – 24.00

Snoopy's Bus; Snoopy's Farm Truck; Snoopy's Lumber Truck; $15.00 – 21.00 each.

Snoopy's Cement Truck, $18.00 – 24.00; Snoopy's Van, $15.00 – 21.00.

• Vilac Toy Company •

In 1990, this French firm exported an assortment of lacquered hard wooden toys, each with a figure of Snoopy. The larger toys have three-dimensional figures while the smaller have two-dimensional figures. They came in a variety of color combinations, all very bright. The boxes, while lacking graphics of the Peanuts characters, still are quite nice to have.

Prices are based on mint-in-the-box condition, with very little wear on the box.

Large Snoopy in car, $35.00 – 50.00;
Small Snoopy in car, $20.00 – 30.00.

Large Snoopy in biplane, $55.00 – 85.00;
Small Snoopy in biplane, $25.00 – 35.00.

Snoopy in sailboat, with his picture on the mast, $75.00 – 110.00.

 # Wind-up Toys

Value is based on mint-in-the-box condition. Due to age, some wear on the box is acceptable. There should be no tears on the box or cellophane, if applicable. All parts should be included, and the toy should work when it is wound.

• Chein •

"Snoopy vs. the Red Baron," two-dimensional cardboard Snoopy sits on top of his plastic, bullet-riddled home, the house hops around after the key is wound, #139, in box $55.00 – 90.00, no box $40.00 – 70.00.

• Aviva Enterprises, Inc., et al •

Aviva Enterprises, Inc. originally issued wind-up walkers in the mid 1970s; the same walkers subsequently were produced under different names: Aviva Toy Company, Inc., Aviva Toy Company, Inc./Hasbro Industries, Inc., and International Trading Technology, Inc. This list is intended as a reference for the styles issued and not necessarily the dates they were introduced. They were packaged in boxes, clear plastic pouches, and blister cards.

Value is based on working condition. The plastic should not be discolored. Finding a box makes that figure worth a couple more dollars.

Small size, approx. 2⅞" tall
$1.00 – 4.00 each

Snoopy, plain figure; Joe Cool wearing sunglasses; Joe Cool wearing sunglasses, 4½"; Flying Ace; Snoopy in a western outfit.

Snoopy in a green tennis visor and shirt, holding a green tennis racket; Snoopy in a football helmet; Snoopy in a red cloth nightcap with a white ball at the end; Woodstock in a red cloth nightcap with a white ball at the end; Woodstock wearing an Indian feather; Woodstock, plain figure; Belle in a pink shirt with blue writing and trim.

Not Pictured
Snoopy in formal attire.
Woodstock holding pink flower.

• Aviva Toy Company/Hasbro Industries, Inc. •

"Snoopy the Drummer,"** Snoopy wears a red hat with a blue and yellow band, he uses drumsticks to play the drum on which Woodstock stands, #833, 1977, in box, $55.00 – 75.00; no box, $30.00 – 45.00; "Snoopy, World's Greatest Cook," Chef Snoopy flips eggs in his skillet, #835, 1977, in box, $45.00 – 65.00; no box, $15.00 – 30.00; "Snoopy the Champ," Snoopy wears boxing gloves, his arms touch the punching bag on which Woodstock stands, #836, 1977, in box, $55.00 – 75.00; no box, $30.00 – 45.00.

"Snoopy Skis,"** Lucy, Charlie Brown, and Snoopy, each on skis; they turn and have moving arms. Woodstock accompanies them. Aviva Toy Company/Hasbro Industries, Inc., series #711, 1979. Charlie Brown in his yellow shirt with black zigzag, black pants, and red ski cap; Lucy in a purple ski sweater, pink pants, and pink ski cap; in box, $24.00 – 36.00 each; no box, $16.00 – 24.00 each.

Not Pictured
Snoopy in a red ski sweater and cap . . . .in box, $30.00 – 42.00
no box, 20.00 – 32.00

• International Trading Technology, Inc. •

"Snoopy Animated Wind-Up with Moving Action,"** set of three figures, each of which moves, Snoopy plays a guitar, Charlie Brown holds a harmonica, and Snoopy plays a drum, #605, 1990, these toys also were sold individually as Style #600, in box, $30.00 – 48.00; no box, $24.00 – 36.00.

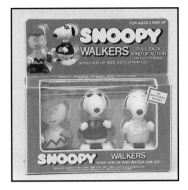

Snoopy Walkers, set of three walkers with pull back wind-up action, Charlie Brown holds baseball in one hand, Joe Cool wears a black turtleneck trimmed in red, and Snoopy holds Woodstock, #340, 1990, in box, $15.00 – 24.00.

 # Wooden Blocks and Playsets

Finding the Peanuts characters on wooden items is rather unusual, so owning a set of wooden blocks is a real treat. For several years, collectors have turned to Japan for the majority of Peanuts items made from wood.

Value assumes all the pieces are in excellent condition. The writing or picture should be legible with bright colors: no shavings or nicks in the wood. The original container, if applicable, should be included.

Snoopy Wooden Puzzle Box, Linus, Marcie, Sally, Franklin, Woodstock, Peppermint Patty, Eudora, Schroeder, Charlie Brown, Belle, Spike, Lucy, several birds, and Woodstock take a ride on a San Francisco trolley, the trolley is a box holding several different-shaped pieces of wood, the object is to fit each piece through the correct opening on the trolley lid, the trolley has wheels and a pull string, Japan, Determined Productions, Inc., #SP-45, 1989, $125.00 – 150.00.

Wooden Letter Blocks, the Peanuts characters appear with letters from the Japanese alphabet, Japan, Determined Productions, Inc., #SL-43, mid to late 1980s, $75.00 – 115.00.

Snoopy Balloons, blocks in a wooden tray, one side of the cubes forms a picture of Snoopy holding balloons, another side has letters, France, Determined Productions, Inc., Vilac, #2168, 1990, $18.00 – 30.00.

 # Yo-Yos
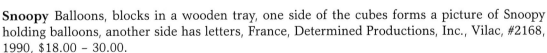

All these yo-yos were produced by Hallmark, a Peanuts licensee since 1960. With the exception of two, each was issued for consumers in the United States.

Value is based on mint condition; in the package or out of the package. The package is quite important, espe-

cially if the yo-yo is from the 1960s, as it includes graphics that show the characters in some of their older incarnations. The yo-yos should be clean with no paint missing or scratches. The picture, normally a decal, should be intact.

Charlie Brown wears a baseball cap and glove, plastic, late 1960s, in package, $15.00 – 22.00; no package, $5.00 – 12.00.

Snoopy Hummingbird Yo-Yo, Snoopy wears a tri-cornered hat and holds his yo-yo, plastic, mid 1970s, in package, $14.00 – 22.00; no package, $10.00 – 16.00.

Snoopy wears an Uncle Sam hat, plastic, mid 1970s, in package, $14.00 – 18.00; no package, $10.00 – 12.00; Woodstock holds a pennant captioned "'76," plastic, mid 1970s, in package, $12.00 – 16.00; no package, $7.00 – 12.00.

Snoopy stands in the middle of his name, plastic, Japan, 1990; Snoopy's name is spelled twice with his face in the middle of the two words, plastic, Japan, 1990; in package, $7.00 – 9.00 each; no package, $4.00 – 7.00 each.

Not Pictured

Snoopy as the World War I Flying Ace sits, plastic, late 1960s. .in package, $17.00 – 24.00
no package, 7.00 – 14.00

Lucy stands, plastic, late 1960s. . . . . .in package, 15.00 – 22.00
no package, 5.00 – 12.00

Linus sucks his thumb and holds his security blanket, plastic, late 1960s. . . . . .in package, 15.00 – 22.00
no package, 5.00 – 12.00

Snoopy Hummingbird Yo-Yo, Snoopy is tangled up in his yo-yo string, late 1960s. . . . . .in package, 10.00 – 14.00
no package, 5.00 – 11.00

Snoopy Yo-Yo for Beginners, Snoopy does some fancy yo-yo tricks, wood, late 1960s. . . . . . .in package, 10.00 – 14.00
no package, 5.00 – 11.00

• Peanuts Puzzler Yo-Yos •

A yo-yo and a little game of skill

Snoopy plays tennis, plastic, #100PF117-8, mid 1970s; Woodstock holds several objects, plastic, mid 1970s; in package, $12.00 – 16.00 each; no package, $8.00 – 11.00 each.

Not Pictured

Snoopy holds the strings of several balloons in one hand and reaches out with the other to Woodstock, plastic, #PF276-5, early 1970s. . . . . .in package, $12.00 – 16.00
. . . . .no package, 8.00 – 11.00

A certain black-and-white dog caught Andrea Podley's eye when she was a youngster, and she fell in love. Her devotion to Snoopy and the rest of the Peanuts gang has grown ever since.

Flash forward to 1983. Andrea's husband, Phil, decided to prove that she was the only adult "silly enough to collect the Peanuts characters." Expecting no response, he placed an ad in a few collector's publications circulating throughout the United States. He soon made a hearty meal of those skeptical words, and he has been choking them down ever since.

Rather than answer each person individually, Phil encouraged Andrea to start a newsletter. That first publication obviously pleased fellow collectors starving for contact with each other. The resulting Peanuts Collector Club quickly went international, continues to expand exponentially (thanks in great part to the World Wide Web), and now has a membership of well over 3,000 fans from all over the world.

Andrea is a leading authority on Peanuts memorabilia. Product line catalogs and magazines from all over the world have featured articles about her, her collection, and the Peanuts Collector Club. She has written numerous articles on this topic for various collector's publications. She and her collection have appeared on both American and Japanese television. The original *Official Price Guide to Peanuts Collectibles*, which she co-authored, is out of print and highly valuable on the secondary market.

Perhaps more than any other honor which has come her way because of this involvement with the Peanuts kids, Andrea cherishes the fact that she was invited to write the foreword to the 1997 HarperCollins book, *Charlie Brown: Not Your Average Blockhead*, by Charles M. Schulz.

Andrea takes pride in the blessings she has received from Charles M. Schulz and United Media, which licenses all the Peanuts characters. She maintains daily contact with Peanuts collectors from all over the world.

She lives in a small, quiet community with Phil and two adorable cats (she'd like to think that even Snoopy would approve of them). When not hunched over a computer and racing to produce the next club newsletter, she enjoys traveling, movies, music, long walks along tree-lined streets, and the company of good friends.

Derrick Bang fled the greater Los Angeles basin — still one of the smartest things he ever did — to attend northern California's UC Davis, loved the area, and decided to remain as a full-time resident after graduating in 1977.

To fill those hours when he wasn't busily writing for any newspaper or magazine foolish enough to publish him, Derrick founded The Game Preserve, a retail game-and-puzzle store, in September 1978. During the next 18 years and a handful of months, he could be found there every day, busily typing away in between intrusive visits from customers. (He finally switched, under protest, to a computer and word-processor instead of an Adler manual typewriter, but little else changed during those years.)

Derrick has written film, television, and general entertainment commentary for all three Davis/Woodland-area newspapers since 1974, and currently supplies regular columns and features to *The Davis Enterprise*. He also has been tantalizing readers for 18 years with a weekly movie trivia column.

He became part of the team that worked on the first *Video Movie Guide*, a mass-market Ballantine Books paperback that debuted in 1987 and became — and remains — a well-respected best-seller in its field. Along with contributing roughly 100 new reviews for each annual edition, he rose through the ranks and now holds the title of associate editor. (That hasn't gotten his name on the spine, but he figures that a few contract sanctions against the two cover-authors might remedy that situation.)

With great regret but recognizing the need to move on to new challenges, Derrick closed his game store in early 1997 and accepted a full-time desk position at *The Davis Enterprise*, where he now toils away as entertainment editor. He still writes the same columns and film reviews, and now wrestles with ballet mothers — two falls out of three — over how much coverage their precious little darlings deserve (he doesn't lose often).

Derrick also produced and starred in a weekly film-review program for Davis Community TV Channel 5 for just over 10 years and taught an annual two-semester bridge class for the city of Davis for 14 years. He has written and produced murder mystery evenings for Yolo County residents, and occasionally plays piano for weddings, amateur theater productions, and city functions. More recently, however, his responsibilities as "resident Web-head" for the Peanuts Collector Club has kept him extremely busy, whether updating the information at the club's World Wide Web site or adding more nuggets of data to the Peanuts Frequently Asked Question (FAQ) file.

When he touches down long enough to be noticed, Derrick shares his home with his wife, Gayna Lamb-Bang (who works for a small local bank), one dog (Winnie the Pooch, who works at shedding copious quantities of fur all over their house), and one cat (Pixie, who works at very little aside from aggressively demanding a lap on which to curl up and fall asleep).

Index

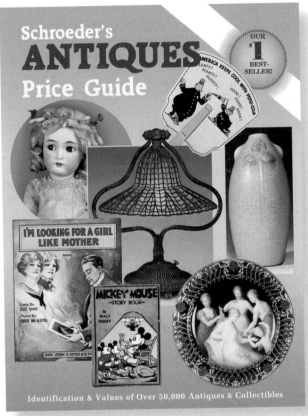